Workshop on Generative AI and Knowledge Graphs (GenAIK)

Abu Dhabi, United Arab Emirates
19 January 2025

ISBN: 979-8-3313-1368-5

Printed from e-media with permission by:

Curran Associates, Inc.
57 Morehouse Lane
Red Hook, NY 12571

CURRAN ASSOCIATES INC. proceedings .com

Some format issues inherent in the e-media version may also appear in this print version.

Association for Computational Linguistics
209 N. Eighth Street
Stroudsburg, Pennsylvania 18360

Phone: 1-570-476-8006
Fax: 1-570-476-0860

acl@aclweb.org

Additional copies of this publication are available from:

Curran Associates, Inc.
57 Morehouse Lane
Red Hook, NY 12571 USA
Phone: 845-758-0400
Fax: 845-758-2633
Email: curran@proceedings.com
Web: www.proceedings.com

COLING 2025

Workshop on Generative AI and Knowledge Graphs (GenAIK)

Proceedings of the Workshop

Abu Dhabi, UAE
January 19, 2025

Preface

Welcome to GenAIK 2025 – The Generative AI and Knowledge Graph Workshop, held in Abu Dhabi, UAE on January 19, 2025.

Generative Artificial Intelligence (GenAI) is a branch of artificial intelligence capable of creating seemingly new, meaningful content, including text, images, and audio. It utilizes deep learning models, such as Large Language Models (LLMs), to recognize and replicate data patterns, enabling the generation of human-like content. Notable families of LLMs include GPT (GPT-3.5, GPT-3.5 Turbo, and GPT-4), LLaMA (LLaMA and LLaMA-2), and Mistral (Mistral and Mixtral). GPT, which stands for Generative Pretrained Transformer, is especially popular for text generation and is widely used in applications like ChatGPT. GenAI has taken the world by storm and revolutionized various industries, including healthcare, finance, and entertainment. However, GenAI models have several limitations, including biases from training data, generating factually incorrect information, and difficulty in understanding complex content. Additionally, their performance can vary based on domain specificity.

In recent times, Knowledge Graphs (KGs) have attracted considerable attention for their ability to represent structured and interconnected information, and have been adopted by many companies in various domains. KGs represent knowledge by depicting relationships between entities, known as facts, usually based on formal ontological models. Consequently, they enable accuracy, decisiveness, interpretability, domain-specific knowledge, and evolving knowledge in various AI applications. The intersection between GenAI and KG has ignited significant interest and innovation in Natural Language Processing (NLP). For instance, by integrating LLMs with KGs during pre-training and inference, external knowledge can be incorporated to enhance the model's capabilities and improve interpretability. When integrated, they offer a robust approach to problem-solving in diverse areas such as information enrichment, representation learning, conversational AI, cross-domain AI transfer, bias, content generation, and semantic understanding. This workshop aims to reinforce the relationships between Deep Learning, Knowledge Graphs, and NLP communities and foster interdisciplinary research in GenAI.

We invited three types of papers: full research papers, short research papers, and position papers. Overall, we received 31 abstract submissions, which were reviewed by 31 members of the Programme Committee. The review process was double-blind. Each paper received three reviews. In total, 15 papers were accepted for publication in this volume, including 12 research papers, 2 short research papers, and 1 position paper.

We would like to express our gratitude to the Organizing Committee and the Program Committee. We would also like to thank our keynote speakers (Kang Liu and Wenya Wang) for accepting our invitations without hesitation and bringing their insights into the importance of knowledge graphs in the age of GenAI. Finally, our gratitude goes also to the sponsor of the conference, NFDI4DataScience, and to the COLING organization team for making the event successful.

January 2025

Genet Asefa Gesese
Harald Sack
Heiko Paulheim
Albert Meroño-Peñuela
Lihu Chen

Organizing Committee

Genet Asefa Gesese, FIZ Karlsruhe, KIT, Germany
Harald Sack, FIZ Karlsruhe, KIT, Germany
Heiko Paulheim, University of Mannheim, Germany
Albert Meroño-Peñuela, King's College London, UK
Lihu Chen, Imperial College London, UK

Program Committee

Paul Groth, University of Amsterdam, The Netherlands
Achim Rettinger, University of Trier, Germany
Cassia Trojahn, Institut de Recherche en Informatique de Toulouse, France
Gerard de Melo, Hasso Plattner Institute, Germany
Pushkar Singh, Google Search Ads AI, United States
Davide Buscaldi, Université Paris 13, France
Pierre-Henri Paris, Paris-Saclay University, France
Mayank Kejriwal, University of Southern California, United States
Finn Arup Nielsen, Technical University of Denmark, Denmark
Marco Bombieri, University of Verona, Italy
Fabien Gandon, Institut national de recherche en informatique et en automatique, France
Giuseppe Rizzo, LINKS Foundation, Italy
Edlira Vakaj Kalemi, Birmingham City University, UK
Vojtech Svatek, Prague University of Economics and Business, Czech Republic
Ondřej Zamazal, Prague University of Economics and Business, Czech Republic
Daniel Garijo, Universidad Politécnica de Madrid, Spain
Sanju Tiwari, TIB Hannover, Germany
Shufan Jiang, FIZ-Karlsruhe, Germany
Jesualdo Fernández-Breis, University of Murcia, Spain
Mauro Dragoni, Fondazione Bruno Kessler, Italy
Kristiina Jokinen, University of Helsinki, Finland
Graham Wilcock, University of Helsinki, Finland
Mathieu d'Aquin, Université de Lorraine, France
Giancarlo Guizzardi, University of Twente, EEMCS, The Netherlands
Oscar Rodríguez Rocha, Institut national de recherche en informatique et en automatique, France
Suvodeep Mazumdar, University of Sheffield, UK
Hiba Arnaout, TU Darmstadt, Germany
Nico Potyka, Cardiff University, UK
Zichao Li, Canoakbit Alliance/University of Waterloo, Canada
Arunav Das, King's College London, UK
Federico Torrielli, University of Turin, Italy

Table of Contents

Effective Modeling of Generative Framework for Document-level Relational Triple Extraction
Pratik Saini and Tapas Nayak 1

Learn Together: Joint Multitask Finetuning of Pretrained KG-enhanced LLM for Downstream Tasks
Anastasia Martynova, Vladislav Tishin and Natalia Semenova 13

GNET-QG: Graph Network for Multi-hop Question Generation
Samin Jamshidi and Yllias Chali 20

SKETCH: Structured Knowledge Enhanced Text Comprehension for Holistic Retrieval
Aakash Mahalingam, Vinesh Kumar Gande, Aman Chadha, Vinija Jain and Divya Chaudhary . . 27

On Reducing Factual Hallucinations in Graph-to-Text Generation Using Large Language Models
Dmitrii Iarosh, Alexander Panchenko and Mikhail Salnikov 43

GraphRAG: Leveraging Graph-Based Efficiency to Minimize Hallucinations in LLM-Driven RAG for Finance Data
Mariam BARRY, Gaetan CAILLAUT, Pierre HALFTERMEYER, Raheel QADER, Mehdi MOUAYAD, Fabrice LE DEIT, Dimitri CARIOLARO and Joseph GESNOUIN 54

Structured Knowledge meets GenAI: A Framework for Logic-Driven Language Models
Farida Helmy Eldessouky, Nourhan Ehab, Carolin Schindler, Mervat Abuelkheir and Wolfgang Minker 66

Performance and Limitations of Fine-Tuned LLMs in SPARQL Query Generation
Thamer Mecharnia and Mathieu d'Aquin 69

Refining Noisy Knowledge Graph with Large Language Models
Na Dong, Natthawut Kertkeidkachorn, Xin Liu and Kiyoaki Shirai 78

Can LLMs be Knowledge Graph Curators for Validating Triple Insertions?
André Gomes Regino and Julio Cesar dos Reis 87

Text2Cypher: Bridging Natural Language and Graph Databases
Makbule Gulcin Ozsoy, Leila Messallem, Jon Besga and Gianandrea Minneci 100

KGFakeNet: A Knowledge Graph-Enhanced Model for Fake News Detection
Anuj Kumar, Pardeep Kumar, Abhishek Yadav, Satyadev Ahlawat and Yamuna Prasad 109

Style Knowledge Graph: Augmenting Text Style Transfer with Knowledge Graphs
Martina Toshevska, Slobodan Kalajdziski and Sonja Gievska 123

Entity Quality Enhancement in Knowledge Graphs through LLM-based Question Answering
Morteza Kamaladdini Ezzabady and Farah Benamara 136

Multilingual Skill Extraction for Job Vacancy–Job Seeker Matching in Knowledge Graphs
Hamit Kavas, Marc Serra-Vidal and Leo Wanner 146

Workshop Program

8:45–8:55 ***Welcome and Opening***

8:55–10:30 **Session 1**

8:55–9:35 ***Keynote 1: Could We Locate Knowledge in Large Language Models?***

09:35–09:55 *Effective Modeling of Generative Framework for Document-level Relational Triple Extraction*
Pratik Saini and Tapas Nayak

9:55–10:10 *Learn Together: Joint Multitask Finetuning of Pretrained KG-enhanced LLM for Downstream Tasks*
Anastasia Martynova, Vladislav Tishin and Natalia Semenova

10:10–10:25 *GNET-QG: Graph Network for Multi-hop Question Generation*
Samin Jamshidi and Yllias Chali

11:00–12:45 **Session 2**

11:00–11:20 *SKETCH: Structured Knowledge Enhanced Text Comprehension for Holistic Retrieval*
Aakash Mahalingam, Vinesh Kumar Gande, Aman Chadha, Vinija Jain and Divya Chaudhary

11:20–11:40 *On Reducing Factual Hallucinations in Graph-to-Text Generation Using Large Language Models*
Dmitrii Iarosh, Alexander Panchenko and Mikhail Salnikov

11:40–12:00 *GraphRAG: Leveraging Graph-Based Efficiency to Minimize Hallucinations in LLM-Driven RAG for Finance Data*
Mariam BARRY, Gaetan CAILLAUT, Pierre HALFTERMEYER, Raheel QADER, Mehdi MOUAYAD, Fabrice LE DEIT, Dimitri CARIOLARO and Joseph GESNOUIN

12:00–12:15 *Structured Knowledge meets GenAI: A Framework for Logic-Driven Language Models*
Farida Helmy Eldessouky, Nourhan Ehab, Carolin Schindler, Mervat Abuelkheir and Wolfgang Minker

12:15–12:35 *Performance and Limitations of Fine-Tuned LLMs in SPARQL Query Generation*
Thamer Mecharnia and Mathieu d'Aquin

13:40–15:30 **Session 3**

13:40–14:20 ***Keynote 2: Can LLMs function as, enhance and benefit from Knowledge Bases?***

14:20–14:40 *Refining Noisy Knowledge Graph with Large Language Models*
Na Dong, Natthawut Kertkeidkachorn, Xin Liu and Kiyoaki Shirai

14:40–15:00 *Can LLMs be Knowledge Graph Curators for Validating Triple Insertions?*
André Gomes Regino and Julio Cesar dos Reis

15:00–15:20 *Text2Cypher: Bridging Natural Language and Graph Databases*
Makbule Gulcin Ozsoy, Leila Messallem, Jon Besga and Gianandrea Minneci

16:00–17:20 **Session 4**

16:00–16:20 *KGFakeNet: A Knowledge Graph-Enhanced Model for Fake News Detection*
Anuj Kumar, Pardeep Kumar, Abhishek Yadav, Satyadev Ahlawat and Yamuna Prasad

16:20–16:40 *Style Knowledge Graph: Augmenting Text Style Transfer with Knowledge Graphs*
Martina Toshevska, Slobodan Kalajdziski and Sonja Gievska

16:40–17:00 *Entity Quality Enhancement in Knowledge Graphs through LLM-based Question Answering*
Morteza Kamaladdini Ezzabady and Farah Benamara

17:00–17:20 *Multilingual Skill Extraction for Job Vacancy–Job Seeker Matching in Knowledge Graphs*
Hamit Kavas, Marc Serra-Vidal and Leo Wanner

17:20–17:40 ***Closing***

Effective Modeling of Generative Framework for Document-level Relational Triple Extraction

Pratik Saini and Tapas Nayak
TCS Research, India
{pratik.saini, nayak.tapas}@tcs.com

Abstract

Document-level relational triple extraction (DocRTE) is a complex task that involves three key sub-tasks: entity mention extraction, entity clustering, and relational triple extraction. Past work has applied discriminative models to address these three sub-tasks, either by training them sequentially in a pipeline fashion or jointly training them. However, while end-to-end discriminative or generative models have proven effective for sentence-level relational triple extraction, they cannot be trivially extended to the document level, as they only handle relation extraction without addressing the remaining two sub-tasks, entity mention extraction or clustering. In this paper, we propose a three-stage generative framework leveraging a pre-trained BART model to address all three tasks required for document-level relational triple extraction. Tested on the widely used DocRED dataset, our approach outperforms previous generative methods and achieves competitive performance against discriminative models.

1 Introduction

Extracting relational triples—composed of a subject entity, an object entity, and the relation between them—from documents is a vital yet challenging task in natural language processing (NLP). Unlike sentence-level relation extraction tasks (Zheng et al., 2017; Zeng et al., 2018; Nayak and Ng, 2020), the challenges in document-level extraction increase significantly. The first major challenge is the extended context of documents, which requires capturing long-distance dependencies between entities across larger spans of text. Another challenge is that an entity may appear multiple times in a document with different surface forms, making entity resolution crucial. This complexity is less pronounced in sentence-level tasks, where entities are generally mentioned only once within a shorter context. An example of document-level relational triple extraction (DocRTE) is shown in Table 1 to demonstrate the complexity of this task.

Generative models (Zeng et al., 2018; Nayak and Ng, 2020) have shown strong performance in sentence-level relational triple extraction. Building on this, Cabot and Navigli (2021) proposed REBEL for document-level relational triple extraction using the DocRED dataset (Yao et al., 2019). REBEL introduced a linearization scheme that encodes all triples in a document as a sequence of tokens, using BART-large as the base model. The model's decoder then generates a token sequence, from which triples are extracted through straightforward post-processing. However, REBEL's linearization scheme does not fully address the entity mention extraction and entity clustering sub-tasks within DocRTE. It only captures the initial mentions of entities involved in relations and does not handle the extraction of mentions with different surface forms. In contrast, Giorgi et al. (2022) proposed an alternative linearization scheme for DocRTE, including all mentions of subject and object entities in the output sequence for each relational triple. This approach partially addresses some challenges of mention extraction and entity clustering. However, it redundantly extracts entity clusters multiple times if they are involved in multiple relational triples, which increases sequence length without added value. It also overlooks clusters that do not appear in any relation.

In contrast, JEREX (Eberts and Ulges, 2021) proposed a three-stage approach to address the tasks of entity mention extraction, entity clustering, and relational triple extraction, which can be trained either in a pipeline or jointly. The first stage employs a span-based classifier to identify entity mentions within the document. The second stage uses pairwise classification between entity mentions for clustering, and the third stage applies a relation classifier to determine relationships, or 'no relation,' between pairs of entity clusters. TAG (Zhang

Proceedings of the Generative AI and Knowledge Graph Workshop (GenAIK), pages 1–12
January 19, 2025. ©2025 International Committee on Computational Linguistics (ICCL)

Document: Washington Place (William Washington House) is one of the first homes built by freed slaves after the Emancipation Proclamation of 1863 in Hampshire County , West Virginia , United States . Washington Place was built by William and Annie Washington in north Romney between 1863 and 1874 on land given to Annie by her former owner , Susan Blue Parsons of Wappocomo plantation . William Washington later acquired other properties on the hills north of Romney along West Virginia Route 28 and became the first African - American land developer in the state of West Virginia . One of his subdivisions is the " Blacks Hill " neighborhood of Romney , adjacent to the Washington Place homestead . Washington Place was bought and restored by Ralph W. Haines , a local attorney and historic preservationist .
Entity Clusters: C1: (['Washington Place', 'William Washington House','Washington Place', 'Washington Place', 'Washington Place'], 'LOC'), C2: (['Emancipation Proclamation'], 'MISC'), C4: (['Hampshire County'], 'LOC'), C5: (['West Virginia', 'West Virginia'], 'LOC'), C6: (['United States'], 'LOC'), C7: (['William', 'William Washington'], 'PER'),C8: (['Annie Washington', 'Annie'], 'PER'), C9: (['Romney', 'Romney', 'Romney'], 'LOC'), C12: (['Susan Blue Parsons'], 'PER'), C13: (['Wappocomo plantation'], 'LOC'), C15: (['West Virginia Route 28'], 'LOC'), C18: (['Blacks Hill'], 'MISC'), C19: (['Ralph W. Haines'], 'PER')
Relational Triples: ['C2', 'C6', 'country'], ['C4', 'C5', 'located in the administrative territorial entity'],['C4', 'C6', 'country'], ['C5', 'C4', 'contains administrative territorial entity'], ['C5', 'C6', 'located in the administrative territorial entity'], ['C5', 'C6', 'country'], ['C6', 'C5', 'contains administrative territorial entity'], ['C7', 'C6', 'country of citizenship'], ['C8', 'C6', 'country of citizenship'], ['C14', 'C6', 'country of citizenship'], ['C15', 'C5', 'located in the administrative territorial entity'], ['C15', 'C6', 'country'], ['C19', 'C6', 'country of citizenship'], ['C1', 'C6', 'country'], ['C12', 'C6', 'country of citizenship'], ['C13', 'C6', 'country'], ['C9', 'C6', 'country']

Table 1: Example of the DocRTE Task. Entity mentions of the same entity cluster are marked using same colors.

et al., 2023) adopted a span-based mention extractor and a table-filling approach for the entity clustering and relation classification sub-tasks. However, these classification and table-filling methods face issues with an excess of negative samples; for n identified entity mentions, there are $O(n^2)$ mention pairs to classify for clustering, most of which do not belong to the same cluster. A similar problem exists for relation classification, where relations are first identified at the entity mention pair level and then aggregated to the entity cluster pair level. This class imbalance issue is common in discriminative approaches for this task. In contrast, generative frameworks avoid this imbalance by design, as they inherently focus on extracting only positive samples—pairs that belong to the same cluster or share a relation — while ignoring negative samples.

As discussed, the single-stage generative approach does not address two key sub-tasks of DocRTE — mention extraction and entity clustering — while discriminative approaches face class imbalance issues due to their structural design. To overcome these challenges, we propose a novel three-stage generative framework, 3G-DocRTE, for DocRTE that effectively integrates both paradigms. In the first stage, we use a generative model to extract all entity mentions by linearizing mentions from the documents. In the second stage, we mark the identified mentions within the input documents and use a generative approach to normalize varying surface forms of the same entity into a unified entity cluster representation, with the first mention's surface form serving as the cluster representative. In the third stage, we employ the REBEL linearization scheme (Cabot and Navigli, 2021) to extract relational triples within the document. Our experiments on the DocRED dataset show that our approach outperforms previous generative models on all three sub-tasks of DocRTE and achieves competitive performance compared to SOTA discriminative models.

2 Task Formulation

Given a document D composed of L tokens, represented as $D = \{t_1, t_2, \ldots, t_L\}$, our objective is to perform document-level relation extraction. This task encompasses following three structured sub-tasks:

Entity Mention Extraction (EME): This task extracts all possible mention spans $M = \{m_i\}_{i=1}^{|M|}$ from the document, where each mention m_i is defined as a continuous sequence of tokens. Mathematically, a mention m_i is represented as $m_i = (t_s, t_{s+1}, \ldots, t_e)$, where $1 \leq s \leq e \leq L$ and $t_s, \ldots, t_e \in D$.

Entity Clustering and Typing (ECT): This task groups the extracted mentions into entity clusters and assigns an entity type, $E = \{(e_j, \tau_j)\}_{j=1}^{|E|}$. Mathematically, each cluster e_j is a set of mentions that are assumed to refer to the same real-world entity, i.e., $e_j = \{m_i | m_i \in M \text{ and } m_i \text{ refers to entity } j\}$, and the type of each cluster is defined as $\tau_j \in \mathcal{T}$, where $\mathcal{T}$ is the set of all possible entity types.

Relational Triple Extraction (RTE): This task generates a set of relational triples $T = \{(e_j, r_{jk}, e_k) \mid e_j, e_k \in E,\ r_{jk} \in R \cup \{\perp\}\}$, where e_j and e_k are entity clusters, r_{jk} is selected from a predefined set $R \cup \{\perp\}$, with $\perp$ denoting the absence of any relation. The goal is to identify and specify the relations r_{jk} between each pair of entity clusters (e_j, e_k).

3 Proposed Framework: 3G-DocRTE

We introduce a three-step, multi-level generative framework, 3G-DocRTE, for Document-level relational triple Extraction (DocRTE), comprising (i) Entity Mention Extraction, (ii) Entity Clustering, and (iii) Relational Triple Extraction. First, we process documents containing multiple sentences to extract entity mentions. Next, we cluster these mentions to form entities along with their respective types. Finally, in the third stage, we generate relational triples present within the input document at the entity level.

A generative sequence-to-sequence model, such as BART (Lewis et al., 2019) models the probability of each output token o_i in the output sequence o based on the input sequence x and the previously generated output tokens $o_{<i}$: $\prod_{i=i}^{n} P(o_i \mid o_{<i}, x)$. The model is trained by maximizing the log-likelihood of the output tokens in the training data. We model this input and output sequence in an effective way for the three stages in our framework.

3.1 Entity Mention Extraction (EME)

Entity mentions can be extracted in a text either by using their specific tokens or by using their token index within the text. The same surface forms of an entity may appear multiple times throughout a document, making it difficult to ascertain precisely which unique instance is being referred to in token-based representation. Index-based representation of mentions can uniquely identify each occurrence. Given this advantage, we opt for an index-based approach to mention extraction in our framework.

We illustrate our index-based mention extraction strategy in Table 2 with an example. Each mention is identified by its start and end index position in the text. We append the start and end token index positions of all the mentions in a sequence separated by space. To maintain a consistent order during decoding, mentions are sorted according to their appearance in the input document. This enhances decoding efficiency by minimizing the token count. During decoding, we retain pairs of index positions, discarding single indexes if present at the end. Using these extracted start and end positions, we reconstruct the original surface form of each mention. To make index extraction easier for the pre-trained model, we follow Mallick et al. (2023) and insert the index of each token in the input document as well. Although, this increases the effective length of the document, but it helps the model during the mention generation.

Washington 0 Place 1 (2 William 3 Washington 4 House 5) 6 is 7 one 8 of 9 the 10 first 11 homes 12 built 13 by 14 freed 15 slaves 1 6 after 17 the 18 Emancipation 19 Proclamation 20 of 21 1863 22 in 23 Hampshire 24 County 25 , 26 West 27 Virginia 28 , 29 United 30 States 31 . 32 Washington 33 Place 34 was 35 built 36 by 37 William 38 and 39 Annie 40 Washington 41 in 42 north 43 Romney 44 between 45 1863 46 and 47 1874 48 on 49 land 50 given 51 to 52 Annie 53 by 54 her 55 former 56 owner 57 , 58 Susan 59 Blue 60 Parsons 61 of 62 Wappocomo 63 plantation 64 ...
0 1 3 5 19 20 22 22 24 25 27 28 30 31 33 34 38 38 40 41 44 44 46 46 48 48 53 53 59 61 63 64

Table 2: Example of input text and linearized output for mention extraction framework.

3.2 Entity Clustering & Typing (ECT)

To facilitate entity-level relational triple extraction, it is crucial to group local mentions of the same entity into document-level entity clusters, especially considering entities may have multiple mentions scattered throughout the input document and may exhibit various surface forms. Similar to our approach for mention extraction, we have introduced a linearization scheme tailored to enable entity clustering, also outputting cluster type information.

On the input side, we specify all mentions using start and end marker tags, denoted as <m> and </m>, respectively. For the output sequence of entity clustering framework, we use a linearization scheme where we replace each mention with the cluster-label/cluster-center. Additionally, we insert the entity type specific tags before and after each mention of that entity, as illustrated in Table 3. To simplify the decoding process and enhance efficiency, we opt to utilize the cluster center or cluster label rather than the entire cluster, thereby minimizing the number of tokens required. We decide to use the entity mention that appears first in the document for an entity cluster as the cluster-label/cluster-center.

For instance, In the example shown in Table 3, "<m> William Washington House </m>" is replaced by "<loc> Washington Place </loc>", where "Washington Place" serves as the first occurring

<m>Washington Place </m>(<m>William Washington House </m>) is one of the first homes built by freed slaves after the <m>Emancipation Proclamation </m>of <m>1863 </m>in <m>Hampshire County </m>, <m>West Virginia </m>, <m>United States </m>. <m>Washington Place </m>was built by <m>William </m>and <m>Annie Washington </m>in north <m>Romney </m>between <m>1863 </m>and <m>1874 </m>on land given to <m>Annie</m>by her former owner , <m>Susan Blue Parsons </m>of <m>Wappocomo plantation </m>...
<loc>Washington Place </loc>(<loc>Washington Place </loc>) is one of the first homes built by freed slaves after the <misc>Emancipation Proclamation </misc>of <time>1863 </time>in <loc>Hampshire County </loc>, <loc>West Virginia </loc>, <loc>United States </loc>. <loc>Washington Place </loc>was built by <per>William </per>and <per>Annie Washington </per>in north <loc>Romney </loc>between <time>1863 </time>and <time>1874 </time>on land given to <per>Annie </per>by her former owner , <per>Susan Blue Parsons </per>of <loc>Wappocomo plantation </loc>...

Table 3: Example of input and out representation for entity clustering stage.

<loc>Washington Place </loc>(<loc>Washington Place </loc>) is one of the first homes built by freed slaves after the <misc>Emancipation Proclamation </misc>of <time>1863 </time>in <loc>Hampshire County </loc>, <loc>West Virginia </loc>, <loc>United States </loc>. <loc>Washington Place </loc>was built by <per>William </per>and <per>Annie Washington </per>in north <loc>Romney </loc>between <time>1863 </time>and <time>1874 </time>on land given to <per>Annie </per>by her former owner , <per>Susan Blue Parsons </per>of <loc>Wappocomo plantation </loc>...
<triple>Washington Place <subj>United States <obj>country <triple>Emancipation Proclamation <subj>United States <obj>country <triple>Hampshire County <subj>West Virginia <obj>located in the administrative territorial entity <subj>United States <obj>country <triple>West Virginia <subj>Hampshire County <obj>contains administrative territorial entity <subj>United States <obj>located in the administrative territorial entity <subj>United States <obj>country <triple>United States <subj>West Virginia <obj>contains administrative territorial entity ...

Table 4: Example of input and output representation for RTE. Note that the blue-colored triple actually comprises two nested triples sharing the same subject/head entity.

mention for the cluster, with the entity type denoted as "<loc>".

During the decoding phase, each mention in the input document has a corresponding cluster label and a cluster type. We utilise these cluster labels to assign mentions to their respective clusters. Mentions sharing the same cluster label are grouped to form a cluster.

After this stage, the documents are normalized with respect to entity mentions as we replace the mentions with the corresponding cluster labels, and these are then enclosed within entity type marker tags. This normalization of the documents serves a dual purpose. Firstly, it simplifies the task of the subsequent entity triple extraction step. Secondly, it eliminates the need to output entire entity clusters with all their mentions, thereby effectively reducing the number of tokens required to be processed. This streamlined approach enhances both the efficiency and accuracy of the subsequent relational triple extraction stage.

3.3 Relational Triple Extraction (RTE)

In the final stage of our approach, namely relational triple Extraction, we focus on generating entity-level relational triples present within the documents. A relational triple comprises head and tail entities along with a relation from a predefined relation set. It's worth noting that a single document may express multiple relations between the same head and tail entities.

This stage builds upon the output of the previous entity clustering stage. To achieve effective linearization and denote all relational triples concisely, we adopt the linearization scheme proposed in the REBEL (Cabot and Navigli, 2021) paper as shown in Table 4. REBEL introduces a set of marker tokens for this purpose. Triples are grouped by the head entity, with the <triple> tag indicating the beginning of a new triple for a specific head entity, succeeded by the head entity itself. The <subj> tag marks the conclusion of the head entity, followed by the object entity. Subsequently, the <obj> tag signifies the conclusion of the tail entity and the initiation of the relation between the head and tail entities. In cases where there are multiple objects or relations of the same head entity, the <subj> tag marks the termination of the preceding relation, followed by the subsequent object entity. This process is repeated as needed for additional objects and relations. Once all relations involving a particular head entity have been processed, a fresh set of relations begins with the subsequent appearing head entity in the text. This iterative process continues until all triples have been linearized.

However, their proposed linearization scheme only utilizes the first occurring mention and disregards any remaining mentions of that entity. They extract mentions solely if they participate in one of the relational triples. Consequently, they do not comprehensively address the entity mention extraction and entity clustering sub-tasks.

To overcome this limitation, we opt to utilize the cluster label of the entities instead of solely relying on the first occurring mention of an entity. It's noteworthy that we have already extracted entity clusters along with entity types in the previous stage, and we can retrieve the entity cluster using the cluster label.

Each stage of our framework builds upon the results of the previous stage. By the conclusion of the third stage in our proposed framework, we can deduce all the relational triples present in the input document using the output of all three stages along with all entity mentions and entity clusters in the documents. In this way our proposed three-stage generative framework 3G-DocRTE solves all three sub-tasks of document-level relational triple extraction.

4 Experiments

4.1 Dataset & Evaluation Metric

We conduct our experiments using the manually annotated part of DocRED dataset (Yao et al., 2019) and use the splits provided by JEREX (Eberts and Ulges, 2021). JEREX removed 45 erroneous document from training set, used 3,008 documents for the training. They randomly split the 1,000 documents in the original dev set into two parts: 300 documents as validation set, and 700 documents for the test set. The specific statistics for these JEREX splits are detailed in Table 5.

Split	#Doc	#Men	#Ent	#Rel
Train	3,008	78,677	58,708	37,486
Dev	300	7,702	5,805	3,678
Test	700	17,988	13,594	8,787

Table 5: DocRED dataset split used for DocRTE.

As the dataset split, we use the evaluation methodology of Eberts and Ulges (2021) for this task. We adopt a strict evaluation criteria for all three sub-tasks of DocRTE. An **entity mention** is considered correct if its surface form is an exact match with a ground truth mention's surface form. An **entity cluster** is considered correct only if it exactly matches a ground truth entity cluster. This includes — all mentions within the generated cluster matching exactly with those in a ground truth cluster — and the cluster type also matching with the ground truth type. We generate relational triples at entity-cluster-level. A **relational triple** is considered as correct if the head and tail entities, as well as the relation itself, are correct and matches with the ground truth relational triple. For each of these sub-tasks, we report precision, recall, and F1 scores.

4.2 Baselines

For baselines, we use two generative approaches: REBEL (Cabot and Navigli, 2021) and Seq2Rel (Giorgi et al., 2022), two discriminative approaches: JEREX (Eberts and Ulges, 2021) and TAG (Zhang et al., 2023) for comparison.

REBEL (Cabot and Navigli, 2021): REBEL uses a BART (Lewis et al., 2019) model to generate the relational triples in a sequence-to-sequence fashion. They use a linearization scheme where entities and relations are represented as tokens separated by special tags. However, this approach cannot solve the mention extraction and entity clustering sub-tasks for the DocRTE.

Seq2Rel (Giorgi et al., 2022): This is another Seq2Seq approach where they use BERT encoder and LSTM decoder to generate the relational triples using a pre-defined linearization scheme. They designed the linearization scheme in such a way that it can extract the entity clusters along with the triples. But this approach only includes those entity mentions and entity clusters that participate in some relational triples. Entity mentions and clusters that are not part of any relational triples are ignored in their linearization scheme. Also, they extract an entity cluster as many times as they participate in as many triples. Additionally, there is a significant amount of redundant entity cluster generation in this approach.

JEREX (Eberts and Ulges, 2021): This is a 3-step discriminative approach for the DocRTE task. First, they extract the entity mentioned using a span-based classifier. Next, they classify each pair of extracted mentions if they belong to the same entity cluster or not. In the third step, they classify the relations or no relation among all possible pairs of entity clusters. They can train these three stages either in a pipeline fashion or in a joint fashion.

TAG (Zhang et al., 2023): This model proposed a table-filling approach for DocRTE. First, it identifies the entity mention spans and creates a table where rows and columns of the table represent each mention. Each cell of this table is then filled with values that represent if they belong to the same cluster or not and the relations between the mentions. Some aggregation mechanism is used to obtain the entity cluster pair-level relations from the mention pair level relations.

4.3 Parameter Settings

For training, we mostly follow the REBEL paper (Cabot and Navigli, 2021). We use BART-large (Lewis et al., 2019) as our base model and fine-tune it separately on the DocRED human annotated dataset for each sub-task of DocRTE with sub-task specific linearization schemes. We used batch size of 4 and AdamW (Loshchilov and Hutter, 2019) optimizer with learning rate at 1e-05, the weight decay at 1e-03. Additionally, The REBEL paper (Cabot and Navigli, 2021) released a pre-trained version of BART-large, which was fine-tuned on a relational triple dataset derived from Wikipedia hyperlinks. We also utilize this pre-trained BART-large model for our experiments, referring to it with the '-pt' suffix.

5 Experimental Results

The performance comparison of generative models and discriminative models are summarized in Table 6.

Entity Mention Extraction: In the entity mention extraction sub-task, both the 3G-DocRTE and 3G-DocRTE-pt models demonstrate competitive performance, each achieving an F1-score of 0.930, closely matching other baseline models. This performance indicates that our 3G-DocRTE framework effectively identifies correct mention spans across various document contexts.

Entity Clustering & Typing: In entity clustering & typing, the 3G-DocRTE framework shows strong performance with an F1-score of more than 80%. This represents an almost 30% higher F1 score than that achieved by the REBEL framework for this task. When type information is not considered in evaluation like TAG does, our approach achieves competitive performance. These results highlight the robustness of our framework in effectively grouping mentions into accurate clusters. However, our performance is slightly lagging—about 5% in F1 score—behind the best result in EC.

Relational Triple Extraction: In relational triple extraction, generative models generally exhibit lower F1-scores compared to discriminative models as evident from Table 6. 3G-DocRTE-pt records the highest F1-score among generative models at 0.405 under the strict evaluation criterion. Under the relaxed criterion, TAG model achieves the highest F1 score of 43.2%, whereas our approach achieves around 41.2% F1 score. The general performance gap between the discriminative and generative models underscores the challenges and potential trade-offs inherent in generative approaches, highlighting a critical area for further improvement. Particularly, our generative approach achieves significantly lower performance in the entity clustering task which needs more attention in future.

Overall, while discriminative models tend to show slight advantages in specific sub-tasks, particularly in Entity Clustering, our 3G-DocRTE framework, particularly in its pre-trained variant, consistently delivers competitive and balanced performance across all sub-tasks. The consistent performance of our framework underscores its potential to advance the state-of-the-art in document-level relation extraction, highlighting its capability to handle complex relational data effectively.

6 Analysis & Discussion

6.1 Discriminative vs Generative Performance

From Table 6, it is evident that discriminative models generally outperform generative models. This discrepancy can likely be attributed to the inherent design choices between these paradigms, which affect the volume of effective training samples. Discriminative models train on all possible pairs of entity clusters to identify relations, using a larger number of training samples per document. During inference, they identify relations from these pairs and aggregate these into document-level triples. In contrast, generative models are trained directly on documents; a single document outputs a set of triples. Considering the DocRED training data, which comprises approximately 3,000 documents with about 58,000 entity clusters, the effective training sample size for discriminative models significantly exceeds that of generative models. This considerable difference may be a reason for the better performance observed in discriminative models.

6.2 Copy vs Reasoning in 3G-DocRTE

We analyze how generative frameworks perform in tasks that involve only copying versus those requiring some reasoning. In the case of the Marker-Inserted linearization scheme (see Table 7) for entity mention extraction, our model simply needs to copy the input tokens and insert <m> tags where entity mentions occur. Identifying a mention is

	EME			ECT			RTE		
Model	P	R	F1	P	R	F1	P	R	F1
REBEL	0.844	0.444	0.582	0.727	0.367	0.488	0.237	0.223	0.230
REBEL-pt	0.837	0.449	0.584	0.720	0.362	0.482	0.251	0.249	0.250
Seq2Rel	-	-	-	-	-	-	0.440	0.338	0.382
JEREX	0.933	0.927	0.930	0.798	0.804	0.801	0.428	0.383	0.404
TAG	0.929	0.928	0.929	0.811	0.798	0.804	0.428	0.395	0.411
3G-DocRTE	0.933	0.926	0.930	0.810	0.807	0.808	0.385	0.376	0.381
3G-DocRTE-pt	0.930	0.930	0.930	0.802	0.805	0.804	0.413	0.397	0.405

Table 6: Performance comparison of generative/discriminative models against 3G-DocRTE framework on JEREX split of DocRED. Models marked with '-pt' denote a BART-large model variant that is post-trained using the REBEL dataset.

a localized task that does not require reasoning across documents. Hence, in this task, our framework achieves a very high F1 score of around 93%. Contrarily, for the entity clustering task, the linearization scheme used in Table 3, our generative framework must not only copy most tokens from the input text but also resolve co-references among different mentions. This co-reference resolution involves long-term reasoning across the entire document. As shown in Table 6, our model achieves an F1 score of approximately 80% in the entity clustering task, which is 10% lower in terms of absolute F1 score compared to the mention extraction task. This performance difference between the two tasks indicates that auto-regressive generative models struggle with reasoning tasks while decoding the output sequence.

6.3 Ablation for Entity Mention Extraction

To optimize mention extraction strategies within the 3G-DocRTE model, we conducted ablation studies focusing on different linearization schemes. Apart from the index-based scheme discussed in Section 4.1, we explored both the marker-inserted and marker-separated schemes. In the marker-inserted scheme, the start and end of all the entity mentions in the document are marked by <m> and </m> tags. An example of this approach can be seen in row 2 of Table 7. The marker-separated scheme includes only the entity mention tokens in the output sequence, marking the start of each mention with a <m> tag. An example of this can be found in row 3 of Table 7. The performances of these schemes are reported in Table 8, showing comparable results. Additionally, we evaluated an adaptation of the index-based scheme that omits the token index in the input document. This approach (see Table 12 in Appendix) resulted in a significant drop in the F1 score for the mention extraction task, as shown in row 4 of Table 8). We use the Index Based linearization for the final model as it achieves high F1 score with fewer output tokens.

Washington Place (William Washington House) is one of the first homes built by freed slaves after the Emancipation Proclamation of 1863 in Hampshire County , West Virginia , United States ...
Marker-Inserted: <m>Washington Place </m>(<m> William Washington House </m>) is one of the first homes built by freed slaves after the <m>Emancipation Proclamation </m>of <m>1863 </m>in ...
Marker-Separated: <m>Washington Place <m>William Washington House <m>Emancipation Proclamation <m>1863 ...

Table 7: Example of token-based linearization strategy for Mention Extraction using start (<m>) and end (</m>) marker tags.

	EME		
Linearization Scheme	P	R	F1
Marker-Inserted	0.939	0.929	0.934
Marker-Separated	0.925	0.924	0.925
Index Based	0.930	0.930	0.930
- w/o index in document	0.532	0.527	0.529

Table 8: Performance comparison of two linearization scheme for entity mention extraction.

6.4 Ablation for Entity Clustering & Typing

In addition to the entity clustering linearization scheme described in Section 4.2 (referred to as Type-Marker-Inserted), we experiment with another scheme, referred to as Type-Marker-Separated, similar to the previous scheme. For every tagged mention in input text, we extract an entity type marker tag followed by the cluster label for that mention. We choose the first appearing mention of a cluster as a cluster label. The performance comparison of these two linearization schemes is reported in Table 10. Results indicate that the Type-Marker-Inserted scheme slightly outperforms the Type-Marker-Separated scheme. The results of our evaluation indicate that the Type-Marker-Inserted scheme slightly outperforms the Type-Marker-Separated scheme. This performance difference suggests that the Type-Marker-Inserted approach forms a coherent and meaningful text compared to the disconnected and divided format of the Type-Marker-Separated scheme which may facilitate better understanding by the model and enables effective grouping of the mentions.

Type-Marker-Separated: <loc>Washington Place <loc>Washington Place <misc>Emancipation Proclamation <time>1863 <loc>Hampshire County <loc>West Virginia <loc>United States <loc>Washington Place <per>William <per>Annie Washington <loc>Romney <time>1863 <time>1874 <per>Annie <per>Susan Blue Parsons <loc>Wappocomo plantation ...

Table 9: Type-Marker-Separated scheme for ECT using the same input format as described in Table 3.

	ECT		
Linearization Scheme	**P**	**R**	**F1**
Type-Marker-Separated	0.792	0.796	0.794
Type-Marker-Inserted	0.802	0.805	0.804

Table 10: Performance comparison of two different linearization schemes for ECT task.

6.5 Ablation for Relational Triple Extraction

Before REBEL Cabot and Navigli (2021), Nayak and Ng (2020) proposed another linearization scheme with their Word Decoder model where each triple is separated by a special tag and the components of a triples (head entity, tail entity, and a relation) are separated by another special tag (see Table 13 in Appendix for more details). We experimented with such representation for the relational triple extraction stage of 3G-DocRTE and include the results in Table 11. The evaluation shows that the REBEL representation yields better performance compared to the Word Decoder representation. It is compact and requires significantly fewer tokens to represent all the relational triples in a document.

	RTE		
Linearization Scheme	**P**	**R**	**F1**
Word Decoder	0.363	0.395	0.378
REBEL	0.413	0.397	0.405

Table 11: Performance comparison of RTE task with two different output representations.

6.6 Unified EME and ECT Approach

As document-level tasks involve a large number of tokens, maximum token length often becomes a performance bottleneck for any pre-trained model such as BART. Implementing all three steps—mention extraction, entity clustering, and relation extraction—within a single linearization process can increase token length and lead to unnecessary repetition of clusters. So we propose three stages for three sub-tasks of DocRTE.

But **Is it possible to reduce the number of steps in the pipeline?** Of the three stages in our proposed 3G-DocRTE framework, it appears feasible to combine the first two stages—mention extraction and entity clustering—into a single step and use a single generative model which takes plain text as input and generates output similar to the output of the second stage of 3G-DocRTE. Our goal is to replace each mention of an entity in the documents with corresponding cluster labels enclosed by entity-type markers. Although the generative approach can perform this combined task, but a significant challenge was to map these cluster labels back to the original mentions in documents as cluster labels and their mentions are not always of the same token length. The BART tokenizer alters the text by removing what it perceives as extra spaces, and it can split tokens into sub-tokens or merge them, complicating the recovery of the original tokens. So we believe that it is more effective and intuitive to use two different stages of the generative approach for these two sub-tasks of mention extraction and entity clustering in DocRTE.

7 Related Work

Relational Triple extraction (RTE) is a crucial task for extracting knowledge from text, where this knowledge is represented in triple form, consisting of two entities (subject and object) and a directed relation from the subject to the object. These triples can be added to knowledge bases (KBs) to enrich them. There are two distinct approaches to addressing this task: (i) Relation Classification (RC) and (ii) Relational Triple Extraction (RTE). In the relation classification approach, entities are pre-identified, and models are required to identify the relations, or 'no relation', between pairs of entities. In the relational triple Extraction approach, models simultaneously extract corresponding entity pairs and their relations. Recently, RTE approaches have gained popularity as they provide an end-to-end solution for this task.

Mintz et al. (2009) introduced the distant supervision method to generate large-scale datasets for relation Classification task without the need for human annotations. It has significantly fostered the research in this area. Following the introduction of word embeddings in NLP (Mikolov et al., 2013; Pennington et al., 2014), numerous neural models were proposed to address this task. Zeng et al. (2014, 2015) introduced CNN-based models for classifying relations or 'no relation' between two entities within a short sentence-level context. Additionally, Jat et al. (2018); Nayak and Ng (2019) proposed attention models for the same task.

Relational triple extraction is relatively new task and Zheng et al. (2017) was very first to introduce a tagging-based approach for this task, while Zeng et al. (2018); Nayak and Ng (2020) explored sequence-to-sequence learning for the same task. Eberts and Ulges (2021) used a pre-trained BART based model that represents relational triples using a linearization mechanism. The BART decoder of their model can generate this representation in an auto-regressive manner. Recent models have leveraged pre-trained transformers like BERT (Devlin et al., 2019) to encode the sentences to get a better representation. Models such as TPLinker (Wang et al., 2020b), CasRel (Wei et al., 2020), TDEER (Li et al., 2021), PRGC (Zheng et al., 2021), PFN (Yan et al., 2021), GRTE (Ren et al., 2021), OneRel (Shang et al., 2022), and BiRTE (Ren et al., 2022) have proposed various neural architectures based on BERT to address RTE at the sentence level.

Recently, with the introduction of the DocRED dataset (Yao et al., 2019), document-level relation extraction has gained significant traction in the research community. Initially, in this field, most research work focused on relation classification at the entity levels within documents. Nan et al. (2020); Wang et al. (2020a); Zeng et al. (2020, 2021); Xu et al. (2021b,a) introduced various attention models and graph convolution models for this task. More recently, researchers have explored the document-level relational triple extraction task on the DocRED dataset. This task is notably more challenging than its sentence-level counterpart, as it involves longer context lengths, requires coreference resolution across the longer text, and the models need to perform multi-hop reasoning to extract triples. REBEL (Cabot and Navigli, 2021) and Seq2Rel (Giorgi et al., 2022) have proposed sequence-to-sequence models for document-level relational triple extraction using a linearized triple representation. Alternatively, JEREX (Eberts and Ulges, 2021), Joint-M (Xu and Choi, 2022), and TAG (Zhang et al., 2023) have proposed multi-stage discriminative approaches for the same task.

8 Conclusion

In this work, we propose an effective way of using generative frameworks for the document-level relational triple extraction task (DocRTE). Our approach completely addresses all three sub-tasks of DocRTE: entity mention extraction, entity clustering, and relational triple extraction, whereas, the previous generative approaches exhibit significant deficiencies in managing these sub-tasks. On the DocRED dataset, our proposed framework surpasses earlier generative models. Additionally, when compared with multi-stage discriminative approaches on the same dataset, our method achieves competitive performance across the three sub-tasks of DocRTE.

9 Ethics Statement

There is no ethical issues concerning this research work.

10 Limitations

Due to limited GPU availability, we can only finetune the BART model at this time. To achieve broader applicability, fine-tuning other encoder-decoder models like T5 would be advantageous.

Another potential limitation of our approach is the significant increase in document length when additional tokens are inserted. While this does not pose an issue for the DocRED dataset, it could become problematic for longer documents. Specifically, the additional tokens may exceed the maximum token limit allowed in the encoder.

References

Pere-Lluís Huguet Cabot and Roberto Navigli. 2021. Rebel: Relation extraction by end-to-end language generation. In *EMNLP*.

Jacob Devlin, Ming-Wei Chang, Kenton Lee, and Kristina Toutanova. 2019. BERT: Pre-training of deep bidirectional transformers for language understanding. In *NAACL*.

Markus Eberts and Adrian Ulges. 2021. An end-to-end model for entity-level relation extraction using multi-instance learning. In *Conference of the European Chapter of the Association for Computational Linguistics*.

John Giorgi, Gary D Bader, and Bo Wang. 2022. A sequence-to-sequence approach for document-level relation extraction. In *Workshop on Biomedical Natural Language Processing*.

Sharmistha Jat, Siddhesh Khandelwal, and Partha Pratim Talukdar. 2018. Improving distantly supervised relation extraction using word and entity based attention. *AKBC*.

Mike Lewis, Yinhan Liu, Naman Goyal, Marjan Ghazvininejad, Abdel rahman Mohamed, Omer Levy, Veselin Stoyanov, and Luke Zettlemoyer. 2019. Bart: Denoising sequence-to-sequence pre-training for natural language generation, translation, and comprehension. In *Annual Meeting of the Association for Computational Linguistics*.

Xianming Li, Xiaotian Luo, Cheng Jie Dong, Daichuan Yang, Beidi Luan, and Zhen He. 2021. TDEER: An efficient translating decoding schema for joint extraction of entities and relations. In *EMNLP*.

Ilya Loshchilov and Frank Hutter. 2019. Decoupled weight decay regularization. In *ICLR*.

Prabir Mallick, Tapas Nayak, and Indrajit Bhattacharya. 2023. Adapting pre-trained generative models for extractive question answering. In *GEM Workshop at EMNLP*.

Tomas Mikolov, Kai Chen, Greg Corrado, and Jeffrey Dean. 2013. Efficient estimation of word representations in vector space. In *Proceedings of the International Conference on Learning Representations*.

Mike Mintz, Steven Bills, Rion Snow, and Dan Jurafsky. 2009. Distant supervision for relation extraction without labeled data. In *Proceedings of the 47th Annual Meeting of the Association for Computational Linguistics and the 4th International Joint Conference on Natural Language Processing*.

Guoshun Nan, Zhijiang Guo, Ivan Sekulic, and Wei Lu. 2020. Reasoning with latent structure refinement for document-level relation extraction. In *Proceedings of the 58th Annual Meeting of the Association for Computational Linguistics*.

Tapas Nayak and Hwee Tou Ng. 2019. Effective attention modeling for neural relation extraction. In *Proceedings of the Conference on Computational Natural Language Learning*.

Tapas Nayak and Hwee Tou Ng. 2020. Effective modeling of encoder-decoder architecture for joint entity and relation extraction. In *Proceedings of The Thirty-Fourth AAAI Conference on Artificial Intelligence*.

Jeffrey Pennington, Richard Socher, and Christopher D. Manning. 2014. Glove: Global vectors for word representation. In *Empirical Methods in Natural Language Processing (EMNLP)*.

Feiliang Ren, Longhui Zhang, Shujuan Yin, Xiaofeng Zhao, Shilei Liu, Bochao Li, and Yaduo Liu. 2021. A novel global feature-oriented relational triple extraction model based on table filling. In *EMNLP*.

Feiliang Ren, Longhui Zhang, Xiaofeng Zhao, Shujuan Yin, Shilei Liu, and Bochao Li. 2022. A simple but effective bidirectional framework for relational triple extraction. *Proceedings of the Fifteenth ACM International Conference on Web Search and Data Mining*.

Y. Shang, Heyan Huang, and Xian-Ling Mao. 2022. OneRel: Joint entity and relation extraction with one module in one step. In *AAAI*.

Difeng Wang, Wei Hu, Ermei Cao, and Weijian Sun. 2020a. Global-to-local neural networks for document-level relation extraction. In *Proceedings of the 2020 Conference on Empirical Methods in Natural Language Processing (EMNLP)*.

Yucheng Wang, Bowen Yu, Yueyang Zhang, Tingwen Liu, Hongsong Zhu, and Limin Sun. 2020b. TPLinker: Single-stage joint extraction of entities and relations through token pair linking. In *COLING*.

Zhepei Wei, Jianlin Su, Yue Wang, Yuan Tian, and Yi Chang. 2020. A novel cascade binary tagging framework for relational triple extraction. In *ACL*.

Liyan Xu and Jinho Choi. 2022. Modeling task interactions in document-level joint entity and relation extraction. In *Proceedings of the 2022 Conference of the North American Chapter of the Association for Computational Linguistics: Human Language Technologies*, pages 5409–5416, Seattle, United States. Association for Computational Linguistics.

Wang Xu, Kehai Chen, and Tiejun Zhao. 2021a. Discriminative reasoning for document-level relation extraction. In *Findings of the Association for Computational Linguistics: ACL-IJCNLP 2021*.

Wang Xu, Kehai Chen, and Tiejun Zhao. 2021b. Document-level relation extraction with reconstruction. *Proceedings of the AAAI Conference on Artificial Intelligence*, 35(16):14167–14175.

Zhiheng Yan, Chong Zhang, Jinlan Fu, Qi Zhang, and Zhongyu Wei. 2021. A partition filter network for joint entity and relation extraction. In *EMNLP*.

Yuan Yao, Deming Ye, Peng Li, Xu Han, Yankai Lin, Zhenghao Liu, Zhiyuan Liu, Lixin Huang, Jie Zhou, and Maosong Sun. 2019. DocRED: A large-scale document-level relation extraction dataset. In *Proceedings of ACL 2019*.

Daojian Zeng, Kang Liu, Yubo Chen, and Jun Zhao. 2015. Distant supervision for relation extraction via piecewise convolutional neural networks. In *Proceedings of the 2015 Conference on Empirical Methods in Natural Language Processing*.

Daojian Zeng, Kang Liu, Siwei Lai, Guangyou Zhou, and Jun Zhao. 2014. Relation classification via convolutional deep neural network. In *Proceedings of the 25th International Conference on Computational Linguistics*.

Shuang Zeng, Yuting Wu, and Baobao Chang. 2021. SIRE: Separate intra- and inter-sentential reasoning for document-level relation extraction. In *Findings of the Association for Computational Linguistics: ACL-IJCNLP 2021*.

Shuang Zeng, Runxin Xu, Baobao Chang, and Lei Li. 2020. Double graph based reasoning for document-level relation extraction. In *Proceedings of the 2020 Conference on Empirical Methods in Natural Language Processing (EMNLP)*.

Xiangrong Zeng, Daojian Zeng, Shizhu He, Kang Liu, and Jun Zhao. 2018. Extracting relational facts by an end-to-end neural model with copy mechanism. In *Proceedings of the 56th Annual Meeting of the Association for Computational Linguistics*.

Ruoyu Zhang, Yanzeng Li, and Lei Zou. 2023. A novel table-to-graph generation approach for document-level joint entity and relation extraction. In *Annual Meeting of the Association for Computational Linguistics*.

Heng Zheng, Rui Wen, Xi Chen, Yifan Yang, Yunyan Zhang, Ziheng Zhang, Ningyu Zhang, Bin Qin, Ming Xu, and Yefeng Zheng. 2021. PRGC: Potential relation and global correspondence based joint relational triple extraction. In *ACL*.

Suncong Zheng, Feng Wang, Hongyun Bao, Yuexing Hao, Peng Zhou, and Bo Xu. 2017. Joint extraction of entities and relations based on a novel tagging scheme. In *Proceedings of the 55th Annual Meeting of the Association for Computational Linguistics*.

A Appendix

A.1 Examples of Linearization

We include some examples of linearization schemes used in our ablation studies here. Details are included in the respective caption.

Washington Place (William Washington House) is one of the first homes built by freed slaves after the Emancipation Proclamation of 1863 in Hampshire County , West Virginia , United States . Washington Place was built by William and Annie Washington in north Romney between 1863 and 1874 on land given to Annie by her former owner , Susan Blue Parsons of Wappocomo plantation ...
0 1 3 5 19 20 22 22 24 25 27 28 30 31 33 34 38 38 40 41 44 44 46 46 48 48 53 53 59 61 63 64

Table 12: Example of input text and linearized output for mention extraction framework where we do not insert the token index in the input documents.

<loc>Washington Place </loc>(<loc>Washington Place </loc>) is one of the first homes built by freed slaves after the <misc>Emancipation Proclamation </misc>of <time>1863 </time>in <loc>Hampshire County </loc>, <loc>West Virginia </loc>, <loc>United States </loc>. <loc>Washington Place </loc>was built by <per>William </per>and <per>Annie Washington </per>in north <loc>Romney </loc>between <time>1863 </time>and <time>1874 </time>on land given to <per>Annie </per>by her former owner , <per>Susan Blue Parsons </per>of <loc>Wappocomo plantation </loc>...
<triple>Washington Place <subj>United States <obj>country <triple>Emancipation Proclamation <subj>United States <obj>country <triple>Hampshire County <subj>West Virginia <obj>located in the administrative territorial entity <subj>United States <obj>country <triple>West Virginia <subj>Hampshire County <obj>contains administrative territorial entity <subj>United States <obj>located in the administrative territorial entity <subj>United States <obj>country <triple>United States <subj>West Virginia <obj>contains administrative territorial entity ...
<triple>Washington Place <subj>United States <obj:>country <triple>... <triple>Hampshire County <subj:>West Virginia <obj:>located in the administrative territorial entity <triple>Hampshire County <subj:>United States <obj:>country <triple>...

Table 13: Example of input and output representation for RTE for REBEL and Word Decoder models. First row represents the input document format used for both of these two models. Row 2 represents the REBEL (Cabot and Navigli, 2021) representation for output triples. Row 3 shows the Word Decoder (Nayak and Ng, 2020) representation for triples. In REBEL representation if you look at the blue-colored triple, you see that two triples are nested which share the same subject/head entity. But the same two triples in Word Decoder representation are flattened for simpler representation.

Learn Together: Joint Multitask Finetuning of Pretrained KG-enhanced LLM for Downstream Tasks

Anastasia Martynova
Sber AI, HSE
Moscow, Russia
ans.martynova@gmail.com

Vladislav Tishin
Sber AI / Moscow, Russia
ITMO / St. Petersburg, Russia
vvikttishin@sberbank.ru

Natalia Semenova
Sber AI, AIRI
Moscow, Russia
semenova.bnl@gmail.com

Abstract

Recent studies have shown that a knowledge graph (KG) can enhance text data by providing structured background knowledge, which can significantly improve the language understanding skills of the LLM. Besides, finetuning of such models shows solid results on commonsense reasoning benchmarks. In this work, we introduce expandable Joint Multitask Finetuning of Pretrained KG-enchanced LLM approach for Question Answering (QA), Machine Reading Comprehension (MRC) and Knowledge Graph Question Answering (KGQA) tasks. Extensive experiments show competitive performance of joint finetuning QA+MRC+KGQA over single task approach with a maximum gain of 30% accuracy.

1 Introduction

Large language models (LLMs), pretrained on extensive text corpus, have demonstrated high performance across a wide range of natural language processing (NLP) tasks. However, despite their success in various applications, these models have notable shortcomings. Studies show that LLMs frequently fail to accurately recall factual information and tend to generate hallucinations - statements that are false or misleading. Furthermore, LLMs pretrained on general text data may not effectively apply domain-specific knowledge without additional training on relevant datasets.

To improve the efficiency of large language models (LLMs) and address the aforementioned challenges, a promising solution is to integrate LLMs with knowledge graphs (KGs). Knowledge graphs represent factual information in a structured format, using triples composed of a head entity, a relation, and a tail entity. KGs are widely applied across various domains due to their structured, interconnected representation of data, offering a more comprehensive and interpretable view of information and facilitating easier interaction with it.

There are several strategies to integrate LLMs with KGs (Pan et al., 2024). The first approach involves enhancing large language models using knowledge graphs. In this approach, KGs can be incorporated during the pretraining and inference stages of the LLM to enrich its linguistic representations with external knowledge and provide insights into its reasoning process. For example, the ERNIE (Zhang et al., 2019) and KALM (Corby Rosset, 2021) architectures leverage this method by feeding pairs of sentences and corresponding entities from the knowledge graph into the LLM, subsequently training the model to predict relationships between these entities.

The second approach takes the opposite direction—strengthening knowledge graphs using LLMs. This technique aims to enhance the productivity of KGs and improve their performance in KG-related tasks. For example, the authors of the QA-GNN (Yasunaga et al., 2021) architecture employ a graph neural network (GNN)-based model to jointly analyze the input context and KG information through message passing. The input text information is transformed into a special node via a pooling operation and then connected with other entities in the KG. Another model, GreaseLM (Zhang et al., 2021), facilitates deeper interaction between text tokens and KG entities. Information from both modalities propagates to each other, allowing representations of linguistic context to be grounded in structured world knowledge and enabling linguistic nuances in context to inform graph knowledge representations.

Another increasingly popular way to leverage the benefits of LLMs and KGs simultaneously is to integrate these models into a single framework where they can mutually reinforce each other. In this framework, LLMs are used to understand natural language, while KGs serve as a knowledge base providing factual information. The DRAGON

Proceedings of the Generative AI and Knowledge Graph Workshop (GenAIK), pages 13–19
January 19, 2025.

(Deep Bidirectional Language-Knowledge Graph Pretraining) architecture (Yasunaga et al., 2022) exemplifies this approach by pretraining a deeply integrated language-knowledge foundation model using both text and KGs at scale. This self-supervised model processes text segments and their corresponding KG subgraphs, integrating information from both modalities bidirectionally.

Since DRAGON demonstrated superior performance in commonsense reasoning and tasks involving complex reasoning compared to the QA-GNN and GreaseLM baselines, we decided to investigate the effectiveness of this model within the frameworks of the Machine Reading Comprehension (MRC) task, the Knowledge Graph Question Answering (KGQA) task, and the combined MRC+QA+KGQA task. This study tests the hypothesis that training on the combined MRC+QA+KGQA task will yield better performance, as the model learns to solve tasks of different types, which in turn aids in solving each task individually. By leveraging the complementary strengths of both textual and structured knowledge understanding, the integrated approach is expected to enhance the model's reasoning capabilities.

2 Related Work

In this work, we consider tasks from the field of natural language processing, such as MRC, QA and KGQA. These tasks are crucial as they represent key challenges in language understanding, demanding models to comprehend, interpret, and interact with text in a meaningful way. Addressing these tasks advances neural networks' capabilities in processing human language.

The Machine Reading Comprehension (MRC) task involves developing systems capable of automatically understanding and processing textual passages to accurately answer questions about the content. This necessitates advanced natural language processing techniques to capture the semantics, context, and nuances of the text, facilitating effective question answering. Prominent large language models, including GPT-4 (Achiam et al., 2023), PaLM 2 (Anil et al., 2023), and Claude 2 from Anthropic, have demonstrated consistently high performance in this domain.

Question answering (QA) is the process of providing answers to asked questions, while refraining from attempting to answer questions outside the context provided. In addition to large language models trained using few-shot learning (similar to the MRC task), architectures with fewer parameters can also handle the QA task effectively.

For example, GrapeQA (Taunk et al., 2023) enhances commonsense question-answering by combining pretrained Language Models with Knowledge Graphs reasoning. It addresses two key challenges faced by typical approaches: difficulty in capturing all QA information in the Working Graph (WG) and inclusion of irrelevant KG nodes. GrapeQA introduces two improvements to the WG: prominent entities for graph augmentation identifies relevant text chunks from QA pairs and augments the WG with corresponding LM latent representations, and context-aware node pruning removes less relevant nodes. These enhancements allow GrapeQA to consistently outperform its predecessor QA-GNN (Yasunaga et al., 2021), demonstrating notable improvements on datasets such as OpenBookQA (Mihaylov et al., 2018) and CommonsenseQA (Talmor et al., 2019).

Another model, KEAR (Xu et al., 2022), extends the transformer architecture with an external attention mechanism, integrating external knowledge from sources like knowledge graphs, dictionaries, and training data. This additional knowledge is retrieved using the input as the key and then integrated with the input. KEAR achieves this without altering the model architecture, opting for text-level concatenation for external attention.

Knowledge Graph Question Answering (KGQA (Yang et al., 2014)) involves the task of responding to natural language queries by utilizing the structured information stored within a knowledge graph. The goal is to provide accurate and contextually appropriate answers to a wide range of natural language questions by effectively navigating the interconnected nodes and relationships within the knowledge graph.

Methods for solving KGQA problems can be broadly categorized into two types: Information Retrieval-based (IR-based) and Semantic Parsing-based (SP-based). SP-based methods adopt a parse-then-execute approach, starting with semantic analysis to parse the relations and entities in complex questions. Next, they construct logical formulas by translating the subgraph into an executable format, such as SPARQL. Finally, these methods use the query language to interact with the Knowledge Graph, retrieving and presenting the results. While SP-based methods are often praised for their interpretability due to the intermediate step of generating detailed logic forms, they face computational challenges, especially with complex questions that involve multiple relations. This results in a larger search space and increased computational cost.

IR-based approaches to Knowledge Graph Question Answering (KGQA) typically involve several steps. First, they extract a question-specific subgraph from the knowledge graph, including all relevant entity nodes and relation edges without generating an executable logic formula. Next, they use a question representation module to encode user-question tokens into low-dimensional vectors. Following this, an extracted-graph-based reasoning module applies a semantic matching algorithm to aggregate information from the subgraph, concentrating on the neighborhood of the central entity. Finally, an answer-ranking module ranks the entity scores within the subgraph to predict the top-ranked entities as the final answers.

In developing our own approach for multitask finetuning, which integrates a language model with a knowledge graph, several foundational IR-based methods for the KGQA task were considered. For instance, Rce-KGQA (Jin et al., 2022) focuses on enhancing reasoning by leveraging both explicit and implicit relational chains within the knowledge graph. EmbedKGQA (Saxena et al., 2020) addresses knowledge graph sparsity by integrating external knowledge and utilizing KG embedding techniques, which improves performance in multi-hop KGQA tasks. SRN (Qiu et al., 2020) approaches KGQA as a sequential decision problem and employs reinforcement learning to effectively search for paths within knowledge graphs. Additionally, KVMemNN (Eric et al., 2017) introduces a key-value retrieval mechanism that enables neural dialogue agents to interact seamlessly with knowledge bases across various domains. These methods were considered for their valuable concepts to form a strategy for finetuning the model on the KGQA and joint task. Our study is not intended to be a direct comparison with all the models listed in this section.

3 Methodology

3.1 Encoders

DRAGON, as previously described, is the basis for all experiments conducted in this study. At the first stage of the study, we tested the lightweight T5-base (Raffel et al., 2020) encoder but we received insufficient results. We used RoBERTa-large (Liu et al., 2019) encoder for input text data and text data from the knowledge graph.

3.2 Datasets & Metrics

Variations of the basic DRAGON method with different encoders are pretrained on a dataset consisting of pairs of "text data + knowledge graph data." The pretraining dataset was derived from the large text corpus BookCorpus and the ConceptNet knowledge graph. BookCorpus is a comprehensive English-language dataset containing 11,038 unpublished books (approximately 74 million sentences) across 16 different subgenres, including romance, history, adventure, and others. ConceptNet is one of the most widely used general knowledge graphs, comprising about 300,000 nodes. Preprocessing involved extracting a subgraph from ConceptNet, containing all concepts mentioned in each line of text from BookCorpus. This process took approximately two weeks and was executed on a CPU.

After that we finetune and evaluate the pretrained DRAGON general domain model[1] on three downstream tasks: Question Answering, Machine Reading Comprehension and Knowledge Graph Question Answering as single tasks and also make joint finetuning. Finetuning was carried out on monolingual (English) datasets. We followed the commonsense reasoning benchmark setup with accuracy metric (Talmor et al., 2019).

The following datasets were used for finetuning on the QA task:

1. CommonsenseQA (Talmor et al., 2019) is a dataset for multiple-choice question answering, designed to assess various facets of commonsense knowledge necessary for predicting correct answers. It contains 12,102 questions with four distractor answers and one correct answer.

2. OpenBookQA (Mihaylov et al., 2018), inspired by open book exams, assesses human understanding in specific subjects. It contains 5,957 elementary-level science questions, probing comprehension of 1,326 core science facts and their applications. The dataset maps each question to a core fact for targeted training.

To finetune on the MRC task, the subsequent dataset was utilized:

[1] https://github.com/michiyasunaga/dragon

1. DREAM (Sun et al., 2019) is a multiple-choice Dialogue-based REAding comprehension exaMination dataset, distinct from existing reading comprehension datasets by its focus on comprehensive multi-turn multi-party dialogue comprehension. It comprises 10,197 multiple-choice questions extracted from 6,444 dialogues, sourced from English-as-a-foreign-language exams curated by human experts.

Finally, for KGQA task finetuning we used the following dataset:

1. KQA Pro (Cao et al., 2022) is a large-scale dataset designed for intricate question answering over knowledge base. Its questions are remarkably diverse and demanding, calling for various reasoning abilities, such as compositional reasoning, multi-hop reasoning, quantitative comparison and set operations. The target knowledge base of KQA Pro comprises a dense subset of Wikidata. The dataset is divided into training, validation, and test sets, with 94376, 11797, and 11797 questions respectively.

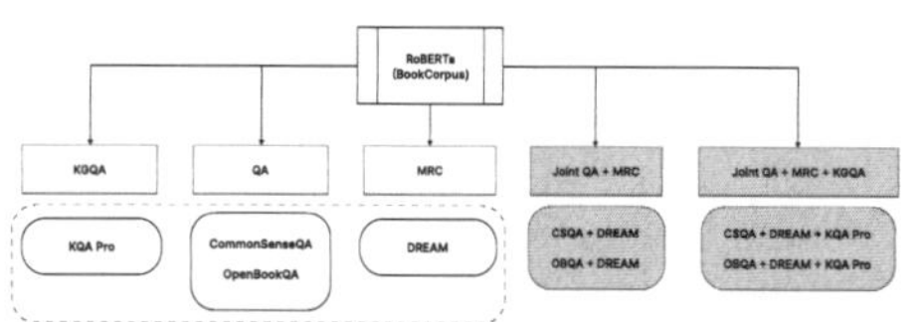

Figure 1: Scheme for finetuning the basic approach with variations of encoders on datasets for QA, MRC, KGQA tasks and their combinations.

3.3 Data Preprocessing

Note that all of the listed datasets for the QA and MRC tasks were also preprocessed with the ConceptNet graph. Specifically, for each question and answer choices, concepts from the original knowledge graph were searched and a subgraph was compiled. KG node embeddings in the case of finetuning on the QA and MRC datasets were initialized with pre-computed ConceptNet entity embeddings as proposed in the MHGRN (Feng et al., 2020) method. This scheme involves converting triplets from KG into sentences. The resulting sentences are then passed to BERT-Large (Devlin et al., 2019) to calculate the embeddings for each sentence. Finally, for each entity, all sentences containing that entity are collected, all token representations of the entity's mention spans in those sentences are retrieved, and the average pooling of these representations is returned.

In the case where the dataset contained only the correct answer, 4 incorrect answer choices for each question were generated using the Meta-Llama-3-8B-Instruct model in order to follow the pattern of questions and answers used in other datasets.

To train model on KGQA task, a subset containing 12,102 questions was extracted from the KQA Pro dataset, since the original KQA Pro is too large. This approach resolved the issue of dataset size discrepancies across tasks and simplified the selection of learning rate and batch size for training. Preprocessing for the KQA Pro subset was performed using a subgraph from the Wikidata knowledge graph that was provided by the authors of KQA Pro which we matched by entities and links to ConceptNet to make a proper grounding.

3.4 Joint MRC & QA finetuning

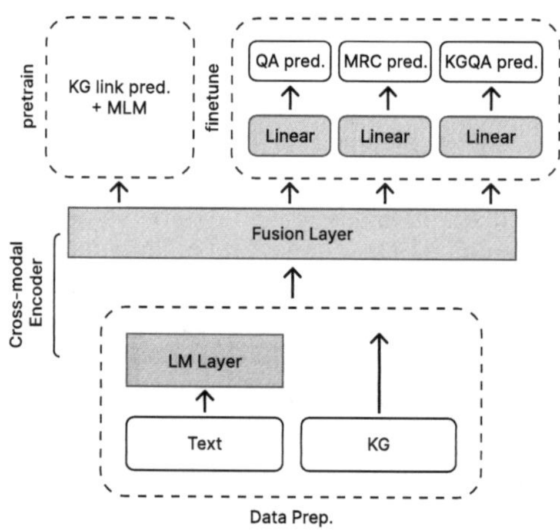

Figure 2: Multitask finetuning scheme for joint MRC+QA+KGQA task. The framework provides training the main KG-enchanced LLM.

Figure 2 depicts our approach to finetuning DRAGON pretrained model on QA, MRC and KGQA tasks, except for the grounding step where we put together text tokens and KG nodes. After that, we fed these pairs to the fusion layer, which is a cross-modal encoder that bidirectionally exchanges information between text and node representations. We used a linear combination of Cross

Entropy loss (Good, 1952) for each task in the following way:

$$\mathcal{L} = \mathcal{L}_{QA} + \mathcal{L}_{MRC} + \mathcal{L}_{KGQA} \quad (1)$$

3.5 Experiments & Results

Dataset Combination	Dev Acc.	Test Acc.
CSQA	0.755	0.689
CSQA + DREAM	**0.783**	**0.73**
CSQA + DREAM + KQA Pro	0.7707	0.6954

Table 1: Comparison of accuracy metrics resulting from finetuning on only one QA task (on the CSQA dataset) and metrics resulting from finetuning on a combination of tasks (DREAM, ARC - MRC task, KQA Pro - KGQA task). Validation and testing was performed on the QA task.

Dataset Combination	Dev Acc.	Test Acc.
OBQA	0.62	0.632
OBQA + DREAM	**0.744**	**0.720**
OBQA + DREAM + KQA Pro	0.67	0.678

Table 2: Comparison of accuracy metrics resulting from finetuning on only one QA task (on the OBQA dataset) and metrics resulting from finetuning on a combination of tasks (DREAM, ARC - MRC task). Validation and testing was performed on the QA task.

Dataset Combination	Dev Acc.	Test Acc.
DREAM	0.4098	0.419
DREAM + CSQA	0.704	0.722
DREAM + OBQA	0.702	0.696
DREAM + CSQA + KQA Pro	**0.7225**	**0.7227**

Table 3: Comparison of accuracy metrics resulting from finetuning on only one MRC task (on the DREAM dataset) and metrics resulting from finetuning on a combination of tasks (CSQA, OBQA - MRC task, KQA Pro - KGQA task). Validation and testing was performed on the MRC task.

Based on the results, DRAGON with a RoBERTa-large encoder was chosen as the most efficient architecture with which further experiments were carried out.

Tables 1-4 show overview of performance DRAGON with the RoBERTa-large encoder on QA, MRC, KGQA, QA+MRC and QA + MRC + KGQA tasks.

With finetuning on the CSQA (QA task), DREAM (MRC task) and KQA Pro (KGQA task)

Dataset Combination	Dev Acc.	Test Acc.
KQA Pro	0.5512	0.5728
KQA Pro + CSQA	0.5611	0.6
KQA Pro + DREAM	0.5610	0.5702
KQA Pro + CSQA + DREAM	**0.6085**	**0.6211**

Table 4: Comparison of accuracy metrics resulting from finetuning on only one KGQA task (on the KQA Pro dataset) and metrics resulting from finetuning on a combination of tasks (DREAM - MRC task, CSQA - QA task). Validation and testing was performed on the KGQA task.

datasets, a significant increase in the metric was shown when testing the model for the MRC task. Finetuning only for the MRC task on the DREAM dataset allows us to achieve an accuracy metric of 41.9%. With finetuning for QA and KGQA tasks, the metric becomes equal to 72.27%. Training on the CSQA+DREAM+KQA Pro datasets also gave an increase for the KGQA task. The metric increased from 57.28% to 62.11%.

Significant gains were demonstrated on the CSQA+DREAM dataset for the QA task. Accuracy with multi-task finetuning increased by 4.1% compared to finetuning only for the QA task on the CSQA dataset (from 68.9% to 73%).

Detailed analysis revealed that KG-pretrained model finetuned on QA task improved the generalization of MRC in our experiments. Unlike QA datasets MRC task assumes to proceed with rather large text passages which is challenging for LLM even with KG-pretraining. Our experiments reported that using long enough texts from the MRC dataset improves the ability of the model to answer more complicated questions. Our code is available at github repository[2]

4 Discussion & Limitations

All finetuning experiments were performed on English-language datasets. This is due to the fact that searching for datasets with overlapping languages for all three tasks (QA, MRC and KGQA) is difficult. Thus, there are a large number of multilingual datasets for QA and MRC tasks, and a limited number of such datasets for the KGQA task, which is associated with the difficulty of translating the entire knowledge graph into another language. At the moment, we were only able to use the QALD-9-Plus (Perevalov et al., 2022) dataset, which con-

[2]Github repository

tains questions in 10 languages, but has a small size (about 1.5 thousand questions), as well as the MLPQ (Tan et al., 2023) dataset, which covers only Chinese, English and French, but contains about 300 thousand questions.

Moreover, we made a test to check if the expand of data for the same task can make the same improvement as the adding other nlp-task. We trained our backbone on two QA datasets - CSQA and OBQA but the performance become 6 to 10% worse than both of them in pair with MRC dataset DREAM.

5 Conclusion & Future work

The paper presented expandable Joint Multitask Finetuning on Pretrained KG-enhanced LLM approach which aims to improve the performance of language models in a variety of language understanding tasks. We proposed a new multitask learning framework which jointly finetunes a language model with a knowledge graph enhanced objective on a few tasks and easily expanded to new nlp-tasks. The paper provides a detailed description of the proposed approach and presents experimental results demonstrating its effectiveness. Our results show strong improvements of synergized QA, MRC and KGQA tasks on each other with a maximun gain of 30% accuracy. We plan to extend our experimental setup by pretrained LLaMa v2 encoder. We also plan to conduct finetuning experiments on multilingual datasets containing English, Chinese, French, and other languages.

References

OpenAI Josh Achiam, Steven Adler, and Sandhini Agarwal et al. 2023. Gpt-4 technical report.

Rohan Anil, Andrew M. Dai, Orhan Firat, and Melvin Johnson et al. 2023. Palm 2 technical report. *ArXiv*, abs/2305.10403.

Shulin Cao, Jiaxin Shi, Liangming Pan, Lunyiu Nie, Yutong Xiang, Lei Hou, Juanzi Li, Bin He, and Hanwang Zhang. 2022. KQA Pro: A large diagnostic dataset for complex question answering over knowledge base. In *ACL'22*.

Minh Phan Xia Song Paul Bennett Saurabh Tiwary Corby Rosset, Chenyan Xiong. 2021. Knowledge-aware language model pretraining. arXiv:2007.00655. Version 2.

Jacob Devlin, Ming-Wei Chang, Kenton Lee, and Kristina Toutanova. 2019. BERT: pre-training of deep bidirectional transformers for language understanding. In *Proceedings of the 2019 Conference of the North American Chapter of the Association for Computational Linguistics: Human Language Technologies, NAACL-HLT 2019, Minneapolis, MN, USA, June 2-7, 2019, Volume 1 (Long and Short Papers)*, pages 4171–4186. Association for Computational Linguistics.

Mihail Eric, Lakshmi Krishnan, Francois Charette, and Christopher D. Manning. 2017. Key-value retrieval networks for task-oriented dialogue. In *Proceedings of the 18th Annual SIGdial Meeting on Discourse and Dialogue*, pages 37–49, Saarbrücken, Germany. Association for Computational Linguistics.

Yanlin Feng, Xinyue Chen, Bill Yuchen Lin, Peifeng Wang, Jun Yan, and Xiang Ren. 2020. Scalable multihop relational reasoning for knowledge-aware question answering. In *Proceedings of the 2020 Conference on Empirical Methods in Natural Language Processing, EMNLP 2020, Online, November 16-20, 2020*, pages 1295–1309. Association for Computational Linguistics.

I. J. Good. 1952. Rational decisions. *Journal of the Royal Statistical Society. Series B (Methodological)*, 14(1):107–114.

Weiqiang Jin, Biao Zhao, Hang Yu, Xi Tao, Ruiping Yin, and Guizhong Liu. 2022. Improving embedded knowledge graph multi-hop question answering by introducing relational chain reasoning. *Data Mining and Knowledge Discovery*.

Yinhan Liu, Myle Ott, Naman Goyal, Jingfei Du, Mandar Joshi, Danqi Chen, Omer Levy, Mike Lewis, Luke Zettlemoyer, and Veselin Stoyanov. 2019. Roberta: A robustly optimized BERT pretraining approach. *CoRR*, abs/1907.11692.

Todor Mihaylov, Peter Clark, Tushar Khot, and Ashish Sabharwal. 2018. Can a suit of armor conduct electricity? a new dataset for open book question answering. In *Proceedings of the 2018 Conference on Empirical Methods in Natural Language Processing*, pages 2381–2391, Brussels, Belgium. Association for Computational Linguistics.

Shirui Pan, Linhao Luo, Yufei Wang, Chen Chen, Jiapu Wang, and Xindong Wu. 2024. Unifying large language models and knowledge graphs: A roadmap. *IEEE Transactions on Knowledge and Data Engineering*, 36(7):3580–3599.

Aleksandr Perevalov, Dennis Diefenbach, Ricardo Usbeck, and Andreas Both. 2022. Qald-9-plus: A multilingual dataset for question answering over dbpedia and wikidata translated by native speakers. *2022 IEEE 16th International Conference on Semantic Computing (ICSC)*, pages 229–234.

Yunqi Qiu, Yuanzhuo Wang, Xiaolong Jin, and Kun Zhang. 2020. Stepwise reasoning for multi-relation question answering over knowledge graph with weak supervision. In *Proceedings of the 13th International*

Conference on Web Search and Data Mining, WSDM '20, page 474–482, New York, NY, USA. Association for Computing Machinery.

Colin Raffel, Noam Shazeer, Adam Roberts, Katherine Lee, Sharan Narang, Michael Matena, Yanqi Zhou, Wei Li, and Peter J. Liu. 2020. Exploring the limits of transfer learning with a unified text-to-text transformer. *J. Mach. Learn. Res.*, 21:140:1–140:67.

Apoorv Saxena, Aditay Tripathi, and Partha Talukdar. 2020. Improving multi-hop question answering over knowledge graphs using knowledge base embeddings. In *Proceedings of the 58th Annual Meeting of the Association for Computational Linguistics*, pages 4498–4507.

Kai Sun, Dian Yu, Jianshu Chen, Dong Yu, Yejin Choi, and Claire Cardie. 2019. DREAM: A challenge data set and models for dialogue-based reading comprehension. *Transactions of the Association for Computational Linguistics*, 7:217–231.

Alon Talmor, Jonathan Herzig, Nicholas Lourie, and Jonathan Berant. 2019. CommonsenseQA: A question answering challenge targeting commonsense knowledge. In *Proceedings of the 2019 Conference of the North American Chapter of the Association for Computational Linguistics: Human Language Technologies, Volume 1 (Long and Short Papers)*, pages 4149–4158, Minneapolis, Minnesota. Association for Computational Linguistics.

Yiming Tan, Yongrui Chen, Guilin Qi, Weizhuo Li, and Meng Wang. 2023. Mlpq: A dataset for path question answering over multilingual knowledge graphs. *Big Data Res.*, 32:100381.

Dhaval Taunk, Lakshya Khanna, Siri Venkata Pavan Kumar Kandru, Vasudeva Varma, Charu Sharma, and Makarand Tapaswi. 2023. Grapeqa: Graph augmentation and pruning to enhance question-answering. In *Companion Proceedings of the ACM Web Conference 2023*, WWW '23 Companion, page 1138–1144, New York, NY, USA. Association for Computing Machinery.

Yichong Xu, Chenguang Zhu, Shuohang Wang, Siqi Sun, Hao Cheng, Xiaodong Liu, Jianfeng Gao, Pengcheng He, Michael Zeng, and Xuedong Huang. 2022. Human parity on commonsenseqa: Augmenting self-attention with external attention. In *Proceedings of the Thirty-First International Joint Conference on Artificial Intelligence, IJCAI-22*, pages 2762–2768. International Joint Conferences on Artificial Intelligence Organization.

Min-Chul Yang, Nan Duan, Ming Zhou, and Hae-Chang Rim. 2014. Joint relational embeddings for knowledge-based question answering. In *Proceedings of the 2014 Conference on Empirical Methods in Natural Language Processing (EMNLP)*, pages 645–650, Doha, Qatar. Association for Computational Linguistics.

Michihiro Yasunaga, Antoine Bosselut, Hongyu Ren, Xikun Zhang, Christopher D. Manning, Percy Liang, and Jure Leskovec. 2022. Deep bidirectional language-knowledge graph pretraining. In *Neural Information Processing Systems (NeurIPS)*.

Michihiro Yasunaga, Hongyu Ren, Antoine Bosselut, Percy Liang, and Jure Leskovec. 2021. QA-GNN: Reasoning with language models and knowledge graphs for question answering. In *Proceedings of the 2021 Conference of the North American Chapter of the Association for Computational Linguistics: Human Language Technologies*, pages 535–546. Association for Computational Linguistics.

Xikun Zhang, Antoine Bosselut, Michihiro Yasunaga, Hongyu Ren, Percy Liang, Christopher D Manning, and Jure Leskovec. 2021. Greaselm: Graph reasoning enhanced language models. In *International Conference on Learning Representations*.

Zhengyan Zhang, Xu Han, Zhiyuan Liu, Xin Jiang, Maosong Sun, and Qun Liu. 2019. ERNIE: Enhanced language representation with informative entities. In *Proceedings of the 57th Annual Meeting of the Association for Computational Linguistics*, pages 1441–1451, Florence, Italy. Association for Computational Linguistics.

GNET-QG: Graph Network for Multi-hop Question Generation

Samin Jamshidi
University of Lethbridge
Department of Computer Science
jamshidisamin73@gmail.com

Yllias Chali
University of Lethbridge
Department of Computer Science
yllias.chali@uleth.ca

Abstract

Multi-hop question generation is a challenging task in natural language processing (NLP) that requires synthesizing information from multiple sources. We propose GNET-QG, a novel approach that integrates Graph Attention Networks (GAT) with sequence-to-sequence models, enabling structured reasoning over multiple information sources to generate complex questions. Our experiments demonstrate that GNET-QG outperforms previous state-of-the-art models across several evaluation metrics, particularly excelling in METEOR, showing its effectiveness in enhancing machine reasoning capabilities.

1 Introduction

Question generation (QG) is the task of producing a natural language question given an input context and an answer. While recent neural models have achieved considerable success in QG, they often fail to generate complex, multi-hop questions that require reasoning across multiple contexts. Unlike simple questions that rely on a single fact, multi-hop questions demand the integration of knowledge from multiple pieces of information to formulate a coherent query.

Multi-hop question generation is not only a challenging task but also a critical one, with applications ranging from improving query suggestions for search engines to enhancing educational tools for reading comprehension (Zamani et al., 2020; Heilman and Smith, 2010) . Despite advancements in models like MulQG (Su et al., 2020) and CQG (Fei et al., 2022), existing methods still struggle to consistently generate high-quality multi-hop questions across diverse contexts.

To address this gap, we introduce GNET-QG, a model that incorporates Graph Attention Networks (GAT) to identify and focus on relevant entities within a context. By enriching the input context using GAT and combining it with a powerful sequence-to-sequence model, GNET-QG is able to generate more complex, coherent, and answerable questions. Our method shows significant improvements over existing techniques, especially in the METEOR metric, indicating better semantic alignment in generated questions.

Context1:
The Oberoi family is an Indian family that is famous for its involvement in hotels, namely through The Oberoi Group .

Context2:
The Oberoi Group is a hotel company with its head office in Delhi .

Answer: Delhi

Simple Question: Where is the head office of The Oberoi Group ?

Complex Question: Oberoi family is part of a hotel company that has a head office in what city?

Figure 1: Example of multi-hop question generation. Context 1 introduces the Oberoi family and their connection to The Oberoi Group, while Context 2 provides information about the group's head office location. A simple question asks for the head office location directly, while a multi-hop question integrates information from both contexts to identify the head office city. In this context, 'complexity' refers to the need for synthesizing information from multiple contexts. This example is adapted from the HotpotQA dataset (Yang et al., 2018).

2 Related Work

Early research in question generation focused on rule-based methods for single-hop QG, transforming declarative sentences into questions via handcrafted rules (Heilman and Smith, 2010). Neu-

Proceedings of the Generative AI and Knowledge Graph Workshop (GenAIK), pages 20–26
January 19, 2025. ©2025 International Committee on Computational Linguistics (ICCL)

ral methods soon emerged, leveraging sequence-to-sequence models to improve reading comprehension QG, but struggled with multi-hop reasoning due to their reliance on local context (Du and Cardie, 2017).

Recent approaches, such as MulQG (Su et al., 2020) and CQG (Fei et al., 2022), have incorporated graph-based models to address multi-hop QG. MulQG used Graph Convolutional Networks (GCNs) to represent context and perform multi-hop encoding fusion, while CQG utilized a controlled framework to focus on key entities during question generation. Building upon these methods, Lin et al. (2024) introduced a type-aware semantics extraction-based chain-of-thought (TASE-CoT) approach for few-shot multi-hop QG. This approach begins by identifying question types and key semantic phrases from the provided documents and answer, then utilizes a three-step chain-of-thought template to generate multi-hop questions based on the extracted information. Despite these advancements, there remains a need for models that consistently perform well across different datasets and contexts.

GNET-QG builds on this body of work by integrating Graph Attention Networks (GAT) into the question generation process. GAT enables our model to focus attention on important entities within the input context, providing better entity representation for complex reasoning tasks.

3 Research Methodology

3.1 Motivation and Overview

Multi-hop question generation (QG) requires reasoning across multiple interconnected information pieces in a document. Traditional transformer models perform well in single-hop QG but struggle with multi-hop tasks due to limitations in capturing long-range dependencies and complex entity relationships. Existing methods often overlook explicit modeling of these relationships, leading to less coherent questions that lack true multi-hop reasoning.

Moreover, many current approaches are tightly coupled with specific models, lacking the flexibility to adapt to newer or different large language models (LLMs). This rigidity hinders leveraging advancements in the field and limits applicability across diverse architectures.

To address these limitations, we propose **GNET-QG**, a model integrating a graph entity network with a transformer-based architecture. Our approach enhances the quality and complexity of generated questions by explicitly modeling semantic relationships between entities through an entity graph and enriching the input context for the question generation model. Crucially, the architecture is designed to be compatible with various transformer-based models due to its text-based enriched input context, allowing greater flexibility and adaptability.

In our experiments, GNET-QG demonstrates significant improvements over baseline models in generating coherent and complex multi-hop questions. We successfully integrate both BART and T5 models within our architecture, evidencing its compatibility and effectiveness with different LLMs.

3.2 Constructing the Entity Graph

To capture the relationships essential for multi-hop reasoning, we construct an entity graph where nodes represent entities extracted from the document, and edges represent relationships between these entities. Entities are identified using a BERT-based Named Entity Recognition (NER) model, resulting in a set $E = \{e_0, e_1, \ldots, e_n\}$, Entities and relationships are derived from the preprocessed data provided by MULQG (Su et al., 2020).

Edges between nodes are defined as follows:

- **Same Sentence Co-occurrence**: Nodes are connected if they appear within the same sentence, capturing immediate contextual relationships.

- **Paragraph Title Relations**: Nodes are connected if a paragraph's title contains an entity that also appears within the paragraph, highlighting hierarchical and topical associations.

- **Cross-Paragraph Entity Consistency**: Entities appearing in different paragraphs but referring to the same concept are linked, ensuring consistency across the document.

3.3 Enriching the Input Context

To effectively leverage the constructed entity graph, we use a Graph Attention Network (GAT) to enhance node representations. The GAT computes attention scores and updates node features as follows:

$$\alpha_{ij} = \frac{\exp(\text{LeakyReLU}(\mathbf{a}_i^T[Wh_i \parallel Wh_j]))}{\sum_{k\in\mathcal{N}(i)}\exp(\text{LeakyReLU}(\mathbf{a}_i^T[Wh_i \parallel Wh_k]))} \quad (1)$$

$$h_i' = \sigma\left(\sum_{j\in\mathcal{N}(i)} \alpha_{ij} W h_j\right) \quad (2)$$

In these equations, h_i and h_j represent the feature vectors of nodes i and j, respectively. $\mathcal{N}(i)$ denotes the set of neighbors of entity i, while W is a weight matrix that transforms input features into a new space. The updated representation h_i' for node i is computed by aggregating information from its neighbors. The attention coefficient α_{ij} represents the importance of node j's features in updating node i. The learnable vector $\mathbf{a}_i$ projects the concatenated feature vector $[Wh_i \parallel Wh_j]$ into a scalar score, allowing the model to compute the relevance of neighboring nodes.

To further enhance the contextual information, we apply multi-head attention at each step. This mechanism allows the model to capture different aspects of the neighbors' features across multiple attention "heads." Multi-head attention is defined as follows:

$$\text{MultiHead}(h_i) = \text{Concat}(\text{head}_1, \ldots, \text{head}_h), \quad (3)$$

where each head is computed as:

$$\text{head}_k = \sigma\left(\sum_{j\in\mathcal{N}(i)} \alpha_{ij}^{(k)} W^{(k)} h_j\right). \quad (4)$$

Here, h denotes the number of attention heads, and $W^{(k)}$ is the weight matrix for the k-th head, and $\alpha_{ij}^{(k)}$ is the attention coefficient for the k-th head. This multi-head setup allows the GAT to capture a richer representation by focusing on different aspects of the input.

After applying the multi-head GAT, we flatten the updated node features H' and pass them through a linear transformation followed by a sigmoid activation function:

$$H_{\text{flat}} = \text{Flatten}(H') \quad (5)$$

$$H_{\text{linear}} = W_l H_{\text{flat}} + b_l \quad (6)$$

$$P = \sigma(H_{\text{linear}}) \quad (7)$$

In these equations, W_l and b_l are learnable parameters of the linear layer, and σ represents the sigmoid activation function, which outputs probability scores for each node. Nodes with probability scores greater than 0.5 are selected:

$$E_{\text{sub}} = \{h_i' \in H' \mid P_i > 0.5\} \quad (8)$$

Here, the selected nodes E_{sub} are the textual representations of entities. These textual representations of entities are concatenated with the original context C and the answer A to form the "enriched input context":

$$C_{\text{enriched}} = [C; A; E_{\text{sub}}] \quad (9)$$

The enriched input context, now in textual form, is subsequently fed into the transformer encoder for question generation, enhancing the model's ability to integrate multi-hop reasoning with focused entity relationships.

3.4 Encoder-Decoder Framework

The enriched input context is fed into the encoder of a pre-trained transformer model, such as BART or T5. The encoder generates contextualized embeddings that provide a compact representation of the input. Incorporating the enriched context enhances the encoder's ability to process long-range dependencies and relationships.

The decoder generates the output question autoregressively, utilizing the encoder's embeddings. It applies masked self-attention to ensure each token prediction considers only previously generated tokens, producing coherent and contextually appropriate multi-hop questions.

Figure 2 illustrates the encoder component of GNET-QG with a BART backbone. Initially, entities (nodes) from the contexts (C) are identified and labeled as E_0. A graph is created using these entities, capturing their relationships based on co-occurrence and paragraph structure. The entity graph is then passed to the Graph Attention Network (GAT), which processes the entity features. After applying flattening, a linear transformation, and a sigmoid activation, the resulting entity representations are concatenated with the contexts to form the enriched input context. This enriched input is subsequently fed into the BART encoder.

4 Implementation Details

In the task of multi-hop question generation, we implemented **GNET-QG** by integrating the GAT from this GitHub repository[1] with an encoder-decoder

[1] https://github.com/HLTCHKUST/MulQG

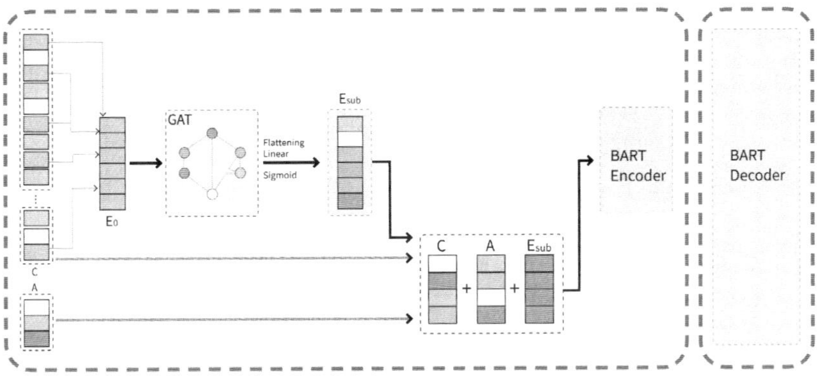

Figure 2: Full architecture of GNET-QG with BART backbone. C represents the original context extracted from the input, A denotes the answer provided as input to the model, and E_{sub} consists of the selected textual entities derived from the input context using the Graph Attention Network (GAT). These components are concatenated to form the enriched input context fed into the BART encoder.

model as the main backbone. We connected the untrained GAT architecture with pre-trained versions of both BART and T5 models to generate the multi-hop questions, leveraging the filtered HotpotQA dataset, following the preprocessing approach outlined in the MULQG (Su et al., 2020).

The GAT and the transformer models (BART and T5) were trained **end-to-end**. During training, gradients were backpropagated through both the GAT and the transformer model, allowing the entire network to learn jointly. This approach enables the model to effectively incorporate the structural information captured by the GAT into the question generation process.

Our candidate pre-trained models for the proposed architecture were the `bart-squad-qg-hl`[2] version of the BART model and the `t5-base-finetuned-question-generation-ap`[3] version of the T5 model. These models were selected due to their proven efficacy in question generation tasks and their availability for fine-tuning on domain-specific datasets.

4.1 Automatic Evaluation

To evaluate GNET-QG's effectiveness, we employed automated evaluation metrics to assess its predictions on samples from the test dataset, comparing the generated questions from the model with the reference questions from the dataset. The metrics used include BLEU (Papineni et al., 2002), ROUGE-L (Lin, 2004), and METEOR (Lavie and Agarwal, 2007), chosen for their extensive adoption in the question-generation research field. This evaluation allows us to directly compare GNET-QG's performance with previous studies on multi-hop question generation.

In Table 1, we present comparative results of GNET-QG with BART backbones against other models, including BART by Lewis et al. (2019), MulQG by Su et al. (2020), CQG by Fei et al. (2022), and TASE-CoT by Lin et al. (2024).

Our model demonstrates superior performance, particularly in the METEOR metric. This improvement can be attributed to GNET-QG's ability to generate questions that are semantically richer and more closely aligned with the reference questions. METEOR places greater emphasis on semantic similarity, synonymy, and recall, rewarding models that capture the meaning of the reference even if the exact wording differs. By explicitly modeling semantic relationships between entities and enriching the input context through the graph entity network, GNET-QG generates questions that include relevant synonyms, paraphrases, and morphological variants, all of which METEOR recognizes and rewards. This focus on semantic richness and relevance allows our model to outperform others in METEOR, highlighting its effectiveness in producing high-quality, semantically accurate multi-hop questions.

Furthermore, the enriched input context enables our model to capture more of the necessary information required to formulate comprehensive questions, increasing recall, a component heavily weighted in METEOR. In contrast, other models

[2] `https://github.com/p208p2002/Transformer-QG-on-SQuAD`

[3] `https://github.com/patil-suraj/question_generation`

Model	BLEU-1	BLEU-2	BLEU-3	BLEU-4	ROUGE-L	METEOR
MulQG	40.15	26.71	19.73	15.20	35.30	20.51
CQG	49.71	37.04	29.93	25.09	**41.83**	27.45
BART	41.41	30.90	24.39	19.75	36.13	25.20
TASE-CoT	45.89	34.06	27.11	22.37	39.68	23.39
GNET-QG (BART backbone)	**49.72**	**38.95**	**32.88**	**27.93**	40.25	**49.87**

Table 1: Automatic evaluation results on HotpotQA. The table compares the performance of various models across multiple metrics, including BLEU, ROUGE-L, and METEOR.

may excel in n-gram precision metrics like BLEU but may not capture the deeper semantic nuances that METEOR evaluates. Therefore, GNET-QG's superior performance in METEOR underscores its capability to generate questions that are not only grammatically correct but also semantically meaningful and contextually appropriate.

4.2 Human Evaluation

To comprehensively assess the performance of our model, we performed a human evaluation comparing the questions generated from three sources: the baseline BART model, our proposed GNET-QG model and human-generated questions. We evaluated the questions based on four metrics:

- **Fluency**: Grammatical correctness and readability.
- **Completeness**: Whether the questions are fully formed and coherent.
- **Answerability**: If the questions are answerable based on the given context.
- **Multi-hop Relevance**: Whether the questions require synthesizing information from multiple contexts (binary classification).

Each metric, except for Multi-hop Relevance, was rated on a scale from 1 to 5, with higher scores indicating better performance. Five annotators evaluated 50 randomly sampled test cases from the test set.

The results are summarized in Tables 2 and 3. GNET-QG achieved a 76% rate of generating multi-hop questions, significantly higher than BART's 54%. In terms of question quality, GNET-QG scored higher in Completeness (4.14) and Answerability (4.18) compared to BART's scores of 3.96 and 3.97, respectively. Although GNET-QG showed improvements in fluency over BART, it still fell slightly short of human-generated questions, suggesting room for further refinement.

Models	Yes	No	Percentage (% Yes)
BART	27	23	54.0
GNET-QG	**38**	**12**	**76.0**
Human	40	10	80.0

Table 2: Counts and percentages of multi-hop questions generated by each model.

Models	Completeness	Answerability	Fluency
BART	3.96	3.97	3.86
GNET-QG	**4.14**	**4.18**	**3.94**
Human	4.28	4.42	4.30

Table 3: Mean ratings for Completeness, Answerability, and Fluency.

4.3 Model Compatibility and Experimental Evidence

A key advantage of our GNET-QG architecture is its compatibility with various large language models (LLMs). Since the enriched input context is text-based, it integrates seamlessly with any transformer-based model capable of processing text input. To demonstrate this flexibility, we implemented GNET-QG using both BART and T5 backbones and compared the results against standard fine-tuned versions of BART and T5.

For the baseline models, we utilized BART as proposed by Lewis et al. (2019) and the fine-tuned version of T5, specifically `t5-base-finetuned-question-generation-ap`[4]. We evaluated the models on the HotpotQA dataset to ensure a fair comparison. The results are presented in Table 4, which shows the superior performance of GNET-QG, especially in terms of METEOR scores, in both the BART and T5 backbones.

These results highlight the architecture's ability to enhance performance across different transformer models, validating its effectiveness and flex-

[4]https://github.com/patil-suraj/question_generation

Model	BLEU-1	BLEU-2	BLEU-3	BLEU-4	ROUGE-L	METEOR
BART Baseline	41.41	30.90	24.39	19.75	36.13	25.20
GNET-QG (BART backbone)	**49.72**	**38.95**	**32.88**	**27.93**	**40.25**	**49.87**
T5 Baseline	32.08	22.04	17.26	13.68	30.78	27.72
GNET-QG (T5 backbone)	42.10	31.92	26.42	22.05	34.38	42.51

Table 4: Comparison of performance metrics (BLEU-1 to BLEU-4, ROUGE-L, and METEOR) for question generation on HotpotQA dataset. GNET-QG shows significant improvements with both BART and T5 backbones.

ibility.

5 Conclusion

In this work, we introduced **GNET-QG**, a graph-based approach to multi-hop question generation that effectively reduces model complexity without sacrificing performance. By explicitly modeling semantic relationships between entities and enriching the input context for transformer-based models, GNET-QG addresses the limitations of existing methods. A key contribution of GNET-QG is its ability to reduce the model size by approximately 7.5 million parameters compared to CQG, a highly competitive model in this space. This substantial reduction leads to improvements in computational efficiency, lower memory usage, and faster inference speeds, making GNET-QG a more practical and scalable solution for real-world applications. Despite the smaller parameter size, our experimental results demonstrate that GNET-QG outperforms CQG in terms of the quality of generated questions, highlighting its effectiveness and efficiency.

Furthermore, we validated the versatility of our architecture by integrating well-known sequence-to-sequence frameworks such as BART and T5. The consistent performance improvements across these models underscore GNET-QG's compatibility with different large language models and its ability to generate high-quality, complex multi-hop questions requiring sophisticated reasoning over multiple interconnected pieces of information.

Future research could focus on enhancing the model's reasoning capabilities to better address abstract or causal questions and extending its application to other NLP tasks like summarization or machine translation. Additionally, exploring GNET-QG's performance on non-English datasets could unlock its potential for multilingual question generation, further broadening its impact.

References

Xinya Du and Claire Cardie. 2017. Identifying where to focus in reading comprehension for neural question generation. In *Proceedings of the 2017 conference on empirical methods in natural language processing*, pages 2067–2073.

Zichu Fei, Qi Zhang, Tao Gui, Di Liang, Sirui Wang, Wei Wu, and Xuan-Jing Huang. 2022. Cqg: A simple and effective controlled generation framework for multi-hop question generation. In *Proceedings of the 60th Annual Meeting of the Association for Computational Linguistics (Volume 1: Long Papers)*, pages 6896–6906.

Michael Heilman and Noah A Smith. 2010. Good question! statistical ranking for question generation. In *Human Language Technologies: The 2010 Annual Conference of the North American Chapter of the Association for Computational Linguistics*, pages 609–617.

Alon Lavie and Abhaya Agarwal. 2007. METEOR: An Automatic Metric for MT Evaluation with High Levels of Correlation with Human Judgments. In *Proceedings of the Second Workshop on Statistical Machine Translation*, pages 228–231, Prague, Czech Republic. Association for Computational Linguistics.

Mike Lewis, Yinhan Liu, Naman Goyal, Marjan Ghazvininejad, Abdelrahman Mohamed, Omer Levy, Ves Stoyanov, and Luke Zettlemoyer. 2019. Bart: Denoising Sequence-to-Sequence Pre-training for Natural Language Generation, Translation, and Comprehension.

Chin-Yew Lin. 2004. ROUGE: A Package for Automatic Evaluation of Summaries. In *Text Summarization Branches Out*, pages 74–81, Barcelona, Spain. Association for Computational Linguistics.

Zefeng Lin, Weidong Chen, Yan Song, and Yongdong Zhang. 2024. Prompting few-shot multi-hop question generation via comprehending type-aware semantics. In *Findings of the Association for Computational Linguistics: NAACL 2024*, pages 3730–3740.

Kishore Papineni, Salim Roukos, Todd Ward, and Wei-Jing Zhu. 2002. Bleu: A Method for Automatic Evaluation of Machine Translation. In *Proceedings of the 40th Annual Meeting on Association for Computational Linguistics*, ACL '02, page 311–318, USA. Association for Computational Linguistics.

Dan Su, Yan Xu, Wenliang Dai, Ziwei Ji, Tiezheng Yu, and Pascale Fung. 2020. Multi-hop question generation with graph convolutional network. *arXiv preprint arXiv:2010.09240*.

Zhilin Yang, Peng Qi, Saizheng Zhang, Yoshua Bengio, William W Cohen, Ruslan Salakhutdinov, and Christopher D Manning. 2018. Hotpotqa: A dataset for diverse, explainable multi-hop question answering. *arXiv preprint arXiv:1809.09600*.

Hamed Zamani, Susan Dumais, Nick Craswell, Paul Bennett, and Gord Lueck. 2020. Generating clarifying questions for information retrieval. In *Proceedings of the web conference 2020*, pages 418–428.

SKETCH: Structured Knowledge Enhanced Text Comprehension for Holistic Retrieval

Aakash Mahalingam[1], Vinesh Kumar Gande[1], Aman Chadha[2,3,†], Vinija Jain[2,4,‡], Divya Chaudhary[1]
[1]Northeastern University, [2]Stanford University, [3]Amazon AI, [4]Meta
mahalingam.aa@northeastern.edu, gande.vi@northeastern.edu, hi@aman.ai, hi@vinija.ai, d.chaudhary@northeastern.edu

Abstract

Retrieval-Augmented Generation (RAG) systems have become pivotal in leveraging vast corpora to generate informed and contextually relevant responses, notably reducing hallucinations in Large Language Models. Despite significant advancements, these systems struggle to efficiently process and retrieve information from large datasets while maintaining a comprehensive understanding of the context. This paper introduces SKETCH, a novel methodology that enhances the RAG retrieval process by integrating semantic text retrieval with knowledge graphs, thereby merging structured and unstructured data for a more holistic comprehension. SKETCH, demonstrates substantial improvements in retrieval performance and maintains superior context integrity compared to traditional methods. Evaluated across four diverse datasets: QuALITY, QASPER, NarrativeQA, and Italian Cuisine—SKETCH consistently outperforms baseline approaches on key RAGAS metrics such as answer_relevancy, faithfulness, context_precision and context_recall. Notably, on the Italian Cuisine dataset, SKETCH achieved an answer relevancy of 0.94 and a context precision of 0.99, representing the highest performance across all evaluated metrics. These results highlight SKETCH's capability in delivering more accurate and contextually relevant responses, setting new benchmarks for future retrieval systems.

Keywords: RAG, Semantic Chunking, Knowledge Graph, RAGAS

1 Introduction

Large Language Models (LLMs), despite their growing size and capabilities, often lack sufficient domain-specific knowledge for certain tasks [27], and their encoded facts can quickly become outdated due to the dynamic nature of information. Updating the knowledge within LLMs through fine-tuning or editing is a complex and resource-intensive process, especially when dealing with extensive text corpora [32]. An alternative approach is Retrieval Augmented Generation (RAG) [45], which involves indexing large volumes of text, divided into smaller segments, in a separate information retrieval system [12]. Retrieved information is then provided to the LLM along with the query as context, enabling more factually updated answers [6]. This method offers benefits such as access to current, domain-specific knowledge, improved interpretability, and provenance tracking, which are often lacking in the opaque parametric knowledge of LLMs [47].

However, existing RAG methods have notable limitations [17]. They typically retrieve only a few short, contiguous text segments, limiting their ability to represent and leverage large-scale discourse structures. This limitation is particularly problematic for complex queries that require integrating knowledge from multiple parts of a text, such as synthesizing information across chapters or drawing conclusions from dispersed data in scientific literature. Moreover, these methods often struggle with multi-hop reasoning, where answering a query necessitates combining information from multiple, non-adjacent text segments, leading to incomplete or inaccurate answers and reducing their usefulness in applications that demand comprehensive understanding and synthesis.

To address these challenges, we introduce SKETCH, a novel methodology that enhances the retrieval process in RAG systems by integrating semantic text retrieval with knowledge graphs [16; 30]. This integration merges structured data (knowledge graphs) and unstructured data (text embeddings), enabling a holistic comprehension

[†]This work does not relate to the position at Amazon AI.
[‡]This work does not relate to the position at Meta.

Proceedings of the Generative AI and Knowledge Graph Workshop (GenAIK), pages 27–42
January 19, 2025. ©2025 International Committee on Computational Linguistics (ICCL)

of the dataset and facilitating the retrieval of relevant information across multiple contexts. By combining these approaches, SKETCH can perform multi-hop reasoning and retrieve contextually relevant information even if it is dispersed throughout the corpus. We evaluate SKETCH on diverse datasets, including QuALITY [3; 34], QAER [2; 8], NarrativeQA [1; 24], and an Italian Cuisine corpus, covering a range of domains and presenting various challenges. Our results demonstrate significant improvements in answer relevancy and context precision metrics compared to baseline methods. SKETCH outperforms traditional RAG approaches by maintaining context integrity and delivering more precise, contextually enriched responses, setting new benchmarks for RAG systems in handling large-scale discourse structures and complex queries across various domains.

2 Related Work

2.1 Retrieval Augmented Generation

RAG is a technique that enhances the capabilities of large language models (LLMs) by integrating external knowledge sources into the generation process [9; 25]. This approach addresses several limitations inherent in LLMs, such as their reliance on static training data and the potential for generating outdated or inaccurate information. By incorporating real-time, domain-specific knowledge, RAG systems can provide more accurate, relevant, and contextually enriched responses. This method not only improves the factual accuracy of the generated content but also enhances interpretability and provenance tracking, which are often lacking in traditional LLMs [13].

2.2 Retrieval Strategies

Retrieval methods have evolved from traditional term-based techniques like TF-IDF [21] to advanced strategies utilizing large language models as retrievers [10; 23; 26; 31; 41]. Innovations such as Fusion-in-Decoder (FiD) [20], combining DPR and BM25, and RETRO [5], employing cross-chunked attention and chunkwise retrieval, represent significant advancements. However, many models still rely on conventional techniques like chunking text corpora and using BERT-based retrievers, which have limitations in capturing the semantic depth of text [28], often leading to context loss in technical or scientific documents [7; 29; 46]. RAPTOR (Recursive Abstractive Processing for Tree-Organized Retrieval) [36] addresses these limitations by constructing a hierarchical tree structure that recursively embeds, clusters, and summarizes text chunks using SBERT [35] and Gaussian Mixture Models (GMMs) [11; 14; 40].

2.2.1 Semantic Chunking

Semantic chunking is a relatively new technique used to divide text into semantically meaningful units, significantly improving the efficiency and accuracy of information retrieval in RAG systems [22]. Unlike traditional chunking methods based on simple rules or statistical models, semantic chunking leverages the inherent meaning of the text. The process begins by splitting the text into individual sentences, which are then grouped with neighboring sentences based on a window size k, representing the number of sentences before and after the current sentence to form a window. Vector embeddings are calculated for each window, and the cosine distance between sequential windows is evaluated. Window-merging strategies, such as calculating the 95th percentile of distance differences to set a threshold T as mentioned in [22], are employed. When the cosine distance difference between sequential windows is within this threshold T, the windows are merged into one chunk, and this process repeats until the threshold is breached, resulting in reformed documents within the corpus.

2.3 Knowledge Graphs

Knowledge graphs are powerful tools for representing and reasoning over structured knowledge by modeling entities and their relationships in a graph structure, enabling integration of information from diverse sources and facilitating knowledge discovery [15]. They provide rich context for understanding and retrieving information [4], with roots in semantic networks and conceptual graphs. Developments in the Semantic Web and standards like RDF and OWL have enhanced their utility [19; 33], leading to prominent examples like DBpedia, Wikidata, and the Google Knowledge Graph. Knowledge graphs have applications in domains such as question answering, recommender systems [38], and natural language processing tasks [18]. Research has focused on knowledge graph construction [39], embedding [37], completion [43], and reasoning [44], as well as integrating them with deep learning models for enhanced performance and explainable AI.

An approach of adding a semantic theme to chunking and creating hybrid retrievers with combination of structured data through knowledge graphs and unstructured data through semantic chunks are new and introduced through SKETCH.

3 SKETCH

3.1 Overview

3.1.1 Semantic Chunking

In SKETCH, Semantic Chunking is crucial for enhancing the retrieval process by ensuring that text is segmented into semantically coherent units. Unlike traditional chunking methods that may disrupt the flow of ideas by splitting text arbitrarily, our Semantic Chunking approach preserves the thematic integrity of the content. This means each chunk represents a complete and meaningful segment of information, which is essential for accurate semantic embedding and retrieval. By maintaining the semantic continuity within chunks, SKETCH ensures that important contextual cues are not lost, which often happens with naive splitting techniques. This is particularly important when dealing with complex queries that require a deep understanding of the content. Semantic Chunking lays a strong foundation for the unstructured retrieval component of SKETCH, enabling more precise matching between queries and relevant text segments.

Moreover, this approach complements the structured retrieval provided by Knowledge Graphs. While Knowledge Graphs capture the relationships between entities, Semantic Chunking ensures that the unstructured text associated with these entities remains contextually rich and semantically intact. Together, they enable SKETCH to perform more accurate and contextually relevant retrievals, effectively handling complex queries that span multiple contexts within the corpus. By integrating Semantic Chunking into the SKETCH framework, we enhance the system's ability to understand and process large volumes of text, leading to significant improvements in retrieval accuracy and overall system performance.

3.1.2 Knowledge Graphs

In SKETCH, Knowledge Graphs (KGs) are integral to enhancing the retrieval process by providing a structured representation of entities and their interrelationships within the corpus. We use LLM to derive the main subject or entities from a text snippet and then KGs to represent entities as nodes and their relationships as edges. In SKETCH, entity refers to the main subject that is under discussion in a sentence whereas the edges are the relationship that they have to other subjects in that sentence.

By encoding relationships between entities, KGs provide additional context that is not easily captured by text embeddings alone. This enriched context helps in understanding complex queries and retrieving more accurate information. When a user submits a query, SKETCH employs the KG for structured retrieval. We perform Named Entity Recognition (NER) [42] on the query using GPT-4 to extract relevant entities. These entities correspond to nodes in the KG. We then construct cypher queries to traverse the KG and retrieve pertinent nodes and their relationships based on the extracted entities. More specifically, KGs enable multi-hop reasoning, allowing the system to traverse multiple relationships to infer new information. When it comes to multi-context questions, the multi-hop feature of KG's fits perfectly in helping retrieve the required information that is potentially missed out during naive or even semantic chunking due to the distance between the texts in the corpus. This capability is particularly useful for answering complex, multi-faceted queries that require synthesizing information from various sources.

3.1.3 Rationale for Combining Semantic Chunking and Knowledge Graphs

The innovative fusion of Semantic Chunking and Knowledge Graphs in SKETCH marks a significant leap forward in the field of Retrieval-Augmented Generation (RAG) systems. This strategic integration addresses core challenges in information retrieval, enabling SKETCH to deliver unprecedented accuracy and depth in handling complex queries across large corpora.

Semantic chunking ensures that text chunks are semantically coherent for a specific entity, while Knowledge Graphs (KGs) provide structured context about the relationships between entities. KGs enable multi-hop reasoning, which helps address complex queries that require integrating information from multiple distant sources. Additionally, Knowledge Graphs offer clear traceability of information, making it easier to understand the flow of retrieval. The combination of Semantic Chunking and Knowledge Graphs creates a synergistic effect that amplifies the strengths of each approach while mitigating their individual limitations. This integration allows SKETCH to:

- **Maintain Semantic Integrity**: Ensuring that each chunk represents a semantically coherent unit reduces the risk of misinterpretation and enhances the quality of embeddings used for retrieval.
- **Enable Complex Reasoning**: Knowledge Graphs empower SKETCH to navigate the intricate web of relationships between entities, facilitating the retrieval of information that requires understanding multiple layers of context.
- **Enhance Retrieval Accuracy**: The dual approach ensures that both the depth (through semantic coherence) and breadth (through relational mapping) of information are captured, leading to more accurate and relevant retrieval results.

When merging results, SKETCH prioritizes semantic alignment: tokens that appear in both structured and unstructured contexts are treated as confirmation signals, reinforcing their relevance and importance. Therefore, integrating Semantic Chunking and Knowledge Graphs offers a more holistic context for each entity, enhancing the overall comprehension of the complete dataset.

3.2 Approach and Reproducibility

Refer Figure 2 to understand the architecture of SKETCH and how documents are pre-processed and embeddings are created and finally how user queries are processed through hybrid retrievers.

3.2.1 Indexing

3.2.1.1 Document Loading and Initialization: We load the dataset which serves as the initial corpus for indexing and retrieval. Additionally, two separate text splitters are initialized: a semantic text splitter and a recursive character text splitter. These splitters are responsible for dividing the text into meaningful chunks for further processing.

3.2.1.2 Semantic Text Splitting: The loaded documents are processed through a semantic text splitter. This segments the text based on semantic content rather than arbitrary lengths like paragraphs or sentences, ensuring each segment maintains thematic consistency. A new set of documents are created, where each document chunk represents a coherent semantic unit. This step is crucial for preserving the context and meaning within each chunk, enhancing the quality of information retrieval.

3.2.1.3 Recursive Text Splitting: The semantically segmented documents are further processed using a recursive character text splitter. This splitter divides the text into chunks of 100 tokens with a overlapping window of 16 tokens, ensuring that even large documents are broken down into smaller, more manageable pieces. By maintaining a chunk size of 100 tokens, the recursive text splitter ensures that the chunks remain contextually coherent, preventing the loss of important information that might occur if sentences were instead arbitrarily cut off.

3.2.1.4 Embedding and Vector Store: The embeddings generated after the recursive text splitting process are stored in a vector database, FAISS. These embeddings represent the semantic meaning of the text chunks and are used for efficient similarity-based retrieval during the querying phase.

3.2.1.5 Knowledge Graph: The initial set of documents is converted into graph documents. This involves parsing the text and identifying entities, attributes, and relationships, which are then structured into a graph format. Using the graph documents, a comprehensive Knowledge Graph (KG) is constructed. The KG captures the intricate relationships and connections between various entities, providing a structured representation of the information contained within the documents. Refer Figure 3 to understand the KG representation for the Italian Cuisine dataset. Each node here represents the entities that are retrieved from the Italian Cuisine corpus and their relationships are represented here as edges. Each node stores the smaller context of the corpus.

3.2.2 Querying

3.2.2.1 Structured Retriever: The first step in the structured retriever is Named Entity Recognition (NER). We identify all the plausibe entities present in the user query and create a cypher query based out of it, treating each entity as a node. We perform NER by passing the user query through GPT-4 and extracting a list of all entities in the sentence. The cypher query is designed to access and retrieve the relevant nodes and their relationships from the KG based on the extracted entities and relationships from the user's query.

3.2.2.2 Unstructured Retriever: This component queries the vector embeddings of the text chunks created during the recursive text splitting phase. By leveraging similarity-based retrieval technique, cosine similarity, the unstructured retriever can identify and retrieve the most relevant text chunks based on their semantic similarity to the user's query.

3.2.2.3 Hybrid Retrieval: The system combines the results from both the structured and unstructured retrievers to create a comprehensive and contextually rich retrieval mechanism. The retrieved results from these two components are then combined, forming a unified context that is subsequently fed to the Large Language Model (LLM) for generating answers to the user's queries. By leveraging the contextual coherence of semantically meaningful text chunks and the structured relationships captured in the Knowledge Graph, the system can provide more accurate and relevant information to the LLM, ultimately improving the quality of the generated responses.

3.3 Datasets

We evaluate the performance of SKETCH using four diverse datasets that present various challenges: a small "Italian Cuisine and Heritage" dataset and three large-scale datasets—QuALITY, QASPER, and NarrativeQA. These datasets test SKETCH's ability to handle long documents, multi-context questions, domain-specific knowledge, and multi-hop reasoning.

The Italian Cuisine dataset, consisting of 6,000 tokens across three text files, serves as an initial testbed for our methodology. We generated multi-context questions and ground truth data using the RAGAS framework and evaluated the approaches using RAGAS metrics: answer_relevancy, faithfulness, context_precision, and context_recall.

QuALITY [3; 34] is a multiple-choice question answering dataset designed for long document comprehension, with passages averaging 5,000 tokens. It tests the system's ability to process lengthy texts and answer deep comprehension questions that require understanding the entire passage. We used the training set, containing approximately 2,090 entries, for our experiments.

QASPER [2; 8] focuses on question answering over scientific papers, comprising 5,049 questions on 1,585 NLP papers. The questions cover methodology, results, and conclusions, requiring navigation through complex scientific texts and multi-hop reasoning to arrive at correct answers. We evaluated our approaches on the validation set, which contains 281 entries with questions, answers, and ground truths.

NarrativeQA [1; 24] involves question answering on long-form narrative texts, including 1,567 stories (books and movie scripts) and 46,765 question-answer pairs. The dataset challenges systems to understand and reason about complex narratives involving character relationships, plot developments, and thematic elements. Answers are free-form, allowing for nuanced and detailed responses. We used the validation set, containing approximately 3,460 entries, for our comparisons.

Table 1: Performance Comparison of Different Approaches against Italian Cuisine Dataset

Approach	Answer Relevancy	Faithfulness	Context Precision	Context Recall	F1 Score
Naive RAG	0.61	**1.00**	0.81	**0.88**	0.84
Semantic	0.84	0.86	0.92	0.83	**0.87**
KG	0.94	0.21	0.77	0.33	0.46
RAPTOR	0.75	0.73	0.38	0.71	0.50
SKETCH	**0.94**	0.87	**0.99**	0.72	0.83

4 Results and Discussion

We evaluated the performance of SKETCH across four diverse datasets: the "Italian Cuisine" dataset, QuALITY, QASPER, and NarrativeQA. Our analysis focused on comparing the effectiveness of SKETCH in enhancing retrieval accuracy and contextual relevance against existing approaches, including Naive RAG, RAPTOR, Semantic-only, and KG-only methods. To ensure a comprehensive evaluation, we assessed four key RAGAS metrics:

answer_relevancy, faithfulness, context_precision, and context_recall. GPT-3.5-turbo-16k served as the evaluation judge for all datasets, ensuring consistency in assessing the quality of responses generated by each method.

The results, visualized in Figure 2, clearly demonstrate SKETCH's significant advantage over other models in retrieval performance. SKETCH consistently performed better across multiple datasets, showing particular strength in answer relevancy, context precision metrics, making it a superior choice for accurate and contextually rich retrieval. Each plot in Figure 2 contrasts SKETCH with baseline models, providing a detailed visual representation of how SKETCH excels in various metrics, further emphasizing its robustness and balanced capability compared to the other tested approaches.

4.1 Italian Cuisine Dataset

The "Italian Cuisine" dataset, consisting of 6,000 tokens distributed across three text files, served as an ideal testbed to assess the core capabilities of SKETCH in a controlled environment. This dataset enabled us to evaluate SKETCH's performance in retrieving accurate and contextually relevant information. We generated a set of 9 multi-context questions that have answers spanning across different parargraphs in three files using the RAGAS framework to facilitate a comprehensive performance comparison.

- **Controlled Complexity for Initial Testing**: The dataset encompasses a variety of topics within the domain of Italian cuisine, such as regional dishes, traditional ingredients, culinary techniques, and cultural heritage. This diversity within a confined scope allows us to test SKETCH's ability to handle multi-faceted queries that require integrating information from different parts of the text.

- **Multi-Context Retrieval Challenges**: By generating a set of 9 multi-context questions using the RAGAS framework, we designed queries whose answers span across different paragraphs and even across multiple files.

- **Domain Diversity**: Including a dataset from a different domain ensures that our evaluation of SKETCH covers a broader spectrum of content types. While the other datasets—QuALITY, QASPER, and NarrativeQA—are centered around long-form narratives and scientific papers, the Italian Cuisine dataset represents a domain with unique characteristics.

- **Complexity Without Overhead**: The dataset strikes a balance between complexity and computational efficiency. It is rich enough to present significant retrieval challenges but small enough to allow for rapid iteration and testing. This is particularly beneficial during the development phase, where quick feedback loops are essential.

Table 1 presents the comparative metrics for the Italian Cuisine dataset across all five retrieval approaches: Naive RAG, RAPTOR, SKETCH, Semantic-only, and KG-only. SKETCH demonstrated clear superiority, achieving the highest Answer Relevancy score of 0.94, comparable only to the KG-only approach. However, SKETCH outperformed KG in Faithfulness (0.87 vs. 0.21) and Context Recall (0.72 vs. 0.33), highlighting SKETCH's ability to maintain context consistency more effectively. Compared to Naive RAG, SKETCH delivered a 54.1% improvement in Answer Relevancy, and it also exceeded RAPTOR by 26%. On the Context Precision metric, SKETCH outperformed RAPTOR by 160% and achieved an 22% higher score than Naive RAG. Although SKETCH's context-F1 score (0.83) was competitive, the Semantic-only approach slightly outperformed it in this metric (0.87), suggesting that while SKETCH excels in most areas, there may be room for further optimization in balancing precision and recall.

Figures 4, 5, 6, 7 and 8 illustrate the performance heatmaps for Naive RAG, RAPTOR, Semantic-only, and KG-only and SKETCH approaches, respectively. These heatmaps provide a deeper understanding of how each approach handled the 9 questions in the test set. SKETCH consistently demonstrated a higher level of answer relevancy and contextual accuracy compared to the other methods, emphasizing its capability to deliver precise and contextually rich responses. The additional heatmaps for Semantic-only and KG-only approaches further illustrate that SKETCH excels in providing well-rounded

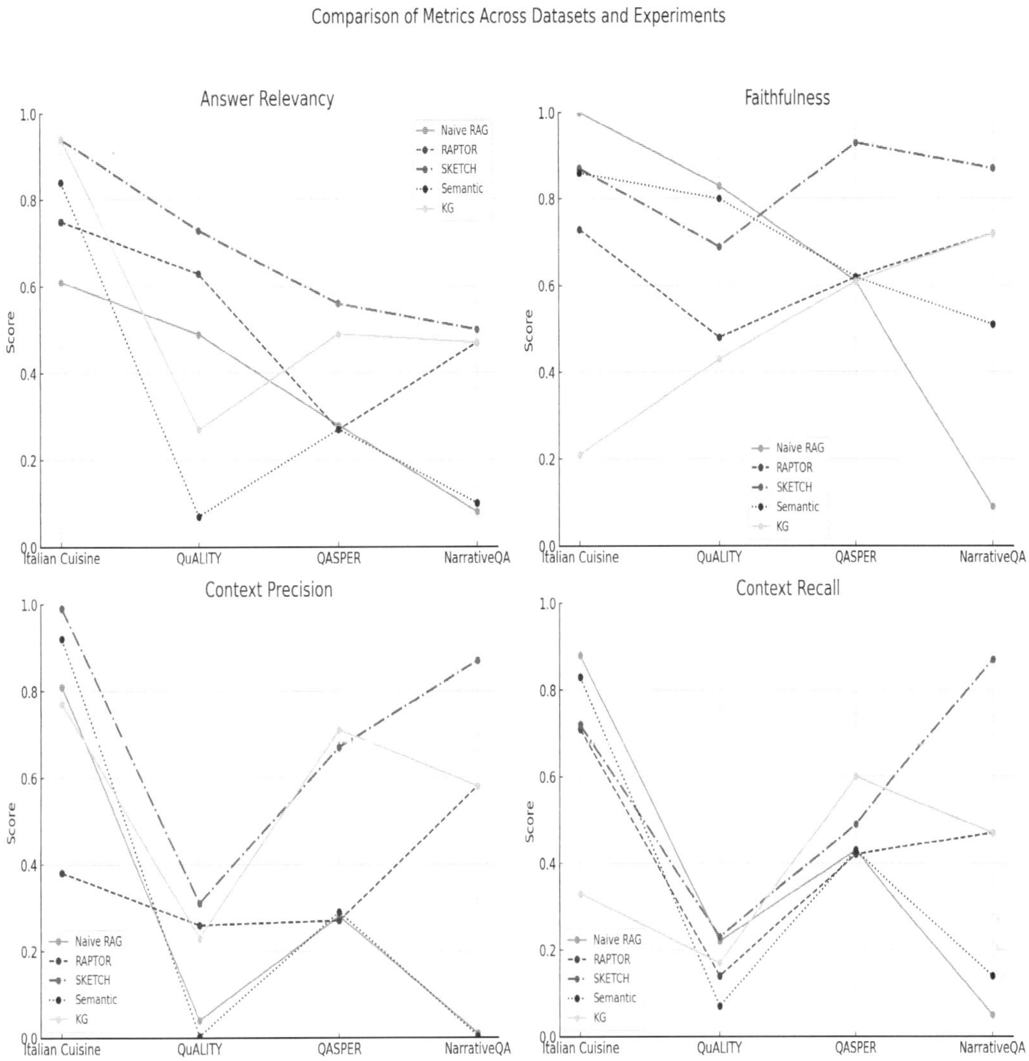

Figure 1: **RAGAS metrics against all datasets and approaches**

retrieval results, surpassing the limitations seen in isolated semantic or structured retrieval methods.

4.2 QuALITY Dataset

The QuALITY validation dataset, designed for long-form document comprehension, provided a challenging evaluation ground for retrieval-augmented systems. Despite the complexity of extended passages, SKETCH outperformed all baseline methods, demonstrating its capability to retrieve and integrate context effectively. Table 2 compares SKETCH and other approaches across key performance metrics.

For Answer Relevancy, SKETCH achieved a score of 0.73, representing a 49% improvement over Naive RAG (0.49) and a 15.87% improvement over RAPTOR (0.63). The Semantic-only and KG-only approaches scored significantly lower at 0.07 and 0.27, respectively. In terms of Faithfulness, SKETCH recorded 0.69, while Naive RAG performed better with 0.83. Although Naive RAG had higher faithfulness, SKETCH's strong performance across other metrics gave it an overall edge. The Semantic-only and KG-only approaches scored 0.80 and 0.43, respectively. This demonstrates SKETCH's effectiveness in synthesizing relevant information from different parts of long passages.

Regarding Context Precision, SKETCH achieved 0.31, a 675% improvement over Naive RAG's 0.04 and a 19.23% improvement over RAPTOR's 0.26. SKETCH also surpassed the KG-only approach, which scored 0.23. For Context Recall, SKETCH recorded 0.23, comparable to Naive RAG's 0.22. RAPTOR, Semantic-only, and KG-only scored 0.14, 0.07, and 0.17, respectively. Compared to other approaches, SKETCH's superior context based F1 score underscores its ability to provide both accurate and contextually consistent retrieval, even in the face of complex, long-form content. These results illustrate SKETCH's superior performance across key metrics, reinforcing its effectiveness as an integrated retrieval mechanism for comprehending long and complex documents over other baseline approaches and showcasing SKETCH's advantage in accurately pinpointing relevant context.

Table 2: Performance Comparison of Different Approaches against QuALITY Dataset

Approach	Answer Relevancy	Faithfulness	Context Precision	Context Recall	F1 score
Naive RAG	0.49	**0.83**	0.04	0.22	0.07
RAPTOR	0.63	0.48	0.26	0.14	0.18
Semantic	0.07	0.80	0.003	0.07	0.01
KG	0.27	0.43	0.23	0.17	0.20
SKETCH	**0.73**	0.69	**0.31**	**0.23**	**0.26**

4.3 QASPER

The QASPER dataset, consisting of scientific papers, presented a challenging environment due to its complexity and technical nature. Despite these challenges, SKETCH demonstrated strong capabilities, outperforming all baseline methods across several key metrics, as shown in Table 3.

For Answer Relevancy, SKETCH achieved a score of 0.56, significantly surpassing Naive RAG's 0.28 a 100% improvement and outperforming RAPTOR's 0.27 by 107.41%. The Semantic-only and KG-only approaches scored 0.27 and 0.49, respectively. On the Faithfulness metric, SKETCH scored an impressive 0.93, exceeding Naive RAG (0.61) by approximately 52.46% and RAPTOR (0.62) by 50%. Regarding Context Precision, SKETCH achieved 0.67, outperforming Naive RAG's 0.28 by 139.29% and RAPTOR's 0.27 by 148.15%. While the KG-only approach achieved a slightly higher precision at 0.71, SKETCH's performance was more balanced across all metrics.

For Context Recall, SKETCH recorded a score of 0.49, improving over Naive RAG's 0.43 by 13.95%. Although the KG-only approach scored higher at 0.60, SKETCH demonstrated superior balance, excelling in relevancy, faithfulness, and precision. Although KG-only achieves the highest F1 score (0.65), SKETCH still maintains a strong F1 performance at 0.57, reflecting its balanced effectiveness. These results indicate that SKETCH consistently outperforms other approaches in the QASPER dataset, emphasizing its strength in providing accurate, faithful, and contextually precise retrieval, particularly in challenging scientific content.

Table 3: Performance Comparison of Different Approaches against QASPER Dataset

Approach	Answer Relevancy	Faithfulness	Context Precision	Context Recall	F1 score
Naive RAG	0.28	0.61	0.28	0.43	0.34
RAPTOR	0.27	0.62	0.27	0.44	0.33
Semantic	0.27	0.62	0.29	0.43	0.35
KG	0.49	0.61	**0.71**	**0.60**	**0.65**
SKETCH	**0.56**	**0.93**	0.67	0.49	0.57

4.4 NarrativeQA

The NarrativeQA dataset posed unique challenges requiring deep narrative understanding, including handling plot development and character interactions across extended text passages. SKETCH demonstrated a notable advantage in addressing these complexities compared to baseline methods, as detailed in Table 4.

For Answer Relevancy, SKETCH achieved a score of 0.50, significantly surpassing Naive RAG's 0.08 (a 525% improvement) and slightly outperforming RAPTOR and KG-only, both at 0.47. The Semantic-only approach scored 0.10. In Faithfulness, SKETCH recorded 0.87, outshining Naive RAG (0.09) by 866.67% and improving over RAPTOR and KG-only, both at 0.72, by 20.83%. Regarding Context Precision, SKETCH achieved 0.51, better than Naive RAG's 0.10 and RAPTOR's

0.30. Although KG-only slightly outperformed SKETCH with 0.58, SKETCH's overall balanced performance ensured its superiority. For Context Recall, SKETCH scored 0.46, significantly higher than Naive RAG's 0.05 (an 800% improvement) and surpassing RAPTOR (0.16) and Semantic-only (0.14), with KG-only slightly ahead at 0.47.

These results indicate that SKETCH consistently outperformed baseline methods in answer relevancy and faithfulness. While KG-only showed slightly better scores in context precision and recall, SKETCH's balanced excellence across all metrics made it the most effective approach for retrieving and synthesizing narrative content. This demonstrates SKETCH's ability to provide contextually rich and accurate retrieval in the NarrativeQA dataset, confirming its superiority in comprehending and generating answers from complex narrative passages.

Table 4: Performance Comparison of Different Approaches against NarrativeQA Dataset

Approach	Answer Relevancy	Faithfulness	Context Precision	Context Recall	F1 score
Naive RAG	0.08	0.09	0.10	0.05	0.07
RAPTOR	0.10	0.46	0.30	0.16	0.21
Semantic	0.10	0.51	0.004	0.14	0.01
KG	0.47	0.72	**0.58**	**0.47**	**0.52**
SKETCH	**0.50**	**0.87**	0.51	0.46	0.48

5 Conclusion and Limitations

This research introduced SKETCH, an innovative methodology that enhances Retrieval-Augmented Generation (RAG) systems by combining semantic chunking with knowledge graphs. By integrating structured and unstructured data, SKETCH addresses the limitations of traditional retrieval methods, such as context loss in large datasets and limited comprehension of complex queries. Our experiments on diverse datasets—including Italian Cuisine, QuALITY, QASPER, and NarrativeQA—demonstrate SKETCH's superior ability to maintain context integrity and generate highly relevant responses, consistently outperforming baseline methods like Naive RAG, RAPTOR, Semantic-only, and KG-only approaches.

SKETCH achieved remarkable improvements across key metrics, showcasing its adaptability to both short and long documents and its effectiveness in navigating complex texts. For instance, on the Italian Cuisine dataset, it achieved an answer relevancy score of 0.94 and context precision of 0.99, improving over Naive RAG by 54.1% and 22.2%, respectively. On the QuALITY dataset, SKETCH improved answer relevancy by 49%, and on the QASPER dataset, it doubled the answer relevancy score over Naive RAG while increasing context precision by 139.29%. Even on the challenging NarrativeQA dataset, SKETCH delivered balanced performance with a 525% improvement in answer relevancy and an 866.67% increase in faithfulness over Naive RAG. While KG achieved the highest F1 score (0.52), SKETCH closely followed with 0.48, demonstrating its balanced effectiveness despite the complexity of narrative content. These findings confirm that SKETCH's combined approach offers a robust framework for advancing RAG systems, setting new benchmarks in accuracy, context comprehension, and cross-domain xapplicability, and paving the way for future advancements in natural language processing.

Limitations While SKETCH significantly improved Answer Relevancy and Context Precision, certain limitations remain. Faithfulness, though better than most baselines, still lags behind Naive RAG on QuALITY (0.69 vs. 0.83, a 16.9% shortfall). Scalability and cost are also concerns, as constructing large-scale knowledge graphs is labor-intensive, and relying on paid LLMs like GPT-4 for semantic evaluation increases expenses. Furthermore, SKETCH's dependence on GPT models for query parsing and RAGAS evaluation can introduce errors and variance due to sampling randomness, prompt sensitivity, and occasional hallucinations, potentially affecting reproducibility. Employing sampling strategies (e.g., multiple runs) and aggregating judgments could help mitigate these issues. Future work should focus on reducing computational costs, refining knowledge graph construction, and improving metrics like Context Recall and Faithfulness to achieve more consistent, high-quality, and stable retrieval results.

Acknowledgments

This research was supported by an OpenAI Research Grant through Researcher Access Program.

References

[1] Deepmind authored Hugging Face NarrativeQA dataset. Narrativeqa.

[2] AllenAI authored Hugging Face QASPER dataset. Qasper.

[3] EMozilla authored Hugging Face QuALITY dataset. Quality.

[4] Jinheon Baek, Alham Fikri Aji, Jens Lehmann, and Sung Ju Hwang. 2023. Direct fact retrieval from knowledge graphs without entity linking. *Preprint*, arXiv:2305.12416.

[5] Sebastian Borgeaud, Arthur Mensch, Jordan Hoffmann, Trevor Cai, Eliza Rutherford, Katie Millican, George van den Driessche, Jean-Baptiste Lespiau, Bogdan Damoc, Aidan Clark, Diego de Las Casas, Aurelia Guy, Jacob Menick, Roman Ring, Tom Hennigan, Saffron Huang, Loren Maggiore, Chris Jones, Albin Cassirer, Andy Brock, Michela Paganini, Geoffrey Irving, Oriol Vinyals, Simon Osindero, Karen Simonyan, Jack W. Rae, Erich Elsen, and Laurent Sifre. 2022. Improving language models by retrieving from trillions of tokens. *Preprint*, arXiv:2112.04426.

[6] Chi-Min Chan, Chunpu Xu, Ruibin Yuan, Hongyin Luo, Wei Xue, Yike Guo, and Jie Fu. 2024. Rq-rag: Learning to refine queries for retrieval augmented generation. *Preprint*, arXiv:2404.00610.

[7] Arman Cohan and Nazli Goharian. 2017. Contextualizing citations for scientific summarization using word embeddings and domain knowledge. In *Proceedings of the 40th International ACM SIGIR Conference on Research and Development in Information Retrieval*, SIGIR '17, page 1133–1136, New York, NY, USA. Association for Computing Machinery.

[8] Pradeep Dasigi, Kyle Lo, Iz Beltagy, Arman Cohan, Noah A. Smith, and Matt Gardner. 2021. A dataset of information-seeking questions and answers anchored in research papers. *Preprint*, arXiv:2105.03011.

[9] Databricks. Why rag.

[10] Dani Yogatama Luke Zettlemoyer Joelle Pineau Manzil Zaheer Devendra Singh Sachan, Mike Lewis. Questions are all you need to train a dense passage retriever.

[11] Raftery A. E. Fraley, C. Model-based clustering, discriminant analysis, and density estimation.

[12] Yunfan Gao, Yun Xiong, Xinyu Gao, Kangxiang Jia, Jinliu Pan, Yuxi Bi, Yi Dai, Jiawei Sun, Meng Wang, and Haofen Wang. 2024. Retrieval-augmented generation for large language models: A survey. *Preprint*, arXiv:2312.10997.

[13] GCP. Why rag.

[14] David Peel Geoffrey McLachlan. Finite mixture models.

[15] Aidan Hogan. Levels of text splitting.

[16] Aidan Hogan, Eva Blomqvist, Michael Cochez, Claudia D'amato, Gerard De Melo, Claudio Gutierrez, Sabrina Kirrane, José Emilio Labra Gayo, Roberto Navigli, Sebastian Neumaier, Axel-Cyrille Ngonga Ngomo, Axel Polleres, Sabbir M. Rashid, Anisa Rula, Lukas Schmelzeisen, Juan Sequeda, Steffen Staab, and Antoine Zimmermann. 2021. Knowledge graphs. *ACM Computing Surveys*, 54(4):1–37.

[17] Yizheng Huang and Jimmay Huang. 2024. A survey on retrieval-augmented text generation for large language models. *Preprint*, arXiv:2404.10981.

[18] Ali Hur, Naeem Janjua, and Mohiuddin Ahmed. 2021. A survey on state-of-the-art techniques for knowledge graphs construction and challenges ahead. *Preprint*, arXiv:2110.08012.

[19] IBM. What is a knowledge graph??

[20] Gautier Izacard and Edouard Grave. 2022. Distilling knowledge from reader to retriever for question answering. *Preprint*, arXiv:2012.04584.

[21] Sparck Jones. A statistical interpretation of term specificity and its application in retrieval.

[22] Greg Kamradt. Levels of text splitting.

[23] Urvashi Khandelwal, Omer Levy, Dan Jurafsky, Luke Zettlemoyer, and Mike Lewis. 2020. Generalization through memorization: Nearest neighbor language models. *Preprint*, arXiv:1911.00172.

[24] Tomáš Kočiský, Jonathan Schwarz, Phil Blunsom, Chris Dyer, Karl Moritz Hermann, Gábor Melis, and Edward Grefenstette. 2017. The narrativeqa reading comprehension challenge. *Preprint*, arXiv:1712.07040.

[25] Patrick Lewis, Ethan Perez, Aleksandra Piktus, Fabio Petroni, Vladimir Karpukhin, Naman Goyal, Heinrich Küttler, Mike Lewis, Wen tau Yih, Tim Rocktäschel, Sebastian Riedel, and Douwe Kiela. 2021. Retrieval-augmented generation for knowledge-intensive nlp tasks. *Preprint*, arXiv:2005.11401.

[26] Daliang Li, Ankit Singh Rawat, Manzil Zaheer, Xin Wang, Michal Lukasik, Andreas Veit, Felix Yu, and Sanjiv Kumar. 2022. Large language models with controllable working memory. *Preprint*, arXiv:2211.05110.

[27] Chen Ling, Xujiang Zhao, Jiaying Lu, Chengyuan Deng, Can Zheng, Junxiang Wang, Tanmoy Chowdhury, Yun Li, Hejie Cui, Xuchao Zhang, Tianjiao Zhao, Amit Panalkar, Dhagash Mehta, Stefano Pasquali, Wei Cheng, Haoyu Wang, Yanchi Liu, Zhengzhang Chen, Haifeng Chen, Chris White, Quanquan Gu, Jian Pei, Carl Yang, and Liang Zhao. 2024. Domain specialization as the key to make large language models disruptive: A comprehensive survey. *Preprint*, arXiv:2305.18703.

[28] Inderjeet Nair, Aparna Garimella, Balaji Vasan Srinivasan, Natwar Modani, Niyati Chhaya, Srikrishna Karanam, and Sumit Shekhar. 2023. A neural CRF-based hierarchical approach for linear text segmentation. In *Findings of the Association for Computational Linguistics: EACL 2023*, pages 883–893, Dubrovnik, Croatia. Association for Computational Linguistics.

[29] Benjamin Newman, Luca Soldaini, Raymond Fok, Arman Cohan, and Kyle Lo. 2023. A question answering framework for decontextualizing user-facing snippets from scientific documents. *Preprint*, arXiv:2305.14772.

[30] Yixin Nie, Songhe Wang, and Mohit Bansal. 2019. Revealing the importance of semantic retrieval for machine reading at scale. *Preprint*, arXiv:1909.08041.

[31] Sosuke Nishikawa, Ryokan Ri, Ikuya Yamada, Yoshimasa Tsuruoka, and Isao Echizen. 2022. Ease: Entity-aware contrastive learning of sentence embedding. *Preprint*, arXiv:2205.04260.

[32] Oded Ovadia, Menachem Brief, Moshik Mishaeli, and Oren Elisha. 2024. Fine-tuning or retrieval? comparing knowledge injection in llms. *Preprint*, arXiv:2312.05934.

[33] Dr Jeff Pan. How do we encode knowledge to use at scale in open, evolving, decentralised systems?

[34] Richard Yuanzhe Pang, Alicia Parrish, Nitish Joshi, Nikita Nangia, Jason Phang, Angelica Chen, Vishakh Padmakumar, Johnny Ma, Jana Thompson, He He, and Samuel R. Bowman. 2022. Quality: Question answering with long input texts, yes! *Preprint*, arXiv:2112.08608.

[35] Nils Reimers and Iryna Gurevych. 2019. Sentence-BERT: Sentence embeddings using Siamese BERT-networks. In *Proceedings of the 2019 Conference on Empirical Methods in Natural Language Processing and the 9th International Joint Conference on Natural Language Processing (EMNLP-IJCNLP)*, pages 3982–3992, Hong Kong, China. Association for Computational Linguistics.

[36] Parth Sarthi, Salman Abdullah, Aditi Tuli, Shubh Khanna, Anna Goldie, and Christopher D. Manning. 2024. Raptor: Recursive abstractive processing for tree-organized retrieval. *Preprint*, arXiv:2401.18059.

[37] Sanat Sharma, Mayank Poddar, Jayant Kumar, Kosta Blank, and Tracy King. 2024. *Augmenting KG Hierarchies Using Neural Transformers*, page 298–303. Springer Nature Switzerland.

[38] Amit Sheth, Swati Padhee, and Amelie Gyrard. 2020. Knowledge graphs and knowledge networks: The story in brief. *Preprint*, arXiv:2003.03623.

[39] Lenka Tětková, Teresa Karen Scheidt, Maria Mandrup Fogh, Ellen Marie Gaunby Jørgensen, Finn Årup Nielsen, and Lars Kai Hansen. 2024. Knowledge graphs for empirical concept retrieval. *Preprint*, arXiv:2404.07008.

[40] Cinzia Viroli and Geoffrey J. McLachlan. 2017. Deep gaussian mixture models. *Preprint*, arXiv:1711.06929.

[41] Sewon Min Patrick Lewis Ledell Wu Sergey Edunov Danqi Chen Wen-tau Yih Vladimir Karpukhin, Barlas Oguz. Dense passage retrieval for open-domain question answering.

[42] Shuhe Wang, Xiaofei Sun, Xiaoya Li, Rongbin Ouyang, Fei Wu, Tianwei Zhang, Jiwei Li, and Guoyin Wang. 2023. Gpt-ner: Named entity recognition via large language models. *Preprint*, arXiv:2304.10428.

[43] Yuqi Wang, Boran Jiang, Yi Luo, Dawei He, Peng Cheng, and Liangcai Gao. 2024. Reasoning on efficient knowledge paths:knowledge graph guides large language model for domain question answering. *Preprint*, arXiv:2404.10384.

[44] Shenghao Yang, Weizhi Ma, Peijie Sun, Min Zhang, Qingyao Ai, Yiqun Liu, and Mingchen Cai. 2024. Common sense enhanced knowledge-based recommendation with large language model. *Preprint*, arXiv:2403.18325.

[45] Hao Yu, Aoran Gan, Kai Zhang, Shiwei Tong, Qi Liu, and Zhaofeng Liu. 2024. Evaluation of retrieval-augmented generation: A survey. *Preprint*, arXiv:2405.07437.

[46] Shiyue Zhang, David Wan, and Mohit Bansal. 2023. Extractive is not faithful: An investigation of broad unfaithfulness problems in extractive summarization. In *Proceedings of the 61st Annual Meeting of the Association for Computational Linguistics (Volume 1: Long Papers)*, pages 2153–2174, Toronto, Canada. Association for Computational Linguistics.

[47] Penghao Zhao, Hailin Zhang, Qinhan Yu, Zhengren Wang, Yunteng Geng, Fangcheng Fu, Ling Yang, Wentao Zhang, Jie Jiang, and Bin Cui. 2024. Retrieval-augmented generation for ai-generated content: A survey. *Preprint*, arXiv:2402.19473.

A Appendix

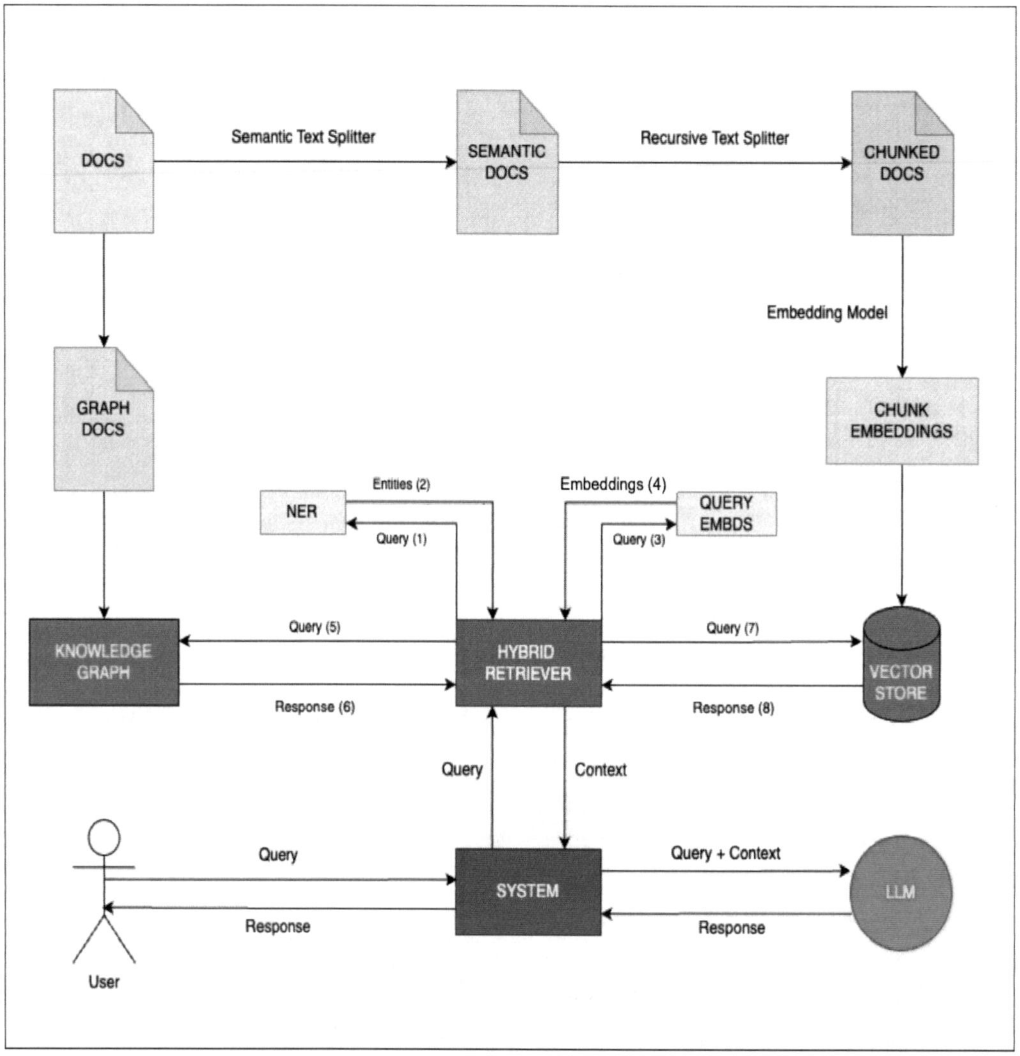

Figure 2: Architecture of SKETCH with a Hybrid Retriever combining structured and unstructured retrievers

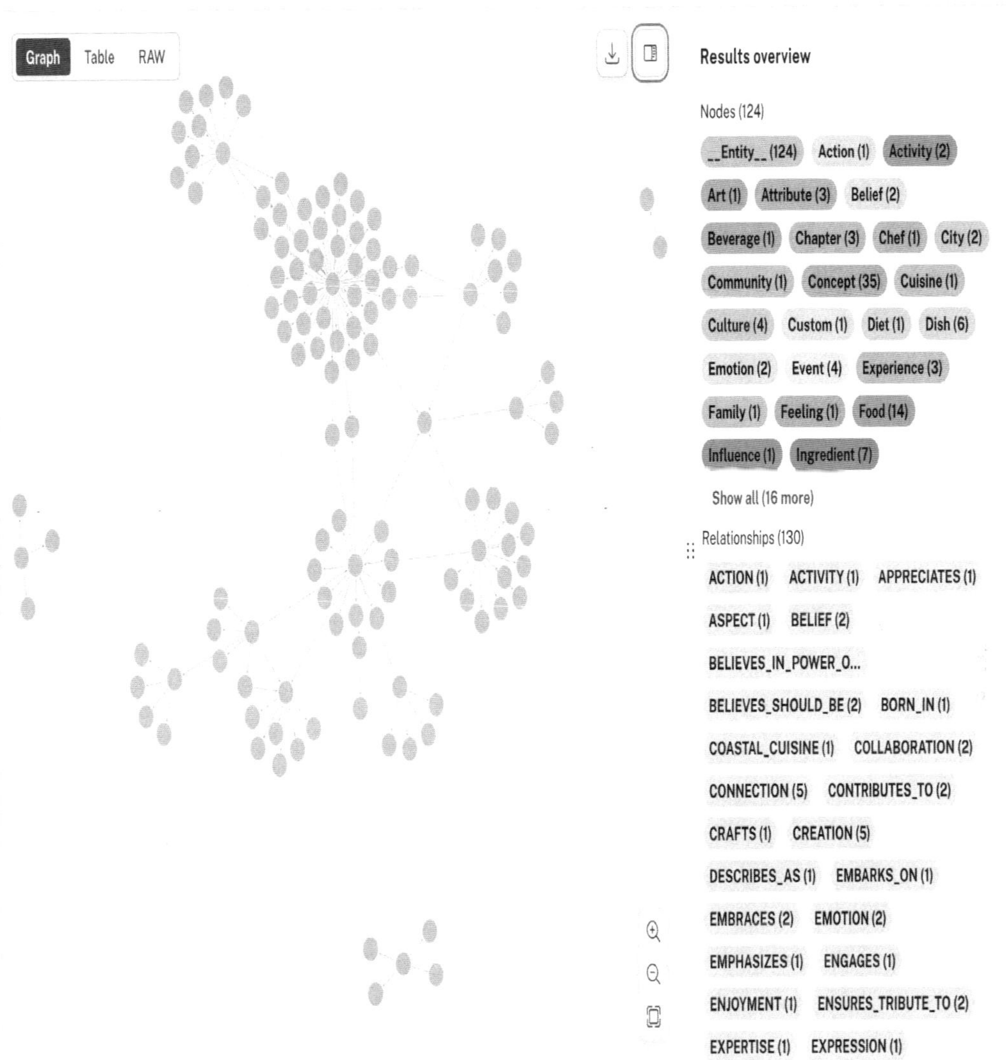

Figure 3: Italian Cuisine KG Representation

Figure 4: Naive RAG Italian Cuisine Performance Heatmap

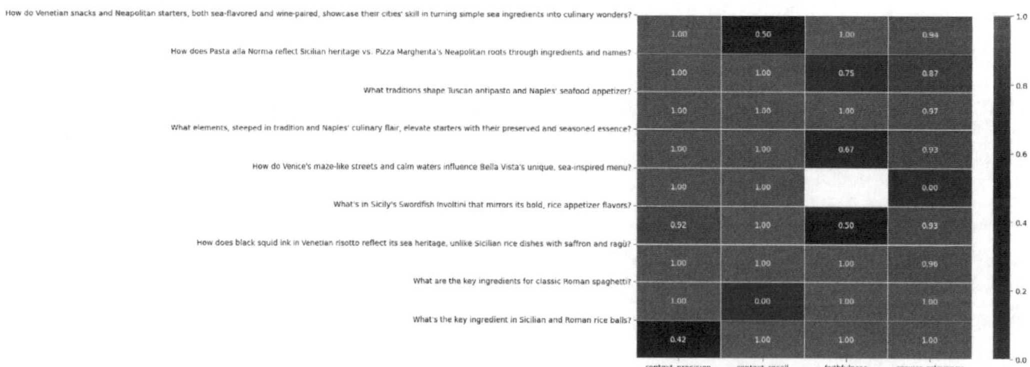

Figure 5: Semantic only Italian Cuisine Performance Heatmap

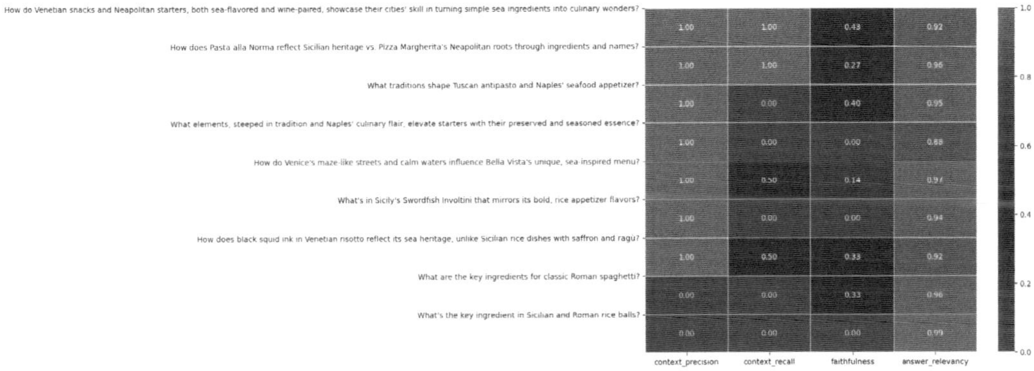

Figure 6: KG only Italian Cuisine Performance Heatmap

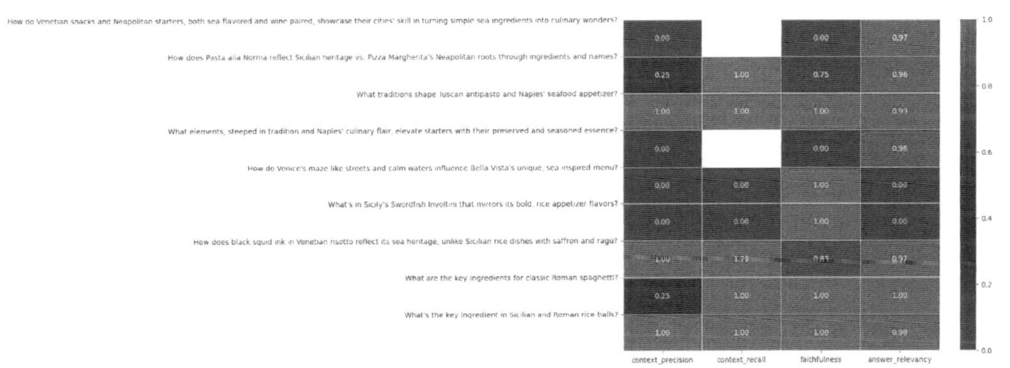

Figure 7: RAPTOR Italian Cuisine Performance Heatmap

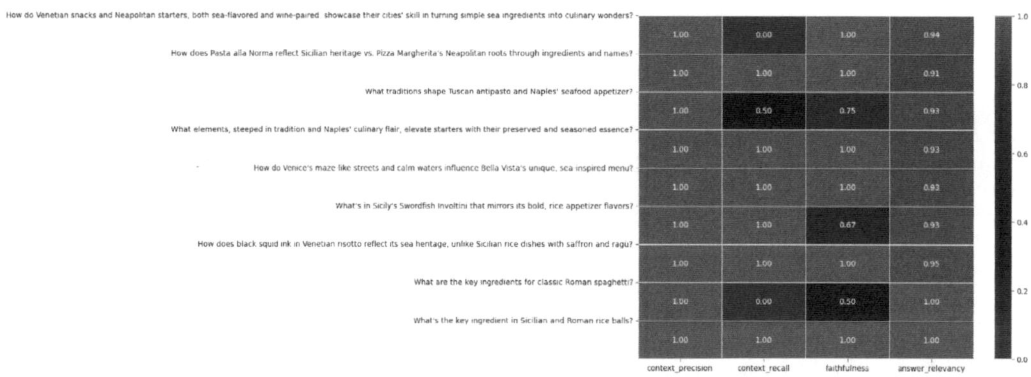

Figure 8: SKETCH Italian Cuisine Performance Heatmap

On Reducing Factual Hallucinations in Graph-to-Text Generation using Large Language Models

Dmitrii Iarosh[1, 3] **Alexander Panchenko**[1, 2] **Mikhail Salnikov**[2, 1]
[1]Skoltech [2]AIRI [3]Saint Petersburg State University
{D.Yarosh, A.Panchenko, Mikhail.Salnikov}@skol.tech

Abstract

Recent work in Graph-to-Text generation has achieved impressive results, but it still suffers from hallucinations in some cases, despite extensive pretraining stages and various methods for working with graph data. While the commonly used metrics for evaluating the quality of Graph-to-Text models show almost perfect results, it makes it challenging to compare different approaches. This paper demonstrates the challenges of recent Graph-to-Text systems in terms of hallucinations and proposes a simple yet effective approach to using a general LLM, which has shown state-of-the-art results and reduced the number of factual hallucinations. We provide step-by-step instructions on how to develop prompts for language models and a detailed analysis of potential factual errors in the generated text.

1 Introduction

Knowledge Graphs KG have become a powerful tool for organizing and representing complex data due to their ability to easily manage trusted information and are used in various industries such as education, healthcare, and social media (Peng et al., 2023). They can be used in conjunction with modern Large Language Models (LLMs) to create Retrieval-Augmented Generation (RAG) systems or to validate the information generated or retrieved. Due to the better validation and understanding of data, it is important to properly translate them into text. This process, known as Graph-to-Text generation, has recently seen success in creating knowledge-grounded chatbots (Zhou et al., 2018; Peng et al., 2024) and Question Answering systems (Razzhigaev et al., 2023; Agarwal et al., 2021; Salnikov et al., 2023). Belikova et al. (2024) demonstrated that integrating various external resources, particularly linearized subgraphs, and employing a marginal probability-based selection method significantly enhanced the effectiveness of the RAG setup.

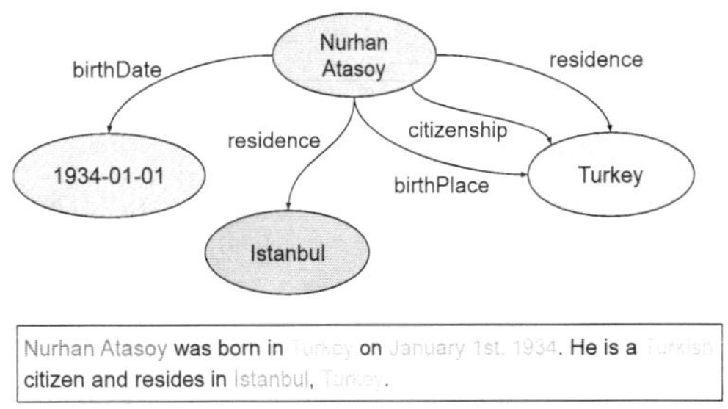

Figure 1: An example of a knowledge graph and its corresponding Graph-to-Text generation that describes the entities and their relationships in the provided graph.

Graph-to-Text involves the processing of Knowledge Graph triplets (subject, property, object) data, into a natural textual representation that should include all the factual information from these triplets and nothing else, as shown in the Figure 1.

In this work, we focus on evaluating the abilities of modern Large Language Models, such as ChatGPT[1], LLaMA-3 (Dubey et al., 2024) and Gemma 2 (Rivière et al., 2024), to solve the Graph-to-Text problem, and specifically on the potential hallucinations that are totally unacceptable for such problems.

Recent studies have produced state-of-the-art results in the Graph-to-Text generation task. They used complex pipelines to organize graphs in a specific order to generate correct text (Guo et al., 2020), or used graph aware approaches (Colas et al., 2022). All of these methods required complex training stages, but they provided the best results according to the leaderboards[2].

Despite the impressive results, these Graph-to-Text methods can still experience hallucinations and may omit certain elements of the graph in the

[1]https://openai.com/chatgpt/overview/
[2]https://synalp.gitlabpages.inria.fr/webnlg-challenge/challenge_2020

Proceedings of the Generative AI and Knowledge Graph Workshop (GenAIK), pages 43–53
January 19, 2025.

resulting text which are difficult to detect with the common metrics used on popular leaderboards. In this paper, we focus on this issue and provide a detailed analysis of state-of-the-art methods, comparing them with general Language Models.

Our contribution are two-fold:

- We provide a detailed guide to our prompt engineering strategy for LLMs in the Graph-to-Text domain, which allows users to achieve state-of-the-art results using a general LLM without the need for complex setup stages, fine-tuning, etc.

- We evaluate state-of-the-art methods and modern large language models (LLMs) on the popular Graph-to-Text dataset, WebNLG (Gardent et al., 2017b), and provide a new and detailed analysis to estimate the hallucinations of these methods which showed limitations of various Natural Language Generation (NLG) metrics.

We make our code publically available to provide reproducible results and motivate future researchers.[3]

2 Related work

In this section, we will provide a brief overview of Knowledge Graphs, their representation and linearization, as well as existing Graph-to-Text algorithms and the potential use of Large Language Models for this task.

2.1 Knowledge Graphs

Knowledge Graphs, such as Wikidata (Vrandečić and Krötzsch, 2014) or DBPedia (Lehmann et al., 2015), represent knowledge about their entities in a structured format. Connection between entities are labelled with properties and together they form triples (subject, property, object). Each triple describes a single fact about its entities without any unnecessary information. This type of knowledge organization helps to provide a brief description of each KG node by summarizing its neighbours. Additionally, Knowledge Graphs are easy to edit in order to keep the data in them up-to-date. There are two main ways to use Knowledge Graphs in conjunction with Language Models. The first one is to feed the graph directly into specially pretrained Graph Convolution Network and then use graph encoded version as input for language model decoder (Zhao et al., 2020). This approach save all the information about the graph structure but requires training a custom model. Other way is to linearize the graph in the special order: it can be connected with graph traversal (Ribeiro et al., 2020; Li et al., 2021) or selected by custom neural network (Guo et al., 2020). Such approach can lose information about two or more steps connections because of unstructured information representation in the Large Language Models context, but can be used with general purpose Large Language Model.

2.2 Graph-to-Text

Problem of Graph-to-Text generation started from lexicalisation task — converting individual Knowledge Graph triples into verb phrase templates. In the first presented solution text was generated based on the predefined templates (Goldberg et al., 1994). This algorithm is simple but requires custom human created templates for each task and can be applied only in a few specific areas. Future development in this area led to creation of algorithms for autonomous extraction of such templates from training data source (Duma and Klein, 2013; Perera and Nand, 2015). While such algorithms provide first fully autonomous generation pipeline, quality was still not enough to compare it with human-written results. Next step in this topic was done by WEBNLG dataset (Gardent et al., 2017a) for Graph-to-Text and vice versa generation. This dataset was based on DBpedia (Lehmann et al., 2015) and provides enough training data for ability to apply fine-tuned pretrained data-driven ML models for Graph-to-Text task. One of the first solutions based on this data was an LSTM transformer based model for sequence to sequence translation (Gardent et al., 2017b). Other approach used graph convolution network (GCN) as encoder which can process graph without linearization to save it structure (Marcheggiani and Perez-Beltrachini, 2018). Further develop of this solution led to the usage of graph attention networks as an encoder to provide more modelling power and improved performance (Koncel-Kedziorski et al., 2019). Another close solution (Beck et al., 2018) where graph-based encoder is also used, replaces GCN with Gated Graph Neural Network (Li et al., 2015). With active development of pretrained language models (PLMs) it was shown that is it possible to use graph embeddings by graph neural network as the input word embeddings of PLM for gener-

[3] https://github.com/s-nlp/llm-g2t

ating text after their representation alignment (Li et al., 2021). Relation-biased breadth first search was used to linearize the graph structure for PLM sequence decoder as it saves information about nodes at the same level with relevant semantics and forces more human-like order of description for relations. Another solution (Guo et al., 2020) proposes a relational graph convolutional network which is used as a planner to linearize the graph in the correct order before feeding it to the pretrained T5 model (Raffel et al., 2020) for the final text generation. This solution shows the best quality in the WEBNLG 2020 challenge. PLM can provide high quality result for the task of Graph-to-Text generation even without special graph-based neural networks (Ribeiro et al., 2020). Fine-tuned for a few epochs BART (Lewis et al., 2020) and T5 models were evaluated on the WEBNLG and AGENDA (Koncel-Kedziorski et al., 2019) datasets with linear traversal graph linearization. While such models as T5 and BART required extra fine-tuning on the task dataset modern general purpose Large Language Models like ChatGPT can provide comparable quality results for the Graph-to-Text translation even in zero-shot mode (Axelsson and Skantze, 2023). Comparison of ChatGPT and GPT-3 (Brown et al., 2020) Large Language Models with pretrained T5 and BART models shows that Large Language Models provide comparable quality results, but tend to generate text with hallucinations and irrelevant information (Yuan and Färber, 2023). In this work we will show that this problem can be solved by prompt engineering and replacing Large Language Model by modern one.

2.3 Large Language Models

Large language models such as Chat-GPT and GPT-3 are based on the transformer decoder architecture (Vaswani et al., 2017). They were designed to provide even zero-shot text generation for user request based on the huge train dataset and large amount of tuned parameters used in their training process. Development of these models by OpenAI lead to the next generation model called GPT-4 [4]. It demonstrates better quality on creative and long context tasks but it is also not open-source and OpenAI doesn't publish any paper about its architecture and training process. An alternative to the GPT-4 model was provided by Meta AI with their Llama 3 models family (Dubey et al., 2024). This Large Language Model is open-source and enough powerful to be used instead of GPT-4, according to provided results of comparison. At the same time Gemma 2 model (Rivière et al., 2024) was introduced by Google. It beats Llama 3 models of the nearly same size and even can be competitive among models with larger amount of parameters. It was also published to open-source.

Quality of Large Language Model answers can be enriched not only by applying new training techniques and increasing of train dataset or model parameters amount but also by different prompting techniques during evaluation of the user request. Providing Large Language Model with a few examples of processing the requested task can lead to the better performance and model adaptation to the new kinds of tasks (Brown et al., 2020). Such method is also known as few-shot prompting. Large Language Model are different from people in their process of thinking, so it is important to generate intermediate thoughts to provide better final quality of generation (Wei et al., 2022). It is called Chain-of-Thoughts method and can be applied both to zero-shot prompt using "Think step by step" phrase or even to a few-shot prompt by including examples with intermediate steps.

2.4 Fact Verification Metric

Employing modern Large Language Models for tasks like text summarization or graph-to-text translation produces favorable results; nevertheless, these models still have the propensity to hallucinate, and such hallucinations can be particularly harmful when they arise in factual statements. To detect factual inconsistency in the Large Language Models output factual consistency metrics such as AlignScore (Zha et al., 2023) can be used. AlignScore is based on RoBERTa (Liu et al., 2019) model which was trained to estimate the information alignment score between two arbitrary text pieces: context and claim. Given text pieces *context* and *claim*, *claim* is aligned with *context* if *context* contains all information from *claim* and *claim* does not contradict *context*. AlignScore was trained on several fact verification datasets (Schuster et al., 2021; Nie et al., 2019) that consist of claims paired with relevant contexts derived from Wikipedia [5] pages, alongside labels indicating the veracity of the claims. To enhance the metric's ability for continuous prediction, semantic text similar-

[4] https://openai.com/index/gpt-4

[5] https://www.wikipedia.org

ity datasets (Marelli et al., 2014; Cer et al., 2017) were incorporated into AlignScore's training corpus. These datasets consist of sentence pairs and corresponding similarity scores, illustrating the degree of semantic relatedness or independence between the sentences.

3 Proposed Framework

We propose a universal and easy-to-use framework for the Graph-to-Text task that does not require fine-tuning or the use of specialized trained modules or models, yet still achieves state-of-the-art results. We use common instruction-based Large Language Models, such as LLaMA 3 (Dubey et al., 2024), Gemma 2 (Rivière et al., 2024) or GPT-4o[6], to generate comprehensive, natural-style text from KG triplets using carefully selected prompt with various prompting techniques.

In our work, as with any system development, we start from a simple zero-shot baseline and simply ask the LLM to convert KG triples into text using the following prompt: *"Translate from graph to text"*. This straightforward approach suffers from a lot of hallucinations, so we asked the model not to hallucinate: *"Describe all nodes of the graph with edges as a connected text. Talk only about items from graph and use information only if graph contains it. Write only description without headers and titles."*, and it actually works, with better results. After that, we tried adding some general hacks, such as a few short learning examples and a chain of thoughts, to improve it. Finally, we provided the following prompt template:

Act as a system which describes all nodes of the graph with edges as a connected text. Follow the examples. Talk only about items from graph and use information only if graph contains it. Validate each written fact and correct it if mistake is found, do it silently without extra notes. Let's think step by step. For each step show described triple and check that all words from it is used in your description.

Task:

Graph: LINEARIZED GRAPH FROM EXAMPLE 1 Model answer:

Step-by-step solution:

MODEL STEP BY STEP SOLUTION FROM EXAMPLE 1

Description: MODEL GRAPH DESCRIPTION FROM EXAMPLE 1

... (Here comes more examples) ...

Now provide answer for the next task yourself.

Task:

Graph: LINEARIZED GRAPH

Model answer:

Step-by-step solution:

It actually works efficiently with the small LLaMA-3-8B-Instruct model and the big proprietary GPT-4o model. Examples of generated outputs for small graph, consisting of two triples (Figure 2), are presented in Table 1.

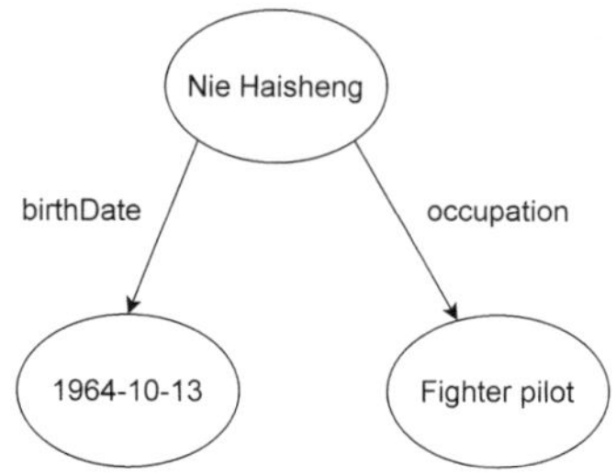

Figure 2: Visualization of the graph described in the Table 1

4 Experiments

Opposite to the previous works (Axelsson and Skantze, 2023; Yuan and Färber, 2023) for the evaluation we have used more actual Large Language Models such as open-source LLaMA-3-8B-Instruct, gemma-2-9b and proprietary gpt-4o and gpt-4o-mini. As a source of Knowledge Graphs we have chosen WEBNLG 2020 English dataset as it is one of the main benchmarks for the Graph-to-Text task. All models were evaluated on the test set using modified tripleset — graph description in the triple form where some predicates are replaced according to the official WEBNLG recommendation[7]. It helps models better understand directions of the links between entities. Each graph was linearized in the order triples are stated in the dataset. Example of the final graph input format is [graph][head] Expect a Miracle [relation] runtime [tail] 3274.0</s>, where [graph] and </s> denote start and end of the graph description and [head], [relation] and [tail] divide parts of the triple. We also replaced all underscore symbols by spaces to prevent Large Language Model from generation incorrect object names.

[6] https://openai.com/index/gpt-4

[7] https://synalp.gitlabpages.inria.fr/webnlg-challenge/docs/#triple-modification

G2T Model	Prompt	BLEU↑	BERTScore F1↑	Example
Reference	–	1	1	Nie Haisheng, born on October 13, 1964, worked as a fighter pilot.
Llama-3-8B-Instruct	zero-shot (simple)	0.1402	0.9455	Nie Haisheng is a person born on October 13, 1964. As a Fighter pilot, he is a professional aviator.
Llama-3-8B-Instruct	zero-shot (anti-hallucinations)	0.5548	0.9771	Nie Haisheng, born on October 13, 1964, is a Fighter pilot.
Llama-3-8B-Instruct	few-shot	0.2647	0.9754	Nie Haisheng is a fighter pilot born on October 13, 1964.
Llama-3-8B-Instruct	CoT few-shot	0.2370	0.9458	The fighter pilot Nie Haisheng was born on October 13, 1964.
Gemma-2-9b	zero-shot (simple)	< 0.0001	0.9124	Nie Haisheng's birthdate is 1964-10-13. Nie Haisheng's occupation is Fighter pilot.
Gemma-2-9b	zero-shot (anti-hallucinations)	< 0.0001	0.9238	Nie Haisheng was born on 1964-10-13. Nie Haisheng's occupation is Fighter pilot.
Gemma-2-9b	few-shot	< 0.0001	0.9541	Nie Haisheng was born on 1964-10-13 and is a Fighter pilot.
Gemma-2-9b	CoT few-shot	< 0.0001	0.9235	Fighter pilot Nie Haisheng was born on 1964-10-13.
GPT-4o	zero-shot (simple)	0.3388	0.9673	Nie Haisheng was born on October 13, 1964, and hisoccupation is a fighter pilot.
GPT-4o	zero-shot (anti-hallucinations)	0.3388	0.9673	Nie Haisheng was born on October 13, 1964, and hisoccupation is a fighter pilot.
GPT-4o	few-shot	0.4572	0.9797	Nie Haisheng was born on October 13, 1964, and works as a fighter pilot.
GPT-4o	CoT few-shot	**0.6407**	**0.9839**	Nie Haisheng, born on October 13, 1964, is a fighter pilot.

Table 1: Examples of Large Language Model outputs with different prompts on the graph, consisting of two triples. Blue text means model hallucinations.

To measure the results we have used standard WEBNLG metrics:Meteor (Banerjee and Lavie, 2005), BLEU (Papineni et al., 2002), Chrf (Popovic, 2015), TER (Snover et al., 2006) and BertScore (Zhang et al., 2020). Moreover, we additionally computed AlignScore metric (Zha et al., 2023) to detect factual inconsistency in the model answers.

For comparison reasons we have also evaluated GAP (Colas et al., 2022) and calculated metrics for the P^2 model (Guo et al., 2020), which is top-1 solution from WEBNLG 2020 competition, based on the model outputs published by authors[8]. Results of our evaluation are presented in the Table 2.

While by some metrics we can easily define the better model, it can be seen that BERTScore F1 is nearly equal both for Large Language Models and P^2 and requires more detailed analysis.

5 Analytics

While by classical translation metrics Large Language Models are slightly worse that the P^2 model, it was expected as fine-tuned models were adopted for the style of reference answers during training on the train part of the dataset and these metrics reward word match (Axelsson and Skantze, 2023). On one hand it gives P^2 advantage, but on the other hand it can't be applied to another dataset without extra fine-tuning process, while Large Language Models can be evaluated just with other examples in few-shot part of the prompt. As difference between Large Language Models and P^2 by BERTScore F1 is at the margin of statistical error we go deeper and compared factual consistency of the generated results with AlignScore. While Large Language Models all as one show high score by this metric, P^2 demonstrates much worse quality. It can be explained by hallucinations or missed facts in the model answers. To define the reasons of such problems with factual consistency we reviewed examples from the dataset where P^2 suffers from fact inconsistency, but two best of compared Large Language Models (Gemma 2 and GPT-4o) still provide high-quality results. One pattern we detected is that P^2 model tends to hallucinate if graph contains multiple triples with the same subject and property but different objects. Examples of the such graph

[8]https://github.com/QipengGuo/P2_WebNLG2020/blob/main/output.txt

G2T Model	Setup	AlignScore↑	Meteor↑	BLEU↑	Chrf↑	TER↓	BERTScore F1↑
GAP	task-specific	0.7797	0.5333	0.2398	0.5985	70.4437	0.9298
P^2	task-specific	0.1511	**0.6286**	**0.4054**	0.6434	**44.2396**	**0.9549**
Llama-3-8B-Instruct	zero-shot	0.8959	0.5507	0.2690	0.6312	66.7051	0.9381
Gemma-2-9b	zero-shot	0.9100	0.5816	0.3148	0.6363	55.4666	0.9448
GPT-4o	zero-shot	0.8909	0.5970	0.2872	**0.6559**	69.0469	0.9455
GPT-4o-mini	zero-shot	0.8826	0.5940	0.2916	0.6488	66.8438	0.9442
Llama-3-8B-Instruct	CoT few-shot	0.9021	0.5487	0.2492	0.6136	62.5371	0.9432
Gemma-2-9b	CoT few-shot	0.9459	0.5818	0.3298	0.6300	48.2942	0.9517
GPT-4o	CoT few-shot	**0.9514**	0.6079	0.3402	0.6536	52.8860	0.9520
GPT-4o-mini	CoT few-shot	0.9436	0.5873	0.3036	0.6417	53.9540	0.9509

Table 2: Comparison of modern Large Language Models Graph-to-Text evaluation on WEBNLG 2020 dataset using simple zero-shot prompts and CoT few-shot prompts which also ask model not to hallucinate; AlignScore (Roberta-base).

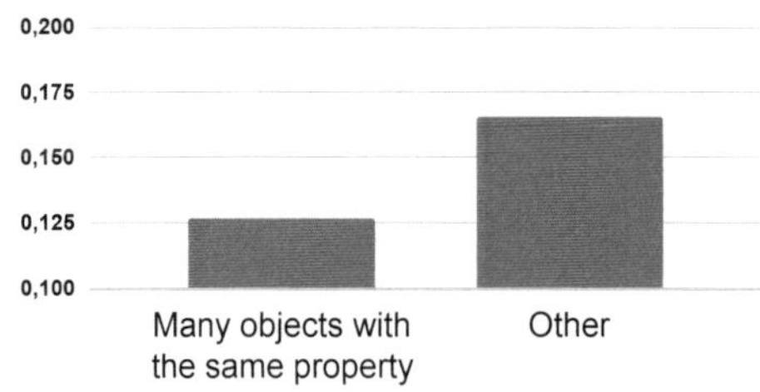

Figure 3: Comparison of AlignScore of P^2 model on graphs which contains multiple triples with the same subject and property but different objects and graphs without such triples.

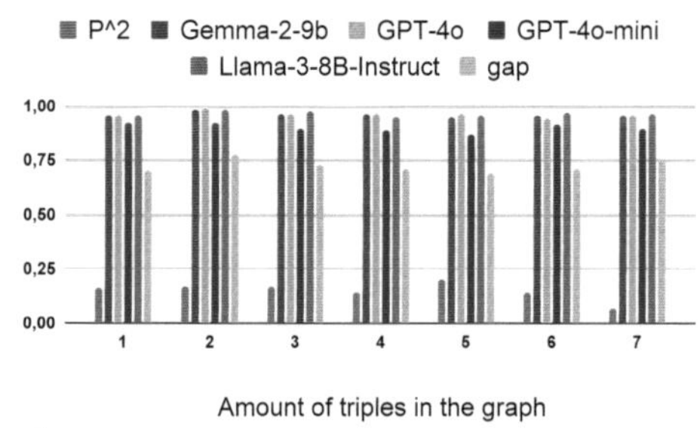

Figure 4: Comparison of AlignScore for P^2 and CoT few-shot prompted Large Language Models grouped by the graphs size in triples.

are provided in the Table 4. To prove this point we aggregated AlignScore results by cases where the graph satisfies this condition and cases where such triplets are absent. The comparison is shown in the Figure 3. It can be seen that P^2 shows 24% less quality in such situations.

Another problem is connected with the size of the graph provided to the model. While Large Language Models show stable quality on any number of triples in the graph P^2 loses more than 50% of quality on the graphs with seven triples. Example of such graph and models output are presented in the Table 3. Comparison of AlignScore for graphs with different triples count is provided in th Figure 4. We have also detected that even on smaller graphs P^2 often skips one of the facts from the graph which led to great but not full description. Examples are given in Table 3 and 5.

To sum up, P^2 shows great results by classic translation metrics because of special graph reordering and language model fine-tuning which makes model answer similar to the references, but still suffers from hallucinations more than modern Large Language Models because of the under the hood T5 model limitations. While generating the result with P^2 requires less computational resources it can be used in further processing only after factual consistency check to detect possible skipped or incorrect facts.

6 Conclusion

We have shown how to select prompt for the modern Large Language Model to show competitive results in Graph-to-Text task with top-1 specialized model fine-tuned for the specific dataset. We provide final few-shot prompt based on the Chain-of-Thoughts technique. Also we evaluated four modern Large Language Models on the graph-to-text task and compared their results with state-of-the-art solution in this task. Based on these evaluation we provided detailed analytics about potential factual errors which can be caused by model hallucinations. Moreover, we described how they can be omitted behind classic translation metrics on the example of the P^2 model.

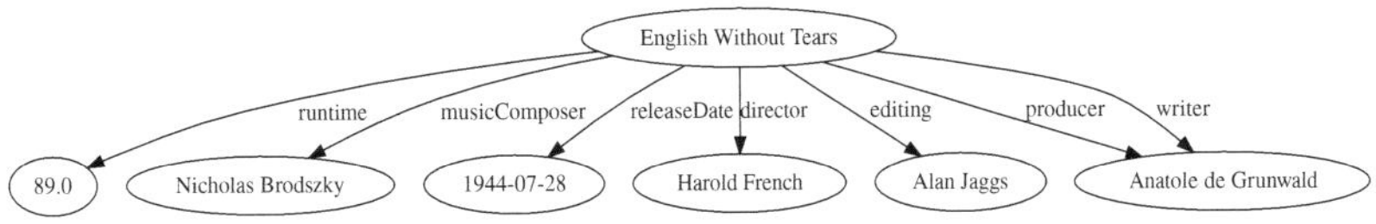

Reference	English Without Tears is a 89 minute film that was written and produced by Anatole de Grunwald. The movie was released on July 28th, 1944. Nicholas Brodszky was the musical composer and Harold French was the director. The editing was done by Alan Jaggs.
P^2	English Without Tears was produced by Anatole de Grunwald and written by Nicholas Brodszky. It was edited by Alan Jaggs and released on 28th July 1944. It has a runtime of 89.0 and was directed by Harold French.
GPT-4o	Released on July 28, 1944, "English Without Tears" runs for 89 minutes. The film was directed by Harold French and edited by Alan Jaggs. The music was composed by Nicholas Brodszky. Anatole de Grunwald contributed as both the producer and the writer.
Gemma2	*English Without Tears*, released on 1944-07-28, is a film with a runtime of 89.0 minutes. It was directed by Harold French and written by Anatole de Grunwald who also produced it. The music was composed by Nicholas Brodszky and edited by Alan Jaggs.

Table 3: Example of the graph with seven triples where P^2 made a factual incorrect statement. Red text means incorrect fact detected by AlignScore, green text marks correct description

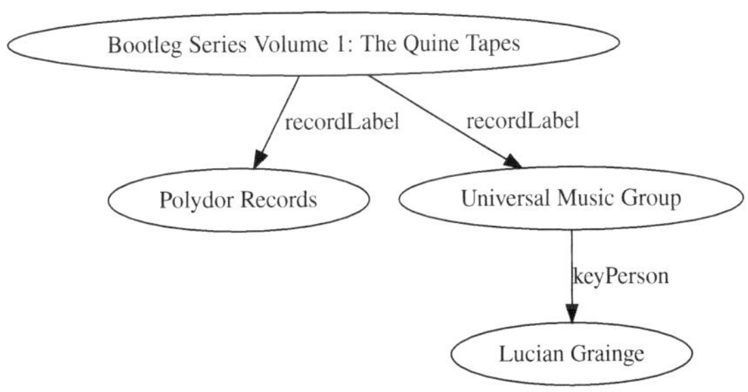

Reference	Bootleg Series Volume 1: The Quine Tapes was released by Universal Music Group, a record label run by key person Lucian Grainge. Polydor Records recorded Bootleg Series Volume 1: The Quine Tapes.
P^2	Lucian Grainge is a key person at Universal Music Group, the label that signed Bootleg Series Volume 1: The Quine Tapes to Polydor Records.
GPT-4o	Bootleg Series Volume 1: The Quine Tapes is associated with Polydor Records and Universal Music Group. A key person in Universal Music Group is Lucian Grainge.
Gemma2	Bootleg Series Volume 1: The Quine Tapes was released by both Polydor Records and Universal Music Group. Lucian Grainge is a significant figure at Universal Music Group.

Table 4: Example of the graph with multiple triples with the same subject and property but different objects. Red text means incorrect fact detected by AlignScore, green text marks correct description

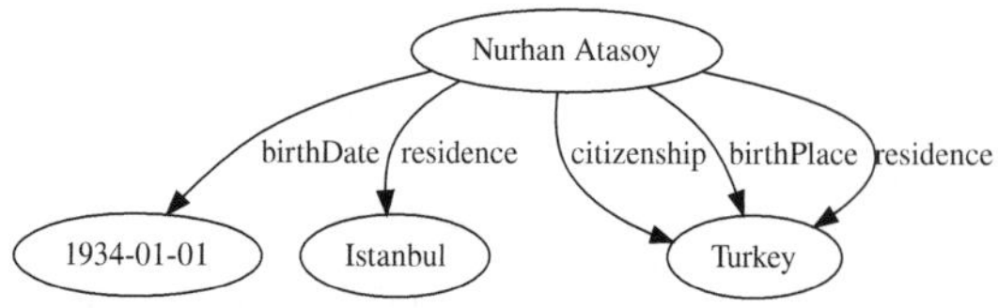

Reference	Nurhan Atasoy was born in Turkey on January 1st, 1934. He is a Turkish citizen and resides in Istanbul, Turkey.
P^2	Nurhan Atasoy was born in Turkey on January 1st 1934. He resides in Istanbul and has Turkish citizenship.
GPT-4o	Nurhan Atasoy, born in Turkey on January 1, 1934, holds Turkish citizenship and resides in Istanbul, Turkey.
Gemma2	Nurhan Atasoy, who was born on 1934-01-01 in Turkey, is Turkish and lives in Istanbul and Turkey.

Table 5: Examples of graph to text generation with various models. The P^2 model omits one of the facts.

7 Limitations

The presented approach of Graph-to-Text translation using Large Language Models requires more computational resources than the state-of-the-art solution. Additionally, it is possible to measure the amount of model hallucinations using human evaluation in addition to the AlignScore.

References

Oshin Agarwal, Heming Ge, Siamak Shakeri, and Rami Al-Rfou. 2021. Knowledge graph based synthetic corpus generation for knowledge-enhanced language model pre-training. In *Proceedings of the 2021 Conference of the North American Chapter of the Association for Computational Linguistics: Human Language Technologies*, pages 3554–3565, Online. Association for Computational Linguistics.

Agnes Axelsson and Gabriel Skantze. 2023. Using large language models for zero-shot natural language generation from knowledge graphs. In *Proceedings of the Workshop on Multimodal, Multilingual Natural Language Generation and Multilingual WebNLG Challenge (MM-NLG 2023)*, pages 39–54, Prague, Czech Republic. Association for Computational Linguistics.

Satanjeev Banerjee and Alon Lavie. 2005. METEOR: an automatic metric for MT evaluation with improved correlation with human judgments. In *Proceedings of the Workshop on Intrinsic and Extrinsic Evaluation Measures for Machine Translation and/or Summarization@ACL 2005, Ann Arbor, Michigan, USA, June 29, 2005*, pages 65–72. Association for Computational Linguistics.

Daniel Beck, Gholamreza Haffari, and Trevor Cohn. 2018. Graph-to-sequence learning using gated graph neural networks. In *Proceedings of the 56th Annual Meeting of the Association for Computational Linguistics (Volume 1: Long Papers)*, pages 273–283, Melbourne, Australia. Association for Computational Linguistics.

Julia Belikova, Evegeniy Beliakin, and Vasily Konovalov. 2024. JellyBell at TextGraphs-17 shared task: Fusing large language models with external knowledge for enhanced question answering. In *Proceedings of TextGraphs-17: Graph-based Methods for Natural Language Processing*, pages 154–160, Bangkok, Thailand. Association for Computational Linguistics.

Tom B. Brown, Benjamin Mann, Nick Ryder, Melanie Subbiah, Jared Kaplan, Prafulla Dhariwal, Arvind Neelakantan, Pranav Shyam, Girish Sastry, Amanda Askell, Sandhini Agarwal, Ariel Herbert-Voss, Gretchen Krueger, Tom Henighan, Rewon Child, Aditya Ramesh, Daniel M. Ziegler, Jeffrey Wu, Clemens Winter, Christopher Hesse, Mark Chen, Eric Sigler, Mateusz Litwin, Scott Gray, Benjamin Chess, Jack Clark, Christopher Berner, Sam McCandlish, Alec Radford, Ilya Sutskever, and Dario Amodei. 2020. Language models are few-shot learners. In *Advances in Neural Information Processing Systems 33: Annual Conference on Neural Information Processing Systems 2020, NeurIPS 2020, December 6-12, 2020, virtual*.

Daniel M. Cer, Mona T. Diab, Eneko Agirre, Iñigo Lopez-Gazpio, and Lucia Specia. 2017. Semeval-2017 task 1: Semantic textual similarity - multilingual and cross-lingual focused evaluation. *CoRR*, abs/1708.00055.

Anthony M. Colas, Mehrdad Alvandipour, and Daisy Zhe Wang. 2022. GAP: A graph-aware language model framework for knowledge graph-to-text generation. In *Proceedings of the 29th International Conference on Computational Linguistics, COLING 2022, Gyeongju, Republic of Korea, October 12-17, 2022*, pages 5755–5769. International Committee on Computational Linguistics.

Abhimanyu Dubey, Abhinav Jauhri, Abhinav Pandey, Abhishek Kadian, Ahmad Al-Dahle, Aiesha Letman, Akhil Mathur, Alan Schelten, Amy Yang, Angela Fan, Anirudh Goyal, Anthony Hartshorn, Aobo Yang, Archi Mitra, Archie Sravankumar, Artem Korenev, Arthur Hinsvark, Arun Rao, Aston Zhang, Aurélien Rodriguez, Austen Gregerson, Ava Spataru, Baptiste Rozière, Bethany Biron, Binh Tang, Bobbie Chern, Charlotte Caucheteux, Chaya Nayak, Chloe Bi, Chris Marra, Chris McConnell, Christian Keller, Christophe Touret, Chunyang Wu, Corinne Wong, Cristian Canton Ferrer, Cyrus Nikolaidis, Damien Allonsius, Daniel Song, Danielle Pintz, Danny Livshits, David Esiobu, Dhruv Choudhary, Dhruv Mahajan, Diego Garcia-Olano, Diego Perino, Dieuwke Hupkes, Egor Lakomkin, Ehab AlBadawy, Elina Lobanova, Emily Dinan, Eric Michael Smith, Filip Radenovic, Frank Zhang, Gabriel Synnaeve, Gabrielle Lee, Georgia Lewis Anderson, Graeme Nail, Grégoire Mialon, Guan Pang, Guillem Cucurell, Hailey Nguyen, Hannah Korevaar, Hu Xu, Hugo Touvron, Iliyan Zarov, Imanol Arrieta Ibarra, Isabel M. Kloumann, Ishan Misra, Ivan Evtimov, Jade Copet, Jaewon Lee, Jan Geffert, Jana Vranes, Jason Park, Jay Mahadeokar, Jeet Shah, Jelmer van der Linde, Jennifer Billock, Jenny Hong, Jenya Lee, Jeremy Fu, Jianfeng Chi, Jianyu Huang, Jiawen Liu, Jie Wang, Jiecao Yu, Joanna Bitton, Joe Spisak, Jongsoo Park, Joseph Rocca, Joshua Johnstun, Joshua Saxe, Junteng Jia, Kalyan Vasuden Alwala, Kartikeya Upasani, Kate Plawiak, Ke Li, Kenneth Heafield, Kevin Stone, and et al. 2024. The llama 3 herd of models. *CoRR*, abs/2407.21783.

Daniel Duma and Ewan Klein. 2013. Generating natural language from linked data: Unsupervised template extraction. In *Proceedings of the 10th International Conference on Computational Semantics (IWCS 2013) – Long Papers*, pages 83–94, Potsdam, Germany. Association for Computational Linguistics.

Claire Gardent, Anastasia Shimorina, Shashi Narayan, and Laura Perez-Beltrachini. 2017a. Creating training corpora for NLG micro-planners. In *Proceedings of the 55th Annual Meeting of the Association for Computational Linguistics (Volume 1: Long Papers)*, pages 179–188, Vancouver, Canada. Association for Computational Linguistics.

Claire Gardent, Anastasia Shimorina, Shashi Narayan, and Laura Perez-Beltrachini. 2017b. The WebNLG challenge: Generating text from RDF data. In *Proceedings of the 10th International Conference on Natural Language Generation*, pages 124–133, Santiago de Compostela, Spain. Association for Computational Linguistics.

E. Goldberg, N. Driedger, and R.I. Kittredge. 1994. Using natural-language processing to produce weather forecasts. *IEEE Expert*, 9(2):45–53.

Qipeng Guo, Zhijing Jin, Ning Dai, Xipeng Qiu, Xiangyang Xue, David Wipf, and Zheng Zhang. 2020. P^2: A plan-and-pretrain approach for knowledge graph-to-text generation. In *Proceedings of the 3rd International Workshop on Natural Language Generation from the Semantic Web (WebNLG+)*, pages 100–106, Dublin, Ireland (Virtual). Association for Computational Linguistics.

Rik Koncel-Kedziorski, Dhanush Bekal, Yi Luan, Mirella Lapata, and Hannaneh Hajishirzi. 2019. Text Generation from Knowledge Graphs with Graph Transformers. In *Proceedings of the 2019 Conference of the North American Chapter of the Association for Computational Linguistics: Human Language Technologies, Volume 1 (Long and Short Papers)*, pages 2284–2293, Minneapolis, Minnesota. Association for Computational Linguistics.

Rik Koncel-Kedziorski, Dhanush Bekal, Yi Luan, Mirella Lapata, and Hannaneh Hajishirzi. 2019. Text generation from knowledge graphs with graph transformers. In *Proceedings of the 2019 Conference of the North American Chapter of the Association for Computational Linguistics: Human Language Technologies, NAACL-HLT 2019, Minneapolis, MN, USA, June 2-7, 2019, Volume 1 (Long and Short Papers)*, pages 2284–2293. Association for Computational Linguistics.

Jens Lehmann, Robert Isele, Max Jakob, Anja Jentzsch, Dimitris Kontokostas, Pablo N. Mendes, Sebastian Hellmann, Mohamed Morsey, Patrick van Kleef, S. Auer, and Christian Bizer. 2015. Dbpedia - a large-scale, multilingual knowledge base extracted from wikipedia. *Semantic Web*, 6:167–195.

Mike Lewis, Yinhan Liu, Naman Goyal, Marjan Ghazvininejad, Abdelrahman Mohamed, Omer Levy, Veselin Stoyanov, and Luke Zettlemoyer. 2020. BART: denoising sequence-to-sequence pre-training for natural language generation, translation, and comprehension. In *Proceedings of the 58th Annual Meeting of the Association for Computational Linguistics, ACL 2020, Online, July 5-10, 2020*, pages 7871–7880. Association for Computational Linguistics.

Junyi Li, Tianyi Tang, Wayne Xin Zhao, Zhicheng Wei, Nicholas Jing Yuan, and Ji-Rong Wen. 2021. Few-shot knowledge graph-to-text generation with pretrained language models. In *Findings of the Association for Computational Linguistics: ACL/IJCNLP 2021, Online Event, August 1-6, 2021*, volume ACL/IJCNLP 2021 of *Findings of ACL*, pages 1558–1568. Association for Computational Linguistics.

Yujia Li, Daniel Tarlow, Marc Brockschmidt, and Richard S. Zemel. 2015. Gated graph sequence neural networks. *arXiv: Learning*.

Yinhan Liu, Myle Ott, Naman Goyal, Jingfei Du, Mandar Joshi, Danqi Chen, Omer Levy, Mike Lewis, Luke Zettlemoyer, and Veselin Stoyanov. 2019. Roberta: A robustly optimized BERT pretraining approach. *CoRR*, abs/1907.11692.

Diego Marcheggiani and Laura Perez-Beltrachini. 2018. Deep graph convolutional encoders for structured data to text generation. In *Proceedings of the 11th*

International Conference on Natural Language Generation, pages 1–9, Tilburg University, The Netherlands. Association for Computational Linguistics.

Marco Marelli, Stefano Menini, Marco Baroni, Luisa Bentivogli, Raffaella Bernardi, and Roberto Zamparelli. 2014. A SICK cure for the evaluation of compositional distributional semantic models. In *Proceedings of the Ninth International Conference on Language Resources and Evaluation, LREC 2014, Reykjavik, Iceland, May 26-31, 2014*, pages 216–223. European Language Resources Association (ELRA).

Yixin Nie, Haonan Chen, and Mohit Bansal. 2019. Combining fact extraction and verification with neural semantic matching networks. In *The Thirty-Third AAAI Conference on Artificial Intelligence, AAAI 2019, The Thirty-First Innovative Applications of Artificial Intelligence Conference, IAAI 2019, The Ninth AAAI Symposium on Educational Advances in Artificial Intelligence, EAAI 2019, Honolulu, Hawaii, USA, January 27 - February 1, 2019*, pages 6859–6866. AAAI Press.

Kishore Papineni, Salim Roukos, Todd Ward, and Wei-Jing Zhu. 2002. Bleu: a method for automatic evaluation of machine translation. In *Proceedings of the 40th Annual Meeting of the Association for Computational Linguistics, July 6-12, 2002, Philadelphia, PA, USA*, pages 311–318. ACL.

Boci Peng, Yun Zhu, Yongchao Liu, Xiaohe Bo, Haizhou Shi, Chuntao Hong, Yan Zhang, and Siliang Tang. 2024. Graph retrieval-augmented generation: A survey. *CoRR*, abs/2408.08921.

Ciyuan Peng, Feng Xia, Mehdi Naseriparsa, and Francesco Osborne. 2023. Knowledge graphs: Opportunities and challenges. *Artif. Intell. Rev.*, 56(11):13071–13102.

Rivindu Perera and Parma Nand. 2015. A multi-strategy approach for lexicalizing linked open data. In *Computational Linguistics and Intelligent Text Processing*, pages 348–363, Cham. Springer International Publishing.

Maja Popovic. 2015. chrf: character n-gram f-score for automatic MT evaluation. In *Proceedings of the Tenth Workshop on Statistical Machine Translation, WMT@EMNLP 2015, 17-18 September 2015, Lisbon, Portugal*, pages 392–395. The Association for Computer Linguistics.

Colin Raffel, Noam Shazeer, Adam Roberts, Katherine Lee, Sharan Narang, Michael Matena, Yanqi Zhou, Wei Li, and Peter J. Liu. 2020. Exploring the limits of transfer learning with a unified text-to-text transformer. *J. Mach. Learn. Res.*, 21:140:1–140:67.

Anton Razzhigaev, Mikhail Salnikov, Valentin Malykh, Pavel Braslavski, and Alexander Panchenko. 2023. A system for answering simple questions in multiple languages. In *Proceedings of the 61st Annual Meeting of the Association for Computational Linguistics (Volume 3: System Demonstrations)*, pages 524–537, Toronto, Canada. Association for Computational Linguistics.

Leonardo F. R. Ribeiro, Martin Schmitt, Hinrich Schütze, and Iryna Gurevych. 2020. Investigating pretrained language models for graph-to-text generation. *CoRR*, abs/2007.08426.

Morgane Rivière, Shreya Pathak, Pier Giuseppe Sessa, Cassidy Hardin, Surya Bhupatiraju, Léonard Hussenot, Thomas Mesnard, Bobak Shahriari, Alexandre Ramé, Johan Ferret, Peter Liu, Pouya Tafti, Abe Friesen, Michelle Casbon, Sabela Ramos, Ravin Kumar, Charline Le Lan, Sammy Jerome, Anton Tsitsulin, Nino Vieillard, Piotr Stanczyk, Sertan Girgin, Nikola Momchev, Matt Hoffman, Shantanu Thakoor, Jean-Bastien Grill, Behnam Neyshabur, Olivier Bachem, Alanna Walton, Aliaksei Severyn, Alicia Parrish, Aliya Ahmad, Allen Hutchison, Alvin Abdagic, Amanda Carl, Amy Shen, Andy Brock, Andy Coenen, Anthony Laforge, Antonia Paterson, Ben Bastian, Bilal Piot, Bo Wu, Brandon Royal, Charlie Chen, Chintu Kumar, Chris Perry, Chris Welty, Christopher A. Choquette-Choo, Danila Sinopalnikov, David Weinberger, Dimple Vijaykumar, Dominika Rogozinska, Dustin Herbison, Elisa Bandy, Emma Wang, Eric Noland, Erica Moreira, Evan Senter, Evgenii Eltyshev, Francesco Visin, Gabriel Rasskin, Gary Wei, Glenn Cameron, Gus Martins, Hadi Hashemi, Hanna Klimczak-Plucinska, Harleen Batra, Harsh Dhand, Ivan Nardini, Jacinda Mein, Jack Zhou, James Svensson, Jeff Stanway, Jetha Chan, Jin Peng Zhou, Joana Carrasqueira, Joana Iljazi, Jocelyn Becker, Joe Fernandez, Joost van Amersfoort, Josh Gordon, Josh Lipschultz, Josh Newlan, Ju-yeong Ji, Kareem Mohamed, Kartikeya Badola, Kat Black, Katie Millican, Keelin McDonell, Kelvin Nguyen, Kiranbir Sodhia, Kish Greene, Lars Lowe Sjösund, Lauren Usui, Laurent Sifre, Lena Heuermann, Leticia Lago, and Lilly McNealus. 2024. Gemma 2: Improving open language models at a practical size. *CoRR*, abs/2408.00118.

Mikhail Salnikov, Hai Le, Prateek Rajput, Irina Nikishina, Pavel Braslavski, Valentin Malykh, and Alexander Panchenko. 2023. Large language models meet knowledge graphs to answer factoid questions. In *Proceedings of the 37th Pacific Asia Conference on Language, Information and Computation*, pages 635–644, Hong Kong, China. Association for Computational Linguistics.

Tal Schuster, Adam Fisch, and Regina Barzilay. 2021. Get your vitamin c! robust fact verification with contrastive evidence. In *Proceedings of the 2021 Conference of the North American Chapter of the Association for Computational Linguistics: Human Language Technologies, NAACL-HLT 2021, Online, June 6-11, 2021*, pages 624–643. Association for Computational Linguistics.

Matthew G. Snover, Bonnie J. Dorr, Richard M. Schwartz, Linnea Micciulla, and John Makhoul. 2006. A study of translation edit rate with targeted human annotation. In *Proceedings of the 7th Conference of the Association for Machine Translation in the Americas: Technical Papers, AMTA 2006, Cambridge, Massachusetts, USA, August 8-12, 2006*, pages 223–231. Association for Machine Translation in the Americas.

Ashish Vaswani, Noam Shazeer, Niki Parmar, Jakob Uszkoreit, Llion Jones, Aidan N. Gomez, Lukasz Kaiser, and Illia Polosukhin. 2017. Attention is all you need. In *Advances in Neural Information Processing Systems 30: Annual Conference on Neural Information Processing Systems 2017, December 4-9, 2017, Long Beach, CA, USA*, pages 5998–6008.

Denny Vrandečić and Markus Krötzsch. 2014. Wikidata: a free collaborative knowledgebase. *Commun. ACM*, 57(10):78–85.

Jason Wei, Xuezhi Wang, Dale Schuurmans, Maarten Bosma, Brian Ichter, Fei Xia, Ed H. Chi, Quoc V. Le, and Denny Zhou. 2022. Chain-of-thought prompting elicits reasoning in large language models. In *Advances in Neural Information Processing Systems 35: Annual Conference on Neural Information Processing Systems 2022, NeurIPS 2022, New Orleans, LA, USA, November 28 - December 9, 2022*.

Shuzhou Yuan and Michael Färber. 2023. Evaluating generative models for graph-to-text generation. In *Recent Advances in Natural Language Processing*.

Yuheng Zha, Yichi Yang, Ruichen Li, and Zhiting Hu. 2023. Alignscore: Evaluating factual consistency with A unified alignment function. In *Proceedings of the 61st Annual Meeting of the Association for Computational Linguistics (Volume 1: Long Papers), ACL 2023, Toronto, Canada, July 9-14, 2023*, pages 11328–11348. Association for Computational Linguistics.

Tianyi Zhang, Varsha Kishore, Felix Wu, Kilian Q. Weinberger, and Yoav Artzi. 2020. Bertscore: Evaluating text generation with BERT. In *8th International Conference on Learning Representations, ICLR 2020, Addis Ababa, Ethiopia, April 26-30, 2020*. OpenReview.net.

Chao Zhao, Marilyn Walker, and Snigdha Chaturvedi. 2020. Bridging the structural gap between encoding and decoding for data-to-text generation. In *Proceedings of the 58th Annual Meeting of the Association for Computational Linguistics*, pages 2481–2491, Online. Association for Computational Linguistics.

Hao Zhou, Tom Young, Minlie Huang, Haizhou Zhao, Jingfang Xu, and Xiaoyan Zhu. 2018. Commonsense knowledge aware conversation generation with graph attention. In *Proceedings of the Twenty-Seventh International Joint Conference on Artificial Intelligence, IJCAI 2018, July 13-19, 2018, Stockholm, Sweden*, pages 4623–4629. ijcai.org.

GraphRAG: Leveraging Graph-Based Efficiency to Minimize Hallucinations in LLM-Driven RAG for Finance Data

Mariam Barry[1], Gaëtan Caillaut[2], Pierre Halftermeyer[3], Raheel Qader[2], Mehdi Mouayad[1], Dimitri Cariolaro[4], Fabrice Le Deit [5], Joseph Gesnouin [6],
[1]BNP Paribas - IT Group - AI & IT Innovation, [2]Lingua Custodia, [3]NEO4J,
[4]Graph Thinking Consulting, [5]BNP Paribas - IT Group - Production, [6]BNP Paribas - Cash Management

Abstract

This study explores the integration of graph-based methods into Retrieval-Augmented Generation (RAG) systems to enhance efficiency, reduce hallucinations, and improve explainability, with a particular focus on financial and regulatory document retrieval. We propose two strategies—FactRAG and HybridRAG—which leverage knowledge graphs to improve RAG performance. Experiments conducted using Finance Bench, a benchmark for AI in finance, demonstrate that these approaches achieve a 6% reduction in hallucinations and an 80% decrease in token usage compared to conventional RAG methods. Furthermore, we evaluate HybridRAG by comparing the Digital Operational Resilience Act (DORA) from the European Union with the Federal Financial Institutions Examination Council (FFIEC) guidelines from the United States. The results reveal a significant improvement in computational efficiency, reducing contradiction detection complexity from $O(n^2)$ to $O(k \cdot n)$—where n is the number of chunks—and a remarkable 734-fold decrease in token consumption. Graph-based retrieval methods can improve the efficiency and cost-effectiveness of large language model (LLM) applications, though their performance and token usage depend on the dataset, knowledge graph design, and retrieval task.

1 Introduction

Generative Artificial Intelligence (GenAI), exemplified by Large Language Models (LLMs) such as OpenAI's GPT series (Brown et al., 2020; OpenAI, 2023), Meta's LLaMA models (Touvron et al., 2023), and Mistral's Mixtral (AI, 2023), has gained prominence in various fields, including healthcare, finance, and education. These models, while highly capable of producing coherent and contextually relevant responses, face challenges in generating factually accurate content—a phenomenon referred to as hallucination (Ji et al., 2023; Bang et al., 2023).

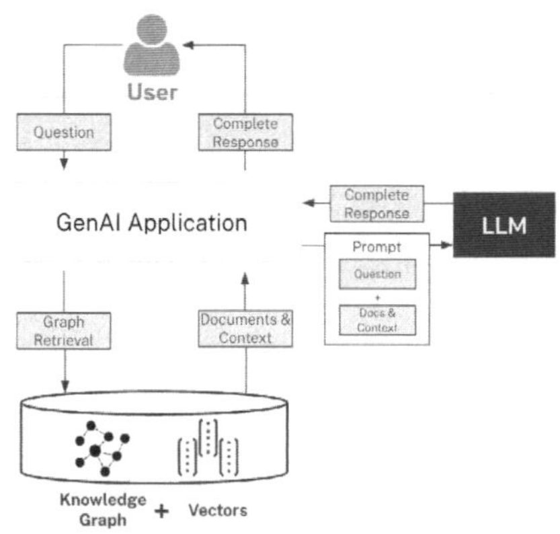

Figure 1: Graph RAG Pattern (Rathle)

Hallucination arises from LLMs' reliance on potentially outdated or domain-general training data, leading to inaccuracies in real-world applications where precision is critical (Dziri et al., 2022).

To address the issue of hallucinations, *Retrieval-Augmented Generation* (RAG) has emerged as a promising approach. Introduced by Lewis et al. (2020), RAG combines a retriever that identifies relevant documents and a generator that creates coherent responses from this information. By combining LLMs with external knowledge bases, RAG systems can enhance response accuracy and relevance by dynamically incorporating up-to-date and verifiable information into generated outputs (Kang and Lee, 2023). The original approach suggested dividing documents into 100-word disjoint chunks, but this can disrupt semantics and lead to hallucinations, as noted by Qian et al. (2024). To mitigate these issues, enhancements like sliding window chunking, sentence-level splitting with surrounding context, and incorporating metadata such as document titles have been proposed to improve the

Proceedings of the Generative AI and Knowledge Graph Workshop (GenAIK), pages 54–65
January 19, 2025.

quality and relevance of the generated outputs (Gao et al., 2023).

While RAG often improves the relevance of language model outputs, it faces notable limitations in real-world applications:

1. **Neglect of Structured Relationships**: Traditional RAG focuses on textual relevance and often overlooks structured relationships critical in domains like citation networks, limiting its effectiveness for complex, interconnected data (Yao et al., 2021).

2. **Redundancy and Lengthy Contexts**: Concatenated text snippets in RAG can lead to redundancy and excessively lengthy inputs, causing the model to lose focus and obscure key information (Longpre et al., 2021).

3. **Limited Global Context**: RAG's restricted retrieval scope hinders its ability to capture broader contexts necessary for tasks like query-focused summarization (Lewis et al., 2020).

These limitations highlight the need for advanced approaches, such as GraphRAG (Figure 1), to incorporate structured relationships and provide richer, more contextually accurate information, while being more efficient in terms of token usage. To overcome these limitations, we explore several distinct approaches to enhancing RAG systems with graphs, including:

1. **FactRAG**: We propose a graph-based approach, "FactRAG," for a question-answering search engine that is more efficient in term of tokens and reduces hallucinations compared to classical RAG.

2. **KG-RAG**: We introduce a knowledge graph-enhanced technique, "KG-RAG," for document comparison tasks, that significantly improves token efficiency and reduces computational complexity from $O(n^2)$ to $O(k \cdot n)$ in LLM-driven retrieval tasks, where n is the number of chunks/nodes and k the number of clusters in the KNN algorithms specifically for detecting contradictions between documents.

3. **HybridRAG**: We provide open-source code for a graph-based Hybrid RAG, which integrates symbolic and sub-symbolic retrieval for flexible question-answering.

2 Related Work

Knowledge Graphs (KGs) play a crucial role in enhancing the interpretability and factual accuracy of large language models (LLMs) by structuring information as entities and relationships (Hogan et al., 2022; Rosin et al., 2022). The integration of graph structures within Retrieval-Augmented Generation (RAG) frameworks has shown significant improvements in model performance. Zhao et al. (2023) demonstrate that Graph-based Retrieval-Augmented Generation enhances contextual accuracy by allowing systems to retrieve relevant entities and relationships from KGs. Similarly, Yasunaga et al. (2022) highlights the benefits of Graph-based Retrieval-Augmented Language Models for fact verification and knowledge enrichment, ensuring that generated outputs are relevant and accurate. Liu et al. (2022) introduces the concept of Graph Retrieval Augmentation, which enhances contextual and semantic understanding in LLMs, resulting in more coherent and pertinent responses. Furthermore, the work of Guu et al. (2020) illustrates how training in a language model with augmented retrieval with knowledge graphs can improve the accuracy and depth of the answer by using KG for the retrieval and structured data. Graph RAG stands out by retrieving graph elements from a pre-constructed knowledge graph, thereby enriching LLM-generated responses with structured knowledge (Rosin et al., 2022). This structure allows Graph RAG to capture semantic nuances, maintain contextual coherence, and reduce verbosity, making it particularly effective for applications in question-answering, recommendation systems, and complex information retrieval tasks relying on structured knowledge.

3 Problem Statement

Large Language Models (LLMs) augmented by Retrieval-Augmented Generation (RAG) systems have advanced the ability to generate contextually relevant responses. However, despite RAG's potential to reduce inaccuracies by integrating external knowledge, hallucinations – defined as the generation of factually incorrect or fabricated information – remain a significant issue. This paper explores the relevance of a graph-based approach to reduce hallucinations and optimize token consumption in language models.

3.1 Graph-based technique

We identify two key approaches to minimizing hallucinations in RAG systems: **pre-generation** and **post-generation**(Agrawal et al., 2023). The pre-generation approach enhances the input context with high-quality, semantically relevant passages to help the model produce accurate outputs. The post-generation approach, on the other hand, validates and corrects factual accuracy using verification processes(Sansford et al., 2024).

Knowledge graphs (KGs) support both approaches by providing structured knowledge. In pre-generation, KGs can insert accurate facts into the input context. In post-generation, KGs help validate generated content for factual correctness.

However, post-generation faces challenges such as converting text to graph representations and the computational costs of iterative LLM calls (Cabot et al., 2023). Additionally, post-generation corrections may introduce further errors, and the iterative calls to LLMs increase computational costs, making large-scale applications impractical. Given these limitations, our work focuses on the pre-generation approach, aiming to reduce hallucinations by using KGs to provide more accurate and reliable context before generation, improving both factual accuracy and efficiency in RAG systems.

3.2 Problem formalization - Building a RAG system with minimal hallucinations

In Retrieval-Augmented Generation (RAG) systems, hallucinations occur when the language model generates content that is factually incorrect or unsupported by retrieved documents. Given a set of documents $D = \{d_1, d_2, \ldots, d_n\}$ and a set of user queries $Q = \{q_1, q_2, \ldots, q_m\}$, the goal is to design a RAG system that minimizes the generation of hallucinated responses while maximizing response accuracy.

We define a RAG system as a function $RAG : Q \to A$, where each query $q \in Q$ is mapped to an answer $a \in A$ based on retrieved context $C \subseteq D$. Let $C(q) = \{c_1, c_2, \ldots, c_k\}$ represent the set of retrieved documents for a query q, where $C(q) \subseteq D$. Es et al. (2023) define the below evaluation measures:

1. **Hallucination Score**, $H(a)$, for each answer $a \in A$ as the proportion of information in a that is unsupported by $C(q)$:

$$H(a) = \frac{\text{Unsupported Information in } a}{\text{Total Information in } a}$$

2. **Faithfulness Score**, $F(a)$, for each answer $a \in A$ as the proportion of information in a that is directly supported by the retrieved context $C(q)$:

$$F(a) = \frac{\text{Supported Information in } a}{\text{Total Information in } a} = 1 - H(a)$$

Objective We aim to minimize the overall hallucination rate $H(A)$ across all answers $A = \{a_1, a_2, \ldots, a_m\}$ while ensuring that each $a \in A$ remains relevant to the query q. This objective can be formulated as:

$$\min_{RAG} H(A) = \frac{1}{m} \sum_{i=1}^{m} H(a_i)$$

subject to:

$$F(a_i) \geq \delta \quad \forall a_i \in A$$

where δ is a predefined faithfulness threshold (e.g., 0.9), ensuring that each generated answer is primarily supported by the retrieved context $C(q)$.

4 Proposal: Graph-based RAG System

We propose to enhance the classical RAG system with knowledge from graph databases instead of raw texts. To this aim, we build a traditional text RAG system to serve as a baseline, as well as two graph-flavored variants, which we call Facts and KG-RAG in the following.

Reproducibility Code for both text and facts RAG are available on Github[1].

4.1 Text RAG

Our text baseline is very classical, we set up a standard RAG pipeline. We relied on the `unstructured`[2] Python package to extract non-overlapping chunks of approximately 500 characters and we used the `all-MiniLM-L6-v2` model provided by `sentence-transformers`[3] (Reimers and Gurevych, 2019) to embed them. We stored the chunks and their embedding inside a `chromadb`[4] database.

4.2 Facts RAG

Our second system rely on LLM to automatically extract entities and relations from raw text, then

[1]https://github.com/gcaillaut/financebench-graph-rag

[2]https://github.com/Unstructured-IO/unstructured

[3]https://github.com/UKPLab/sentence-transformers

[4]https://github.com/chroma-core/chroma

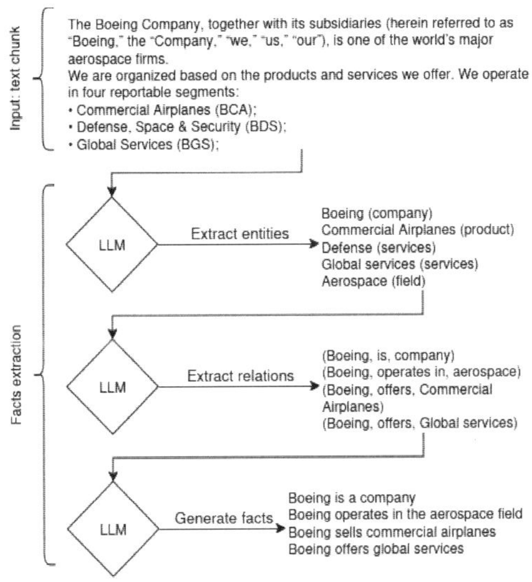

Figure 2: Facts extraction process. We first extract entities from a raw and potentially noisy text. Then we build triples using the text and the extracted entities. Finally, we generate textual description of the triples, which we call *facts*.

convert these triples into short sentences. We call these sentences *facts*. Hence, this system is very similar to our baseline, the difference being an additional step to convert relevant chunks into facts. Practically speaking, we first ask an LLM to extract all entities inside a relevant chunk, then we ask for the relations between them. Finally, the LLM generate triples and a short sentence (the fact) describing the triple in natural language inside a JSON array. The resulting sentences are much more concise, contain less noise, and are more direct. We then provide these generated facts to the LLM instead of the raw chunks. The complete prompt we used to generate these facts is given in Appendix C and the overall process is described in Figure 2.

The purpose of this system is to validate the relevance of LLM-based knowledge graph extraction methods (Zhang and Soh, 2024; Carta et al., 2023) in the context of RAG. While we pointed out the limitations of these approaches in the previous section, we also believe that extracting graphs from text is a powerful summarization and noise filtering tool, as it removes all uninformative tokens and the facts generated are very clear and easy to understand.

4.3 KG-RAG (Knowledge Graph based RAG)

Our third system is based on a graph representation of the document to be queried. The document is processed to extract a knowledge graph, given a predefined graph schema. Then, text chunks and their embeddings are stored inside a node and linked to the entities they contain. More specifically, we rely on the `llm-graph-builder` tool from Neo4j[5] to extract a knowledge graph from pdf files. The tool can also automatically generate a graph schema from raw text, so we use the questions in our dataset (more details in Section 5) to extract a schema suiting our target task.

Finally, we use the user's query to find the most relevant chunks using traditional embedding similarity, then we explore the graph using the chunks as seed to retrieve potentially useful entities and relations, in the form of triples. We limit the exploration of the graph to the direct neighbors of the relevant chunks, but more sophisticated exploration strategies are possible, such as re-ranking documents using graph-based algorithms like PageRank.

4.4 Hybrid RAG

The last system we experimented with aims to leverage explicit and implicit relationships from the knowledge graph using an hybrid architecture. As illustrated in Figure 3.

We introduce a GraphRAG framework that combines explicit (symbolic) and implicit (subsymbolic) retrieval methods to enhance retrieval-augmented generation (RAG) systems. Our approach allows for adaptive retrieval based on the nature of the user question, with Explicit RAG using text-to-Cypher translation for structured queries, while Implicit RAG leverages vector similarity to find k-nearest neighbours. The system employs an LLM to determine the optimal retrieval method, utilizing the retrieved context to generate precise answers, offering a versatile solution for better knowledge retrieval tasks.

Our approach to HybridRAG is tested with a comparative analysis of two regulatory documents: the Digital Operational Resilience Act (DORA) from the European Union and the Federal Financial Institutions Examination Council (FFIEC) guidelines from the United States.

The HybridRAG system is designed to optimize the retrieval and contradiction identification process in large regulatory documents using a knowledge graph-based KNN clustering approach. Traditional Retrieval-Augmented Generation (RAG)

[5]`https://llm-graph-builder.neo4jlabs.com/`

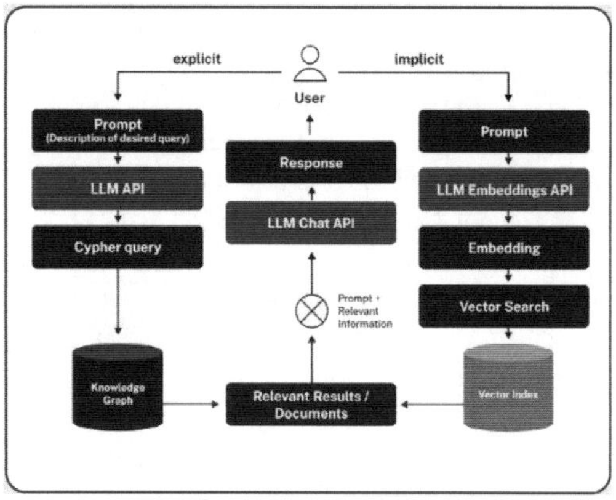

Figure 3: **Hybrid Graph RAG**: Explicit vs. Implicit RAG, *e.g* Symbolic vs. Sub-Symbolic Retrieval. The framework offers two retrieval strategies based on the nature of the user's query.

methods often suffer from high token consumption due to the computationally expensive Cartesian product of document segments. To overcome this, HybridRAG uses KNN clustering to group similar document segments, reducing computational costs. The system captures the context for each document node, generates text embeddings, and clusters nodes based on cosine similarity.

5 Experiments and evaluation

We conducted experiments to address the following two research questions on datasets related to the financial domain.

1. **RQ1:** Does a graph-based RAG system reduce hallucinations compared to a classical RAG system for a question-answering task?
2. **RQ2:** How efficient is Graph/Hybrid RAG in terms of token consumption for retrieval tasks involving document comparison?

5.1 Datasets in Finance Domain

The datasets used in this study include FinanceBench (Islam et al., 2023), a benchmark for evaluating AI systems in finance, which contains various financial documents like regulatory reports and financial statements. Additionally, we utilized DORA (Digital Operational Resilience Act)(European Parliament and Council of the European Union, 2022), a European Union regulation on managing IT risks in the financial sector, and the FFIEC IT Handbook(Federal Financial Institutions Examination Council, 2019), which offers guidelines for IT management in U.S. financial institutions. These data sets were used to assess the performance of the proposed methods in financial document retrieval and contradiction detection.

5.2 Metrics

We will use the metrics of Deep Eval (AI, 2024) to evaluate RQ1. Since we are not interested in assessing the overall RAG quality or the retrieval mechanism, but rather the probability to hallucinate, we focused on the two hallucinations measures available in DeepEval. The Faithfulness Metric first uses an LLM to extract all claims made in the actual_output, before using the same LLM to classify whether each claim is truthful based on the facts presented in the retrieval_context. The Hallucination metric employs an LLM to evaluate each context in a set of contexts, determining whether there are any contradictions with the *actual_output*.

The metrics are calculated according to the following equation:

$$\text{Faithfulness} = \frac{\text{Number of Truthful Claims}}{\text{Total Number of Claims}} \quad (1)$$

the *Number of Truthful Claims* represents the count of accurate statements, and the *Total Number of Claims* represents the overall number of statements evaluated.

$$\text{Hallucination} = \frac{\text{NB of Contradicted Contexts}}{\text{Total Number of Contexts}} \quad (2)$$

5.3 RQ1: Hallucinations of RAG systems (FactRAG & KG-RAG)

Recent studies (Kamalloo et al., 2023; Tan et al., 2023) on LLM show that they are good at answering mainstream, general domain-related questions, without needing any kind of knowledge injection, such as RAG. Hence, we chose to experiment on the Financebench (Islam et al., 2023) dataset, as it contains questions on financial documents from the filings of public companies[6], which are less likely to have been seen and memorized by currently available LLM. The dataset is comprised of 150 questions and 84 documents. For each pair (question, document) in this dataset, we retrieved the 8 most relevant chunks and asked an LLM to

[6]https://www.sec.gov/search-filings

	faithfulness ↑	hallucination ↓
Llama 3.2 3B		
Text RAG	0.844	0.704
Facts RAG	**0.937**	0.679
KG-RAG	0.790	**0.660**
Llama 3.1 8B		
Text RAG	0.843	0.659
Facts RAG	**0.891**	0.658
KG-RAG	0.890	**0.532**
Qwen 2.5 32B		
Text RAG	0.954	**0.395**
Facts RAG	**0.970**	0.594
KG-RAG	0.963	0.407

Table 1: DeepEval scores with GPT4o as a judge.

generate an answer. Finally, we relied on DeepEval[7] to perform the evaluation. DeepEval relies on a *strong* LLM to automatically score RAG systems, we chose `GPT-4o` since it has been reported as being one of the most accurate. In order to evaluate the propensity to hallucinate, we report in the following the *faithfulness* measures from DeepEval, as it quantifies the consistency of the generated answer given contextual information. This is a good proxy for hallucination because we expect the LLM's response to be aligned with the retrieved chunks, and it is also the recommended way to measure hallucination. We also report the *hallucination* measure from DeepEval for completeness.

For each RAG system, we experimented with three LLMs: `Llama 3.2 3B`, `Llama 3.1 8B` (Dubey et al., 2024) and `Qwen 2.5 32B` (Team, 2024). We used these same LLM to generate facts during the facts-RAG experiments.

The results of the DeepEval evaluation are shown in Table 1. We observe an increase in faithfulness when switching from text to graph-based RAG systems, except with the smaller model. This observation fits our prior hypothesis stating that providing contextual information from KG can reduce hallucinations.

We also observe that the gap between Text and Facts RAG is higher with smaller, and supposedly less powerful, models. Since this measure quantifies the consistency between the retrieved context and the generated answer, we conclude that smaller models have some difficulties to filter out noise in

[7]`https://github.com/confident-ai/deepeval`

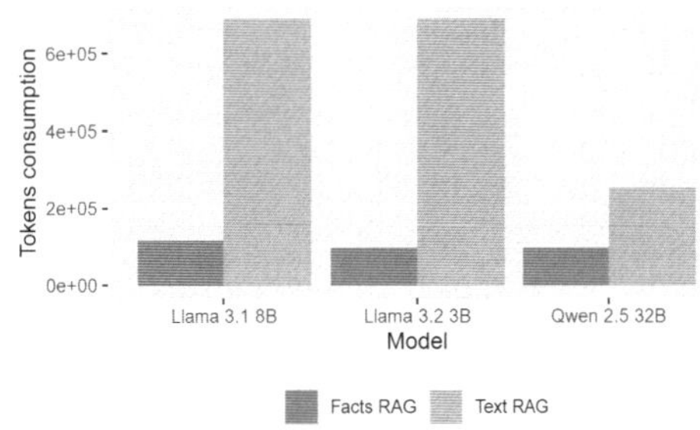

Figure 4: Total number of input tokens consumed during our experiments, for all 150 questions. Facts RAG uses dense and effective prompts while producing less hallucinations than Text RAG.

raw texts, thus providing cleaner facts help them generating more appropriate answers; while larger models have better reasoning capabilities and can filter irrelevant information on their own.

5.3.1 Ablation studies

We conducted ablation studies to measure the individual contribution of text and graph contexts. These experiments focus on our KG-RAG system, we removed either the text chunks or the triples extracted from the KG and we computed the faithfulness and hallucination measures from DeepEval . The results, shown in Table 2, shows that the faithfulness is always better when providing only triples from our KG.

We also observe that the relative differences between all setups (hybrid, no text and no graph) tend to decrease the larger the model is. This validates our previous assumption, large models can filter out irrelevant and useless information by themselves. However, we argue that letting the model do the filtering is suboptimal as it requires to provide every bits of available information to the LLM. We already showed that graph-based RAG improves the overall response by reducing hallucinations, and we show in the following that it also has the benefit of being a lot more efficient in terms of tokens consumption as illustrated in Figure 4.

5.4 RQ2: HybridRAG optimizing tokens usage in Graph-based RAG Systems

This experiment examines GraphRAG's capability to detect contradictions in regulatory language across jurisdictions, specifically between DORA (EU) and FFIEC (US) documents, demonstrating its efficiency in large-scale regulatory analysis.

Using a knowledge-graph-based KNN cluster-

	faithfulness ↑	hallucination ↓
Llama 3.2 3B		
text + graph	0.790	**0.660**
graph only	**0.940**	0.665
text only	0.807	0.690
Llama 3.1 8B		
text + graph	0.890	**0.532**
graph only	**0.965**	0.576
text only	0.866	0.592
Qwen 2.5 32B		
text + graph	0.963	0.407
graph only	**0.988**	0.619
text only	0.945	**0.365**

Table 2: DeepEval scores with GPT4o as a judge when removing text or graph contexts.

ing approach, HybridRAG minimizes token consumption by streamlining contradiction detection. Unlike traditional RAG methods that rely on costly pairwise comparisons ($O(n^2)$ complexity), HybridRAG clusters document segments with KNN ($O(k \cdot n)$ complexity), - where n being the number of chunks - reducing retrieval to targeted, contextually relevant nodes. This approach involves embedding each document node, clustering similar segments, and generating optimized LLM prompts for contradiction detection.

With this clustering method ($k = 10$), API calls decreased from almost 2 million (1 975 944 with the classical approach) to just 2 690, achieving a 734-fold reduction in token consumption. Eight potential contradictions were identified, underscoring GraphRAG's effectiveness in enhancing computational efficiency and cost-effectiveness in regulatory document retrieval.

6 Perspectives and Future Work

6.1 Limitations

This work focuses exclusively on the English language, and as such, we cannot confidently generalize our findings to other languages, even those with high resource availability.

Several limitations are associated with the DeepEval toolkit used for evaluating our RAG systems. Generally speaking, the use of LLM as a judge offers numerous advantages, such as ease of use and the ability to enable reproducible evaluations through hard-coded prompts and standard evaluation pipeline, it also presents some drawbacks. Firstly, it requires a lot of computing power and is impractical for large-scale evaluations due to high latency and potentially prohibitive costs. For instance, evaluating a single system (only 150 questions) necessitates processing approximately 4 million input tokens and 0.4 million output tokens. Secondly, the prompts utilized are often hard-coded in English, which renders the toolkit unsuitable for applications in other languages.

Lastly, even if we showed that introducing knowledge from KG enhances RAG systems, it is important to point out the difficulties of building and querying a graph that suits our target task. The underlying schema of existing KG might not fit the target use case, hence the KG often has to be either hand-crafted (extremely costly and difficult to maintain) or automatically generated (error-prone and compute-intensive). For instance, Mihindukulasooriya et al. (2023) show that precision and recall are very low even when the set of relation's types to extract is restricted.

6.2 Future work

Future work could extend graph-based RAG approaches to handle diverse datasets, including visually rich and multilingual documents, by integrating visual embeddings from Vision-Language Models (Faysse et al., 2024) and heterogeneous data (Sun et al., 2024). Fine-tuning language models with domain-specific knowledge could further reduce hallucination rates. Additionally, incorporating multimodal capabilities (e.g., text and images) could enhance contextual understanding and retrieval precision. Improving the scalability of knowledge graph construction and integrating external sources like ontologies could further reduce hallucinations (Agrawal et al., 2023). Exploring hybrid models combining symbolic reasoning with deep learning (Ambrogio et al., 2023) and advanced post-generation verification (Sansford et al., 2024) could also improve RAG systems.

6.3 Architecture design to industrialize RAG systems in production

We propose a design to smoothly deploy RAG systems in production. The architecture schema in the appendix of Figure 6 demonstrates how modular design can ensure scalability and system reliability.

The RAG logic is composed of most of the app that the user interacts with containing the RAG logic, the models hub (green) which is deployed on its infrastructure mostly based on GPU, the Data Module (red) which consists of the Data ingestion layer of RAG, the Evaluation Module (light blue) which is responsible of all functional evaluations of the RAG and lastly one of the most important parts, the monitoring and the logging (orange), which ensure that our system works well, help with debugging, audits, updates, and gives the entire vision of the RAG. This setup allows each component to operate independently and cohesively, supporting efficient scaling, robust functionality, and clear traceability.

6.4 Lessons learned and best practices for deploying RAG systems in Production

We share some recommendations based on lessons learned in large-scale banking infrastructure.

To maintain efficient operation, several best practices must be followed when deploying RAG systems in production. First, a modular design should be implemented to allow easier maintenance, updates, and scalability (Zhang et al., 2021). Caching frequently accessed queries can help reduce latency and improve performance. Additionally, using an LLM gateway enables switching between models based on task requirements.

Real-time monitoring and logging mechanisms should track system health, latency, error rates, and performance metrics, enabling prompt issue resolution and continuous improvement (Smith and Roberts, 2022). Appropriate evaluation metrics should asses system accuracy and reliability, with faithfulness as a key metric to ensure the generated responses align with the intended outputs (Kumar et al., 2023). Finally, security measures such as input and output guardrails are necessary to maintain ethical boundaries (Patel and Gupta, 2024). Regular backups and audit logging ensure data integrity, traceability, and reproducibility across the system.

7 Conclusion

This study demonstrates three significant contributions of graph-based approaches in enhancing classical RAG systems:

1. **Reduction of Hallucinations**: The use of graph-based structures, such as Fact-RAG, significantly reduces hallucinations by linking contextually relevant information. This leads to more precise and complete responses, with experimental evaluations showing a 6% reduction in hallucinations while using 80% fewer tokens compared to text-only RAG.

2. **Efficiency and Cost Savings**: For document comparison use-case, GraphRAG improves efficiency by filtering out irrelevant data, reducing computational costs, and enhancing scalability. Using semantic clustering, it reduces the complexity of detecting contradictions from $O(n^2)$ to $O(k \cdot n)$ where n is the number of chunks and nodes in the graph.

3. **Enhanced Explainability and Traceability**: HybridRAG, using knowledge graphs, allows users to trace responses back to specific data sources and relationships as shown in Figure 5 (an example of the output of the demo using NEO4J). This transparency is crucial for sectors like finance and banking, enabling better governance, easier audits, and a more thorough understanding of the reasoning behind answers.

This efficiency demonstrates that graph-based retrieval methods can make large-scale LLM applications more cost-effective and accessible. However, their effectiveness depends on factors such as the dataset, knowledge graph modeling, and the specific retrieval task, highlighting that graph-based approaches are not always inherently more efficient.

Acknowledgments

We are grateful to Jean-Luc Billy and Philip Rathle for their insightful discussions on RAG and Knowledge Graphs, and to Virginie Chenal-Laze and Gael Marchand for sharing their domain knowledge on regulatory matters. We also acknowledge Lingua Custodia and BNP Paribas IT Group for providing the computing resources that supported the experiments on large language models (LLMs).

Reproducibility

We open-sourced the code to facilitate adoption and reproducibility of experiments.

HybridRAG Code for HybridRAG demo to compare DORA & FFIEC is available on Github [8].

FactRAG Code for both text and facts RAG used with FinanceBench Data are available on Github[9].

[8] https://github.com/halftermeyer/dora-ffiec-hybrid-rag-neo4j

[9] https://github.com/gcaillaut/financebench-graph-rag

References

Garima Agrawal, Tharindu Kumarage, Zeyad Alghamdi, and Huan Liu. 2023. Can knowledge graphs reduce hallucinations in llms?: A survey. *arXiv preprint arXiv:2311.07914*.

Confident AI. 2024. Deepeval: The evaluation framework for llms.

Mistral AI. 2023. Mixtral model card. `https://mistral.ai`.

M. Ambrogio, D. Garcia, and F. Rodriguez. 2023. Symbolic reasoning meets deep learning for improved nlp models. *Computational Intelligence Review*, 18(2):102–118.

Yejin Bang, Samuel Cahyawijaya, Bryan Wilie Lee, Wenliang Dai, Dan Su, Bryan Wilie, Pascale Fung, et al. 2023. A multitask, multilingual, multimodal evaluation of chatgpt on reasoning, hallucination, and interactivity. In *Proceedings of the International Conference on Learning Representations (ICLR)*.

Tom B Brown, Benjamin Mann, Nick Ryder, Melanie Subbiah, Jared Kaplan, Prafulla Dhariwal, Arvind Neelakantan, Pranav Shyam, Girish Sastry, Amanda Askell, et al. 2020. Language models are few-shot learners. In *Advances in neural information processing systems*.

Pere-Lluís Huguet Cabot, Simone Tedeschi, Axel-Cyrille Ngonga Ngomo, and Roberto Navigli. 2023. Redfm: a filtered and multilingual relation extraction dataset. In *Proceedings of the 61st Annual Meeting of the Association for Computational Linguistics (Volume 1: Long Papers)*, pages 4326–4343.

Salvatore Carta, Alessandro Giuliani, Leonardo Piano, Alessandro Sebastian Podda, Livio Pompianu, and Sandro Gabriele Tiddia. 2023. Iterative zero-shot llm prompting for knowledge graph construction. *arXiv preprint arXiv:2307.01128*.

Abhimanyu Dubey, Abhinav Jauhri, Abhinav Pandey, Abhishek Kadian, Ahmad Al-Dahle, Aiesha Letman, Akhil Mathur, Alan Schelten, Amy Yang, Angela Fan, et al. 2024. The llama 3 herd of models. *arXiv preprint arXiv:2407.21783*.

Nouha Dziri, Alexander Milton, Tiezheng Yu, Mohit Yu, Kevin Bowden, Debanjan Ghosh, Andrea Madotto, and Pascale Fung. 2022. On the origin of hallucinations in conversational models: Is it the datasets or the models? *Transactions of the Association for Computational Linguistics (TACL)*, 10:730–746.

Shahul Es, Jithin James, Luis Espinosa-Anke, and Steven Schockaert. 2023. Ragas: Automated evaluation of retrieval augmented generation. *arXiv preprint arXiv:2309.15217*.

European Parliament and Council of the European Union. 2022. Regulation (EU) 2022/2554 of the European Parliament and of the Council on Digital Operational Resilience for the Financial Sector (DORA). Accessed: 2024-11-13.

L. Faysse, J. Turner, and D. Patel. 2024. Colpali: Efficient document retrieval via vision-language models. Proceedings of the Conference on Document Retrieval.

Federal Financial Institutions Examination Council. 2019. Federal Financial Institutions Examination Council (FFIEC) IT Examination Handbook. Accessed: 2024-11-13.

Yunfan Gao, Yun Xiong, Xinyu Gao, Kangxiang Jia, Jinliu Pan, Yuxi Bi, Yi Dai, Jiawei Sun, Meng Wang, and Haofen Wang. 2023. Retrieval-augmented generation for large language models: A survey. *arXiv preprint arXiv:2312.10997*.

K. Guu, K. Lee, Z. Tung, P. Pasupat, and M. Chang. 2020. Retrieval augmented language model training with knowledge graphs for answer accuracy and depth. In *Proceedings of Empirical Methods in Natural Language Processing (EMNLP)*.

Aidan Hogan, Eva Blomqvist, Michael Cochez, Claudia d'Amato, Gerard De Melo, Claudio Gutierrez, Sabrina Kirrane, Jose Emilio Labra Gayo, Roberto Navigli, Sebastian Neumaier, et al. 2022. Knowledge graphs. *Synthesis Lectures on Data, Semantics, and Knowledge*, 12(2):1–257.

Pranab Islam, Anand Kannappan, Douwe Kiela, Rebecca Qian, Nino Scherrer, and Bertie Vidgen. 2023. Financebench: A new benchmark for financial question answering. *Preprint*, arXiv:2311.11944.

Ziwei Ji, Nayeon Lee, Rita Frieske, Tiezheng Yu, Dan Su, Yanlin Xu, Etsuko Ishii, Yejin Bang, Andrea Madotto, and Pascale Fung. 2023. A survey of hallucination in natural language generation. *ACM Computing Surveys*, 55(12):1–35.

Ehsan Kamalloo, Nouha Dziri, Charles Clarke, and Davood Rafiei. 2023. Evaluating open-domain question answering in the era of large language models. In *Proceedings of the 61st Annual Meeting of the Association for Computational Linguistics (Volume 1: Long Papers)*, pages 5591–5606.

Jihoon Kang and Minji Lee. 2023. Ever-growing knowledge: Integrating retrieval-augmented generation for continuous learning in language models. *IEEE Transactions on Neural Networks and Learning Systems*, 34(8):2591–2603.

P. Kumar et al. 2023. Metrics for evaluating large language models: Precision, recall, and faithfulness. *IEEE Transactions on AI*, 10(2):125–134.

Patrick Lewis, Ethan Perez, Aleksandra Piktus, Fabio Petroni, Vladimir Karpukhin, Naman Goyal, Heinrich Küttler, Mike Lewis, Wen-tau Yih, Tim Rocktäschel, et al. 2020. Retrieval-augmented generation for knowledge-intensive nlp tasks. *Advances in Neural Information Processing Systems*, 33:9459–9474.

J. Liu, C. Xiong, and J. Callan. 2022. Graph retrieval augmentation for enhanced contextual and semantic understanding in large language models. In *Proceedings of the North American Chapter of the Association for Computational Linguistics (NAACL)*.

Shayne Longpre, Yi Lu, Mitchell Wortsman, Tianhao Xia, et al. 2021. Lost in the middle: How length of input affects language models' ability to understand context. In *Proceedings of the 2021 Conference on Empirical Methods in Natural Language Processing (EMNLP)*, pages 1001–1013.

Nandana Mihindukulasooriya, Sanju Tiwari, Carlos F Enguix, and Kusum Lata. 2023. Text2kgbench: A benchmark for ontology-driven knowledge graph generation from text. In *International Semantic Web Conference*, pages 247–265. Springer.

OpenAI. 2023. Gpt-4 technical report. *arXiv preprint arXiv:2303.08774*.

N. Patel and R. Gupta. 2024. Security frameworks for ethical ai deployment. *Journal of AI Ethics*, 3(1):45–62.

H. Qian, M. Chen, Y. Liu, and S. Wang. 2024. Grounding retrieval-augmented generation: Mitigating hallucinations with contextual awareness. In *Proceedings of the Conference on Empirical Methods in Natural Language Processing (EMNLP)*.

Philip Rathle. The graphrag manifesto: Adding knowledge to genai.

Nils Reimers and Iryna Gurevych. 2019. Sentence-bert: Sentence embeddings using siamese bert-networks. In *Proceedings of the 2019 Conference on Empirical Methods in Natural Language Processing*. Association for Computational Linguistics.

Guy Rosin, Ranit Ben Aharon, Marina Litvak, and Daniel Cohen-Or. 2022. Knowledge graphs in natural language processing: A survey. *Journal of Artificial Intelligence Research (JAIR)*, 73:765–826.

Hannah Sansford, Nicholas Richardson, Hermina Petric Maretic, and Juba Nait Saada. 2024. Grapheval: A knowledge-graph based llm hallucination evaluation framework. *arXiv preprint arXiv:2407.10793*.

A. Smith and J. Roberts. 2022. Real-time monitoring and feedback for ai applications. *AI Systems Journal*, 8(3):148–159.

Qiang Sun, Yuanyi Luo, Wenxiao Zhang, Sirui Li, Jichunyang Li, Kai Niu, Xiangrui Kong, and Wei Liu. 2024. Docs2kg: Unified knowledge graph construction from heterogeneous documents assisted by large language models. *arXiv preprint arXiv:2406.02962*.

Yiming Tan, Dehai Min, Yu Li, Wenbo Li, Nan Hu, Yongrui Chen, and Guilin Qi. 2023. Can chatgpt replace traditional kbqa models? an in-depth analysis of the question answering performance of the gpt llm family. In *International Semantic Web Conference*, pages 348–367. Springer.

Qwen Team. 2024. Qwen2.5: A party of foundation models.

Hugo Touvron, Thibaut Lavril, Gautier Izacard, Xavier Martinet, Marie-Anne Lachaux, Timothée Lacroix, Baptiste Roziere, Naman Goyal, Eric Hambro, Faisal Azhar, et al. 2023. Llama: Open and efficient foundation language models. *arXiv preprint arXiv:2302.13971*.

Yifan Yao, Zilu Zhang, Fei Fang, Min Zheng, Lei Li, Linhong Sun, and Jie Tang. 2021. Citationkg: Constructing a citation knowledge graph with contextual information and applications. In *Proceedings of the 2021 Conference of the North American Chapter of the Association for Computational Linguistics (NAACL)*, pages 1234–1245.

M. Yasunaga, X. Wu, D. Radev, and J. Leskovec. 2022. Graph-based retrieval-augmented language models for fact verification and knowledge enrichment. In *Transactions of the Association for Computational Linguistics (TACL)*.

Bowen Zhang and Harold Soh. 2024. Extract, define, canonicalize: An llm-based framework for knowledge graph construction. *arXiv preprint arXiv:2404.03868*.

Y. Zhang et al. 2021. Scalable architectures for large-scale ai systems. *Journal of AI Engineering*, 12(4):250–267.

W. Zhao, C. Wang, X. Zhang, and H. Lin. 2023. Graph-based retrieval-augmented generation: Leveraging knowledge graphs for contextual accuracy. In *Proceedings of the Conference on Knowledge Discovery and Data Mining (KDD)*.

A Reproducibility of HybridRAG demo

Reproducibility The code source for HybridRAG demo is open-sourced [10] to facilitate adoption.

A.1 Use-Case for Efficient Contradiction Detection in Regulatory Documents

The problem focuses on efficiently detecting contradictions between document segments, such as those from regulatory documents (DORA and FFIEC), using a Retrieval-Augmented Generation (RAG) system. The approach consists of two key steps:

1. **KNN Clustering**: A semantic similarity relation is used to group similar document segments based on cosine similarity, reducing the complexity from $O(n^2)$ to $O(k \cdot n)$ by considering only the top k-nearest neighbours for each node, where n is the number of chunks (nodes in the graph).

[10] `https://github.com/halftermeyer/dora-ffiec-hybrid-rag-neo4j`

2. **Contradiction Detection**: An LLM is used to detect contradictions between pairs of similar segments, reducing the number of LLM calls and the associated token consumption.

A.2 Approach: HybridRAG for Optimized Retrieval and Contradiction Identification

Traditional RAG systems often suffer from high token consumption due to the computationally expensive Cartesian product of document segments. HybridRAG addresses this by utilizing a streamlined pipeline that applies KNN clustering :

1. **Optimization of Retrieval and Contradiction Identification:** HybridRAG enhances efficiency in retrieving and identifying contradictions within large regulatory documents.

2. **Knowledge-Graph-Based KNN Clustering:** It utilizes KNN clustering with knowledge graph embeddings to group similar document segments, reducing computational costs.

3. **Context Capture:** Context for each document node is captured, incorporating its content, structural relationships, and citations.

4. **Embedding Creation:** Text embeddings are generated by concatenating contextual information, encapsulating the semantic essence of document segments.

5. **KNN Clustering:** Cosine similarity is applied to cluster document segments, creating labeled edges (e.g., `SIMILAR_TO`) for efficient comparison.

6. **Contradiction Discovery:** LLM prompts are used to assess contradictions between document segments, yielding a simple "Yes" or "No" answer.

B Architectural Design for RAG in Production

We propose a design schema in Figure 6 that demonstrates how modular design can ensure scalability and system reliability.

C Facts extraction on finance data (Islam et al., 2023)

The prompt used to extract a knowledge graph from a text is given below. The first assistant answer is forced, the others are generated by the LLM and are not reported here.

```
## User
Please read the text below, I will ask
you questions afterwards.

{{ INPUT_TEXT }}

## Assistant
I have read the text, I am ready to answer
your questions.

## User
The end goal is to build a knowledge
graph from the text. We will do it
step by step. First, extract all named
entities (persons, organizations, events,
...), dates (times and epochs too) and
locations. Put them in a list.

## Assistant
<list of entities>

## User
Perfect, now generate a list of triples
(subject, predicate, object). Subjects
and objects must come from the list
of entities you extracted beforehand.
Predicates are very short text (up to
3 words) describing the relation between
subjects and objects. Try to extract only
*interesting* triples, do not report too
obvious triples.

## Assistant
<list of triples>

## User
Great, now format the triples as a JSON
list. Add a "text" attribute containing
a sentence in natural language fully
describing the fact held by the triple.
Just write the JSON content.

## Assistant
<JSON content>
```

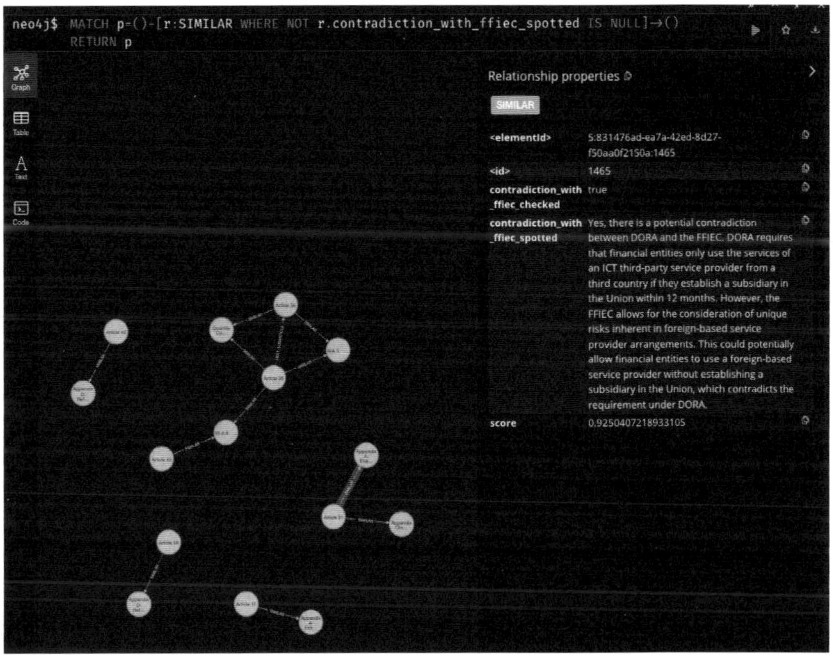

Figure 5: HybridRAG: Example of potential contradiction between articles in DORA and FFIEC

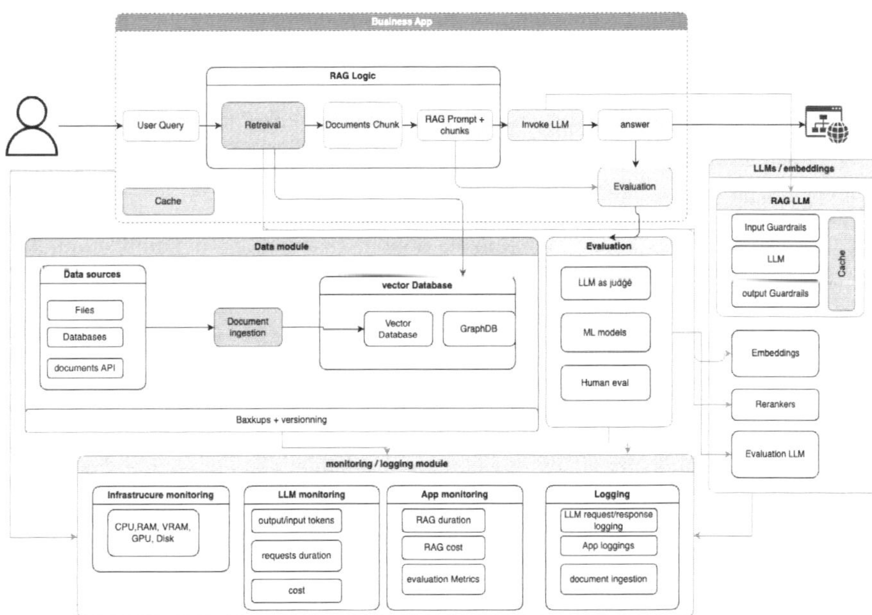

Figure 6: Architectural Design and Components to Deploy RAG in Production

Structured Knowledge meets GenAI: A Framework for Logic-Driven Language Models

Farida Eldessouky[1], Nourhan Ehab[1], Carolin Schindler[2], Mervat Abuelkheir[1], Wolfgang Minker[2]
[1]German University in Cairo, [2]Ulm University
Correspondence: farida.el-dessouky@guc.edu.eg

Abstract

Large Language Models (LLMs) excel at generating fluent text but struggle with context sensitivity, logical reasoning, and personalization without extensive fine-tuning. This paper presents a logical modulator: an adaptable communication layer between Knowledge Graphs (KGs) and LLMs as a way to address these limitations. Unlike direct KG-LLM integrations, our modulator is domain-agnostic and incorporates logical dependencies and commonsense reasoning to achieve contextual personalization. By enhancing KG interaction, this method will produce linguistically coherent and logically sound outputs, increasing interpretability and reliability in generative AI.

1 Introduction

As LLMs gain prominence in generating natural language, surveys point out that their reasoning capabilities become increasingly apparent (Chang et al., 2024). When dealing with critical applications like healthcare (Nazi and Peng, 2024), trust is vital and well-informed decisions need to be guaranteed. Hence, the gaps related to the black box nature of LLMs highlight the need for models that cannot only generate human-like text but also make informed, context-aware decisions. Unlike existing methods that attempt to incorporate KGs as external sources (Sui and Hooi, 2024), our approach centers on a bidirectional mediator that enables a dynamic and adaptable exchange between the LLM and KG. The KG serves as the primary source for grounded, factual, and explainable information, while the LLM provides the necessary fluency and cohesiveness to translate structured data into human-readable language. This framework ensures that responses are not only accurate but also explainable, aligning well with applications where trust and transparency are essential.

2 Related Work

LLMs rely on statistical patterns learned through extensive amounts of data, rather than true logical reasoning. This can lead to errors in context-sensitive tasks (Zhou et al., 2024). This limitation is especially problematic in sensitive fields like medicine and law (Wang et al., 2023), where accuracy and logical consistency are crucial. Approaches following retrieval-augmented generation (RAG) (Lewis et al., 2020) revolutionize factual accuracy by incorporating external knowledge. However, they primarily rely on surface-level matching and embedding similarities, lacking the depth needed for complex reasoning (Mao et al., 2021). Graph-based enhancements of this approach, such as GraphRAG (Peng et al., 2024), offer structured knowledge integration through KGs but reduce KG data to vector embeddings, which strips away important logical dependencies. Some studies explore utilizing KGs as a prompt mechanism to support graph-based reasoning tasks in LLMs. (Zhang, 2023; Huang et al., 2024). They find that embedding graph data into LLM prompts can improve reasoning capabilities, while there is also a key limitation: The integration often fails to retain the full relational structure of the KG, leading to limitations in multi-step reasoning and contextual consistency.

3 A Framework for KG-Enhanced LLM Reasoning

To enhance reasoning and personalization in LLMs, we propose a domain-independent end-to-end framework centered around an independent mediator as shown in Figure 1. This mediator can be perceived as a way to perform the retrieval part of RAG. The main difference in our architecture from traditional methods is that it better structures the reasoning behind the retrieval through a decompositional querying mechanism. This way a more optimal use of structured knowledge can be

Proceedings of the Generative AI and Knowledge Graph Workshop (GenAIK), pages 66–68
January 19, 2025.

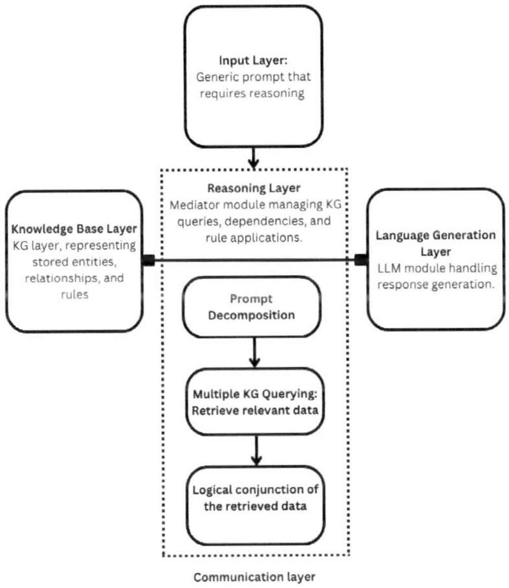

Figure 1: Modular Architecture for our proposed end-end framework for KG-enhanced LLM reasoning.

achieved. The mediator breaks down user inputs into KG queries, interprets KG responses for the LLM by extracting the needed nodes and relationships (which can be not very prose friendly), and handles the back and forth communication between separate LLM and KG modules to achieve comprehensive answers. By coordinating these interactions, the mediator enables the KG to act as the primary source of reasoning, while the LLM provides fluent language generation. This design offers a versatile solution that addresses gaps in LLM reasoning and adapts seamlessly to various domains. Separating the modules in our systems and connecting the dots through our proposed modulator organizes the communication between these modules, making the pipeline more flexible and interpretable. With this approach, we aim at aligning outputs with user-specific data from the KG, preserving logical depth that simpler KG-LLM integrations lack. Moreover, integrating symbolic AI with LLMs supports explainability, a key issue in AI (Longo et al., 2024), by allowing responses to be traced back to specific KG elements and rules, enhancing transparency and fostering trust. Furthermore, we aim for organizing the pipeline by separating the modules and facilitating the communication between them. Unlike retrieval-based approaches (e.g., GraphRAG, LightRAG (Guo et al., 2024)), which reduce KG data to vector representations, our framework directly interacts with the KGs through a dynamic reasoning layer. This hybrid approach combines the structured knowledge of KGs with the linguistic capabilities of LLMs, improving factual accuracy, logical depth, and personalization.

4 Conclusion and Future Work

By introducing a decompositional reasoning layer to interface with KGs, this research offers a novel approach to improve reasoning in LLMs. Our method targets responses that are contextually grounded and linguistically fluent by giving LLMs fine-grained access to structures of KGs. Applications where sophisticated reasoning is crucial are particularly promising for this hybrid architecture. KG-enhanced models that adjust to particular user demands while retaining logical accuracy could be extremely helpful in domains including career development, healthcare planning, and legal advising. These domains offer use-cases to be explored when conducting empirical studies with our approach. Moreover, since knowledge needs to be updated regularly in practical applications, future work includes investigating how KG completion with LLMs can benefit from our proposed reasoning mediator. This way, the bidirectional property of the mediator is leveraged to dynamically enrich the KG with new, contextually relevant knowledge, without the need to manually modify it.

Limitations and Ethical Considerations

Integrating KGs with LLMs, despite its advantages, faces key challenges. Real-time KG querying can introduce latency, especially when responses require multiple reasoning steps or extensive entity retrieval. Accurate entity linking is also complex due to ambiguity, synonyms, and domain-specific terms, requiring advanced learning for reliable mapping, as misalignment can reduce response relevance. Scalability poses further issues, as expanding the KG for broader knowledge increases storage and rule complexity. Additionally, evaluating reasoning quality, particularly for personalized tasks, often demands expert review, limiting scalability. Overcoming these obstacles is crucial for a robust, high-performance KG-augmented LLM system. Ensuring transparency in KG construction, regular bias mitigation, and accountability in how responses are generated will be essential to address ethical concerns.

References

Yupeng Chang, Xu Wang, Jindong Wang, Yuan Wu, Linyi Yang, Kaijie Zhu, Hao Chen, Xiaoyuan Yi, Cunxiang Wang, Yidong Wang, et al. 2024. A survey on evaluation of large language models. *ACM Transactions on Intelligent Systems and Technology*, 15(3):1–45.

Zirui Guo, Lianghao Xia, Yanhua Yu, Tu Ao, and Chao Huang. 2024. Lightrag: Simple and fast retrieval-augmented generation. *arXiv preprint arXiv:2410.05779*.

Wenyu Huang, Guancheng Zhou, Mirella Lapata, Pavlos Vougiouklis, Sebastien Montella, and Jeff Z Pan. 2024. Prompting large language models with knowledge graphs for question answering involving long-tail facts. *arXiv preprint arXiv:2405.06524*.

Patrick Lewis, Ethan Perez, Aleksandra Piktus, Fabio Petroni, Vladimir Karpukhin, Naman Goyal, Heinrich Küttler, Mike Lewis, Wen-tau Yih, Tim Rocktäschel, et al. 2020. Retrieval-augmented generation for knowledge-intensive nlp tasks. *Advances in Neural Information Processing Systems*, 33:9459–9474.

Luca Longo, Mario Brcic, Federico Cabitza, Jaesik Choi, Roberto Confalonieri, Javier Del Ser, Riccardo Guidotti, Yoichi Hayashi, Francisco Herrera, Andreas Holzinger, et al. 2024. Explainable artificial intelligence (xai) 2.0: A manifesto of open challenges and interdisciplinary research directions. *Information Fusion*, 106:102301.

Yuning Mao, Pengcheng He, Xiaodong Liu, Yelong Shen, Jianfeng Gao, Jiawei Han, and Weizhu Chen. 2021. Generation-augmented retrieval for open-domain question answering. In *Proceedings of the 59th Annual Meeting of the Association for Computational Linguistics and the 11th International Joint Conference on Natural Language Processing (Volume 1: Long Papers)*, pages 4089–4100, Online. Association for Computational Linguistics.

Zabir Al Nazi and Wei Peng. 2024. Large language models in healthcare and medical domain: A review. In *Informatics*, volume 11, page 57. MDPI.

Boci Peng, Yun Zhu, Yongchao Liu, Xiaohe Bo, Haizhou Shi, Chuntao Hong, Yan Zhang, and Siliang Tang. 2024. Graph retrieval-augmented generation: A survey. *arXiv preprint arXiv:2408.08921*.

Yuan Sui and Bryan Hooi. 2024. Can knowledge graphs make large language models more trustworthy? an empirical study over open-ended question answering. *arXiv preprint arXiv:2410.08085*.

Cunxiang Wang, Xiaoze Liu, Yuanhao Yue, Xiangru Tang, Tianhang Zhang, Cheng Jiayang, Yunzhi Yao, Wenyang Gao, Xuming Hu, Zehan Qi, et al. 2023. Survey on factuality in large language models: Knowledge, retrieval and domain-specificity. *arXiv preprint arXiv:2310.07521*.

Jiawei Zhang. 2023. Graph-toolformer: To empower llms with graph reasoning ability via prompt augmented by chatgpt. *arXiv preprint arXiv:2304.11116*.

Bo Zhou, Daniel Geißler, and Paul Lukowicz. 2024. Misinforming llms: vulnerabilities, challenges and opportunities. *arXiv preprint arXiv:2408.01168*.

Performance and Limitations of Fine-Tuned LLMs in SPARQL Query Generation

Thamer Mecharnia
LORIA, Université de Lorraine
CNRS, INRIA 54506
Vandœuvre-lès-Nancy, France
thamer.mecharnia@loria.fr

Mathieu d'Aquin
LORIA, Université de Lorraine
CNRS, INRIA 54506
Vandœuvre-lès-Nancy, France
mathieu.daquin@loria.fr

Abstract

Generative AI has simplified information access by enabling natural language-driven interactions between users and automated systems. In particular, Question Answering (QA) has emerged as a key application of AI, facilitating efficient access to complex information through dialogue systems and virtual assistants. The Large Language Models (LLMs) combined with Knowledge Graphs (KGs) have further enhanced QA systems, allowing them to not only correctly interpret natural language but also retrieve precise answers from structured data sources such as Wikidata and DBpedia. However, enabling LLMs to generate machine-readable SPARQL queries from natural language questions (NLQs) remains challenging, particularly for complex questions.

In this study, we present experiments in fine-tuning LLMs for the task of NLQ-to-SPARQL transformation. We rely on benchmark datasets for training and testing the fine-tuned models, generating queries directly from questions written in English (without further processing of the input or output). By conducting an analytical study, we examine the effectiveness of each model, as well as the limitations associated with using fine-tuned LLMs to generate SPARQL.

1 Introduction

In recent years, the interaction between users and automated systems across various domains has become the center of Artificial Intelligence (AI) research. One of the main challenges in this interaction is translating human-written questions into machine-readable formats. This is specifically true for knowledge graphs represented in RDF format. Those contain vast amounts of information on a wide variety of topics, but would generally require a user to write a query in the SPARQL language to use them to answer specific questions. Such queries provide accurate answers from reliable and structured data sources. However, they are accessible only to people with SPARQL knowledge and the time to formulate such queries. This is a significant barrier to the accessibility of information embedded in KGs.

This study explores how LLMs, when fine-tuned, can generate accurate SPARQL queries from NLQ, allowing direct human-friendly interaction with KGs such as DBpedia[1] and Wikidata[2], thus giving access to complicated systems to a wider range of people, including non-specialists. By investigating a range of LLMs, we aim to identify the conditions under which these models produce accurate SPARQL queries, while highlighting their limitations. These limitations include syntactic errors in generated queries, hallucinated identifiers, etc. Our objective is to better understand the capabilities of different LLMs in this task, and to identify potential areas of improvement for future research.

The remainder of this paper is organized as follows. In Section 2, we present related works on QA and LLM development. Then, in Section 3, we present our analytic study and the fine-tuning process of various Meta's LLaMA models to get a new model specialized on transforming NLQ to SPARQL queries, called Llama-KGQA (Llama based model for Knowledge Graph Question Answering). Section 4 presents our results, comparing the fine-tuned models with each other, as well as with other existing QA systems. Finally, Section 5 summarizes our findings and outlines future perspectives to enhance Llama-KGQA's capabilities.

2 Related Works

Question-answering is a branch of Natural Language Processing (NLP) that aims to automatically respond to user questions asked in natural language.

[1] https://www.dbpedia.org/
[2] https://www.wikidata.org/

Proceedings of the Generative AI and Knowledge Graph Workshop (GenAIK), pages 69–77
January 19, 2025.

The goal of QA systems is to provide precise and contextually relevant answers to a wide range of questions by accessing various data sources, such as unstructured text (see, for example, (Nassiri and Akhloufi, 2023)), structured databases (see, for example, (Khanam and Subbareddy, 2017)), or knowledge graphs (see, for example, (Pramanik et al., 2024)). QA systems have become central to many applications, including search engines, intelligent virtual assistants (e.g. Siri, Alexa, etc.), and customer support chatbots.

QA systems are typically classified according to the type of data on which they rely to answer questions: text-based QA systems (TBQA) and knowledge-based QA systems (KBQA). The TBQA systems extract answers from large collections of unstructured or semi-structured text, such as documents, web pages, or research papers. They involve tasks such as document retrieval and answer extraction, relying heavily on NLP techniques such as information retrieval (see, for example, (Arbaaeen and Shah, 2020; Abbasiantaeb and Momtazi, 2021; Otegi et al., 2022), text classification (see, for example, (Fields et al., 2024)), and semantic matching (see, for example, (Zhang et al., 2019)). KBQA systems utilize structured data sources, such as knowledge bases or knowledge graphs, where information is stored in a highly organized manner (such as RDF data). These systems interpret user queries given as NLQ and translate them into formal queries (e.g. SPARQL for RDF-based knowledge graphs) that can directly retrieve factual answers from the knowledge base.

In this paper, we focus specifically on KBQA systems that rely on knowledge graphs. Those systems are discussed later in this section.

Large Language Models (LLMs) have significantly advanced the field of QA by enhancing the ability of AI assistance and chatbots to comprehend and generate natural language responses. LLMs such as GPT (Achiam et al., 2023), BERT (Devlin et al., 2019), Mixtral (Jiang et al., 2024), and Meta-Llama Models (AI@Meta, 2024) are pre-trained on massive datasets that include diverse text sources such as books, web pages, and scientific articles. This extensive pre-training enables LLMs to internalize vast amounts of general knowledge and linguistic structures, allowing them to respond to open-domain questions across various fields with minimal task-specific training. Unlike traditional QA systems that rely on explicit query-to-answer mappings or structured knowledge bases, LLMs can generate nuanced, context-aware responses by leveraging their pre-trained language understanding models.

However, LLMs also face challenges, such as actual generated errors or "hallucination" (Min et al., 2023), where the models generate plausible but incorrect answers due to their reliance on learned patterns rather than factual verification. Despite these challenges, LLM-based QA systems are at the forefront of NLP, offering robust capabilities for applications in virtual assistants, search engines, and more.

Among the research questions that have arisen in recent years is the possibility for LLMs to efficiently generate machine-readable queries from questions written in natural language to interrogate information sources. For knowledge graphs, this involves transforming a question posed (for example) in English into a valid SPARQL queries to a specified KG (Khorashadizadeh et al., 2024). This could significantly improve linking human language with machine-readable data stores, such as KGs. This capability is crucial because KGs, such as DBpedia and Wikidata, store vast amounts of structured information that can be accessed through SPARQL queries. By enabling LLMs to automatically convert user questions into SPARQL, QA systems can provide accurate and rich responses by tapping directly into these vast repositories. Furthermore, automating this process would reduce the need for defining the query manually, which will improve the accessibility to complex data for non-expert users.

This line of research contributes to the development of Knowledge Graph Question Answering (KGQA) systems, which utilize KG to retrieve answers from structured data repositories. To assess the performance of these systems, a KGQA leaderboard has been established, as presented by the authors in (Perevalov et al., 2022c), which allows the evaluation of KGQA systems using benchmark datasets. In this context, several benchmarking frameworks have been proposed, such as GERBIL QA (Usbeck et al., 2019), which is designed to evaluate KGQA systems in a comprehensive way. Among the widely used datasets for KGQA system evaluation, the Question Answering over Linked Data (QALD) dataset series is considered a standard. In particular, the QALD challenge[3] was launched to compare KGQA systems on various benchmarks, including QALD-9-plus (Perevalov et al., 2022b) and QALD-10 (Usbeck et al., 2023). Furthermore, detailed evaluations tracking the progress of KGQA systems are available through the QALD leaderboard[4], providing valuable insights into the evolution of these systems.

3 The analytic study

In this analytic study, we fine-tuned several LLMs, all based on the Llama architecture, including Llama-3-8b[5], Llama-2-7b[6], Llama-3-70b[7], and Mixtral-8x7b[8], to evaluate their performance in generating SPARQL queries from NLQ and compare the results with existing similar systems reported in the KGQA leaderboard[9] and in (Perevalov et al., 2022b). The reason to choose Llama-based LLMs is both their availability, so they could be downloaded and fine-tuned locally, and their relative high performance in NLP related tasks.

The models were trained and tested against two KGs, DBpedia and Wikidata, providing a comprehensive comparison of their capabilities. The latest KGQA benchmark datasets for these KGs are provided in QALD-9-plus[10] and QALD-10[11] respectively.

The proposed method fine-tunes an LLM such as Meta-Llama and MistralAI-Mixtral to transform NLQ into SPARQL queries. The objective is to create a robust NLQ-to-SPARQL transformation system capable of querying complex KGs accurately with minimal human input.

Since we, at this stage, only focus on questions in English, the first step involves filtering training datasets that pair NLQs with their corresponding SPARQL queries, retaining only English-language entries. These datasets, including benchmarks like QALD-9-plus and QALD-10, offer rich annotations for NLQ-to-SPARQL transformations.

Since these LLMs are pre-trained on general language modeling tasks, the next step involves fine-tuning them on the filtered NLQ-SPARQL dataset. The fine-tuning follows a sequence-to-sequence learning paradigm, where the model takes a natural language question as input and generates the corresponding SPARQL query as output. The model learns to align the structure of the NLQ with the syntax of SPARQL queries. To enhance the efficiency of the fine-tuning process, we used the Parameter-Efficient Fine-Tuning[12] (PEFT) library, along with the LoRA technique (Hu et al., 2021), which adapts pre-trained models by fine-tuning only an additional subset of parameters (the adapters). In this LoRA configuration, we have set the lower-rank matrices of the adapter at 16 to save memory and reduce computational cost by training fewer parameters. We also have set the scaling factor for the low-rank matrices at 32 to scale up the impact of adapters to help the model learn the task-specific adjustments more effectively. In order to prevent overfitting, the dropout probability for LoRA layers is set at 0.05. We have also specified the task of the model fine-tuning as "causal language modeling", so the model is trained to predict the next word in a sequence. In this configuration, LoRA is enabled only to adapt attention mechanisms ("k_proj", "q_proj", "v_proj", and "o_proj") and feed-forward layers ("up_proj" and "down_proj"). By selectively adapting only these modules, we focus on the parts of the model most relevant to language generation while preserving computational efficiency. In this configuration, no additional bias terms are learned in the adapters, i.e. the bias is set at "none". This simplifies the structure of the model.

This approach reduces memory consumption and accelerates the fine-tuning process without compromising on model performance.

Once trained, the model performance is validated on a testing set of NLQ-SPARQL pairs. During the testing phase, an execution correctness cycle is applied over 10 attempts, i.e. if a generated SPARQL query contains syntactic errors, the same NLQ is re-processed to generate a different query, thereby improving the chances of generating a valid query.

[3]https://www.nliwod.org/challenge

[4]https://github.com/KGQA/leaderboard?tab=readme-ov-file

[5]https://huggingface.co/meta-llama/Meta-Llama-3-8B-Instruct

[6]https://huggingface.co/togethercomputer/Llama-2-7B-32K-Instruct

[7]https://huggingface.co/meta-llama/Meta-Llama-3-70B-Instruct

[8]https://huggingface.co/mistralai/Mixtral-8x7B-Instruct-v0.1

[9]https://github.com/KGQA/leaderboard?tab=readme-ov-file

[10]https://github.com/KGQA/QALD_9_plus/tree/main/data

[11]https://github.com/KGQA/QALD-10

[12]https://huggingface.co/docs/peft/main/en/index

4 Experiment

All codes were written in Python using the Huggingface Transformer library[13]. The models were trained and tested on two NVIDIA RTX A6000 GPUs with 48 GB GDDR6 memory. During the fine-tuning and the testing phases, we used DBpedia and Wikidata QALD datasets, which both include a training set and a testing set. DBpedia benchmark version is provided in QALD-9-plus as a set of question-query pairs. The question is formulated in many languages, including English that we have used, and the query is the SPARQL translation of the question. QALD-9-plus DBpedia training set contains 408 question-query pairs, and its testing set contains 150 pairs. Wikidata is provided in QALD-10 with a training set that contains 412 pairs and a testing set that contains 395 pairs.

The experimental results, including detailed outputs for various models tested on QALD-9-plus and QALD-10 datasets, are available in the Llama-KGQA GitHub repository[14].

Comparison between LLMs

In this comparison, we evaluate the performance of four LLMs: Llama-3-8b, Llama-2-7b, Mixtral-7b, and Llama-3-70b on the latest DBpedia benchmark version provided in the QALD-9-plus dataset; this benchmark is designed for question-answering over DBpedia KG. We used GERBIL QA metrics[15] to evaluate the accuracy of the models. In this evaluation, we used the micro as well as the macro version of precision (Equation 1), recall (Equation 2), and F-measure (Equation 3), in addition of QALD-specific Macro F1 metric. In all of those metrics, the items considered are the individual responses to SPARQL queries. In other words, the best result is obtained when the generated query gives exactly the same set of answers as the one in the gold standard.

$$Precision = \frac{TP}{TP + FP} \quad (1)$$

$$Recall = \frac{TP}{TP + FN} \quad (2)$$

$$\text{F1-measure} = 2 \cdot \frac{Precision \times Recall}{Precision + Recall} \quad (3)$$

[13]https://huggingface.co/docs/transformers/

[14]https://github.com/ThamerMECHARNIA/Llama-KGQA.

[15]https://github.com/dice-group/gerbil/wiki/Precision,-Recall-and-F1-measure

For micro measures, they are calculated based on the overall counts of true positives (TP), false negatives (FN), and false positives (FP) across all queries, without considering the individual predictions for each query. However, the macro measures are calculated for each query, and returns the average.

The additional Macro F1 QALD metric, which is usually used to compare the models in QALD challenge, is calculated differently. The Macro F1 QALD metric builds upon Equation 3, incorporating additional semantic information as described in (Usbeck et al., 2019); if the golden answer is not empty but the generated query retrieves an empty answer, it is assumed that the model cannot generate a correct query. So, the precision of this query is set to 1 and its recall and F-measure are set to 0.

We fine-tuned each model with different epoch settings: 2, 4, 6, 8, and 10. During the testing phase, we made 5 runs per epoch upon the same testing set, i.e. we asked the model to generate SPARQL queries from the same NLQs in the testing set 5 times. Therefore, we performed 25 runs and used the GERBIL QA tool[16] version 0.2.5 to evaluate the results of each run and calculate the average Macro F1 QALD of the 5 runs per epoch. Table 1 shows that Llama-3-8b with 6 epochs achieves the highest Macro F1 score, demonstrating superior performance in generating SPARQL queries for DBpedia KG. In most other epoch settings (4, 8, and 10), Llama-3-70b has obtained slightly better results than Llama-3-8b. Although this can simply be attributed to Llama-3-70b being a larger model, which enables better handling of intricate language structures and knowledge graph queries, the differences in performance between the two remain small. Llama-2-7b and Mixtral-7b show competitive performance, although with slightly lower Macro F1 scores than Llama-3-8b, indicating an effective yet more limited capacity for precision and recall in this task. This comparison highlights the trade-off between model size and performance, particularly in knowledge-intensive tasks such as KGQA. As a result, we chose Llama-3-8b with 6 epochs as the base model to fine-tune for Llama-KGQA.

Table 2 shows the detailed results obtained by the representative run (the run with the closest Macro F1 QALD to the average Macro F1 QALD) of the Llama-KGQA model that obtained the best results

[16]https://gerbil-qa.aksw.org/gerbil/

	Epoch	Llama-3-8b	Llama-2-7b	Mixtral-7b	Llama-3-70b
Average Macro F1 QALD	2	**52.89%**	49.78%	50.64%	52.57%
	4	56.34%	55.66%	54.73%	**57.75%**
	6	**60.65%**	57.19%	54.88%	58.78%
	8	57.64%	55.95%	55.64%	**59.86%**
	10	57.79%	58.03%	57.78%	**58.38%**

Table 1: Average Macro F1 QALD of Llama-3-8b, Llama-2-7b, Mixtral-7b, and Llama-3-70b on QALD-9-plus DBpedia dataset.

(fine-tuned Llama-3-8b with 6 epochs), as trained and tested on the DBpedia KG. These results are published in GERBIL QA[17].

The experiments indicated that, on average, the model generated SPARQL queries with syntactic errors for approximately 3 questions in this run (the one shown in Table 2) out of 150 questions asked. This represents a 2% error rate. However, prompting the model with the same question again led to successful error correction, yielding a valid SPARQL query within just one additional attempt. This suggests that such errors are rare cases where the model randomly failed to generate a valid SPARQL query, since additional attempts consistently led to correct queries. This iterative querying approach therefore offers a practical solution to improving the accuracy of the LLM-based NLQ-to-SPARQL models.

Comparison with other QA models

We have also compared our results to existing KGQA systems using DBpedia and Wikidata as KG. The results of these models are performed using QALD-9-plus dataset benchmarks for DBpedia and QALD-10 for Wikidata. All results are reported in the QALD leaderboard. The training and the testing sets are both using English questions only for all systems.

Table 3 compares the results obtained by Llama-KGQA, with QAnswer (Diefenbach et al., 2020), DeepPavlov (Burtsev et al., 2018), and Platypus (Pellissier Tanon et al., 2018) using the QALD-9-plus DBpedia dataset. The results of these models are reported in (Perevalov et al., 2022a). We notice that our fine-tuned Llama-3-8b significantly outperforms the top systems of the leaderboard, obtaining 60.68% vs 30.39% of QAnswer. This is a surprising result considering the relatively low effort required to fine-tune Llama3-8b to achieve it. However, this is probably explained by the fact that DBpedia is a well-known resource derived from Wikipedia and using human-readable identifiers. In other words, Llama3-8b likely already had a strong ability to relate to the content of DBpedia from its pre-training, on which the fine-tuning process could rely.

Table 4 compares Llama-KGQA that is fine-tuned this time with QALD-10[18], with the results reported in (Usbeck et al., 2023) that were obtained by (Borroto et al., 2022), QAnswer (Shivashankar et al., 2022), (Baramiia et al., 2022), Gavrilev et al.[19]. This comparison uses the Wikidata dataset in QALD-10. This table shows that Llama-KGQA struggled with Wikidata and only obtained 13.36% Macro F1 QALD. This low performance refers to Wikidata queries in the dataset that use entity identifiers instead of named entities (property and individual names). In other words, our model not having access to or a way to actually query the KG, it could not accurately generate SPARQL queries with valid identifiers in DBpedia. In fact, it would often hallucinate them.

Runtime analysis

This study aims to assess not only accuracy but also the trade-offs in computational efficiency and scalability. To evaluate the efficiency of model fine-tuning, we tracked the training process with Weights & Biases[20] in order to generate the run history and summary. The performance metrics of the model are shown in Figures 1, 2, and 3.

Figure 1 shows the training loss graph of the model with the run that fine-tunes Llama-KGQA. Since the model is configured for causal language model task, it is fine-tuned with the cross-entropy loss function. The X-axis of this graph represents the training steps, each step on this axis reflects a single update to the model parameters during train-

[17] `https://gerbil-qa.aksw.org/gerbil/experiment?id=202410290002`

[18] `https://gerbil-qa.aksw.org/gerbil/experiment?id=202410290003`

[19] Their findings are reported in (Usbeck et al., 2023)

[20] `https://wandb.ai/site`

	Micro F1	Micro Precision	Micro Recall	Macro F1	Macro Precision	Macro Recall	Macro F1 QALD
Llama-KGQA	18.97%	20.00%	18.04%	45.34%	45.82%	46.93%	60.68%

Table 2: Detailed GERBIL QA results for Llama-KGQA.

Model / System	Year	Macro Precision	Macro Recall	Macro F1 QALD
Llama-KGQA	2024	**45.82%**	**46.93%**	**60.68%**
QAnswer	2022	-	-	30.39%
DeepPavlov	2022	-	-	12.40%
Platypus	2022	-	-	15.03%

Table 3: Comparison between Llama-KGQA and QAnswer, DeepPavlov, and Platypus using QALD-9-plus DBpedia benchmarking dataset.

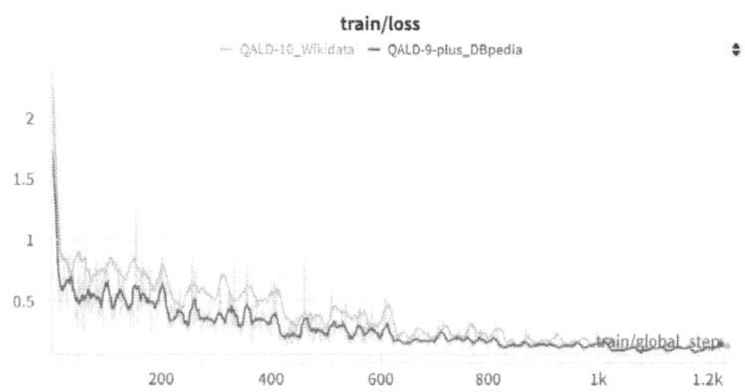

Figure 1: The training loss of Llama-KGQA on QALD-9-plus and QALD-10.

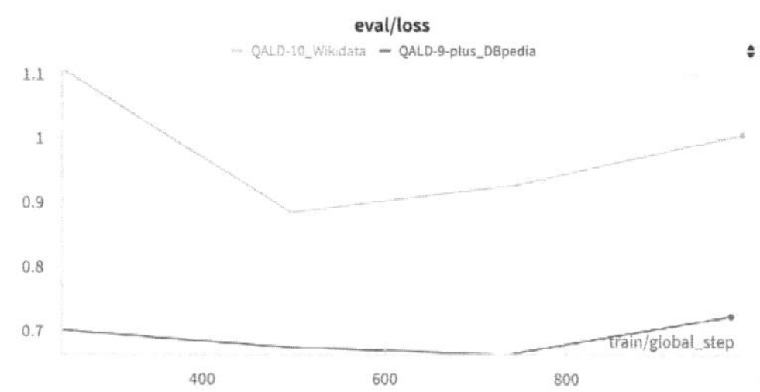

Figure 2: The evaluation loss of Llama-KGQA on QALD-9-plus and QALD-10.

ing, so as the number of steps increases, the model iteratively learns from the training data. The Loss is used in this graph to measure the performance of the model at each step of the training process, i.e. it quantifies the difference between the model's predictions and the actual target values in the training dataset. This graph contains 2 curves for training the model on QALD-9-plus and QALD-10. We notice that in both cases, both curves show a consistent downward trend in losses, suggesting that the model is learning effectively.

Figure 2 shows the evaluation loss (test loss) graph of the same model as Figure 1 (Llama-KGQA) to evaluate it. The evaluation loss is calculated on a separate validation dataset (the testing set) in order to indicate how well the model generalizes to new inputs and to help in monitoring overfitting. We notice in the QALD-10 curve that the loss starts to increase while the training loss in Figure 1 continues to decrease, which means that the model struggles to generate good predictions for the testing data. This overfitting is explained by the fact that the model cannot find the correct entity identifiers from Wikidata because it has no context that incorporates the KG.

The curves of QALD-9-plus in both graphs (training loss and evaluation loss) have a smaller loss than the curves of QALD-10, and the margin becomes bigger in the evaluation loss, which refers to better performance in both training and -especially- testing. This is explained by the model struggling with Wikidata identifiers used in the queries in the training set and the testing set.

Figure 3 shows the utilization of the GPU process and its allocated memory graphs during model fine-tuning. We notice that the memory allocation and the GPU utilization were higher when fine-tuning the model using QALD-9-plus compared to QALD-10. It also takes longer for the model to train with QALD-9-plus (1171s) compared to QALD-10 (1005s).

Limitations of the Approach

While our approach demonstrates promising results in generating SPARQL queries from NLQ, two main limitations warrant discussion. The first limitation is that the performance of our fine-tuned model, Llama-KGQA, is notably lower for Wikidata KG, where content is not transparent due to

Model / System	Year	Macro Precision	Macro Recall	Macro F1 QALD
(Borroto et al., 2022)	2022	45.38%	45.74%	**59.47%**
QAnswer	2022	**50.68%**	**52.38%**	57.76%
(Shivashankar et al., 2022)	2022	32.06%	33.12%	49.09%
(Baramiia et al., 2022)	2022	42.89%	42.72%	42.81%
Gavrilev et al.	2022	14.21%	14.00%	19.48%
Llama-KGQA	2024	7.46%	7.43%	13.36%

Table 4: Comparison between Llama-KGQA and (Borroto et al., 2022), QAnswer, (Shivashankar et al., 2022), (Baramiia et al., 2022), Gavrilev et al. using QALD-10 Wikidata benchmarking dataset.

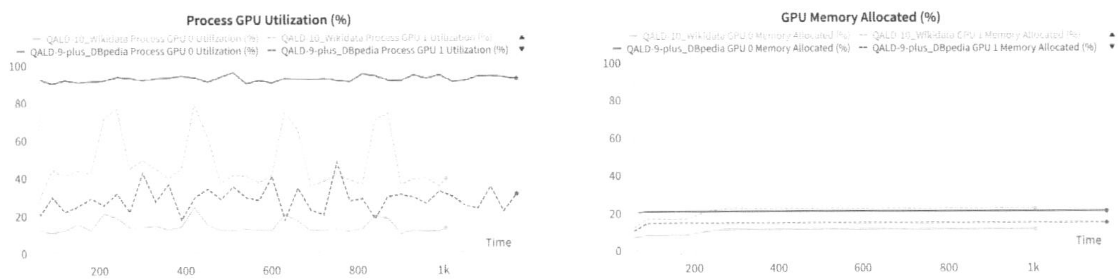

Figure 3: A: GPU process utilization during Llama-KGQA fine-tuning. B: GPU process allocated memory during Llama-KGQA fine-tuning.

the use of non-human-readable identifiers. This limitation underscores the difficulty of interpreting the KG data that was not explicitly available during training. For example, to generate a SPARQL query for the following question in the QALD-10 testing set: "After whom is the Riemannian geometry named?", Llama-KGQA has generated the following SPARQL query:

```
SELECT DISTINCT?uri WHERE {
    <http://www.wikidata.org/
        entity/Q160544> <http://
        www.wikidata.org/prop/
        direct/P31>?uri.
}
```

While the golden query is:

```
...
PREFIX wd: <http://www.wikidata.
   org/entity/>
PREFIX wdt: <http://www.wikidata.
   org/prop/direct/>
SELECT DISTINCT ?result WHERE {
    wd:Q761383 wdt:P138 ?result.
}
```

This example highlights the issue of the model using incorrect identifiers.

Another limitation is that the model occasionally generates SPARQL queries that use incorrect URIs for properties or individuals, leading to inaccurate or invalid results. This issue arises because the model has no access to the target KG, and therefore may not correctly represent the mappings between natural language expressions and the corresponding KG entities. For example, to answer the following question in the QALD-9-plus testing set: "What is the profession of Frank Herbert?", Llama-KGQA has generated the following SPARQL query:

```
PREFIX dbo: <http://dbpedia.org/
   ontology/>
PREFIX res: <http://dbpedia.org/
   resource/>
SELECT DISTINCT?uri WHERE {
     res:Frank_Herbert dbo:
        profession?uri
}
```

While the golden query is:

```
PREFIX dbpedia2: <http://dbpedia.
   org/property/>
PREFIX res: <http://dbpedia.org/
   resource/>
SELECT DISTINCT ?string WHERE {
   res:Frank_Herbert dbpedia2:
      occupation ?string
}
```

This example demonstrates the model's difficulty

in identifying the correct property name used in this KG.

Such limitations highlight the need for improved mechanisms to ensure the correct association between natural language input and the appropriate identifiers or URIs in the target knowledge graph.

5 Conclusion

This study conducted an analysis that compared several Llama-based LLMs for their ability to generate SPARQL queries from NLQ. Our results reveal that Llama-KGQA, the fine-tuned version of Llama-3-8b, has obtained a higher accuracy than larger models like Llama-3-70b, while remaining efficient and scalable for real-world applications. The fine-tuning process using QALD question-answering datasets has shown potential in enhancing the overall effectiveness and adaptability of our new QA model, Llama-KGQA, marking a significant step forward in the application of LLMs within knowledge-driven AI. However, we also showed that for a KG (namely wikidata) which content would not have been transparent to the LLM from its pretraining, especially due to non-human-readable identifiers, the performance Llama-KGQA is dramatically lower.

Future work should therefore further explore incorporating the KG context into LLM fine-tuning, which could improve the model's ability to interpret and generate more accurate queries. This perspective will target the challenges of using fine-tuned LLMs in efficient QA systems powered by knowledge graphs, in particular by enabling the LLM to make use of information about relevant content in the knowledge graph during generation of the SPARQL query.

References

Zahra Abbasiantaeb and Saeedeh Momtazi. 2021. Text-based question answering from information retrieval and deep neural network perspectives: A survey. *Wiley Interdisciplinary Reviews: Data Mining and Knowledge Discovery*, 11(6):e1412.

Josh Achiam, Steven Adler, Sandhini Agarwal, Lama Ahmad, Ilge Akkaya, Florencia Leoni Aleman, Diogo Almeida, Janko Altenschmidt, Sam Altman, Shyamal Anadkat, et al. 2023. Gpt-4 technical report. *arXiv preprint arXiv:2303.08774*.

AI@Meta. 2024. Llama 3 model card.

Ammar Arbaaeen and Asadullah Shah. 2020. Natural language processing based question answering techniques: A survey. In *2020 IEEE 7th International Conference on Engineering Technologies and Applied Sciences (ICETAS)*, pages 1–8. IEEE.

Nikita Baramiia, Alina Rogulina, Sergey Petrakov, Valerii Kornilov, and Anton Razzhigaev. 2022. Ranking approach to monolingual question answering over knowledge graphs. In *NLIWoD@ ESWC*, pages 32–37.

Manuel Borroto, Francesco Ricca, Bernardo Cuteri, and Vito Barbara. 2022. Sparql-qa enters the qald challenge. In *Proceedings of the 7th Natural Language Interfaces for the Web of Data (NLIWoD) co-located with the 19th European Semantic Web Conference, Hersonissos, Greece*, volume 3196, pages 25–31.

Mikhail Burtsev, Alexander Seliverstov, Rafael Airapetyan, Mikhail Arkhipov, Dilyara Baymurzina, Nickolay Bushkov, Olga Gureenkova, Taras Khakhulin, Yurii Kuratov, Denis Kuznetsov, et al. 2018. Deeppavlov: Open-source library for dialogue systems. In *Proceedings of ACL 2018, system demonstrations*, pages 122–127.

Jacob Devlin, Ming-Wei Chang, Kenton Lee, and Kristina Toutanova. 2019. BERT: Pre-training of deep bidirectional transformers for language understanding. In *Proceedings of the 2019 Conference of the North American Chapter of the Association for Computational Linguistics: Human Language Technologies, Volume 1 (Long and Short Papers)*, pages 4171–4186, Minneapolis, Minnesota. Association for Computational Linguistics.

Dennis Diefenbach, Andreas Both, Kamal Singh, and Pierre Maret. 2020. Towards a question answering system over the semantic web. *Semantic Web*, 11(3):421–439.

John Fields, Kevin Chovanec, and Praveen Madiraju. 2024. A survey of text classification with transformers: How wide? how large? how long? how accurate? how expensive? how safe? *IEEE Access*.

Edward J Hu, Yelong Shen, Phillip Wallis, Zeyuan Allen-Zhu, Yuanzhi Li, Shean Wang, Lu Wang, and Weizhu Chen. 2021. Lora: Low-rank adaptation of large language models. *arXiv preprint arXiv:2106.09685*.

Albert Q Jiang, Alexandre Sablayrolles, Antoine Roux, Arthur Mensch, Blanche Savary, Chris Bamford, Devendra Singh Chaplot, Diego de las Casas, Emma Bou Hanna, Florian Bressand, et al. 2024. Mixtral of experts. *arXiv preprint arXiv:2401.04088*.

M Humera Khanam and S Venkata Subbareddy. 2017. Question answering system with natural language interface to database. *International journal of management, IT and engineering*, 7(4):38–48.

Hanieh Khorashadizadeh, Fatima Zahra Amara, Morteza Ezzabady, Frédéric Ieng, Sanju Tiwari, Nandana Mihindukulasooriya, Jinghua Groppe, Soror

Sahri, Farah Benamara, and Sven Groppe. 2024. Research trends for the interplay between large language models and knowledge graphs. *arXiv preprint arXiv:2406.08223*.

Sewon Min, Kalpesh Krishna, Xinxi Lyu, Mike Lewis, Wen-tau Yih, Pang Wei Koh, Mohit Iyyer, Luke Zettlemoyer, and Hannaneh Hajishirzi. 2023. Factscore: Fine-grained atomic evaluation of factual precision in long form text generation. *arXiv preprint arXiv:2305.14251*.

Khalid Nassiri and Moulay Akhloufi. 2023. Transformer models used for text-based question answering systems. *Applied Intelligence*, 53(9):10602–10635.

Arantxa Otegi, Iñaki San Vicente, Xabier Saralegi, Anselmo Peñas, Borja Lozano, and Eneko Agirre. 2022. Information retrieval and question answering: A case study on covid-19 scientific literature. *Knowledge-Based Systems*, 240:108072.

Thomas Pellissier Tanon, Marcos Dias de Assunção, Eddy Caron, and Fabian M Suchanek. 2018. Demoing platypus–a multilingual question answering platform for wikidata. In *The Semantic Web: ESWC 2018 Satellite Events: ESWC 2018 Satellite Events, Heraklion, Crete, Greece, June 3-7, 2018, Revised Selected Papers 15*, pages 111–116. Springer.

Aleksandr Perevalov, Andreas Both, Dennis Diefenbach, and Axel-Cyrille Ngonga Ngomo. 2022a. Can machine translation be a reasonable alternative for multilingual question answering systems over knowledge graphs? In *Proceedings of the ACM Web Conference 2022*, pages 977–986.

Aleksandr Perevalov, Dennis Diefenbach, Ricardo Usbeck, and Andreas Both. 2022b. Qald-9-plus: A multilingual dataset for question answering over dbpedia and wikidata translated by native speakers. In *2022 IEEE 16th International Conference on Semantic Computing (ICSC)*, pages 229–234.

Aleksandr Perevalov, Xi Yan, Liubov Kovriguina, Longquan Jiang, Andreas Both, and Ricardo Usbeck. 2022c. Knowledge graph question answering leaderboard: A community resource to prevent a replication crisis. In *Proceedings of the Thirteenth Language Resources and Evaluation Conference*, pages 2998–3007, Marseille, France. European Language Resources Association.

Soumajit Pramanik, Jesujoba Alabi, Rishiraj Saha Roy, and Gerhard Weikum. 2024. Uniqorn: unified question answering over rdf knowledge graphs and natural language text. *Journal of Web Semantics*, page 100833.

Kanchan Shivashankar, Khaoula Benmaarouf, and Nadine Steinmetz. 2022. From graph to graph: Amr to sparql. In *Proceedings of the 7th Natural Language Interfaces for the Web of Data (NLIWoD) co-located with the 19th European Semantic Web Conference (ESWC 2022), Hersonissos, Greece, 29th May*.

Ricardo Usbeck, Michael Röder, Michael Hoffmann, Felix Conrads, Jonathan Huthmann, Axel-Cyrille Ngonga-Ngomo, Christian Demmler, and Christina Unger. 2019. Benchmarking question answering systems. *Semantic Web*, 10(2):293–304.

Ricardo Usbeck, Xi Yan, Aleksandr Perevalov, Longquan Jiang, Julius Schulz, Angelie Kraft, Cedric Möller, Junbo Huang, Jan Reineke, Axel-Cyrille Ngonga Ngomo, et al. 2023. Qald-10–the 10th challenge on question answering over linked data. *Semantic Web*, (Preprint):1–15.

Xu Zhang, Wenpeng Lu, Fangfang Li, Xueping Peng, and Ruoyu Zhang. 2019. Deep feature fusion model for sentence semantic matching. *Computers, Materials and Continua*.

Refining Noisy Knowledge Graph with Large Language Models

Dong Na[1] **Natthawut Kertkeidkachorn**[1] **Xin Liu**[2] **Kiyoaki Shirai**[1]

[1]Japan Advanced Institute of Science and Technology, Ishikawa, Japan
[2]National Institute of Advanced Industrial Science and Technology, Tokyo, Japan

{s2320036, natt, kshirai}@jaist.ac.jp, xin.liu@aist.go.jp

Abstract

Knowledge graphs (KGs) represent structured real-world information composed by triplets of head entity, relation, and tail entity. These graphs can be constructed automatically from text or manually curated. However, regardless of the construction method, KGs often suffer from misinformation, incompleteness, and noise, which hinder their reliability and utility. This study addresses the challenge of noisy KGs, where incorrect or misaligned entities and relations degrade graph quality. Leveraging recent advancements in large language models (LLMs) with strong capabilities across diverse tasks, we explore their potential to detect and refine noise in KGs. Specifically, we propose a novel method, *LLM_sim*, to enhance the detection and refinement of noisy triples. Our results confirm the effectiveness of this approach in elevating KG quality in noisy environments. Additionally, we apply our proposed method to Knowledge Graph Completion (KGC), a downstream KG task that aims to predict missing links and improve graph completeness. Traditional KGC methods assume that KGs are noise-free, which is unrealistic in practical scenarios. Our experiments analyze the impact of varying noise levels on KGC performance, revealing that LLMs can mitigate noise by identifying and refining incorrect entries, thus enhancing KG quality.

1 Introduction

Knowledge Graphs (KGs) provide a structured framework for representing interconnected data, widely used in research fields such as natural language processing and recommendation systems. However, automated KG construction often introduces noise, leading to inaccurate or misaligned triples that degrade the quality and reliability of downstream tasks like Knowledge Graph Completion (KGC) (Xie et al., 2018). Addressing noise in KGs is crucial for maintaining KGC performance, as this task relies on accurate triples to infer missing links and enhance KG completeness.

Large Language Models (LLMs), which demonstrate impressive capabilities across a variety of tasks like question answering (Lála et al., 2023), summarization (Jin et al., 2024), and translation (Huang et al., 2023), offer a promising solution for KG noise detection. By encoding extensive factual and contextual knowledge, LLMs can evaluate the coherence of entity-relationship pairs based on learned semantic patterns (Petroni et al., 2019). Leveraging LMs for noise detection presents a potential advancement over traditional noise detection methods, which typically depend on KG embedding models or rule-based techniques that may not effectively handle nuanced or context-specific noise.

In this study, we propose a novel approach, *LLM_sim*, which uses a LLM, Llama3[1], to detect and refine erroneous triples in noisy KGs. Our *LLM_sim*, generates candidate triples for detected noise and refines them using contextual similarity, matching them to existing KG triples. Our experiments show that *LLM_sim* is particularly effective under high noise conditions, underscoring the value of LLMs for KG refinement.

The contributions of this paper are as follows:

- We introduce *LLM_sim*, which leverages LLMs to detect and refine noise in KGs, improving downstream KG task performance.
- We validate our approach through experiments on WN18RR[2] and FB15k-237[3].
- We systematically evaluate the impact of various noise levels on KGC, showing our

[1]https://huggingface.co/meta-llama/Meta-Llama-3-8B
[2]https://huggingface.co/datasets/VLyb/WN18RR
[3]https://huggingface.co/datasets/VLyb/FB15k-237

Proceedings of the Generative AI and Knowledge Graph Workshop (GenAIK), pages 78–86
January 19, 2025.

method's robustness under different noise conditions.

The remainder of this paper is organized as follows. Section 2 reviews related work on noise detection and KGC methods. Section 3 explains our proposed method *LLM_sim* for detecting and refining noisy KGs. Section 4 describes the experimental setup, including datasets and model configurations. Section 5 presents experimental results, highlighting the effectiveness of our approach. Finally, Section 6 concludes the paper and outlines future research directions.

2 Related Work

In noise detection research, various approaches have been proposed to demonstrate the effectiveness of their models in detecting noise. These methods can be broadly categorized into three types: traditional KG embedding models, noise detection based on pre-trained language models(PLMs), and unsupervised rule-based noise detection models.

Knowledge Graph Embedding (KGE) models assess the validity of triples by estimating confidence scores for embedded representations, based on the principle that correct triples approximate the vector equation $h + r \approx t$, where h and t represent the head and tail entities, and r represents the relationship. Notable models in this category include TransE (Bordes et al., 2013), RotatE (Sun et al., 2019), DistMult (Yang et al., 2014), and ComplEx (Trouillon et al., 2016). However, noise in training data can degrade embedding quality, as KG embeddings rely on clean data for optimal performance. While KGE models can determine a triple's validity, their performance remains limited due to their sensitivity to noisy data.

PLMs, such as *GPT-2 XL*[4], approach noise detection by assessing the semantic relationship between text and entities within a triple. They evaluate correctness by measuring the model's confidence or probability score for a given triple. However, these models often struggle with domain-specific or temporal knowledge, as they depend on the contexts present in their training data. Additionally, these models primarily rely on associative reasoning rather than causal inference, making it challenging to detect implicit noise in complex knowledge reasoning scenarios. Consequently, such models often have limited capacity for inferring non-explicit relationships and may not effectively detect noise in superficially similar triples.

Unsupervised rule-based noise detection models use predefined rules or constraints to detect anomalies or noise in triples. For example, (Hong et al., 2021) introduced a rule-based triple confidence framework for noise detection in KGE, assigning confidence scores to improve noise filtering and enhance the robustness and accuracy of embedding models. Probabilistic models have also been applied to noisy data (Yi and Wu, 2019; Garg et al., 2021), using statistical methods to quantify uncertainty and model noise, facilitating robust error correction and data refinement, thereby enhancing the quality, usability, and reliability of KGs. However, these models often struggle to intuitively grasp the semantic information of triples and lack a solid foundation of real facts and logical coherence. Although they are not dependent on labeled data, rule-based approaches lose efficacy in dynamic KGs or frequently updated datasets, as fixed rules may become outdated, leading to inefficiency and reduced scalability.

3 Methodology

To effectively detect noise in KGs, which refers to erroneous triples, we propose a novel framework to detect and refine noisy triples in large-scale KGs using LLMs. Our approach consists of two key components: noise detection and noise refinement. Figure 1 illustrates the overall process of noise detection and refinement in KGs. The LLM detection model first identifies noise within the *KG*, which is detected as noise data, *filtered KG* in the figure, which is then passed to the LLM refinement for correction. The *refined KG* along with detected correct triplets, *filtered KG*, forms a new dataset, *renewed KG*, which is subsequently utilized for KGC tasks. The refinement process begins with the LLM generating five candidate triples for a given noisy triple. The candidates are divided into head-relation and relation-tail pairs, which are then matched against the noisy KG. The most suitable candidate is selected based on similarity calculations and used as the final refinement triple.

3.1 Noise Detection

Noise detection plays a crucial role in our proposed method. In this paper, we propose a novel approach that leverages the generative capabilities of LLMs to detect noisy triples. We call this pro-

[4]https://huggingface.co/openai-community/gpt2-xl

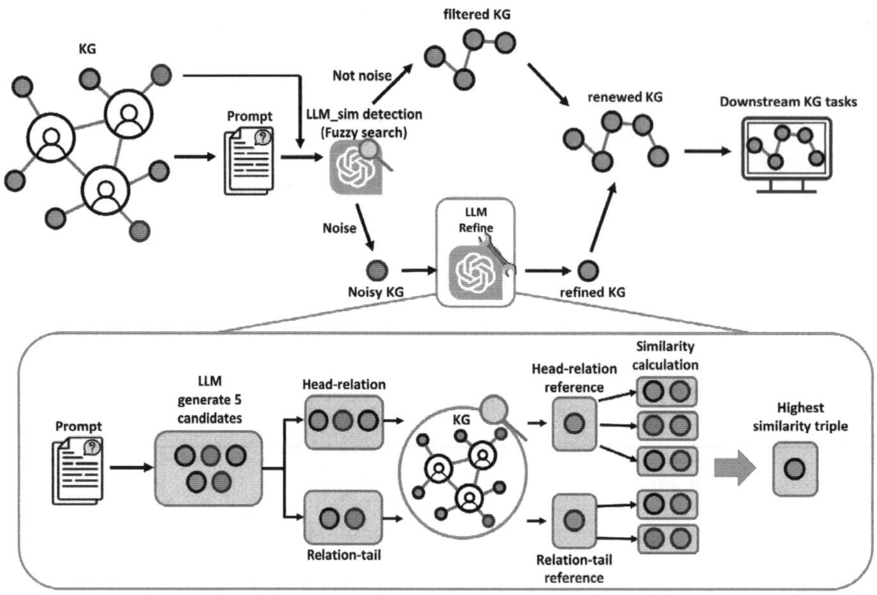

Figure 1: Overview of *LLM_sim*. The red circles represent noisy triples, the blue circles indicate correct triples, and the green circles represent stochastic triples, which may be either correct or noisy.

cess *LLM_sim* detection. To enhance the LLM's evaluation with relevant contextual information, we employ a fuzzy search (Fu et al., 2016) to search similar triplets within the original KG, which is provided as *ADDITIONAL_CONTEXT*. This context includes triples that are structurally and semantically similar to the target triple $\langle E1, R, E2 \rangle$, aiding the LLM in evaluating factual accuracy. Our method involves the following five steps.

Query Vector Construction: We encode the target triple as a query vector $\mathbf{q}$ that captures its semantic information.

$$\mathbf{q} = f(realization(E1, R, E2)), \qquad (1)$$

where $f(\cdot)$ is a function based on the Sentence Transformer model *all-MiniLM-L6-v2*[5], mapping each entity or relation to its corresponding embedding. The function $realization()$ is used to create a simple sentence from a triple into a statement like "$E1\ R\ E2$".

Fuzzy Search in KG: We use the query vector $\mathbf{q}$ to perform a fuzzy search over the KG and identify triples with high semantic similarity, calculated using cosine similarity:

$$\text{cosine}(\mathbf{q}, \mathbf{t}) = \frac{\mathbf{q} \cdot \mathbf{t}}{||\mathbf{q}|| \cdot ||\mathbf{t}||}, \qquad (2)$$

where $\mathbf{t}$ represents embedding vectors of other triples in the KG, as computed by Equation 1.

Selection of Similar Triples: To avoid confusion from multiple contexts, we select the single triple $\langle E1', R', E2' \rangle$ most similar to $\mathbf{q}$ based on similarity scores computed by Equation 2. This selected triple serves as *ADDITIONAL CONTEXT* to support the LLM in assessing the validity of the target triple.

Prompt Design: A structured prompt leverages the *ADDITIONAL CONTEXT* to assist the LLM in accurately evaluating the relationship between entities. The prompt is crafted to ensure the LLM can process and reason through the query effectively. The prompt format is as follows:

> Based on all your knowledge and **the given context** ⟨***ADDITIONAL_CONTEXT***⟩**.** Determine if the ⟨*E1*⟩ has a ⟨*R*⟩ with the ⟨*E2*⟩. Answer the question **by reasoning step-by-step**, and provide your final answer within 'yes' or 'no'.
> **Answer in this format:**
> Final Answer: [yes/no]

[5] https://huggingface.co/sentence-transformers/all-MiniLM-L6-v2

Filtering of Erroneous Triplets : By systematically applying the prompt and interpreting the LLMs' responses, we effectively filter out false triples, thereby enhancing the overall quality and reliability of the data.

3.2 Noise Refinement

The bottom half of Figure 1 illustrates the workflow of refining noisy triples in KGs using LLMs. Starting with a set of noisy triples, despite providing context, directly correcting erroneous triples remains challenging for LLMs. In order to balance model efficiency and prediction accuracy, the LLM generates five candidate triples for each noisy instance. These candidate triples are grouped based on two distinct pairings: Head-relation and relation-Tail. The *KG* is then utilized to compute similarity scores between the candidate triples and the reference triples in the KG. Finally, the candidate triple with the highest similarity score is selected as the optimal refinement for the noisy triple, ensuring improved data quality in the KG. This approach achieves higher accuracy compared to directly using the LLM to correct noisy triples (as demonstrated in our experiments). In summary, this methodology comprises three key steps: candidate generation, grouping strategy, and similarity calculation.

3.2.1 Candidate Generation

To address the noisy triples, we designed a prompt that allows the LLM to automatically refine the mismatches. We designed the prompt as follows:

> The entities in the given triple **do not correctly correspond to each other**. Based on your knowledge, please rectify the triple and generate five correct triples, ensuring that **the original ⟨R⟩ remains unchanged**. Each refined triple should **include either ⟨*E1*⟩ or ⟨*E2*⟩ from the given triple**.
> Please output the refined triples in the following format:
> 1. (entity, relation, entity)
> 2. (entity, relation, entity)
> 3. (entity, relation, entity)
> 4. (entity, relation, entity)
> 5. (entity, relation, entity)

In this prompt, we first need to clearly indicate that the given triples are not correct. In generating refined triples, the task requires the model to retain the original relation while modifying one of the entities. This constraint significantly reduces the likelihood of the LLM producing fabricated or irrelevant information. By grounding the refinement process in the given structure—fixing either the head or tail entity and preserving the original relation, we aim to enhance the factual accuracy of the output and maintain consistency with the KGs.

Each triple consists of a head entity (E_1), a relation (r), and a tail entity (E_2). In cases where the entities and relations within a triple are misaligned, it is often unclear whether the mismatch originates from the E_1 or the E_2. To tackle this uncertainty, our prompt instructs the model to fix one entity and the relation while predicting the other entity. This approach mitigates the risk of LLM hallucination and improves both the prediction accuracy and the efficiency of the model by systematically narrowing down the sources of error within the triples.

3.2.2 Grouping Strategy

To address the uncertainty about whether noise originates from the head or tail entity in a triple, we employ a grouping strategy that enhances the accuracy of LLM predictions for both entities. Specifically, we organize generated candidate triples into two grouping criteria: (1) the "Head-relation" pair (E_1, r), where triples that share the same head entity and relation and (2) the "relation-Tail" pair (r, E_2), where those that share the same relation and tail entity. This grouping process helps to mitigate noise introduced by entity permutations, ensuring that semantically similar triples are compared effectively.

After grouping, we search for similar combinations in the reference dataset, which is the original *KG* in this study. Instead of searching for the complete triple (E_1, r, E_2), we search separately for either the (E_1, r) or the (r, E_2) in the reference dataset.

Without grouping, directly matching entire triples (E_1, r, E_2) may lead to incorrect alignments with unrelated KG entries. Grouping enables a focused comparison on each entity's role, ensuring accuracy and reducing noise.

3.2.3 Similarity Calculation

Both the original noisy triple and its generated candidates are embedded into a dense vector space by converting them into textual representations. For any given triple (E_1, r, E_2), we construct its text representation by concatenating the head entity, relation, and tail entity into a single sequence:

$$T = \text{``}E_1\ r\ E_2\text{''}. \tag{3}$$

To represent these triples in a vector space, we employ the Sentence Transformer model, specifically the `all-MiniLM-L6-v2` variant. The model encodes each triple's textual representation into a dense vector:

$$\mathbf{v}_T = \text{SentenceTransformer}(T). \tag{4}$$

Thus, for the sequence T of the given triple, the corresponding embedding vector $\mathbf{v}_T$ is obtained by encoding its textual representation.

After generating embeddings for candidate and reference triples, we measure their similarity using cosine similarity. For a pair of triples (T_1, T_2), the cosine similarity between their embeddings $\mathbf{v}_{T_1}$ and $\mathbf{v}_{T_2}$ is calculated as:

$$\text{cos\_sim}(\mathbf{v}_{T_1}, \mathbf{v}_{T_2}) = \frac{\mathbf{v}_{T_1} \cdot \mathbf{v}_{T_2}}{\|\mathbf{v}_{T_1}\| \|\mathbf{v}_{T_2}\|}. \tag{5}$$

For each group, we select the candidate triple with the highest cosine similarity to any reference triple, a triple in *KG*. A higher cosine similarity indicates that the textual representations of the two triples are more semantically consistent, suggesting that the entity relationships they express are more closely aligned. Let G_j represent a candidate triple and F_i represent a reference triple from the dataset. We aim to find the candidate triple G_j^* that maximizes the cosine similarity to any reference triple within the group:

$$G_j^* = \arg\max_{G_j \in \text{gen}} \left(\max_{F_i \in \text{ref}} \text{cos\_sim}(\mathbf{v}_j, \mathbf{v}_i) \right), \tag{6}$$

- gen represents the set for all generated candidate triples.
- ref represents the set for all reference triples in the dataset.

Despite the presence of noise in the dataset, the majority of triples remain accurate. Leveraging this fact, our method addresses noise effectively by calculating cosine similarity between generated triples and reference triples. This similarity-based approach allows us to isolate noise from correct data with high accuracy, thereby enhancing the dataset's reliability.

This three-step refinement process aims to effectively enhance the quality of KGs by correcting noisy triples.

4 Experiment

This section describes our experimental setup, including the dataset description, noise construction methods, and evaluation metrics.

4.1 Dataset

We conduct experiments on two datasets, WN18RR and FB15k-237, derived from WordNet (Miller, 1995) and Freebase (Bollacker et al., 2008), respectively, that are widely used for KGC benchmarks. Both datasets contain structured triples representing relationships between entities, making them suitable for evaluating KGC. Table 1 summarizes key statistics for each dataset.

Dataset	**WN18RR**	**FB15k-237**
Entities	40,943	14,541
Relationships	11	237
Train Triples	86,835	272,115
Validation Triples	3,034	17,535
Test Triples	3,134	20,466

Table 1: WN18RR and FB15k-237 Datasets

4.2 Noisy KG Dataset Construction

To simulate real-world conditions where KGs are often noisy, we introduce controlled levels of noise into WN18RR and FB15k-237 by injecting erroneous triples. Specifically, we vary the noise ratio at 10%, 20%, and 30%, based on reported noise levels in real-world datasets (Hasan and Chu, 2022; Song et al., 2022). Noise is introduced by replacing one of the entities in a triple as:

$$G' = (h', r, t) \ or \ (h, r, t'), \tag{7}$$

where h' and t' represent randomly chosen entities that do not relate to t or h in the context of the original relation r.

4.3 Baseline Methods

We evaluate our proposed method, *LLM_sim*, against several baselines categorized as follows:

Pre-trained Language Models: GPT-2 XL, which detects noise based on general language understanding. A prompt used for noise detection:

Is ⟨Entity1⟩ a ⟨relationship⟩ of ⟨Entity2⟩? Answer the question within yes and no:

Note that this prompt differs from the one used for Llama3, as described in subsection 3.1. Initially, we used identical prompts for both GPT-2 XL and Llama3. When Llama3 received prompts designed for GPT-2 XL, the lack of specificity led to irrelevant responses. Similarly, GPT-2 XL struggled with prompts tailored for Llama3, resulting in inadequate answers. Consequently, we developed distinct prompts for each model to better suit their capabilities and improve output quality.

KGE Models: We include TransE, RotatE, and ExpressivE (Pavlović and Sallinger, 2022) as baseline models, where the validity of triples is assessed using embeddings from these models. For TransE, for instance, noise detection is performed by verifying if the norm of $||(\mathbf{h} + \mathbf{r} - \mathbf{t})||$ is less than a threshold γ. After testing various values from 0 to 1, we chose $\gamma = 0.1$ for TransE and RotatE, and $\gamma = 0.2$ for ExpressivE for each score function, respectively.

Rule-based Methods: For WN18RR, we identify noisy triples by assessing the consistency of the part-of-speech tags for the head and tail entities in each relation. In FB15k-237, however, the larger variety of relations makes it impractical to design rules for each one. Instead, we first group triples by relation, apply Named Entity Recognition (NER) within each group, and filter out entities whose types deviate from the dominant entity types, identifying them as noise.

Noise Detection Methods: For robust noise detection, we adopt CAGED (Zhang et al., 2022) as our baseline, a state-of-the-art approach renowned for its effectiveness in identifying and filtering noisy relations. CAGED leverages advanced entity and relation embedding techniques to detect inconsistencies within KGs, providing high precision in distinguishing authentic triples from erroneous data.

4.4 Evaluation Metric

4.4.1 Noise Detection

The performance of noise detection is measured using accuracy, precision, recall, and F1 score.

4.4.2 Noise Refinement

We evaluated the refinement process using two primary methods due to the lack of gold-standard labels, which made direct evaluation challenging. First, we assessed whether the generated triples were present in the original noise-free dataset, referring to this metric as "correctness." This approach offers an initial indication of refinement accuracy by checking alignment with verified data. Second, we performed a manual evaluation, where 100 randomly selected samples were inspected to qualitatively assess refinement accuracy.

4.4.3 KGC task

We use KGC metrics to evaluate the impact of noise detection and noise refinement on the downstream task, selecting the ExpressiveE model to perform KGC on the datasets. Evaluation metrics include Mean Reciprocal Rank (MRR) and Hit@k (Hit@1, Hit@3, and Hit@10), measuring model effectiveness in predicting missing links. Specifically, MRR represents the average of the reciprocal ranks of the correct entities, highlighting how close the predictions are to the top rank. Hit@k calculates the proportion of correct entities ranked within the top k predictions, reflecting the model's ability to rank true triples highly.

We compare the following KGC models using different KGs to systematically compare different noise detection and refinement methods:

KGC: Original KG with injected noise at varying ratios, without any filtering or refinement.

KGC + CAGED: KG filtered using the CAGED model, which removes noisy triples based on domain-specific criteria.

KGC + GPT2: KG filtered using GPT-2 XL, which removes detected noisy triples.

KGC + *LLM_sim:* without context KG filtered using Llama3. Noisy triples are not refined but just removed. The additional context is not used for noise detection.

KGC + *LLM_sim:* detection Similar to KGC + LLM_sim detection without context, but it includes context-based filtering, with neighboring triples providing additional information for noise detection.

KGC + *LLM_sim*: Final refined KG consisting of both filtered and refined triples.

Noise Level	Model	WN18RR				FB15k-237			
		Accuracy	Precision	Recall	F1 score	Accuracy	Precision	Recall	F1 score
10% Noise	TransE	0.473	0.896	0.468	0.615	0.411	0.884	0.398	0.549
	RotatE	0.511	0.900	0.509	0.650	0.464	0.895	0.459	0.606
	ExpressivE	0.603	0.902	0.585	0.709	0.527	0.890	0.521	0.660
	GPT-2 XL	0.823	0.562	0.468	0.511	0.787	0.899	0.860	0.879
	Rule-base	0.672	0.900	0.715	0.797	0.681	**1.000**	0.645	0.784
	CAGED	0.853	0.963	0.856	0.906	**0.839**	0.850	**0.857**	**0.900**
	LLM_sim without context	0.868	**0.980**	0.871	0.922	0.806	0.969	0.810	0.883
	LLM_sim detection	**0.911**	0.934	**0.969**	**0.951**	0.806	0.962	0.816	0.883
20% Noise	TransE	0.335	0.708	0.305	0.426	0.353	0.724	0.325	0.449
	RotatE	0.423	0.774	0.407	0.533	0.438	0.782	0.425	0.551
	ExpressivE	0.593	0.810	0.558	0.661	0.501	0.811	0.501	0.619
	GPT-2 XL	0.786	0.811	0.960	0.829	0.775	0.809	**0.945**	**0.872**
	Rule-base	0.634	0.811	0.715	0.760	0.719	**1.000**	0.653	0.790
	CAGED	0.804	0.933	0.814	0.869	0.712	0.694	0.927	0.794
	LLM_sim without context	0.869	**0.960**	0.875	0.915	**0.798**	0.935	0.807	0.866
	LLM_sim detection	**0.883**	0.894	**0.971**	**0.930**	0.784	0.918	0.806	0.858
30% Noise	TransE	0.310	0.553	0.278	0.370	0.322	0.568	0.291	0.385
	RotatE	0.377	0.630	0.352	0.452	0.403	0.655	0.383	0.483
	ExpressivE	0.504	0.728	0.511	0.600	0.486	0.720	0.483	0.578
	GPT-2 XL	0.712	0.730	0.960	0.829	0.717	0.737	**0.953**	0.831
	Rule-base	0.600	0.730	0.716	0.723	0.749	**1.000**	0.656	0.792
	CAGED	0.734	0.895	0.703	0.788	0.732	0.702	0.892	0.785
	LLM_sim without context	**0.865**	**0.934**	0.875	0.904	**0.798**	0.903	0.809	**0.854**
	LLM_sim detection	0.853	0.850	**0.970**	**0.906**	0.777	0.842	0.855	0.848

Table 2: Comparison of various noise detection models on WN18RR and FB15k-237 with different levels of noise (10%, 20%, 30%).

	WN18RR		FB15k-237	
	correctness	Human evaluation (randomly select 100 refined triple)	correctness	Human evaluation (randomly select 100 refined triple)
10% noise	82.37%	89.00%	87.24%	92.00%
20% noise	80.75%	87.00%	85.27%	88.00%
30% noise	78.46%	82.00%	83.46%	83.00%

Table 3: Results of noise refinement

5 Results and Analysis

In this section, we present the results of our experiments and conduct a thorough analysis to gain insight into the outcomes.

5.1 Result of Noise Detection

We analyze the performance of *LLM_sim* in noise detection for both WN18RR and FB15k-237 datasets, using prior work as a baseline for comparison.

Tables 2 shows the results for WN18RR and FB15k-237 with 10%, 20%, and 30% noise, respectively.

Our experimental results reveal several key insights. First, both the PLMs and the noise detection models outperform KGE models. KGE models perform notably worse in noise detection, likely due to their inability to account for noise during training.

Second, the PLM, represented by GPT-2 XL, performs well in recall but underperforms in other metrics. This could be due to the high proportion of positive samples in the datasets, making it difficult for the model to distinguish between noisy and non-noisy samples.

Third, the performance of *LLM_sim* differs between WN18RR and FB15k-237. In WN18RR, *LLM_sim* detection surpasses *LLM_sim* without context, at 10% and 20% noise. However, at 30% noise, *LLM_sim* without context performs better, possibly due to degraded quality from increased noise. In contrast, *LLM_sim* detection consistently underperforms in FB15k-237 due to low inter-triple correlation, reducing the value of contextual information.

		WN18RR				FB15k-237			
		MRR	Hit@1	Hit@3	Hit@10	MRR	Hit@1	Hit@3	Hit@10
	KGC in clean data	0.506	0.459	0.519	0.597	0.212	0.148	0.235	0.339
10% noise	KGC	0.423	0.375	0.448	0.508	**0.191**	**0.128**	**0.214**	**0.319**
	KGC + CAGED	0.400	0.343	0.429	0.505	0.176	0.117	0.195	0.298
	KGC + GPT2	0.412	0.359	0.433	0.467	0.143	0.106	0.156	0.216
	KGC + *LLM_sim* without context	0.402	0.343	0.430	0.509	0.174	0.116	0.193	0.293
	KGC + *LLM_sim* detection	**0.434**	**0.380**	**0.460**	**0.533**	0.173	0.116	0.190	0.292
	KGC + *LLM_sim*	0.404	0.346	0.431	0.510	0.183	0.122	0.206	0.302
20% noise	KGC	0.363	0.317	0.396	0.435	0.174	0.116	0.192	0.293
	KGC + CAGED	0.351	0.295	0.381	0.450	0.168	0.115	0.185	0.276
	KGC + GPT2	0.338	0.396	0.370	0.404	0.171	0.115	0.188	0.286
	KGC + *LLM_sim* without context	0.370	0.312	0.401	0.473	0.175	0.117	0.196	0.294
	KGC + *LLM_sim* detection	**0.390**	**0.333**	**0.421**	**0.487**	0.170	0.115	0.187	0.284
	KGC + *LLM_sim*	0.376	0.318	0.407	0.481	**0.178**	**0.120**	**0.201**	**0.306**
30% noise	KGC	0.290	0.246	0.324	0.358	0.141	0.109	0.152	0.201
	KGC + CAGED	0.294	0.241	0.327	0.382	0.167	0.116	0.185	0.273
	KGC + GPT2	0.321	0.271	0.356	0.401	0.167	0.114	0.184	0.278
	KGC + *LLM_sim* without context	0.335	0.280	0.367	0.429	0.169	0.115	0.188	0.281
	KGC + *LLM_sim* detection	0.343	0.289	0.375	0.434	0.166	0.113	0.185	0.277
	KGC + *LLM_sim*	**0.370**	**0.312**	**0.391**	**0.463**	**0.177**	**0.119**	**0.199**	**0.295**

Table 4: Performance KGC task for WN18RR and FB15k-237 datasets with different noise conditions

Finally, as the noise ratio increases, the overall model performance declines. Nevertheless, the performance of LLMs remains relatively stable, further demonstrating their robustness in handling noisy datasets.

5.2 Result for Noise Refinement

Table 3 presents the results of both evaluations. The results suggest that our refinement method effectively refines triples to a certain extent. Notably, the manual inspection scores are slightly higher than those of correctness, likely due to dataset incompleteness. This implies that the model may predict correct triples that do not appear in the original dataset, resulting in some cases being marked as incorrect even if they are accurate.

5.3 Result and Analysis for KGC Task

The experimental results offer key insights into the impact of dataset noise on downstream KGC tasks. As expected, increased noise ratios correlate with greater performance degradation in KGC. However, an intriguing exception occurred in the FB15k-237 dataset with 10% noise: the dataset with noise (i.e., KGC) performed better than the data where the noise is detected and corrected. This outcome may be attributed to the relatively small proportion of noise within a large dataset, suggesting that the KGC model can still perform better due to the abundance of correct data.

Additionally, Tables 2 and 4 show a clear relationship that higher noise detection accuracy leads to better KGC performance. This highlights the importance of effective noise detection in improving downstream task accuracy. When the noise detection method is imperfect, filtering out noisy data results in a reduction in the number of good data samples, reducing the effectiveness of the model.

Our *LLM_sim* method also demonstrated distinct effects under varying noise levels. In the low-noise WN18RR dataset, while it achieved slightly better results than the *LLM_sim* without context but did not surpass *LLM_sim* detection. However, in high-noise conditions, *LLM_sim* significantly improved performance, demonstrating its value in noise-heavy scenarios.

Finally, our refinement method showed a substantial positive effect on the FB15k-237 dataset, likely due to the LLM's reliance on factual concepts (in FB15k-237) rather than purely semantic content (in WN18RR). This preference for fact-based knowledge enables LLMs to perform particularly well on datasets that prioritize factual correctness.

6 Conclusion

The results confirmed that our proposed *LLM_sim* method significantly enhanced KG reliability, benefiting downstream tasks such as KGC. These findings underscored the broader potential of LLMs for KG-specific tasks by detecting and refining noise in dynamic, evolving KGs. The demonstrated robustness of LLMs in high-noise settings highlighted their applicability to real-world scenarios where KGs are frequently updated.

Moving forward, we plan to refine our methods to enhance noise detection and refinement capabilities, aiming for improved robustness and adaptability across diverse datasets.

7 Limitations

While our method achieved promising results on the WN18RR and FB15k-237 datasets, we have not yet tested it on real-world datasets. Additionally, our approach is limited by the difficulty of rigorously evaluating refined triples, a common challenge in practical KG applications. As a result, some limitations remain in fully identifying and removing all noise.

Acknowledgments

This work is supported by JSPS Grant-in-Aid for Early-Career Scientists (Grant Number 24K20834). This work was based on results obtained from a project, JPNP20006, commissioned by the New Energy and Industrial Technology Development Organization (NEDO).

References

Kurt Bollacker, Colin Evans, Praveen Paritosh, Tim Sturge, and Jamie Taylor. 2008. Freebase: a collaboratively created graph database for structuring human knowledge. In *Proceedings of the 2008 ACM SIGMOD international conference on Management of data*, pages 1247–1250.

Antoine Bordes, Nicolas Usunier, Alberto Garcia-Duran, Jason Weston, and Oksana Yakhnenko. 2013. Translating embeddings for modeling multi-relational data. *Advances in neural information processing systems*, 26.

Zhangjie Fu, Xinle Wu, Chaowen Guan, Xingming Sun, and Kui Ren. 2016. Toward efficient multi-keyword fuzzy search over encrypted outsourced data with accuracy improvement. *IEEE Transactions on Information Forensics and Security*, 11(12):2706–2716.

Siddhant Garg, Goutham Ramakrishnan, and Varun Thumbe. 2021. Towards robustness to label noise in text classification via noise modeling. In *CIKM 2021*, pages 3024–3028.

Rashida Hasan and Cheehung Chu. 2022. Noise in datasets: What are the impacts on classification performance? In *ICPRAM*.

Yan Hong, Chenyang Bu, and Xindong Wu. 2021. High-quality noise detection for knowledge graph embedding with rule-based triple confidence. In *PRICAI 2021*. Springer.

Hui Huang, Shuangzhi Wu, Xinnian Liang, Bing Wang, Yanrui Shi, Peihao Wu, Muyun Yang, and Tiejun Zhao. 2023. Towards making the most of llm for translation quality estimation. In *CCF International Conference on Natural Language Processing and Chinese Computing*, pages 375–386. Springer.

Hanlei Jin, Yang Zhang, Dan Meng, Jun Wang, and Jinghua Tan. 2024. A comprehensive survey on process-oriented automatic text summarization with exploration of llm-based methods. *arXiv preprint arXiv:2403.02901*.

Jakub Lála, Odhran O'Donoghue, Aleksandar Shtedritski, Sam Cox, Samuel G Rodriques, and Andrew D White. 2023. Paperqa: Retrieval-augmented generative agent for scientific research. *arXiv preprint arXiv:2312.07559*.

George A Miller. 1995. Wordnet: a lexical database for english. *Communications of the ACM*, 38(11):39–41.

Aleksandar Pavlović and Emanuel Sallinger. 2022. Expressive: A spatio-functional embedding for knowledge graph completion. *arXiv preprint arXiv:2206.04192*.

Fabio Petroni, Tim Rocktäschel, Sebastian Riedel, Patrick Lewis, Anton Bakhtin, Yuxiang Wu, and Alexander Miller. 2019. Language models as knowledge bases? In *EMNLP-IJCNLP*, pages 2463–2473.

Hwanjun Song, Minseok Kim, Dongmin Park, Yooju Shin, and Jae-Gil Lee. 2022. Learning from noisy labels with deep neural networks: A survey. *IEEE Transactions*.

Zhiqing Sun, Zhi-Hong Deng, Jian-Yun Nie, and Jian Tang. 2019. Rotate: Knowledge graph embedding by relational rotation in complex space. *arXiv preprint arXiv:1902.10197*.

Théo Trouillon, Johannes Welbl, Sebastian Riedel, Éric Gaussier, and Guillaume Bouchard. 2016. Complex embeddings for simple link prediction. In *International conference on ML*. PMLR.

Ruobing Xie, Zhiyuan Liu, Fen Lin, and Leyu Lin. 2018. Does william shakespeare really write hamlet? knowledge representation learning with confidence. In *AAAI 2018*, volume 32.

Bishan Yang, Wen-tau Yih, Xiaodong He, Jianfeng Gao, and Li Deng. 2014. Embedding entities and relations for learning and inference in knowledge bases. *arXiv preprint arXiv:1412.6575*.

Kun Yi and Jianxin Wu. 2019. Probabilistic end-to-end noise correction for learning with noisy labels. In *CVPR 2019*, pages 7017–7025.

Qinggang Zhang, Junnan Dong, Keyu Duan, Xiao Huang, Yezi Liu, and Linchuan Xu. 2022. Contrastive knowledge graph error detection. In *Proceedings of the 31st ACM International Conference on Information & Knowledge Management*, pages 2590–2599.

Can LLMs be Knowledge Graph Curators for Validating Triple Insertions?

André Gomes Regino
Institute of Computing – University of Campinas – Brazil
Center for Information Technology Renato Archer – Brazil
andre.regino@students.ic.unicamp.br

Julio Cesar dos Reis
Institute of Computing – University of Campinas – Brazil
jreis@ic.unicamp.br

Abstract

As Knowledge Graphs (KGs) become central to modern applications, automated methods for validating RDF triples before insertion into these graphs are essential. The complexity and scalability challenges in manual validation processes have led researchers to explore Large Language Models (LLMs) as potential automated validators. This study investigates the feasibility of using LLMs to validate RDF triples by focusing on four distinct and complementary validation tasks: class and property alignment, URI standardization, semantic consistency, and syntactic correctness. We propose a systematic validation method that uses prompts to guide LLMs through each stage of the triple evaluation of the RDF. In our experiments, four models are evaluated across these tasks. Our results reveal that more advanced models like Llama-3-70B-Instruct offer superior accuracy and consistency. Our findings emphasize the practical open challenges of deploying LLMs in real-world RDF validation scenarios, including domain generalization, semantic drift, and the need for human-in-the-loop interventions. This investigation advances the research on the refinement and integration of LLM-based RDF validation techniques into KG management workflows.

1 Introduction

Knowledge Graphs (KGs) have emerged as essential artifacts to represent structured knowledge in various digital applications, such as search engines, recommendation systems, and question-answering platforms. Having underlying logical and semantically consistent KGs is relevant for applications because they rely on them to improve user experience and help decision making.

At the core of KGs are Resource Description Framework (RDF) triples, which consist of subject-predicate-object expressions that form the basic building blocks of KGs. An RDF triple links a subject to an object through a predicate, encapsulating a single piece of knowledge (Bizer et al., 2023). In this context, ontologies play a significant role in KGs by defining structured schema by ensuring consistency and semantic integrity within KGs. Ontologies specify the classes, properties, and relationships that form the backbone of KGs by guiding the data management and querying processes.

Maintaining the integrity and consistency of KGs as new RDF triples are added is a complex and ongoing challenge. Traditional methods for validating and inserting RDF triples often involve manual efforts by ontology experts, which can be time consuming and prone to human errors. These methods struggle to keep pace with modern data environments' dynamic and large-scale nature. The limitations of current approaches highlight the urgent need for advanced automated tools that can support ontology experts in the management of KG. Automating the identification and elimination of erroneous information improves efficiency and accuracy, reducing the dependency on extensive human intervention.

The insertion of new RDF triples into an existing KG presents issues that can undermine the graph's reliability and usability. First, there is the problem of violating the predefined classes and properties in place, where new triples might not conform to the established ontology schema. Second, URI standardization and duplication pose significant challenges; ensuring that new triples do not introduce redundant or conflicting URIs is essential for maintaining a coherent KG. Third, semantic inconsistency is an issue, as newly added triples might contradict existing knowledge, leading to logical inconsistencies within the graph. Lastly, the syntactic correctness of the triples, respecting a pre-defined language (*e.g.,* n-triples (Beckett et al., 2014) and turtle (Beckett et al., 2014) syntax), avoids malformed triple errors in RDF parsers. These issues collectively impact the overall effectiveness of KGs, compromising their ability to deliver accurate

Proceedings of the Generative AI and Knowledge Graph Workshop (GenAIK), pages 87–99
January 19, 2025. ©2025 International Committee on Computational Linguistics (ICCL)

and reliable knowledge representation.

Recent advancements in Language Models (LLMs) have opened new avenues for addressing the challenges associated with KG management. LLMs, which excel in various natural language processing (NLP) tasks, have demonstrated capabilities in understanding and generating human language with contextual and semantic accuracy (Tang et al., 2023). The intersection of KGs and LLMs presents a promising opportunity to leverage these models to enhance KG management processes (Pan et al., 2024). We originally hypothesized that the advanced semantic understanding of LLMs could assist in identifying violations of classes and properties, standardizing URIs, and ensuring syntactic and semantic consistency of triples. This integration has the potential to significantly improve the efficiency and reliability of KG management, providing ontology experts with powerful tools to maintain high-quality KGs.

This study investigates and evaluates the use of LLMs in validating and inserting RDF triples into existing KGs without negatively impacting their integrity. Specifically, we develop a methodology that ensures new triples are consistent with the existing KG and conform to underlying ontologies.

The broader implications of this research include potential benefits for both academia and industry, such as more reliable KGs and improved data management processes over time. Integrating LLMs into KG curation tasks can lead to more intelligent and automated knowledge management systems, offering enhanced capabilities for handling complex and dynamic data environments.

This article is organized as follows: Section 2 reviews related work, discussing previous approaches for RDF triple validation. Section 3 defines the addressed issues in validating RDF triples. Section 4 outlines our designed method. Section 5 presents the evaluation procedures and obtained results. Section 6 discusses our findings and open research challenges. Finally, Section 7 draws conclusion remarks.

2 Related Work

This section summarizes existing investigations and approaches to validating RDF triples. A recently published survey describing the intersection between LLMs and KGs (Khorashadizadeh et al., 2024) identified KG validation as an essential research venue. KG validation is categorized into two main approaches: fact-checking and inconsistency detection. Our present solution concentrates on inconsistency detection, a relatively underexplored area within the broader context of KG validation. The survey highlights only one significant study in this domain: ChatRule (Luo et al., 2023). ChatRule is a framework that leverages KGs to build LLM prompts, generating rules to detect inconsistencies within the KG. Our work further extends this field by systematically evaluating the capability of LLMs to validate RDF triples in KG insertion operations, focusing on various types of inconsistencies.

Huaman and Fensel presents a methodical approach to improving KG quality without using LLMs (Huaman and Fensel, 2021). The framework integrates existing tools and workflows to ensure correctness, completeness, and usability of KGs. It employs rule-based methods for quality assessment, using metrics like accuracy and completeness. Cleaning tasks involve schema verification through constraint languages (e.g., SHACL, ShEx) and fact validation using internal consistency checks or external sources like Wikipedia. For enrichment, it detects duplicates and resolves conflicts using tools such as SILK and LIMES.

Frey *et al.* (Frey et al., 2023) demonstrated the evaluation of various LLMs, including GPT-4[1] and Claude 2[2], revealing their proficiency in working with Turtle, an RDF triple serialization format. Their study introduced some tasks to assess the models' ability to parse, understand, and create KGs in Turtle syntax. While newer versions of GPT and Claude demonstrate promising capabilities, they frequently struggle with strict output formatting, often including unnecessary explanations, complicating their integration with RDF tools. We face similar problems with our method and despite these challenges, the models show huge potential for assisting in KG engineering.

The Triples Accuracy Assessment (TAA) (Liu et al., 2017) approach offers an automated method for validating RDF triples in a KG using other KGs. Unlike traditional methods that rely on internal information, TAA identifies equivalent resources across different KGs and matches predicates to assess the correctness of triples. A confidence score is generated to indicate the accuracy of each triple, showing promising results with high F-measure

[1]https://openai.com/index/gpt-4/

[2]https://www.anthropic.com/research

scores in evaluations using the FactBench dataset.

Our originality lies in the innovative use of LLMs to validate RDF triples for KG insertion operations, which traditionally solely rely on rule-based methods or external KG interlinks. Unlike prior approaches, such as the Triples Accuracy Assessment (Liu et al., 2017), which leverages other KGs for validation, our study explores the potential of LLMs to bring deeper semantic understanding and context to the validation process. To the best of our knowledge, this study is the first to systematically assess the potential effectiveness of LLMs in this specific application and across various RDF validation tasks. Our study offers new, original insights into LLMs' potential to enhance the accuracy and efficiency of RDF triple validation.

3 Problem Formulation

This section outlines four critical problems our approach addresses when validating and inserting new triples into a KG using LLMs. The rationale behind choosing the following problems is that they align with existing standards and best practices in RDF and ontology management. They are common underlying problems encountered during the construction and maintenance of KGs.

Problem 1: Violation of Predefined Classes and Properties

One fundamental issue in maintaining KG's integrity is ensuring that new triples adhere to the predefined classes and properties outlined in the ontology. During the generation of triples, it is essential to specify which classes and properties the KG structure requires. The critical task is to verify if any generated triple contains classes or properties not part of the predefined list provided by the ontology maintainer.

Let C be the set of essential classes and Pr be the important properties the ontology defines. For each triple $t = (s, p, o)$ in the set of $\mathcal{T}$, the predicate p, and the object o (if it is a class) must be elements of Pr and C, respectively.

For $C = \{Person, Organization, Product\}$, $Pr = \{hasName, isPartOf, produces\}$, $t_1 = (Organization/X, produces, Product/X\_AI)$ and $t_2 = (Person/SteveJobs, born, State/California)$. All the elements from t_1 can be found in C and Pr. If the object "State" is not in C, then t_2 should be flagged.

Problem 2: URI Standardization

The addition of new triples requires no duplicated URIs within the KG. Duplicates and redundancies increase the size of KGs without adding relevant knowledge. This problem arises when different URIs refer to the same real-world entity. Guaranteeing the uniqueness of URIs is vital to maintaining a coherent representation of entities.

For any new triple $t = (s, p, o)$ in $\mathcal{T}$, the subject s and the object o – if it is a URI – must be checked against existing URIs in the KG. Let $\mathcal{U}$ be the set of all URIs in the existing KG. The new URIs s and o must not introduce duplicates.

If the resource $Car/Tesla\_S\_2023$ is present in the KG, then the addition of $t = (Car/Tesla\_S\_23, hasFeature, Electric\_Drive)$ should be flagged since $Car/Tesla\_S\_2023$ and $Car/Tesla\_S\_23$ refer to the same entity.

Problem 3: Semantic Inconsistency

Semantic inconsistency occurs when new triples contradict the existing triples in the KG. A resource cannot simultaneously possess mutually exclusive properties. Ensuring semantic consistency requires checking the logical compatibility of new triples with the existing KG data.

Let $\mathcal{R}$ be a set of semantic statements and constraints the ontology defines. For each new triple $t = (s, p, o)$ in $\mathcal{T}$, we must verify that t does not violate any rule $r \in \mathcal{R}$ based on the existing triples in the KG.

An example of a rule using Semantic Web Rule Language (SWRL) states that a person can not be sibling and married to the same person: $Sibling(?x, ?y) \wedge MarriedTo(?x, ?y) \rightarrow false$.

If $t_1 = (Phone/iPhone\_X, isCompatibleWith, Gadget/USB\_C)$ in $\mathcal{T}$, and there is an existing t_2 in the KG which states that the iPhone X is incompatible with USB C, adding t_1 would create a contradiction with t_2, based on a criterion $r \in \mathcal{R}$ that states that two resources cannot be compatible and incompatible with each other simultaneously.

Problem 4: Syntactic Inconsistency

In addition to semantic checking, ensuring the syntactic correctness of RDF triples is essential to maintaining the structural integrity of a KG. For instance, a syntactically valid RDF triple using the n-triples syntax must have three components: a subject, a predicate, and an object. Any deviation from this, such as triples with fewer or more than three components, constitutes a syntactic error and can disrupt the proper functioning of the KG.

Each triple $t = (s, p, o)$ in $\mathcal{T}$ must adhere to the required syntactic structure. This involves checking that each triple has precisely one subject, predicate, and object.

For instance, an existing triple $t_1 = (Island/Santorini, hasPopulation)$, which lacks an object, would be flagged as a syntactic error. A triple like $t_2 = (Island/Crete, hasArea, 8336, km)$ with an extra component would also be erroneous.

4 Validating Generated RDF Triples based on LLMs

Our proposed method consists of four main steps, each involving a specific prompt and requiring the intervention of an ontology maintainer to ensure correctness. These steps systematically validate and prepare RDF triples for precise insertion into an existing KG. The steps address the critical issues of class and property compliance, URI uniqueness, semantic and syntactic consistency, and challenges explained with more details in Section 3. Figure 1 presents our method to validate RDF triples.

The input is a set of RDF triples formatted as $\mathcal{T} = \{(s_1, p_1, o_1), (s_2, p_2, o_2), ..., (s_n, p_n, o_n)\}$. The output is a set of final validated RDF triples as $T_{final} = \{(s_1, p_1, o_1), (s_2, p_2, o_2), ..., (s_n, p_n, o_n)\}$. Algorithm 1 shows the procedure of our method.

The first step (#1 in Figure 1) aims to verify that $\mathcal{T}$ contains classes and properties listed as necessary by the ontology maintainer. The process begins with the maintainer creating a List of Important Classes and Properties $\mathcal{L}_{c,p}$ (line 2 in Algorithm 1). This list outlines the crucial classes and properties that must be present in the RDF triples.

The list $\mathcal{L}_{c,p}$ is manually curated by the ontology maintainer, who possesses a deep knowledge of the KG's structure and the relevant domain. This list is derived directly from the ontology (cf. Figure 1).

Although the important classes and properties human-curated lists may limit generalizability, they are important for ensuring semantic coherence and alignment with the KGs domain. These curated inputs are minimal compared to the automated processing enabled by LLMs in the pipeline.

The LLM evaluates each triple from all triples $\mathcal{T}$ (line 3 of Algorithm 1) to check for compliance with the provided list. The compliance check is defined as: $\forall(s, p, o) \in \mathcal{T}, (class(s) \in \mathcal{L}_{c,p}) \wedge (property(p) \in \mathcal{L}_{c,p})$.

To materialize this step (line 4 of Algorithm 1), we use the prompt[3] $pr_1 = (i_1, \mathcal{T}, \mathcal{L}_{c,p})$ composed of the following components: an initial instruction i_1 on evaluating the presence of properties and classes, the set of RDF triples to be analyzed $\mathcal{T}$ and the List of Important Classes and Properties $\mathcal{L}_{c,p}$. Line 4 of Algorithm 1 shows a summarized version of i_1.

Any triples containing classes or properties not included in the List of Important Classes and Properties are flagged (lines 5 and 6 of Algorithm 1). The ontology maintainer reviews these non-compliant triples and determines whether they should be removed (line 9 of Algorithm 1). This step ensures that all generated triples adhere to the predefined schema.

The second step (#2 in Figure 1) ensures that new triples do not introduce duplicate resources into the KG. After removing the triples flagged in Step 1, the remaining triples $\mathcal{T}$ are checked for resource duplication.

The LLM performs SPARQL queries on the existing KG to identify similar resources, generating a List of Duplicate Resources $\mathcal{L}_{dr}$ (line 12 of Algorithm 1). Different from $\mathcal{L}_{c,p}$, the generation of $\mathcal{L}_{dr}$ does not require human intervention.

SPARQL queries serve as an interface with the KG. The second step uses SPARQL queries to retrieve resources in the KG similar to those in the triples under analysis. We identify these similar resources by querying the KG with SPARQL and filling $\mathcal{L}_{dr}$ with the results.

The prompt (line 13 of Algorithm 1) for this step $pr_2 = (i_2, \mathcal{T}, \mathcal{L}_{dr})$ includes an initial instruction i_2 on identifying duplicate resources, the set of RDF triples to be checked $\mathcal{T}$ and the List of Duplicate Resources $\mathcal{L}_{dr}$.

The ontology maintainer reviews the flagged duplicates and updates the triples as necessary. If a resource is confirmed as duplicate, the maintainer updates the triples to use the correct, existing resource values (line 18 of Algorithm 1). If a resource is erroneously marked as a duplicate, it is ignored. This step guarantees the uniqueness of URIs in the KG, preventing conflicts and ensuring a coherent representation of entities.

The third step (#3 in Figure 1) ensures that the new triples do not violate predefined semantic restrictions. The ontology maintainer provides a List of Semantic Restrictions $\mathcal{L}_{sr}$ (line 21 of Algorithm

[3] All the prompts listed in this section can be found in https://zenodo.org/records/13712876

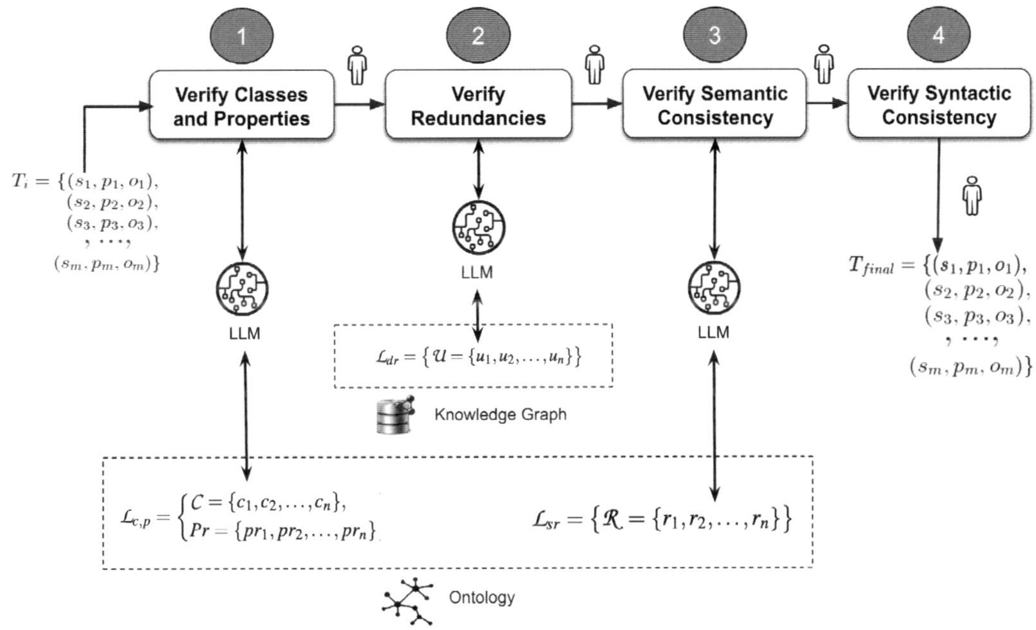

Figure 1: Method to validate RDF triples. The boxes with grey circles represent the steps to transform the initial triples $\mathcal{T}$ in the validated triples T_{final}. Among the steps, the method requires human intervention, represented by the human icon. Steps 1, 2, and 3 use three lists as input: $\mathcal{L}_{c,p}$ and $\mathcal{L}_{sr}$ – part of the ontology – and $\mathcal{L}_{dr}$ – part of the KG.

1), primarily consisting of rules specified in SWRL.

The set of triples modified by the previous steps $\mathcal{T}$ is then compared against these restrictions by the LLM (line 22 of Algorithm 1). The language model identifies any triples that potentially violate the semantic rules.

The prompt for this step $pr_3 = (i_3, \mathcal{T}, \mathcal{L}_{sr})$ includes an initial instruction i_3 on identifying triples with semantic restrictions, the set of RDF triples to be analyzed $\mathcal{T}$ and the List of Semantic Restrictions $\mathcal{L}_{sr}$.

The ontology maintainer reviews the flagged triples and decides whether to remove them (line 27 of Algorithm 1). This step prevents the introduction of logical contradictions, such as an object being simultaneously marked as compatible and incompatible with another object, thus maintaining the semantic integrity of the KG.

The final step (#4 in Figure 1) ensures the syntactic correctness of the RDF triples before they are inserted into the KG. The set of triples modified by the previous steps, $\mathcal{T}$, is provided as input, and the language model checks for any syntactic errors (line 30 of Algorithm 1).

This step does not require additional lists as the previous steps. The language model identifies and flags triples that do not conform to the required RDF structure (line 34 of Algorithm 1), ensuring that only syntactically correct triples are considered for insertion into the KG.

The prompt for this step $pr_4 = (i_4, \mathcal{T})$ includes an initial instruction i_4 about the syntactic validation and the set of RDF triples to be analyzed $\mathcal{T}$.

The ontology maintainer proceeds with a final validation on the flagged triples and T_{final}, ensuring they are ready to be inserted in the KG.

5 Evaluation

This evaluation assesses if the developed method and the designed prompts instructing the LLMs can effectively identify and correct specific issues within the RDF triples. The evaluation focuses on the four distinct problems identified in Section 3 and addressed by our solution (Section 4).

Section 5.1 describes the models, datasets, and procedures used in this evaluation. Section 5.2 demonstrates the obtained results.

5.1 Setup and Procedures

The experimental evaluation used four distinct Language Models: Bloom-176B (Scao et al., 2022), Mixtral-7B-Instruct (Jiang et al., 2024), Gemma2-

9B-Instruct (Team, 2024; Team et al., 2024), and Llama-3-70B-Instruct (AI@Meta, 2024). We chose Bloom because it was one of the first large-scale language models launched, setting a precedent in the open-source community. Among the four models, Bloom is the largest, with 176 billion parameters, which enables it to capture a wide range of linguistic nuances and knowledge. Bloom is free, although it limits the number of tokens generated per minute[4]. These factors were key reasons for including Bloom in our evaluation.

Mixtral was selected for its unique architecture as a mixture of experts (Jiang et al., 2024), differentiating it from the other LLMs. This model combines multiple specialized sub-models, or "experts", to process different input parts, allowing for more efficient computations. Despite being a smaller language model with 7 billion parameters, Mixtral is cost-effective and has demonstrated impressive results, even outperforming some closed-source LLMs like GPT-3.5 (Jiang et al., 2024).

Gemma 2 was included because it originated as an open-source model developed by Google (Team et al., 2024), known for competitive results on public LLM leaderboards. With 9 billion parameters, Gemma 2 balances size and computational cost. Its performance relative to its size, cost, and open-source nature justified its selection for our study.

Finally, Llama-3-70B was chosen because it is one of the top-performing models on the LLM leaderboard[5], especially considering its size of 70 billion parameters. Produced by Meta, Llama-3 inclusion in our evaluation was driven by its leading performance, size, and alignment with the other open-source models in our study. Together, these models represent the current state of open-source LLMs across various scales and architectures.

The dataset consists of 500 records of questions and answers related to product compatibility from ten different e-commerce stores. This dataset was generated in 2023 using random samples of actual customer interactions. These e-commerce stores are customers of GoBots[6], a Brazilian AI startup specializing in e-commerce solutions. The GoBots maintains an existing KG focused on product compatibility, which has been successfully deployed in a production environment. The triples used in our evaluation are sourced directly from this KG. They reflect real-world scenarios and have proven their utility in supporting e-commerce operations.

Each of the 500 records includes (1) A question posed by a customer about the compatibility of a car with a product; (2) An answer provided by a seller indicating compatibility or incompatibility; (3) A set of RDF triples associated with the question-answer pair, representing the car, the product, and their compatibility status[7]. The RDF triples were automatically generated by a system developed by the Brazilian AI startup. This system generates and integrates RDF triples into an existing KG (Sant'Anna et al., 2020).

To evaluate specific aspects of this investigation, noise was randomly introduced into the dataset, targeting particular defined problems. It is important to note that these noises were added automatically, ensuring the randomness of the process and eliminating any possibility of bias that could be attributed to manual interference. This approach was deliberately chosen to ensure a fair and unbiased evaluation of the model's ability to handle data inconsistencies, regardless of how the noise was introduced.

- *Noise type 1*: For 100 randomly chosen records, triples with classes and properties not allowed are added to the existing triples (problem 1);
- *Noise type 2*: For another 100 randomly chosen records, resources similar to existing resources (with minor modifications like year changes) are added (problem 2);
- *Noise type 3*: For another 100 randomly chosen records, RDF triples indicating false compatibility (contradicting existing SWRL rules) are introduced (problem 3);
- *Noise type 4*: For another 100 randomly chosen records, RDF triples with four components are added at the end of the triple list (subject, predicate, object, and a random fourth component), disrupting the syntactic consistency (problem 4);
- *Control*: No noise is added for the remaining 100 records of the dataset, serving as a control group.

[4] https://huggingface.co/bigscience/bloom

[5] https://huggingface.co/spaces/lmsys/chatbot-arena-leaderboard

[6] https://gobots.ai/

[7] An example of a dataset record can be found in https://zenodo.org/records/13722627

Each of the 500 records contains either one type of noise or no noise (in the case of the 100 records from the control group). No record contains more than one type of noise. The evaluation measured each model's accuracy, precision, recall, and F1 score in identifying the introduced noise types.

The evaluation followed the following steps:

1. **Noise Introduction:** Introduced specific types of noise into the dataset to simulate the four problems (as described).

2. **Method Execution:** Apply the corresponding prompts to the dataset:

   - Prompt 1: Identifies triples with classes and properties not allowed by the ontology. We added a noisy RDF triple, indicating the car speed. There is no class or property in the ontology (and consequently in the list of allowed classes and properties) related to car speed;
   - Prompt 2: Detects duplicate resources. We added noisy RDF triples related to the model year of a car. For instance, we added the triple related to the car "HRV 21", expecting that the LLM could detect the duplication with an already existing resource in the KG, "HRV 2021";
   - Prompt 3: Checks semantic consistency by searching for contradictions in compatibility among products and cars. We added the example from Section 4, adding SWRL related to compatible and incompatible products and cars. We added noisy compatibility triples, expecting that the LLM could identify them;
   - Prompt 4: Verifies the correct syntax of triple insertion. We added noisy RDF triples with four components.

3. **Metrics Computation:** Calculate accuracy, precision, recall, and F1 for each prompt by each model, evaluating the number of correctly identified records versus false positives and false negatives. For example, in the case of 100 records with noise from problem 1, a true positive is when the model correctly identifies the problem in a record. A true negative occurs when the model correctly identifies that one of the remaining 400 records has no issues. A false negative would be when the model fails to identify problem 1 in one of the 100 problematic records, while a false positive would occur if the model incorrectly identifies one of the 400 noise-free records as problematic. These values are used to compute the evaluation metrics for each model.

4. **Analysis of Results:** Quantitative analysis to determine the effectiveness of each prompt in addressing the specific problems.

5.2 Results

In evaluating the models across the four RDF validation problems, a clear trade-off emerges between precision, recall, and accuracy. For instance, in the Class and Properties Violation Problem, the Llama-3 70B Instruct model got an accuracy of 0.84, coupled with a balanced precision and recall of 0.78 and 0.89, respectively. This indicates that the model was good at identifying valid triples and minimizing false positives and negatives. On the other hand, Bloom-176B showed a more balance between precision and recall (0.54 vs. 0.56) but at a much lower accuracy (0.55), reflecting difficult-to-maintain consistent results across the scenarios.

We observed that models like Mixtral-7B and Gemma2-9B exhibit higher recall than precision in some instances, such as the "Class and Properties Violation" and "Syntactic Inconsistency Problem". This comes at the cost of higher false positives, reflected in lower precision. The balance between these metrics suggests that selecting a model for RDF validation requires prioritizing the metrics most relevant to the specific validation scenario, whether catching more errors (recall) or ensuring fewer false positives (precision).

The models showed varying degrees of sensitivity to different types of RDF validation issues, revealing insights into their strengths and weaknesses. In the "Syntactic Inconsistency Problem", where adherence to RDF structure is required, Llama-3 70B Instruct outperformed all other models with almost perfect accuracy (0.99) and F1 score (0.98). This indicates that this model is well-suited for tasks requiring precise syntactic validation. However, Bloom-176B struggled with syntactic errors, achieving a low accuracy of 0.36, suggesting it is less adept at handling structural rules.

In the "Semantic Inconsistency Problem" and "URI Standardization", which involves relationships and contextual knowledge, Gemma2-9B showed higher metric values than in syntactic tasks. This could be attributed to their ability to recognize complex ontological relationships, although their recall and F1 scores are behind Llama-3. The results suggest that while some models specialize in specific RDF issues, they face challenges when encountering unfamiliar error types.

6 Discussion and Open Research Challenges

This research inquired how LLMs can be suited to contribute as KG Curators in the operations of triple insertion. This research demonstrated that LLMs for the distinct problems addressed can be applicable as an approach to help ontology engineers address RDF validation. In the following, we underline key findings and challenges regarding several aspects of our experimental results and the consequences of applying our solution to operational settings.

The most performing LLM. Overall, we found that the Llama-3 70B Instruct model consistently outperformed the others across all validation problems, excelling in tasks that demand high precision and recall. Its effectiveness in the "Syntactic Inconsistency Problem" (0.99 accuracy) and "URI Standardization Problem" (0.96 accuracy) underscored its robustness in handling structural data such as RDF triples. In our understanding, this model's success is due to its large parameter size and fine-tuning, which are geared explicitly towards instruction-based tasks, enabling it to generalize across diverse RDF validation scenarios.

Underperformance consistently. Conversely, Bloom-176B consistently underperformed, particularly in the "Semantic Inconsistency Problem" (0.29 accuracy) and "Syntactic Inconsistency Problem" (0.36 accuracy). Its lower accuracy and inconsistent precision-recall balance show its limitations in handling the rule-based nature of RDF validation. The gap in results between Llama-3 and Bloom can be explained by differences in model size, training datasets, domain-specific tuning, and more than two years between the release of both models.

The most challenging problems. Discussing the four validation problems, the "URI Standardization Problem" obtained the best overall results, with a mean accuracy of 0.71. This can be attributed to the nature of 'standardizing URIs', which primarily involves pattern recognition that LLMs are well-equipped to handle. The best model, Llama-3, achieved a near-perfect accuracy of 0.96 for this problem, showing its ability to manage standardized data consistently. On the contrary, the "Syntactic Inconsistency Problem" proved to be the most challenging overall, with an average accuracy of 0.53 and a mean F1 score of 0.47. This difficulty arose from Gemma 2 reaching a precision of 0.08 and accuracy of 0.26, which was the worst precision and accuracy of the evaluation. Mixtral-7B got better results in this task. Comparing the two models with similar sizes, Mixtral outperformed Gemma 2 in semantic-related tasks, and Gemma 2 outperformed Mixtral in syntactic-related tasks.

Cost vs. Accuracy Trade-off. The cost-effectiveness of deploying different LLMs for RDF triple validation is critical for real-world applications. For instance, while the Llama model achieved superior accuracy and overall metrics, it comes with a significant computational cost of $0.88 per million tokens. In contrast, the Gemma-2 9B Instruct model, which costs $0.30 per million tokens, provides a balanced trade-off between cost and accuracy but falls short of achieving the precision needed for more complex scenarios. Mixtral 7B Instruct offers a middle ground in cost and performance at $0.60 per million tokens. At the same time, Bloom is a freely available model that, despite being cost-free, exhibits significantly lower accuracy and reliability. These costs were gathered in two companies that provide LLMs APIs: TogetherAI[8] and Hugging Face[9]. The costs reflect the price found when this manuscript was written - September 2024.

Semantic Drift in Long Triple Chains. One issue encountered in RDF triple validation using LLMs is the potential for semantic drift when evaluating long chains of interconnected triples. In this context, semantic drift refers to the model losing coherence as it processes extended sequences. This drift is increased by the models' limited memory retention and inability to consistently track relationships across multiple triples. Triples involving big and deep ontological hierarchies or chains that span various levels may introduce errors as the models struggle to maintain context. As a future work, addressing this challenge may require fine-tuning LLMs with specific datasets designed to enhance memory retention over long sequences or integrating mechanisms that allow for continuous context tracking in KG context. Without such interventions, long triple chains remain a source of inaccuracy.

[8] https://api.together.ai/models

[9] https://huggingface.co/models

Ontology Complexity and Coverage. The complexity of ontologies, characterized by rich hierarchies, specialized vocabularies, and relationships, introduces significant challenges for LLM-based RDF validation. The method revealed that as ontologies grow more complex, models like Bloom and Mixtral struggle to navigate the intricate set of classes and properties accurately. A notable issue is incomplete ontology coverage, where the models lack sufficient information about specialized vocabularies, leading to false positives or negatives during validation. For example, triples involving lesser-known properties or deep subclass hierarchies often went unrecognized, highlighting gaps in the models' ontological understanding. Addressing this issue may require expanding the training datasets to include more comprehensive ontology samples for future work.

Ontology Size. The experiments conducted in this study did not suffer from token limitation, as the ontology used is relatively small and well within the context size limits of the employed LLMs. However, we acknowledge that scaling the approach to large ontologies remains an open issue. Future work will explore strategies to handle extensive schemas, such as breaking them into subsets or leveraging hierarchical representations to fit within the token constraints of LLMs.

7 Conclusion

Ensuring the quality and consistency of KGs is critical for real-world applications that rely on semantic accuracy. As KGs become more integral to artificial intelligence systems, advancing methods for their automated validation might play a key role in driving accurate, reliable, and scalable semantic solutions. Our study explored using LLMs to validate RDF triples by addressing critical challenges in automating a traditionally manual process. We showcased the strengths and limitations of current LLMs in KG curation by examining the effectiveness of models like Llama-3-70B-Instruct and Bloom-176B across four RDF validation tasks. The Llama-3 model demonstrated competitive results, particularly in maintaining syntactic and semantic consistency, showing the potential for real-world deployment. Our results highlighted the complexity and cost implications, especially in handling errors requiring more context. The findings suggested future research directions, including more sophisticated approaches to reducing semantic drift in longer triple chains and enhancing model generalization across domains. Also, incorporating humans into the loop and refining prompt engineering techniques could enhance LLM results.

Limitations

One limitation found during the development of this investigation is the low accuracy of some models when handling intricate RDF syntax and semantics. For instance, models like Bloom-176B demonstrated considerable inconsistency in detecting syntactic errors, due to their less targeted training. This variability among models indicates that not all LLMs can address complex validation tasks, suggesting a need for further fine-tuning and model selection based on specific KG characteristics.

Another limitation was handling with long triple chains, where models experienced semantic drift. Certain LLMs struggled to retain the necessary context across interconnected triples as the chain increased, leading to validation inaccuracies. Addressing this drift might require models specifically trained to manage extended sequences or incorporate a human-in-the-loop strategy. Additionally, the significant computational cost of more accurate models, like Llama-3-70B, limits scalability in practical applications, where cost-effective but reliable validation solutions are desirable.

We acknowledge that the proposed approach involves some degree of manual effort, mainly through the involvement of the ontology maintainer in providing inputs such as lists of essential classes and properties. However, this involvement is necessary to ensure the RDF's semantic alignment and domain specificity triples with the existing KG and ontology. Although LLM automation significantly reduces the overall workload, human oversight remains essential to maintain the quality and reliability of the KG.

Acknowledgments

This study was financed by the National Council for Scientific and Technological Development - Brazil (CNPq) process number 140213/2021-0. In addition, this research was partially funded by the São Paulo Research Foundation (FAPESP) (grants #2022/13694-0, #2022/15816-5 and #2024/07716-6). The opinions expressed in this work do not necessarily reflect those of the funding agencies. We thank GoBots for providing the infrastructure used in this research.

References

AI@Meta. 2024. Llama 3 model card.

David Beckett, Tim Berners-Lee, Eric Prud'hommeaux, and Gavin Carothers. 2014. Rdf 1.1 turtle. *World Wide Web Consortium*, pages 18–31.

Christian Bizer, Tom Heath, and Tim Berners-Lee. 2023. Linked data-the story so far. In *Linking the World's Information: Essays on Tim Berners-Lee's Invention of the World Wide Web*, pages 115–143.

Johannes Frey, Lars-Peter Meyer, Natanael Arndt, Felix Brei, and Kirill Bulert. 2023. Benchmarking the abilities of large language models for rdf knowledge graph creation and comprehension: How well do llms speak turtle? *arXiv preprint arXiv:2309.17122*.

Elwin Huaman and Dieter Fensel. 2021. Knowledge graph curation: a practical framework. In *Proceedings of the 10th International Joint Conference on Knowledge Graphs*, pages 166–171.

Albert Q Jiang, Alexandre Sablayrolles, Antoine Roux, Arthur Mensch, Blanche Savary, Chris Bamford, Devendra Singh Chaplot, Diego de las Casas, Emma Bou Hanna, Florian Bressand, et al. 2024. Mixtral of experts. *arXiv preprint arXiv:2401.04088*.

Hanieh Khorashadizadeh, Fatima Zahra Amara, Morteza Ezzabady, Frédéric Ieng, Sanju Tiwari, Nandana Mihindukulasooriya, Jinghua Groppe, Soror Sahri, Farah Benamara, and Sven Groppe. 2024. Research trends for the interplay between large language models and knowledge graphs. *arXiv preprint arXiv:2406.08223*.

Shuangyan Liu, Mathieu d'Aquin, and Enrico Motta. 2017. Measuring accuracy of triples in knowledge graphs. In *Language, Data, and Knowledge: First International Conference, LDK 2017, Galway, Ireland, June 19-20, 2017, Proceedings 1*, pages 343–357. Springer.

Linhao Luo, Jiaxin Ju, Bo Xiong, Yuan-Fang Li, Gholamreza Haffari, and Shirui Pan. 2023. Chatrule: Mining logical rules with large language models for knowledge graph reasoning. *arXiv preprint arXiv:2309.01538*.

Shirui Pan, Linhao Luo, Yufei Wang, Chen Chen, Jiapu Wang, and Xindong Wu. 2024. Unifying large language models and knowledge graphs: A roadmap. *IEEE Transactions on Knowledge and Data Engineering*.

Diogo Teles Sant'Anna, Rodrigo Oliveira Caus, Lucas dos Santos Ramos, Victor Hochgreb, and Julio Cesar dos Reis. 2020. Generating knowledge graphs from unstructured texts: Experiences in the e-commerce field for question answering. In *ASLD@ ISWC*, pages 56–71.

Teven Le Scao, Angela Fan, Christopher Akiki, Ellie Pavlick, Suzana Ilić, Daniel Hesslow, Roman Castagné, Alexandra Sasha Luccioni, François Yvon, Matthias Gallé, et al. 2022. Bloom: A 176b-parameter open-access multilingual language model. *arXiv preprint arXiv:2211.05100*.

Xiaojuan Tang, Zilong Zheng, Jiaqi Li, Fanxu Meng, Song-Chun Zhu, Yitao Liang, and Muhan Zhang. 2023. Large language models are in-context semantic reasoners rather than symbolic reasoners. *arXiv preprint arXiv:2305.14825*.

Gemma Team. 2024. Gemma.

Gemma Team, Morgane Riviere, Shreya Pathak, Pier Giuseppe Sessa, Cassidy Hardin, Surya Bhupatiraju, Léonard Hussenot, Thomas Mesnard, Bobak Shahriari, Alexandre Ramé, et al. 2024. Gemma 2: Improving open language models at a practical size. *arXiv preprint arXiv:2408.00118*.

A Appendix - Algorithm

B Appendix - Summary of Results

Table 1 presents the results. It demonstrates varied effectiveness across the four evaluated problems, with differences in accuracy, precision, recall, and F1-score among the four language models.

For **Problem 1**, which focused on detecting violations of predefined classes and properties, Llama-3-70B-Instruct achieved the highest accuracy (0.84) and F1-score (0.80), followed by Mixtral-7B-Instruct with an accuracy of 0.64 and an F1-score of 0.61. The overall mean accuracy for this problem across all models was 0.61, with a mean precision of 0.65, recall of 0.71, and F1-score of 0.58.

Algorithm 1 Our Method for Validating RDF Triples for Knowledge Graph Insertion

Require: Set of RDF triples $\mathcal{T}$, List of Important Classes and Properties $\mathcal{L}_{c,p}$, Knowledge Graph $\mathcal{KG}$, List of Semantic Restrictions $\mathcal{L}_{sr}$

Step 1: Verify Classes and Properties using LLM and Prompt 1
$\mathcal{L}_{c,p} \leftarrow$ createListOfImportantClassesAndProperties() ▷ Created by ontology maintainer
for each $(s,p,o) \in \mathcal{T}$ **do**
    $response \leftarrow$ LLM(Prompt 1: "Check if the triple (s,p,o) violates any predefined classes or properties in $\mathcal{L}_{c,p}$")
    if $response =$ violation **then**
        $flaggedTriples_1 \leftarrow flaggedTriples_1 \cup \{(s,p,o)\}$
    end if
end for
$\mathcal{T} \leftarrow \mathcal{T} \setminus flaggedTriples_1$ ▷ Reviewed by ontology maintainer
Step 2: Verify Redundancies using LLM and Prompt 2
for each $(s,p,o) \in \mathcal{T}$ **do**
    $\mathcal{L}_{dr} \leftarrow$ queryForDuplicateResources($s, o, \mathcal{KG}$)
    $response \leftarrow$ LLM(Prompt 2: "Check if the triple (s,p,o) contains duplicate or similar resources in $\mathcal{L}_{dr}$")
    if $response =$ duplicate **then**
        $flaggedTriples_2 \leftarrow flaggedTriples_2 \cup \{(s,p,o)\}$
    end if
end for
$\mathcal{T} \leftarrow$ updateResourcesInTriples($\mathcal{T}$, $flaggedTriples_2$, $\mathcal{KG}$) ▷ Reviewed by ontology maintainer
Step 3: Verify Semantic Consistency using LLM and Prompt 3
for each $(s,p,o) \in \mathcal{T}$ **do**
    $\mathcal{L}_{sr} \leftarrow$ createListOfRules() ▷ Created by ontology maintainer
    $response \leftarrow$ LLM(Prompt 3: "Check if the triple (s,p,o) violates any semantic restrictions defined in $\mathcal{L}_{sr}$")
    if $response =$ violation **then**
        $flaggedTriples_3 \leftarrow flaggedTriples_3 \cup \{(s,p,o)\}$
    end if
end for
$\mathcal{T} \leftarrow \mathcal{T} \setminus flaggedTriples_3$ ▷ Reviewed by ontology maintainer
Step 4: Verify Syntactic Consistency using LLM and Prompt 4
for each $(s,p,o) \in \mathcal{T}$ **do**
    $response \leftarrow$ LLM(Prompt 4: "Check if the triple (s,p,o) is syntactically correct")
    if $response =$ correct **then**
        $\mathcal{T}_{final} \leftarrow \mathcal{T}_{final} \cup \{(s,p,o)\}$
    else
        $flaggedTriples_4 \leftarrow flaggedTriples_4 \cup \{(s,p,o)\}$
    end if
end for
$\mathcal{T} \leftarrow \mathcal{T} \setminus flaggedTriples_4$ ▷ Reviewed by ontology maintainer
$flaggedTriples \leftarrow flaggedTriples_1 \cup flaggedTriples_2 \cup flaggedTriples_3 \cup flaggedTriples_4$
return $\mathcal{T}_{final}, flaggedTriples$ ▷ Final set of triples ready for insertion into the Knowledge Graph

Concerning **Problem 2**, which involved identifying and standardizing duplicate resources, Llama-3-70B-Instruct achieved the highest results with an accuracy of 0.96, precision of 0.92, recall of 0.97, and F1-score of 0.94. The mean accuracy of each model for this problem was 0.71, with a mean precision of 0.75, recall of 0.73, and F1-score of 0.67.

Table 1: Results of the experimental evaluation. The first column lists the four problems described in Section 3; the second column lists the four LLMs used in the evaluation; the remaining columns show the values of each metric in each model and problem. Bold values represent the best score for each metric and each problem.

Problem	Model	Accuracy	Precision	Recall	F1
1 - Class and Properties Violation	Bloom-176B	0.55	0.54	0.56	0.50
	Mixtral-7B-Instruct	0.64	0.67	0.77	0.61
	Gemma2-9B-Instruct	0.42	0.59	0.61	0.42
	Llama-3-70B-Instruct	**0.84**	**0.78**	**0.89**	**0.80**
	Mean	0.61	0.65	0.71	0.58
2 - URI Standardization	Bloom-176B	0.44	0.50	0.49	0.41
	Mixtral-7B-Instruct	0.52	0.64	0.69	0.51
	Gemma2-9B-Instruct	0.90	**0.93**	0.75	0.80
	Llama-3-70B-Instruct	**0.96**	0.92	**0.97**	**0.94**
	Mean	0.71	0.75	0.73	0.67
3 - Semantic Inconsistency	Bloom-176B	0.29	0.34	0.26	0.26
	Mixtral-7B-Instruct	0.56	0.39	0.36	0.37
	Gemma2-9B-Instruct	0.81	0.83	0.53	0.50
	Llama-3-70B-Instruct	**0.92**	**0.86**	**0.95**	**0.89**
	Mean	0.65	0.61	0.53	0.51
4 - Syntactic Inconsistency	Bloom-176B	0.36	0.32	0.23	0.27
	Mixtral-7B-Instruct	0.50	0.59	0.63	0.49
	Gemma2-9B-Instruct	0.26	0.08	0.37	0.13
	Llama-3-70B-Instruct	**0.99**	**0.99**	**0.97**	**0.98**
	Mean	0.53	0.50	0.55	0.47

Problem 3, focused on detecting semantic inconsistencies, yielded similar trends, with Llama-3-70B-Instruct showing the highest accuracy (0.92) and F1-score (0.89). The mean accuracy across all models for this problem was 0.65, with a precision of 0.61, recall of 0.53, and F1-score of 0.51.

For **Problem 4**, which addressed syntactic inconsistencies in RDF triples, Llama-3-70B-Instruct delivered the best results with an accuracy of 0.99, precision of 0.99, recall of 0.97, and F1-score of 0.98. The mean accuracy for this problem across models was 0.53, with a mean precision of 0.50, recall of 0.55, and F1-score of 0.47.

Figure 2 presents the mean metric values across all four problems, highlighting Llama-3-70B-Instruct as the top-performing model, with a mean accuracy of 0.93, precision of 0.89, recall of 0.95, and F1-score of 0.90. Mixtral-7B-Instruct and Gemma2-9B-Instruct had moderate overall results, with mean accuracies of 0.55 and 0.59, respectively. Mixtral-7B-Instruct exhibited a mean precision of 0.57, recall of 0.61, and F1-score of 0.50, while Gemma2-9B-Instruct achieved a mean precision of 0.60, recall of 0.56, and F1-score of 0.46. Bloom-176B had the lowest mean with an accuracy of 0.41, precision of 0.42, recall of 0.38, and F1-score of 0.36 across all problems.

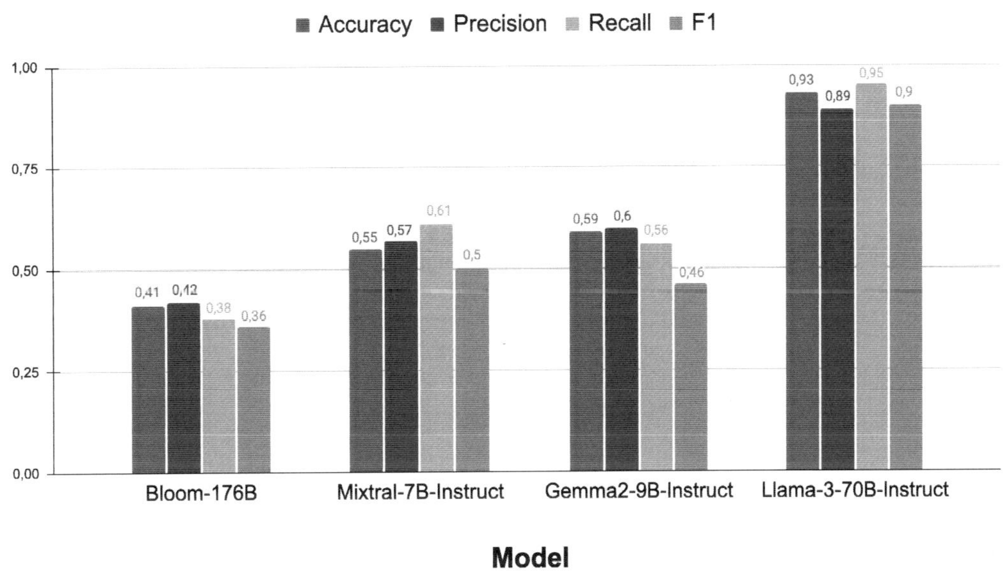

Figure 2: Summarization of the results achieved in the experimental evaluation. The x-axis represents the models. The y-axis represents values in the range [0,1] of each metric. The values shown are the mean values for each metric (accuracy, precision, recall, and F1) across all four problems. For example, the accuracy for Bloom-176B (0.41) was calculated by averaging the accuracy results obtained across the four problems, and similarly for the other metrics and models.

Text2Cypher: Bridging Natural Language and Graph Databases

Makbule Gulcin Ozsoy
Neo4j / London, UK
makbule.ozsoy@neo4j.com

Leila Messallem
Neo4j / Malmö, Sweden
leila.messallem@neo4j.com

Jon Besga
Neo4j / London, UK
jon.besga@neo4j.com

Gianandrea Minneci
Neo4j / London, UK
gianandrea.minneci@neo4j.com

Abstract

Knowledge graphs use nodes, relationships, and properties to represent arbitrarily complex data. When stored in a graph database, the Cypher query language enables efficient modeling and querying of knowledge graphs. However, using Cypher requires specialized knowledge, which can present a challenge for non-expert users. Our work Text2Cypher aims to bridge this gap by translating natural language queries into Cypher query language and extending the utility of knowledge graphs to non-technical expert users. While large language models (LLMs) can be used for this purpose, they often struggle to capture complex nuances, resulting in incomplete or incorrect outputs. Fine-tuning LLMs on domain-specific datasets has proven to be a more promising approach, but the limited availability of high-quality, publicly available Text2Cypher datasets makes this challenging. In this work, we show how we combined, cleaned and organized several publicly available datasets into a total of 44,387 instances, enabling effective fine-tuning and evaluation. Models fine-tuned on this dataset showed significant performance gains, with improvements in Google-BLEU and Exact Match scores over baseline models, highlighting the importance of high-quality datasets and fine-tuning in improving Text2Cypher performance.

1 Introduction

Databases are essential in applications, supporting data storage and knowledge management, and are typically accessed via query languages like SQL (for relational databases) or Cypher (for graph databases). With advancements in LLMs, users can now query databases using natural language through applications that perform tasks such as Text2SQL or Text2Cypher. Consequently, even with minimal technical expertise, users can easily retrieve information, build applications such as dashboards or analytics, or integrate knowledge into other systems, such as Retrieval-Augmented Generation (RAG). The Text2Cypher task converts plain language questions into Cypher query language (see Figure 1). In the figure, a user wants to write a Cypher query for *'What are the movies of Tom Hanks'*. A Text2Cypher model translates the input natural language question into Cypher, i.e., it returns *'MATCH (actor:Person {name: "Tom Hanks"})-[:ACTED_IN]->(movie:Movie) RETURN movie.title AS movies'*. This generated Cypher query can then be used to retrieve relevant data from the database, allowing for utilization based on the needs of the user.

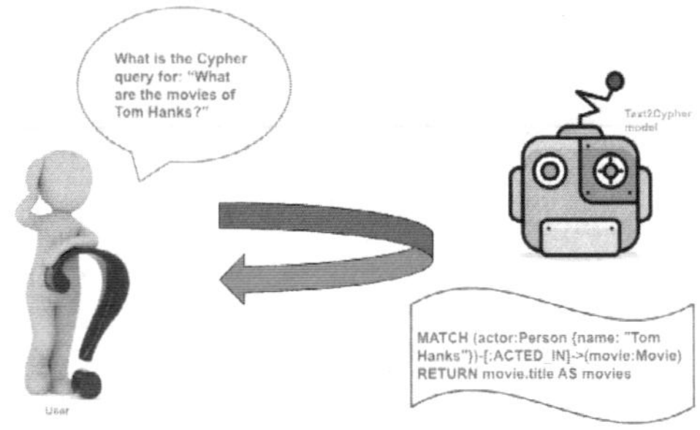

Figure 1: User wants to write a Cypher query for 'What are the movies of Tom Hanks'. A Text2Cypher model translates the input natural language question into Cypher, i.e., 'MATCH (actor:Person {name: "Tom Hanks"})-[:ACTED_IN]->(movie:Movie) RETURN movie.title AS movies'

Foundational large language models (LLMs) can be utilized for Text2Cypher task directly with an appropriate prompt. However, they may struggle with complex queries, leading to incomplete or incorrect outputs which damage the utility of the knowledge graph. Fine-tuning LLMs on domain-specific datasets offers a promising solution but requires high quality data that pairs natural language queries with Cypher translations, plus schema information for greater accuracy. However, creating such a dataset is challenging, as it requires an understand-

Proceedings of the Generative AI and Knowledge Graph Workshop (GenAIK), pages 100–108
January 19, 2025.

ing of graph representation, domain-specific knowledge to formulate effective natural language questions, and proficiency in Cypher syntax. If the training set does not include high-quality, diverse and sufficient examples, the fine-tuned Text2Cypher model may underperform.

The number of publicly available Text2Cypher datasets is limited. A few examples include those created by Neo4jLabs (Neo4jLabs, 2024), datasets converted from Text2SQL sets (Zhao et al., 2023c,b; SemanticParser4Graph, 2024), and others constructed synthetically (Zhong et al., 2024). However, these datasets are prepared independently, which makes it difficult to use them together. In this work, we combine and refine instances from publicly available datasets, creating a large dataset for training and testing, and use it to benchmark and fine-tune foundational models for Text2Cypher.

Our main contributions are as follows:

- We combine instances from publicly available datasets, refining and organizing them to enhance usability. The final dataset includes $44,387$ instances, with a training and test split, of $39,554$ and $4,833$ instances, respectively. The dataset is made available to the public [1].
- We use this new dataset to benchmark foundational and previously fine-tuned models on the Text2Cypher task. The results showed that large-foundational models performed the best, however, the fine-tuned models showed promise for improving performance.
- We fine-tuned a set of selected foundational models using the new dataset and compared their performance to benchmark results. The results showed that all the fine-tuned models achieve better results than their baseline models. One of the fine-tuned models are made publicly accessible [2].

The paper is structured as follows: Section 2 discusses related work on translating natural language to query languages, with a focus on Text2Cypher. Section 3 details the dataset preparation process. Section 4 and Section 5 present our experiments for benchmarking and fine-tuning. Finally, Section 6 concludes the paper.

[1]Dataset: `https://huggingface.co/datasets/neo4j/text2cypher-2024v1`

[2]A finetuned model: `https://huggingface.co/neo4j/text2cypher-gemma-2-9b-it-finetuned-2024v1`

2 Related Work

2.1 Graph Databases and Cypher Language

Graph Database Systems store, manage, and retrieve graph data, where nodes, relationships, and their properties are used for representing real-world knowledge (Zheng et al., 2024). These systems enable efficient querying of relationships and offer easy visualization (Yoon et al., 2017).

Companies specializing in graph databases include Neo4j (Neo4j, 2024), NebulaGraph (Wu et al., 2022), and Amazon Neptune (Bebee et al., 2018). In April 2024, GQL standard (ISO/IEC 39075:2024) (languages – GQL, 2024) was released, providing a unified query language for graph databases. The ISO GQL standard is heavily influenced by Neo4j's Cypher language (both share a large amount of syntax and they are both declarative pattern-matching languages). So while this work focuses on translating natural language into Cypher queries, the general approach will be applicable to GQL when it is more widespread.

2.2 Natural Language to Code Generation

Converting natural language to executable code is essential for applications like database interfaces and virtual assistants (Pasupat and Liang, 2015; Yu et al., 2018; Agashe et al., 2019; Lai et al., 2023; Zhong et al., 2024). Advancements in large language models (LLMs) have enabled significant progress in translating natural language into query languages like SQL or Cypher. This capability allows users to retrieve information, build dashboards, and integrate database knowledge into systems like Retrieval-Augmented Generation (RAG).

There has been extensive research on the Text2SQL task, which translates natural language queries to SQL (Yu et al., 2018; Guo et al., 2019; Rajkumar et al., 2022; Li et al., 2023; Fan et al., 2024; Li et al., 2024). In contrast, there is less work focused on the Text2Cypher task, which translates natural language queries into Cypher. This disparity stems from SQL's dominance in relational databases and traditionally high industry demand (Memgraph, 2024). However, graph-based data representation is not only a more obvious fit for knowledge graphs, but is gaining recognition for addressing issues like hallucinations in RAG models. As such interest in Cypher is increasing, and Cypher's efficiency in expressing complex, interconnected queries makes it a compelling alternative to SQL for knowledge graphs (and other domains).

2.3 Text2Cypher Task

The Text2Cypher task translates natural language queries into Cypher queries (see Figure 1). Large language models (LLMs) can handle this with zero- or few-shot prompts, which have shown promise but are still imperfect (Chen et al., 2021). Fine-tuning LLMs offers a more robust alternative, though it is limited by the scarcity of relevant datasets and high computational costs (Ni et al., 2023). Some research has focused on creating datasets for Text2Cypher, while others have concentrated on model benchmarking and fine-tuning for this task.

Some dataset preparation efforts for Text2Cypher involve translating existing datasets from other query languages, while others focus on creating dedicated datasets. Examples of translations include S2CTrans (Zhao et al., 2023a), which converts SPARQL queries into Cypher in order to handle complex graph queries, and CySpider (Zhao et al., 2023b) and Rel2Graph (Zhao et al., 2023c), which map SQL queries to Cypher and create parallel corpora of natural language-to-Cypher pairs. Specific Text2Cypher datasets include Neo4jLabs datasets (Neo4jLabs, 2024), which are generated via LLMs and their crowd-sourcing tool (Bratanič, 2024c). Opitz and Hochgeschwender (Opitz and Hochgeschwender, 2022) and SyntheT2C (Zhong et al., 2024) used synthetic methods to generate Cypher query data. While several efforts have been made to create datasets for the Text2Cypher task, these datasets are often developed independently. In this work, we aim to compile a well-structured Text2Cypher dataset by combining and structuring instances from publicly available sources.

Some research has focused on benchmarking and fine-tuning models for the Text2Cypher task: Authors from Neo4j (Bratanič, 2024a) released fine-tuned models based on their datasets, using LLMs like LLama and Codestral. GPT4Graph (Guo et al., 2023) evaluated LLMs on graph tasks, including Cypher query generation, using the MetaQA (Zhang et al., 2018) dataset and testing InstructGPT-3 (Ouyang et al., 2022) in zero- and one-shot settings. TopoChat (Xu et al., 2024) developed a material sciences dataset, using prompts to generate Cypher queries with foundational LLMs. Baraki et al. (Baraki, 2024) leveraged Neo4jLabs' crowd-sourced and synthetic datasets to fine-tune models, using the crowd-sourced set for evaluation. TransKGQA (Chong et al., 2024) extracted information from knowledge graphs, using the 'sentence-transformers/all-MiniLM-L12-v2' model to generate Cypher queries. Although these works have provided fine-tuned models, the number of models used was limited. In our work, after constructing a larger and more organized dataset, we benchmark and fine-tune a wider range of baseline LLMs.

Table 1: Data fields

Field name	Description
question	Textual question
schema	The database schema
cypher	Output cypher query
data_source	Alias of the dataset source
database_reference	Alias of the database
instance_id	Incremental index

3 Dataset Construction

While several Text2Cypher datasets exist, many are prepared separately, making them hard to use together. In this work we bring instances from publicly available datasets together, clean and organize them for smoother use. For this purpose, we executed three main steps: (i) Identification and collection of publicly available datasets, (ii) Combining and cleaning the data, and (iii) Creating the training and test splits.

3.1 Identification and collection of publicly available datasets

As the initial step, we identified the datasets which are already publicly available. We have identified 25 different resources from (i) Neo4j resources (including Neo4jLabs) (ii) HuggingFace (HF) datasets and (iii) Academic papers. Out of these resources, we were able to utilize 16 of those datasets, as they met our criteria of including natural language question and Cypher query pairs, as well as database schema information, along with appropriate licensing and accessibility.

3.2 Combining and cleaning the data

After identifying the input datasets, we standardized them into a single format. Each row was reformatted to include fields ["question", "schema", "cypher", "data_source", "database_reference", "instance_id"], as described in Table 1. One of the fields, namely "database_reference", requires particular attention. In some cases within the combined dataset, database access is available where the reference or the generated Cypher queries can be executed. Further details about these databases can be found at the page of Neo4jLabs-Crowdsourcing Initiative (Bratanič, 2024c). The combined dataset is further cleaned in two steps:

- **Manual checks and updates**: This step aims to produce more reliable and error-free output data. Queries are manually reviewed, and errors are corrected through straightforward removals or updates: (i) Updating Cypher queries, such as removing unwanted characters (e.g., back-tick) (ii) Removing irrelevant questions (e.g., "Lorem ipsum ...") (iii) Deduplicating rows based on the ["question", "cypher"] pairs.
- **Syntax validation**: Each Cypher query is checked for syntax errors by running 'EXPLAIN' clauses in a local Neo4j database. Queries that trigger syntax errors are identified and removed from the combined dataset. Additionally, the queries are de-duplicated.

3.3 Creating the training and test splits

Having the cleaned dataset, the final step is to prepare the training and test splits. We have identified 3 groups of datasets: (i) Train-specific datasets: Files with "train" in the name, used for training. (ii) Test-specific datasets: Files with "test" or "dev" in the name, used for testing. (iii) Remaining datasets: Files with no specified use. We assigned Train-specific datasets to the training split and Test-specific datasets to the test split. The remaining datasets were split 90:10 for training and testing, respectively. Each split was shuffled to prevent over-fitting from sequence or repetitive questions.

The data preparation resulted in $44,387$ instances, with $39,554$ instances in the training split and $4,833$ instances in the test split. The train and test splits contain $\sim$89% and $\sim$11% of the overall data, respectively. Their distribution across data sources is similar, as shown in Figure 2. As explained previously, not every instance in the training and test sets has database access, as indicated by the "database_reference" field. Analyzing the distribution of instances with database access reveals that the training set contains $22,093$ such instances (55.85% of the total), while the test set has $2,471$ instances (51.12% of the total). These instances are later used in the experimentation with an additional evaluation procedure.

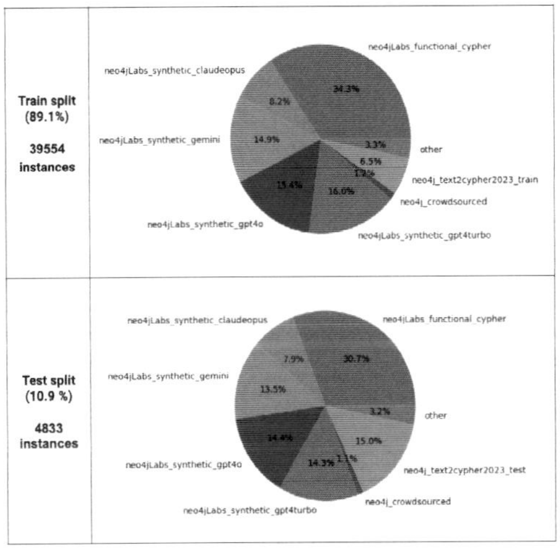

Figure 2: Data distribution: The train and test splits contain $\sim$89% and $\sim$11% of the overall data, respectively.

4 Model Evaluation and Benchmarking

After constructing a larger and more organized dataset, this section presents the benchmarking results.

4.1 Evaluation metrics

Text2Cypher is a type of text-to-text generation task, where natural language questions are translated into Cypher queries. Therefore, evaluation metrics commonly used in other text-to-text tasks, such as machine translation and summarization, can also be applied to this task. Using HuggingFace Evaluate library (HuggingFace, 2024), we computed: (i) Text2Text comparison metrics, such as ROUGE, BLEU, METEOR (ii) Embedding similarity metrics, such as BERTScore, FrugalScore (iii) Text similarity metrics, such as Cosine and Jaro-Winkler similarity, and (iv) Exact Match score. Although we calculated all these metrics, we primarily use Google-BLEU and Exact Match scores throughout the paper.

4.2 Experimental Setup

For benchmarking the models, we used the test split of the larger dataset introduced in Section 3. Closed models were evaluated through APIs provided by the respective companies. For the other models, which are openly accessible via HuggingFace (HF), we utilized HF interfaces. To access GPUs for evaluation, we employed RunPod (RunPod, 2024) environments. Where relevant, we followed the instructions outlined in Table 3, which

Table 2: Models used for benchmarking

Type	Name	Base model
HF	hf_ft_lakkeo_stable_cypher_instruct3B	Stability AI/Stable-code-instruct-3b
HF	hf_ft_tomasonjo_text2cypher	Meta/Llama-3-8b-Instruct
HF	hf_ft_neo4j_text2cypher_23_codellama	Meta/CodeLlama13B
OpenAI	openai_ft_neo4j_text2cypher_23_gpt3_5	OpenAI/GPT3.5
HF	hf_foundational_meta_llama3_1_8B_instruct	Meta/LLama-3.1-8B-instruct
HF	hf_foundational_codeLlama_7B_instruct_hf	Meta/CodeLLama-7B-instruct
HF	hf_foundational_gemma2_9B_it	Google/Gemma-2-9B-it
HF	hf_foundational_codegemma_7B_it	Google/CodeGemma-7B-it
OpenAI	openai_gpt3_5	OpenAI/GPT-3.5
OpenAI	openai_gpt4_o	OpenAI/GPT-4o
OpenAI	openai_gpt4_o_mini	OpenAI/GPT-4o-mini
VertexAI	gemini-1.0-pro-002	Google/Gemini-1.0-Pro
GoogleAIStudio	gemini-1.5-flash-001	Google/Gemini-1.5-Flash
GoogleAIStudio	gemini-1.5-pro-001	Google/Gemini-1.5-Pro

Table 3: Instructions used

Type	Instruction prompt
System Instruct.	Task: Generate Cypher statement to query a graph database. Instructions: Use only the provided relationship types and properties in the schema. Do not use any other relationship types or properties that are not provided in the schema. Do not include any explanations or apologies in your responses. Do not respond to any questions that might ask anything else than for you to construct a Cypher statement. Do not include any text except the generated Cypher statement.
User Instruct.	Generate Cypher statement to query a graph database. Use only the provided relationship types and properties in the schema. Schema: {schema} Question: {question} Cypher output:

were inspired from tips provided by authors from Neo4j (Bratanič, 2024b).

We defined two types of evaluation procedures:

- **Translation-based evaluation**: The generated Cypher queries are compared with the reference Cypher queries based solely on the textual content. The evaluation metrics used for this comparison are detailed in Section 4.1.
- **Execution-based evaluation**: The generated and reference Cypher queries are executed on the target databases, and their outputs are collected. The collected execution results are converted into string representations (ordered lexicographically for consistency). The same evaluation metrics used in the translation-based evaluation are then applied to these outputs.

4.3 Benchmarking results

For benchmarking, we aimed to evaluate not only baseline LLMs but also previously fine-tuned models specifically tailored for the Text2Cypher task. The list of models used for benchmarking purpose are listed in Table 2. In the table, first group includes the fine-tuned models, second group includes the open-weighted models and the last group includes the closed models.

Figure 3 presents the performance comparison of the selected models on the test split. The figure presents Google-BLEU score for translation-based and Exact Match score for execution-based evaluation. Among the previously fine-tuned models, i.e., with different data, HF/tomasonjo_text2cypher performed best, but this may be misleading as it had encountered 14.4% of the test data during training. Among the open-weighted models, Google/Gemma-2-9B-it is the best performing model. Contrary to expectations, the code-focused models (e.g., CodeGemma) did not outperform the baseline models. This may be attributed to the fact that Cypher queries are relatively closer to natural language, reducing the advantage of code-specific models. Among closed-

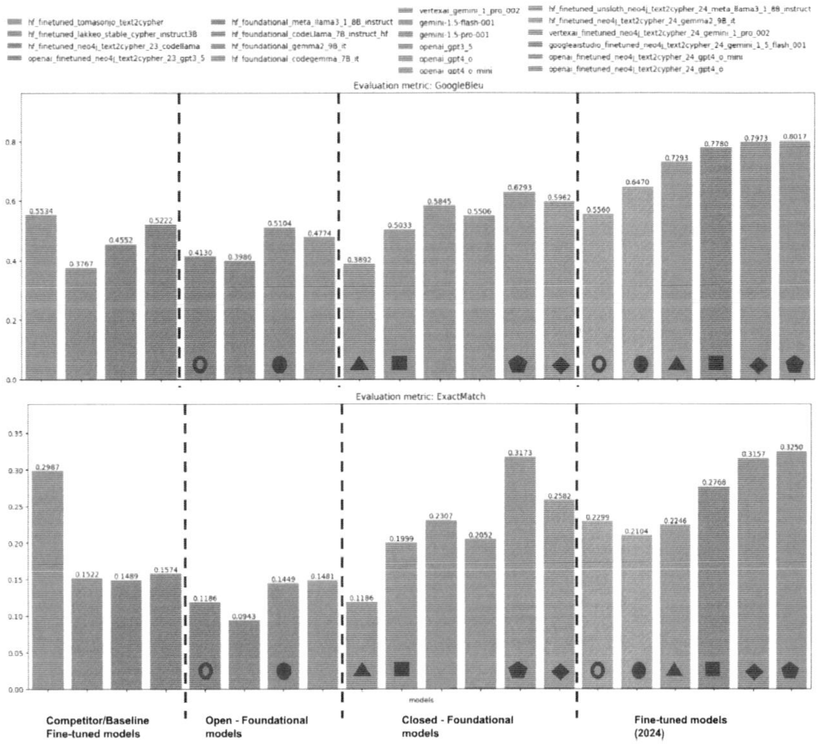

Figure 3: Performance comparison of the baseline and finetuned models. Presents Google-BLEU score for translation-based and Exact Match score for execution-based evaluation.

foundational models, the best performing models are OpenAI/GPT4o, OpenAI/GPT4o-mini, and Google/Gemini-1.5-Pro-001 led in performance, with larger models outperforming smaller ones.

Overall, closed foundational models like GPT and Gemini achieved the best performance, though at higher costs. Fine-tuned models improved baseline open-weighted models. In the next section, we explore the process of fine-tuning models and evaluating them using the new dataset introduced in Section 3.

5 Model Finetuning and Evaluation

Based on the findings of benchmarking, presented in Section 4, we selected six baseline models for our subsequent steps, presented in Table 4. In the table, first group includes the open-weighted models, while the second group includes the closed models. Although some models, such as Google/Gemini-1.5-Pro, demonstrated better performance in the benchmark results, they were unavailable for fine-tuning at the time of this analysis and are therefore not included in this work.

Table 4: Models used for fine-tuning

Type	Base model
HF	Meta/LLama-3.1-8B-instruct
HF	Google/Gemma-2-9B-it
OpenAI	OpenAI/GPT-4o
OpenAI	OpenAI/GPT-4o-mini
VertexAI	Google/Gemini-1.0-Pro
GoogleAIStudio	Google/Gemini-1.5-Flash

5.1 Experimental setup

For the finetuning process, we used the training split of the larger dataset introduced in Section 3. The closed models were trained through APIs provided by their respective companies, while the other models were finetuned using HuggingFace (HF) or Unsloth (Unsloth, 2024) interfaces on GPU machines hosted in RunPod (RunPod, 2024) environments. The evaluation procedures and metrics were identical to those used in benchmarking section, Section 4. The instructions remained consistent with those outlined in Table 3. We used Google-BLEU score for translation-based and Exact Match score for execution-based evaluation.

Table 5: The improvements of the fine-tuned models over the baseline models

Baseline model	ΔGoogle BLEU	ΔExact Match
HF/LLama3.1-8B-it	~0.14	~0.11
HF/Gemma2-9B-it	~0.13	~0.07
VertexAI/Gemini-1.0-Pro-002	~0.34	~0.11
GoogleAIStudio/Gemini-1.5-Flash-001	~0.27	~0.09
OpenAI/Gpt-4o-mini	~0.20	~0.06
OpenAI/Gpt-4o	~0.18	~0.01

5.2 Finetuning results

The evaluation results for all models, including those previously benchmarked, are shown in Figure 3. The last group in the figure highlights the fine-tuned models trained on the dataset introduced in Section 3. For easier comparison, red shapes are used to link each fine-tuned model with its corresponding baseline version. The figure shows that all fine-tuned models achieve better results than their baseline models. The best results are obtained by the Finetuned-OpenAI/Gpt4o, Finetuned-OpenAI/Gpt4o-mini and Finetuned-GoogleAIStudio/Gemini-1.5-Flash-001 models.

The improvements in the fine-tuned models over the baseline models are presented in Table 5. The enhancements for models that have already performed well are relatively smaller than others. For example, OpenAI/Gpt-4 shows an 0.18 increase in the Google-BLEU score, while VertexAI/Gemini-1.0-Pro-002 demonstrates a 0.34 increase. The improvements of the finetuned open-weighted models, i.e. HF/LLama3.1-8B-it and HF/Gemma2-9B-it, are relatively less pronounced. During fine-tuning of these models, our goal was to minimize resource usage (e.g., cost and memory). As a result, with better-tuned parameters, we could potentially achieve even stronger results.

Although all the fine-tuned models showed improvements in Google-BLEU and Exact Match scores, it is important to remain aware of the potential risks and pitfalls associated with fine-tuning.

6 Conclusion

Databases are essential for data storage, management, and retrieval, often accessed through query languages like Cypher. Recent advancements in large language models (LLMs) have made it possible to access databases using natural language through tasks like Text2Cypher. While LLMs can be directly used for this task, they often struggle with complex queries, resulting in incomplete or incorrect Cypher outputs. Fine-tuning LLMs on specific Text2Cypher datasets offers a more effective solution. However, publicly available Text2Cypher datasets are limited and often created independently, making them difficult to combine and use effectively. To address this, we combined and refined several datasets into a unified set of 44,387 instances, with 89% in the training split and 11% in testing. Fine-tuned models trained on this dataset outperformed baselines, achieving up to a 0.34 increase in Google-BLEU score and a 0.11 increase in Exact Match score. This work highlights the importance of dataset and fine-tuning for Text2Cypher task. Future work will refine the dataset further, analyze challenging cases, and explore improvements through prompt engineering and model optimization.

Limitations

The previous sections demonstrated how fine-tuned models significantly boost performance. However, there are several risks and pitfalls that must be considered.

Even though we de-duplicated the dataset by ["question", "cypher"] pairs, it is still possible to have instances where the same "question" appears with different "cypher" outputs. In such cases, these instances may have been split between the training and test sets, meaning that fine-tuned models could have already encountered the same "question" during training. However, since these instances have different "cypher" outputs, even if the fine-tuned models memorize the "cypher" output for the question, their generated response would be incorrect. This essentially penalizes the models for having seen and memorized the question. In the future, we plan to clean the test set of such instances, re-run the evaluation, and assess any performance differences.

Our dataset is constructed by collecting and combining publicly available datasets, which may include paraphrased versions of the same questions. It is known that training on paraphrased examples of the test set may artificially inflate the performance of the fine-tuned model (Yang et al., 2023). Additionally, both the training and test sets are drawn from the same data distribution, sampled from a larger dataset. If the data distribution shifts, the results may not hold up in the same way.

Finally, the dataset used was gathered from publicly available sources. Over time, foundational models may gain access to both the training and test sets, potentially achieving similar or even better performance results in the future.

References

Rajas Agashe, Srinivasan Iyer, and Luke Zettlemoyer. 2019. Juice: A large scale distantly supervised dataset for open domain context-based code generation. *arXiv preprint arXiv:1910.02216*.

Welemhret Welay Baraki. 2024. Leveraging large language models for accurate cypher query generation: Natural language query to cypher statements. Master degree project, University of Skövde. https://www.diva-portal.org/smash/get/diva2:1881385/FULLTEXT01.pdf.

Bradley R Bebee, Daniel Choi, Ankit Gupta, Andi Gutmans, Ankesh Khandelwal, Yigit Kiran, Sainath Mallidi, Bruce McGaughy, Mike Personick, Karthik Rajan, et al. 2018. Amazon neptune: Graph data management in the cloud. In *ISWC (P&D/Industry/BlueSky)*.

Tomaž Bratanič. 2024a. Hf models. https://huggingface.co/tomasonjo.

Tomaž Bratanič. 2024b. Langchain cypher search: Tips and tricks. https://neo4j.com/developer-blog/langchain-cypher-search-tips-tricks/.

Tomaž Bratanič. 2024c. Neo4jlabs crowdsourcing initiative. https://medium.com/@bratanic-tomaz/e65ba51916d4.

Mark Chen, Jerry Tworek, Heewoo Jun, Qiming Yuan, Henrique Ponde De Oliveira Pinto, Jared Kaplan, Harri Edwards, Yuri Burda, Nicholas Joseph, Greg Brockman, et al. 2021. Evaluating large language models trained on code. *arXiv preprint arXiv:2107.03374*.

You Li Chong, Chin Poo Lee, Shahrin Zen Muhd-Yassin, Kian Ming Lim, and Ahmad Kamsani Samingan. 2024. Transkgqa: Enhanced knowledge graph question answering with sentence transformers. *IEEE Access*.

Yuankai Fan, Zhenying He, Tonghui Ren, Can Huang, Yinan Jing, Kai Zhang, and X Sean Wang. 2024. Metasql: A generate-then-rank framework for natural language to sql translation. *arXiv preprint arXiv:2402.17144*.

Jiaqi Guo, Zecheng Zhan, Yan Gao, Yan Xiao, Jian-Guang Lou, Ting Liu, and Dongmei Zhang. 2019. Towards complex text-to-sql in cross-domain database with intermediate representation. *arXiv preprint arXiv:1905.08205*.

Jiayan Guo, Lun Du, Hengyu Liu, Mengyu Zhou, Xinyi He, and Shi Han. 2023. Gpt4graph: Can large language models understand graph structured data? an empirical evaluation and benchmarking. *arXiv preprint arXiv:2305.15066*.

HuggingFace. 2024. Huggingface evaluate. https://huggingface.co/evaluate-metric.

Yuhang Lai, Chengxi Li, Yiming Wang, Tianyi Zhang, Ruiqi Zhong, Luke Zettlemoyer, Wen-tau Yih, Daniel Fried, Sida Wang, and Tao Yu. 2023. Ds-1000: A natural and reliable benchmark for data science code generation. In *International Conference on Machine Learning*, pages 18319–18345. PMLR.

ISO/IEC 39075:2024 Information Technology – Database languages – GQL. 2024. Gql database languages. https://jtc1info.org/slug/gql-database-language/.

Haoyang Li, Jing Zhang, Cuiping Li, and Hong Chen. 2023. Resdsql: Decoupling schema linking and skeleton parsing for text-to-sql. In *Proceedings of the AAAI Conference on Artificial Intelligence*, volume 37, pages 13067–13075.

Jinyang Li, Binyuan Hui, Ge Qu, Jiaxi Yang, Binhua Li, Bowen Li, Bailin Wang, Bowen Qin, Ruiying Geng, Nan Huo, et al. 2024. Can llm already serve as a database interface? a big bench for large-scale database grounded text-to-sqls. *Advances in Neural Information Processing Systems*, 36.

Memgraph. 2024. Graph database vs relational database. https://memgraph.com/blog/graph-database-vs-relational-database.

Neo4j. 2024. Neo4j graph database. https://neo4j.com/.

Neo4jLabs. 2024. Neo4jlabs datasets. https://github.com/neo4j-labs/text2cypher/tree/main/datasets.

Ansong Ni, Srini Iyer, Dragomir Radev, Veselin Stoyanov, Wen-tau Yih, Sida Wang, and Xi Victoria Lin. 2023. Lever: Learning to verify language-to-code generation with execution. In *International Conference on Machine Learning*, pages 26106–26128. PMLR.

Dominik Opitz and Nico Hochgeschwender. 2022. From zero to hero: generating training data for question-to-cypher models. In *Proceedings of the 1st International Workshop on Natural Language-based Software Engineering*, pages 17–20.

Long Ouyang, Jeffrey Wu, Xu Jiang, Diogo Almeida, Carroll Wainwright, Pamela Mishkin, Chong Zhang, Sandhini Agarwal, Katarina Slama, Alex Ray, et al. 2022. Training language models to follow instructions with human feedback. *Advances in neural information processing systems*, 35:27730–27744.

Panupong Pasupat and Percy Liang. 2015. Compositional semantic parsing on semi-structured tables. *arXiv preprint arXiv:1508.00305*.

Nitarshan Rajkumar, Raymond Li, and Dzmitry Bahdanau. 2022. Evaluating the text-to-sql capabilities of large language models. *arXiv preprint arXiv:2204.00498*.

RunPod. 2024. Runpod. `https://www.runpod.io/`.

SemanticParser4Graph. 2024. Semanticparser4graph datasets. `https://github.com/22842219/SemanticParser4Graph/tree/main/sp_data_folder`.

Unsloth. 2024. Unsloth ai - open source fine-tuning for llms. `https://unsloth.ai/`.

Min Wu, Xinglu Yi, Hui Yu, Yu Liu, and Yujue Wang. 2022. Nebula graph: An open source distributed graph database. *arXiv preprint arXiv:2206.07278*.

HuangChao Xu, Baohua Zhang, Zhong Jin, Tiannian Zhu, Quansheng Wu, and Hongming Weng. 2024. Topochat: Enhancing topological materials retrieval with large language model and multi-source knowledge. *arXiv preprint arXiv:2409.13732*.

Shuo Yang, Wei-Lin Chiang, Lianmin Zheng, Joseph E Gonzalez, and Ion Stoica. 2023. Rethinking benchmark and contamination for language models with rephrased samples. *arXiv preprint arXiv:2311.04850*.

Byoung-Ha Yoon, Seon-Kyu Kim, and Seon-Young Kim. 2017. Use of graph database for the integration of heterogeneous biological data. *Genomics & informatics*, 15(1):19.

Tao Yu, Rui Zhang, Kai Yang, Michihiro Yasunaga, Dongxu Wang, Zifan Li, James Ma, Irene Li, Qingning Yao, Shanelle Roman, et al. 2018. Spider: A large-scale human-labeled dataset for complex and cross-domain semantic parsing and text-to-sql task. *arXiv preprint arXiv:1809.08887*.

Yuyu Zhang, Hanjun Dai, Zornitsa Kozareva, Alexander J Smola, and Le Song. 2018. Variational reasoning for question answering with knowledge graph. In *AAAI*.

Zihao Zhao, Xiaodong Ge, Zhihong Shen, Chuan Hu, and Huajin Wang. 2023a. S2ctrans: Building a bridge from sparql to cypher. In *International Conference on Database and Expert Systems Applications*, pages 424–430. Springer.

Ziyu Zhao, Wei Liu, Tim French, and Michael Stewart. 2023b. Cyspider: A neural semantic parsing corpus with baseline models for property graphs. In *Australasian Joint Conference on Artificial Intelligence*, pages 120–132. Springer.

Ziyu Zhao, Wei Liu, Tim French, and Michael Stewart. 2023c. Rel2graph: Automated mapping from relational databases to a unified property knowledge graph. *arXiv preprint arXiv:2310.01080*.

Yingying Zheng, Wensheng Dou, Lei Tang, Ziyu Cui, Yu Gao, Jiansen Song, Liang Xu, Jiaxin Zhu, Wei Wang, Jun Wei, et al. 2024. Testing gremlin-based graph database systems via query disassembling. In *Proceedings of the 33rd ACM SIGSOFT International Symposium on Software Testing and Analysis*, pages 1695–1707.

Ziije Zhong, Linqing Zhong, Zhaoze Sun, Qingyun Jin, Zengchang Qin, and Xiaofan Zhang. 2024. Synthet2c: Generating synthetic data for fine-tuning large language models on the text2cypher task. *arXiv preprint arXiv:2406.10710*.

KGFakeNet: A Knowledge Graph-Enhanced Model for Fake News Detection

Anuj Kumar[1], **Pardeep Kumar**[2], **Abhishek Yadav**[1], **Satyadev Ahlawat**[2], **Yamuna Prasad**[1]
[1]Department of Computer Science & Engineering, Indian Institute of Technology Jammu, India
[2]Department of Electrical Engineering, Indian Institute of Technology Jammu, India
{anuj,pardeep.kumar,2021pcs1015,satyadev.ahlawat,yamuna.prasad}@iitjammu.ac.in

Abstract

The proliferation of fake news on social media has intensified the spread of misinformation, promoting societal biases, hate, and violence. While recent advancements in Generative AI (GenAI), particularly large language models (LLMs), have shown promise, these models often need more structured representation for accurate verification, as they rely on pre-trained data patterns without access to real-time or validated information. This study presents a framework that utilizes Open Information Extractor 6 (OpenIE6) to extract triplet relationships (subject-predicate-object) from statements and justifications to compute the cosine similarity between the Knowledge Graphs (KGs) of the statements and their supporting justification to precisely measure the relevance and alignment between them. This similarity feature is integrated with an attention mechanism over GenAI-generated embeddings to enhance the model's ability to capture semantic features accurately. In addition, a Multi-Layer Perceptron (MLP) classifier is employed to integrate all features, resulting in a 4% improvement in accuracy and a 5% increase in F1-score over state-of-the-art LLM-based approaches.

1 Introduction

> *"A lie gets halfway around the world before the truth has a chance to get its boots on."*
>
> *Attributed to Winston Churchill*

The rapid spread of misleading and factually inaccurate information, commonly called fake news, has become a critical issue in the digital age. Misinformation disrupts democratic processes, distorts public discourse, and misguides individual decision-making (Sharma et al., 2019). With digital platforms serving as the primary source for news consumption, the influence of fake news has grown exponentially, leading to significant societal consequences. These platforms allow for the swift dissemination of information, creating an environment where fake news can influence elections, deepen societal divides, and, in extreme cases, incite violence.

As the volume of information expands, traditional manual fact-checking methods cannot keep pace, highlighting the need for automated detection systems. Moreover, early models for fake news detection(Girgis et al., 2018; Trueman et al., 2021; Long et al., 2017) primarily focused on statement-level analysis, classifying statements as true or false. However, real-world misinformation often blends truth and falsehood, defying simple categorization. This complexity has led to the use of intermediate truth classifications—such as "half true," "barely true," and "mostly false"—which better capture the nuanced nature of many news items and emphasize the need for more sophisticated detection models.

To address this, the LIAR dataset by (Wang, 2017), sourced from POLITIFACT[1], introduced a more granular classification approach, categorizing statements across six levels of truthfulness, from "true" to "pants on fire". Models using the LIAR dataset have utilized linguistic features such as emotional tone, hedging, and speaker-related attributes (Thorne and Vlachos, 2018) to improve detection. However, while the LIAR dataset supports nuanced classification, it lacks external evidence. To address this gap, the LIAR-PLUS dataset (Alhindi et al., 2018) extends LIAR by providing additional contextual information, including justifications and detailed fact-checking verdicts for each labeled statement.

With the growing prominence of Generative AI (GenAI) models (Brown et al., 2020; AI, 2024) in Natural Language Processing (NLP) tasks such as machine translation, text classification, and data extraction, these models have also been explored

[1]https://www.politifact.com/

Proceedings of the Generative AI and Knowledge Graph Workshop (GenAIK), pages 109–122
January 19, 2025. ©2025 International Committee on Computational Linguistics (ICCL)

for applications in fake news detection (Hu et al., 2022). Although powerful, GenAI models, particularly large language models (LLMs), are limited by their lack of structured representation, as they largely rely on patterns from pre-trained datasets without access to real-time, validated information sources. This limitation raises concerns about the reliability of GenAI models in fact-checking tasks, as they lack the capability to cross-reference real-world facts dynamically. Recent research has addressed this limitation by integrating knowledge graphs (KGs) with GenAI models (Gu and Krenn, 2024), utilizing KG-structured, entity-based representations to enrich models with factual and contextually relevant information.

Knowledge Graph (KG) embeddings allow models to capture relationships and concepts in a structured format, storing entities (like "Paris" or "Einstein") and their relationships (e.g., "is the capital of," "was born in") in a graph form that enables efficient retrieval of factual information. By leveraging KG embeddings capture structured relationships that enhance verification, helping reduce hallucinations and improve accuracy. Moreover, Open Information Extraction (OpenIE) (Banko et al., 2007) has become essential for transforming unstructured text into structured knowledge. OpenIE6[2] (Kolluru et al., 2020), the latest research, enables the extraction of factual statements by identifying subject-predicate-object triplets, which form the backbone of knowledge graphs. OpenIE6 surpasses earlier versions with improved contextual accuracy and scalability, making it particularly effective for large-scale data sources. By allowing dynamic extraction of factual relationships directly from a wide array of sources, OpenIE6 equips models with up-to-date, contextually relevant information—a valuable trait for domains requiring dynamic knowledge updates.

Our proposed framework, KGNewsNet, leverages OpenIE6 to extract triplet relationships from statements and justifications, generating Knowledge Graphs (KGs) that capture structured semantic relationships. Afterwards, the cosine similarity between the statement and justification KGs is computed to generate a feature that quantifies alignment between statement and their justifications. The KG embeddings and OpenIE6 reduce hallucinations by grounding answers in structured data. Combined with GenAI-generated embeddings and enhanced by an attention mechanism, this feature enables our model to prioritize relevant aspects of the statement-justification pairs, improving overall detection accuracy. Additionally, a Multi-Layer Perceptron (MLP) classifier integrates these features, yielding substantial improvements in detection performance. Our model achieves a 4% increase in accuracy and a 5% boost in F1-score over existing LLM-based approaches, demonstrating the efficacy of KG-enhanced fact-checking. The key contributions of this work are as follows:

- **OpenIE6-Driven Knowledge Graph Integration:** We integrate KGs generated by OpenIE6 to provide structured, context-rich knowledge that strengthens the structured representation of the GenAI model, enhancing statement verification.

- **Enhanced statement-justification Alignment:** Our framework employs an attention mechanism that emphasizes critical aspects of statement-justification pairs, utilizing a specialized attention module within the GenAI model to improve semantic comprehension of misinformation. Additionally, a cosine similarity feature derived from the Knowledge Graph further refines the alignment, enhancing the model's ability to verify statements accurately.

- **Enhanced Detection Performance with Multi-Layer Perceptron (MLP) Classifier:** Integrating KG-based features, GenAI embeddings, and attention yields substantial performance improvements, achieving a 45.4% accuracy in six-class classification and outperforming established GenAI models.

2 Related Work

Identifying fake news has evolved through extensive research, progressing from traditional fact-checking approaches to advanced machine learning and deep learning techniques. Initial methods primarily relied on manual fact-checking and information retrieval, but as the volume of online misinformation increased, the demand for automated solutions became imperative. Research in this area has largely focused on combining natural language processing (NLP) with machine learning to identify linguistic and thematic patterns indicative of fake news. For example, Latent Dirichlet Allocation (LDA) (Casillo et al., 2021) has been employed

[2]https://github.com/dair-iitd/openie6

to reveal hidden topics within news content, highlighting patterns that suggest deceptive intent. This early content-based approach has provided a foundational technique for detecting inconsistencies in fabricated stories. Supervised learning algorithms, including support vector machines (SVMs) and random forests, have also demonstrated effectiveness in misinformation classification, leveraging labeled data to identify fake news.

The advent of deep learning methods, such as convolutional neural networks (CNNs) and bidirectional long short-term memory networks (BiLSTMs), further improved detection by capturing nuanced textual features. Introducing pre-trained language models (PLMs) like BERT (Devlin et al., 2019; Kotonya and Toni, 2020; Shu et al., 2019; Yang et al., 2022a; Atanasova et al., 2020) marked a significant advancement in the field, as these models harness vast corpora to recognize complex language structures, capturing subtler cues of misinformation. Recent studies have also explored the role of influential users in amplifying misinformation, contributing valuable perspectives for detection systems targeting social network effects.

Label	Train	Validation	Test
Barely True	1654	237	212
False	1995	263	249
Half True	2114	248	265
Mostly True	1962	251	241
Pants on Fire	839	116	92
True	1676	169	208
Total	**10240**	**1284**	**1267**

Table 1: Dataset Statistics showing the distribution of labels across training, validation, and test splits.

The automated fact-checking systems have emerged as essential tools for combating misinformation, scaling up the verification process by cross-referencing claims with authoritative sources. Complementary approaches, including source verification, metadata analysis, and digital forensics, enhance these systems by assessing the credibility of information sources. A prominent advancement in this area involves integrating external knowledge bases (KBs) with PLMs to improve claim verification. Models like ERINE (Zhang et al., 2019) and TagMe (Ferragina and Scaiella, 2010) leverage structured factual data from repositories such as WikiData (Vrandečić and Krötzsch, 2014), allowing for more robust fact-checking by anchoring statements in verified, external data. However, despite improved accuracy, challenges remain in ensuring that relevant knowledge is effectively applied to specific statements, with issues often arising from the overgeneralization or irrelevance of incorporated knowledge. Addressing these limitations requires a balance between leveraging external data and maintaining relevance to the context of the claims being verified.

The rise of Generative AI (GenAI) models has introduced new possibilities for scalable misinformation detection by utilizing advanced language understanding and generation capabilities (Hu et al., 2022). Instruction-following models like InstructGPT (Ouyang et al., 2022) and Self-Instruct (Wang et al., 2023) have demonstrated efficacy in validating content by following structured prompts, combining data analysis with instruction-based guidelines to enhance claim verification. ChatGPT (OpenAI, 2024) adds a conversational aspect to fact-checking, enabling real-time, interactive validation through human-like dialogue, though its proprietary constraints limit customization for broader research applications.

Open-source alternatives, such as Stanford's Alpaca (Taori et al., 2023) built on the LLaMA framework (Touvron et al., 2023), offer more flexible options, allowing researchers to integrate external knowledge sources and customize models for specific applications. Recent research continues to explore instruction-following GenAI for misinformation detection, as seen in (Cheung and Lam, 2023), where external evidence retrieval is combined with instruction-based models, and in (Wang et al., 2024), which employs prompt-based modules to generate claim justifications. However, these models still face significant challenges with hallucinations, particularly in cases lacking structured, factual grounding. Integrating GenAI models with knowledge-rich databases can help mitigate this issue by supporting accuracy and consistency in generated responses, providing a clearer factual foundation for misinformation detection.

Our work, KGNewsNet, builds upon these advancements by addressing key limitations in GenAI-based misinformation detection models, particularly the insufficient integration of external evidence in models like (Cheung and Lam, 2023). KGNewsNet enhances fake news detection by combining knowledge graphs (KGs) with the LIAR-PLUS dataset, leveraging KG embeddings and attention mechanisms to incorporate structured,

Index	Column	Liar-Plus
1	ID	11972.json
2	Label	TRUE
3	Statement	Building a wall on the U.S.-Mexico border will take literally years.
4	Subject	Immigration
5	Speaker	Rick Perry
6	Job Title	Governor
7	State Info	Texas
8	Party Affiliation	Republican
9	True Counts	30
10	Mostly True Counts	30
11	Half True Counts	42
12	False Counts	23
13	Pants on Fire Counts	18
14	Context	Radio interview
15	Justification	Meantime, engineering experts agree the wall would most likely take years to complete. Keep in mind, too, that it took more than six years to build roughly 700 miles of fence and barriers along the roughly 2,000-mile U.S.-Mexico border.

Table 2: Example entry from the LIAR-PLUS dataset, showcasing metadata such as speaker details, historical truthfulness counts, and a justification for the claim.

external data into the model more effectively. This approach provides a grounded, contextually relevant framework that addresses gaps in existing PLM-based models. Our experimental results indicate a substantial improvement, with KGNewsNet achieving an accuracy of 0.454, outperforming comparable models and demonstrating its effectiveness in misinformation detection.

3 Preliminaries

3.1 Problem Definition

This work aims to develop a model that can accurately classify statements into multiple truthfulness categories by leveraging external knowledge and justifications. Let $S = \{s_1, s_2, \ldots, s_n\}$ and $J = \{j_1, j_2, \ldots, j_n\}$ represent the set of statements and justification to be classified, where each statement s_i and j_i is associated with a truthfulness label, the goal is to predict its truthfulness label $y_i \in \{c_1, c_2, \ldots, c_k\}$, with $k = 6$ corresponding to the six truthfulness categories (e.g., true, mostly true, half-true, barely true, false, and pants on fire) by considering; The textual content of the statement s_i. The corresponding justification J_i provides factual support or context for the statement. External knowledge K is derived from a knowledge graph (KG) that includes relevant factual information. Metadata M, such as the speaker information and context.

Thus, the classification function can be defined as:

$$\hat{y}_i = f(s_i, J_i, K, M)$$

Where f is the model that learns to map the combination of the statement, justification, external knowledge, and metadata to the correct truthfulness category.

The model aims to minimize the classification error across all statements in the dataset:

$$\mathcal{L} = \frac{1}{n} \sum_{i=1}^{n} \mathcal{L}(f(s_i, J_i, K, M), y_i)$$

Where $\mathcal{L}$ is the loss function (e.g., categorical cross-entropy loss) and n is the number of statements.

3.2 Dataset

The development of our advanced fact-checking model began with the use of the LIAR-PLUS dataset(Alhindi et al., 2018), an enhanced version of the original LIAR dataset(Wang, 2017). Compiled by Alhindi et al.(Alhindi et al., 2018), LIAR-PLUS consists of approximately 12.8K annotated short statements. This dataset extends beyond the original LIAR dataset by incorporating justifications, which provide essential context and explanations for each statement's truthfulness classification.

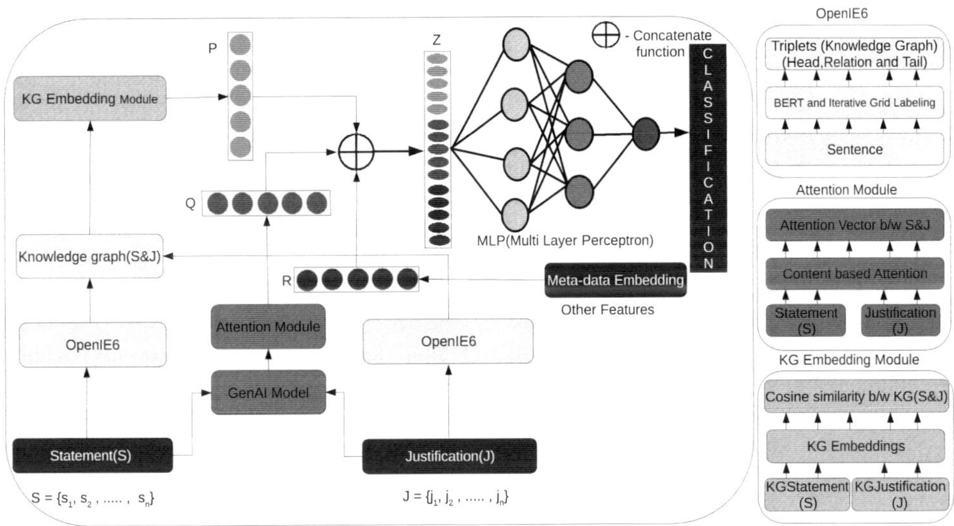

Figure 1: This framework represents the architecture of KGNewsNet computes value P (from TransE embeddings) and Q (from GPT (Black et al., 2022) embeddings) using attention mechanisms. These, along with metadata vector R, are concatenated into Z and passed through an MLP for final classification.

The LIAR-PLUS dataset is divided into three distinct subsets as shown in table **??**, each of which plays a crucial role in model training, validation, and testing. A key feature of the LIAR-PLUS dataset is the inclusion of a "Justification" column, which offers textual explanations or evidence supporting each statement's verdict. This addition enhances the fact-checking process by providing contextual information that the model can leverage when determining the truthfulness of a statement. By incorporating these justifications, the model can make more informed and accurate decisions based on the statement and the rationale behind the verdict.

Table 2 outlines the feature structure in the LIAR dataset, where rows 1 to 15 represent various data points. Feature 1 provides the label, while Feature 2 includes the main statement or news text, which forms the primary content analyzed for truthfulness. Contextual details are provided by features $\{4, 5, 6, 7, 8, 15\}$: feature 4 specifies the subject, offering insight into the topic; feature 5 identifies the speaker, establishing the source; feature 6 includes the speaker's job title, adding professional background; feature 7 provides state information, offering geographical context; feature 8 denotes the speaker's party affiliation; and feature 15 offers additional context to enrich the background of the statement. Additionally, features $\{9, \ldots, 13\}$ detail the speaker's historical truthfulness record by counting previous statements categorized by veracity, which is crucial for assessing credibility and adds an essential dimension to the analysis.

The wealth of information in the LIAR-PLUS dataset offered us a unique opportunity to delve deeper into fact-checking. It allowed our model to harness the statement's words and underlying justifications, producing a more nuanced and accurate understanding of truth in an age where misinformation often spreads unchecked.

4 Methodology

This section describes the methodology used to develop our proposed model, KGNewsNet, shown in Figure 1. The model integrates multiple layers of textual analysis, knowledge graph embeddings, and metadata, including sentiment analysis, to improve the accuracy of fake news detection.

4.1 Attention Module

Let S_i and J_i represent the i-th statement and its corresponding justification, respectively, where each has up to n_i tokens. Each token in S_i and J_i is using GPT-NeoX(Black et al., 2022) to get token embeddings. Let $\mathbf{s}_{i,t} \in \mathbb{R}^D$ and $\mathbf{j}_{i,t} \in \mathbb{R}^D$ denote the embedding vectors for the t-th tokens in the i-th statement S_i and justification J_i, respectively.

Thus, we have

$$S_i = \{\mathbf{s}_{i,1}, \mathbf{s}_{i,2}, \ldots, \mathbf{s}_{i,n_i}\}$$

$$J_i = \{\mathbf{j}_{i,1}, \mathbf{j}_{i,2}, \ldots, \mathbf{j}_{i,n_i}\}$$

where $n_i = 512$ is the number of tokens in S_i and J_i and padding is applied if S_i or J_i contains fewer than n_i tokens.

To capture the alignment between each statement-justification pair, we compute a matrix of attention weights α_i between S_i & J_i. The attention weight $\alpha_{i,t,u}$ between the t-th token in S_i and the u-th token in J_i is given by

$$\alpha_{i,t,u} = \frac{\exp\left(\frac{\mathbf{s}_{i,t}\cdot\mathbf{j}_{i,u}}{\sqrt{D}}\right)}{\sum_{t=1,v=1}^{n_i}\exp\left(\frac{\mathbf{s}_{i,t}\cdot\mathbf{j}_{i,v}}{\sqrt{D}}\right)} \quad (1)$$

where $\mathbf{s}_{i,t} \cdot \mathbf{j}_{i,u}$ denotes the dot product between the t-th token embedding in S_i and the u-th token embedding in J_i, computed as

$$\mathbf{s}_{i,t} \cdot \mathbf{j}_{i,u} = \sum_{p=1}^{D} s_{i,t,p}\, j_{i,u,p} \quad (2)$$

and $D = 150$ is the dimensionality of the embeddings. The softmax normalization ensures that $\alpha_{i,t,u}$ forms a probability distribution over the tokens in J_i for each token in S_i, capturing the relative alignment of each justification token with respect to each statement token.

Next, we construct a context-aware representation $\mathbf{c}_{i,t}$ for each token $\mathbf{s}_{i,t}$ in the statement S_i by computing a weighted sum of the token embeddings in J_i based on the attention weights:

$$\mathbf{c}_{i,t} = \sum_{u=1}^{n_i} \alpha_{i,t,u}\,\mathbf{j}_{i,u} \quad (3)$$

where $\mathbf{c}_{i,t} \in \mathbb{R}^D$ is the attended representation of the t-th token in S_i, taking into account its alignment with each token in J_i.

To obtain a single content-based attention vector Q_i for each statement S_i that incorporates the context from the justification J_i, we aggregate the $\mathbf{c}_{i,t}$ vectors across all tokens in S_i. We use average pooling over the $\mathbf{c}_{i,t}$ vectors to produce Q_i:

$$Q_i = \frac{1}{n_i}\sum_{t=1}^{n_i} \mathbf{c}_{i,t} \quad (4)$$

Where $Q_i \in \mathbb{R}^D$ is the content-based attention vector that summarizes the alignment between each statement S_i and its corresponding justification J_i across all tokens. This process effectively captures token-level alignment for multiple statement-justification pairs, yielding a context-aware representation for each statement based on its justification.

4.2 Knowledge Graph Extraction and Embedding Module

Our dataset contains n statement-justification pairs, where each statement S_i has a corresponding justification J_i. For each i-th statement-justification pair, we use OpenIE6(Kolluru et al., 2020) to extract structured knowledge graphs in the form of triplets (h, r, t), where h is the head entity, r is the relation, and t is the tail entity. For more information about OpenIE6, please refer to Appendix A.3.

Since a single statement or justification can yield multiple triplets, we limit the number of extracted triplets to a maximum of m_1 for statements and m_2 for justifications, where m_1 = 3 and m_2 = 6 as expressed in (Kolluru et al., 2020) it reflects the length of statements and justifications. Let the sets of triplets extracted from the i-th statement S_i and justification J_i be represented as:

$$\text{KG}_{S_i} = \{(h_{i,k}^S, r_{i,k}^S, t_{i,k}^S)\}_{k=1}^{\min(n_{S_i}, m_1)}$$

$$\text{KG}_{J_i} = \{(h_{i,l}^J, r_{i,l}^J, t_{i,l}^J)\}_{l=1}^{\min(n_{J_i}, m_2)}$$

where n_{S_i} and n_{J_i} are the total number of possible triplets extracted by OpenIE6 from S_i and J_i, respectively.

Each triplet (h, r, t) is then represented by embeddings $\mathbf{h}$, $\mathbf{r}$, and $\mathbf{t}$ using TransE. The TransE model ensures that the relationship holds by approximating the translation:

$$\mathbf{h} + \mathbf{r} \approx \mathbf{t} \quad (5)$$

where $\mathbf{h}$, $\mathbf{r}$, and $\mathbf{t}$ are the vector representations for the head, relation, and tail entities, respectively, typically in $\mathbb{R}^D$ where D is the embedding dimensionality.

For each possible pair of triplets from KG_{S_i} and KG_{J_i}, we compute the cosine similarity (CS) between their embeddings. This results in a total of $m_1 \times m_2 = M$ cosine similarity values for each statement-justification pair. Each pairwise cosine similarity is computed as follows:

$$\text{CS}((h_{i,k}^S, r_{i,k}^S, t_{i,k}^S), (h_{i,l}^J, r_{i,l}^J, t_{i,l}^J)) = \frac{\mathbf{h}_{i,k}\cdot\mathbf{t}_{i,l}}{\sqrt{\|\mathbf{h}_{i,k}\|^2}\cdot\sqrt{\|\mathbf{t}_{i,l}\|^2}} \quad (6)$$

Models	**Accuracy**	**F1-Score**
LSTM(Girgis et al., 2018)	0.224	0.217
Hybrid CNN(Girgis et al., 2018)	0.247	0.274
SNN (LM + KG + KG-ENTITY)(Koloski et al., 2022)	0.267	0.267
KnowBert-W+W(Whitehouse et al., 2022)	0.294	0.289
CofCED(Yang et al., 2022b)	0.294	0.295
AC-BiLSTM(Trueman et al., 2021)	0.338	0.351
P_Bi_LSTM(Alhindi et al., 2018)	0.374	0.361
CapsulNet(Goldani et al., 2021)	0.395	-
Hybrid LSTM(Long et al., 2017)	0.407	0.415
DSNDM + Att.(Chernyavskiy and Ilvovsky, 2020)	0.412	0.402
Generative AI Model Performances		
ChatGPT(OpenAI, 2024)	0.263	0.251
FactLLaMA(Cheung and Lam, 2023)	0.304	0.299
FactLLaMA$_{know}$(Cheung and Lam, 2023)	0.313	0.304
L-Defense$_{LLaMA2}$(Wang et al., 2024)	0.328	0.314
L-Defense$_{ChatGPT}$(Wang et al., 2024)	0.311	0.305
Proposed KGNewsNet without KG	0.441	0.436
Proposed KGNewsNet	**0.454**	**0.450**

Table 3: Comparison of the proposed KGNewsNet with previous state-of-the-art models. Results are evaluated based on Accuracy and F1-Score. The proposed KGNewsNet achieves the best performance.

where $\mathbf{h}_{i,k}$ and $\mathbf{t}_{i,l}$ are the embeddings of the head and tail entities in each pair of triplets from KG_{S_i} and KG_{J_i}, respectively, and $\|\mathbf{h}_{i,k}\|$ denotes the Euclidean norm of vector $\mathbf{h}_{i,k}$.

The final output of this module for each i-th statement-justification pair is a vector $\mathbf{P}_i \in \mathbb{R}^M$, containing cosine similarity scores:

$$\mathbf{P}_i = \left[\text{CS}((h^S_{i,k}, r^S_{i,k}, t^S_{i,k}), (h^J_{i,l}, r^J_{i,l}, t^J_{i,l}))\right]^{m_1,m_2}_{k=1,l=1} \tag{7}$$

This vector $\mathbf{P}_i$ captures the alignment between each combination of triplet pairs across the statement and justification. By iterating through each of the n statement-justification pairs, we maintain consistency and manageability in the knowledge graph representations while capturing detailed relational alignment within the text.

4.3 Feature Vector Construction and Classification

To build the final feature vector, we concatenate the attention module vector $\mathbf{Q}$, KG module vector $\mathbf{P}$, and metadata features $\mathbf{R}$. The metadata features $\mathbf{R}$ include the information shown in Table 2, such as speaker information, party affiliation, and count information that details the speaker's historical truthfulness record. This information, derived by counting previous statements categorized by veracity, is crucial for assessing credibility and adds an essential dimension to the analysis. The final feature vector $\mathbf{Z}$, which is a concatenation of all the above vectors, is defined as:

$$\mathbf{Z} = [\mathbf{Q}\|\mathbf{P}\|\mathbf{R}] \tag{8}$$

The feature vector $\mathbf{Z}$ is then passed into a Multi-Layer Perceptron (MLP) for classification, where the veracity prediction output $\hat{y}$ is calculated as:

$$\hat{y} = \frac{\exp(\mathbf{w}^T\mathbf{Z} + b)}{\sum_k \exp(\mathbf{w}_k^T\mathbf{Z} + b_k)} \tag{9}$$

where $\mathbf{w}$ and b represent the weight vector and bias for each class in the MLP, and $\mathbf{w}_k$ and b_k are the weight vector and bias for each potential class k. To optimize the model, we use categorical cross-entropy loss:

$$L = -\sum_{i=1}^{N}\sum_{k=1}^{K} y_{i,k}\log(\hat{y}_{i,k}) \tag{10}$$

where y_i is the true label for sample i and $\hat{y}_i$ is the predicted probability for the true class.

The KGNewsNet algorithm, as outlined in Algorithm 1, provides a detailed implementation of the methodology described in this work. The algorithm highlights how features from attention and KG alignment are fused with metadata and processed through a Multi-Layer Perceptron (MLP)

Algorithm 1 KGNewsNet: Fake News Detection

Data: $S = \{S_i\}$: Statements, $J = \{J_i\}$: Justifications, $\mathbf{R}$: Metadata, Knowledge Graph Triplets (Head, Relation, Tail)

Result: Veracity predictions $\hat{y} = \{\hat{y}_i\}$

Initialize Embed, attention mechanism, KG embedding lookup, and MLP classifier Set loss function L

for *epoch* $= 1$ *to* N **do**

  foreach *batch* $(S_i, J_i, \mathbf{R}_i)$ **do**

    Step 1: Compute token embeddings for statements and justifications:

    $\mathbf{S}_{i,t} = \text{Embed}(s_{i,t}), \quad \mathbf{J}_{i,t} = \text{Embed}(j_{i,t})$

    Step 2: Compute attention weights between tokens in S_i and J_i:

    $\alpha_{i,t,u} = \frac{\exp(\frac{\mathbf{s}_{i,t} \cdot \mathbf{j}_{i,u}}{\sqrt{D}})}{\sum_{t=1,v=1}^{n_i} \exp(\frac{\mathbf{s}_{i,t} \cdot \mathbf{j}_{i,v}}{\sqrt{D}})}$

    Step 3: Compute context-aware representation of S_i:

    $Q_i = \frac{1}{n_i} \sum_{t=1}^{n_i} \sum_{u=1}^{n_i} \alpha_{i,t,u} \mathbf{j}_{i,u}$

    Step 4: Retrieve KG embeddings for S_i and J_i from the lookup dictionary & Compute cosine similarity between all triplet pairs:

    $\text{CS}((h_{i,k}^S, r_{i,k}^S, t_{i,k}^S), (h_{i,l}^J, r_{i,l}^J, t_{i,l}^J)) = \frac{\mathbf{h}_{i,k} \cdot \mathbf{t}_{i,l}}{\sqrt{\|\mathbf{h}_{i,k}\|^2} \cdot \sqrt{\|\mathbf{t}_{i,l}\|^2}}$ Construct the cosine similarity vector:

    $\mathbf{P}_i = \left[\text{CS}((h_{i,k}^S, r_{i,k}^S, t_{i,k}^S), (h_{i,l}^J, r_{i,l}^J, t_{i,l}^J))\right]_{k=1,l=1}^{m_1,m_2}$

    Step 5: Concatenate features from attention, KG embeddings, and metadata:

    $Z_i = [Q_i \| \mathbf{P}_i \| \mathbf{R}_i]$

    Step 6: Perform classification using MLP:

    $\hat{y}_i = \text{Softmax}(\mathbf{W} Z_i + \mathbf{b})$

    Step 7: Compute loss and update model parameters:

    $L = -\sum_{i=1}^{N} \sum_{k=1}^{K} y_{i,k} \log(\hat{y}_{i,k})$

  end

  Step 8: Evaluate metrics on validation data

end

Result: Compute $\hat{y}_i$ for unseen S_i, J_i using trained parameters.

for final classification. By following the step-by-step process.

Time Complexity: The overall time complexity of KGNewsNet algorithm 1 is $O(N \cdot B \cdot (T \cdot E + T^2 \cdot D + T^2 \cdot D + m_1 \cdot m_2 \cdot D + D + L \cdot D^2))$, where N is the number of epochs, B is the batch size, T is the token sequence length, E is the embedding computation cost, D is the embedding dimensions, m_1 and m_2 are the numbers of triplets in statements and justifications, and L is the number of MLP layers.

5 Experiments and Results

In this section, we present the experimental setup and results of our proposed model, KGNewsNet, as well as its comparison with other state-of-the-art models for fake news detection. The experiments are conducted on the LIAR-PLUS dataset, and the results demonstrate how the integration of statement, justification, and external knowledge representations leads to significant performance improvements. We use accuracy and F1-score as the evaluation metrics to benchmark KGNewsNet's performance.

5.1 Experimental Setup

The experiments were conducted in a cloud environment with 40 vCPUs, a Tesla V100-PCIE GPU with 32GB of memory, and 256GB of RAM, providing ample resources for efficient model training. We used the LIAR-PLUS dataset (Alhindi et al., 2018) for veracity prediction, leveraging tokenization, padding or truncating to a fixed length, and embedding generation as outlined in the Methodology section. KGNewsNet was trained using the LIAR-PLUS dataset (Alhindi et al., 2018), with preprocessing and embedding techniques outlined in the Methodology section. Additional details regarding the parameter details for result replication are provided in Appendix A.1.

5.2 Results

Table 3 presents the performance of KGNewsNet compared with previous state-of-the-art models, including traditional models, advanced architectures, and recent Generative AI approaches. Traditional models such as LSTM (Girgis et al., 2018), Hybrid CNN (Girgis et al., 2018), and KnowBert-W+W (Whitehouse et al., 2022) achieve moderate accuracy scores of 0.224, 0.247, and 0.294, respectively. Their limited performance can be attributed to the absence of structured knowledge integration, which restricts their ability to capture contextual and relational nuances in statements and justifications.

Advanced architectures, such as CapsuleNet (Goldani et al., 2021) and Hybrid LSTM (Long et al., 2017), introduce richer representational techniques, achieving accuracy scores of 0.395 and 0.407, respectively. Generative AI models like FactLLaMA$_{know}$ (Cheung and Lam, 2023) and L-Defense$_{LLaMA2}$ (Wang et al., 2024) show incremental gains, with accuracies of 0.313 and 0.328. However, these models struggle to match KGNewsNet's performance due to their lack of explicit knowledge integration. Generative models rely on pre-trained contextual embeddings but lack mechanisms to align statements with external knowledge, making it difficult to validate claims effectively. Furthermore, their probabilistic nature and sensitivity to prompt design often result in inconsistent performance, particularly for claims requiring nuanced reasoning or factual grounding.

KGNewsNet demonstrates the effectiveness of integrating Knowledge Graph (KG) embeddings to address these limitations. By leveraging KG triplets, the model achieves an accuracy of 0.454 and an F1-score of 0.450, outperforming all other methods. This improvement underscores the importance of knowledge grounding in aligning statements and justifications. The KG module enhances token-level alignment and enriches the content-based attention vector, enabling the model to capture complex relationships effectively.

As outlined in Algorithm 1, KGNewsNet's computational complexity. Unlike traditional models with linear operations or generative models relying on token embeddings, KGNewsNet introduces additional computational cost through explicit pairwise alignment between statements and justifications. This higher complexity enables superior performance in tasks requiring structured support and nuanced veracity detection.Additionally, Appendix A.2 illustrates triplet alignment and prediction results (Tables 4 and 5), showing strong alignment in "true" cases and partial alignment in "barely-true" or "half-true" cases. These examples highlight KGNewsNet's ability to capture contextual relationships while revealing challenges in distinguishing closely related truthfulness categories, pointing to potential refinements for interpreting nuanced distinctions.

6 Conclusion

This paper presents KGNewsNet, a model for fake news detection that harnesses statements, justifications, metadata, and external knowledge graph embeddings to enhance classification performance. The results indicate that incorporating external knowledge sources and meticulously extracting features from both statements and justifications are pivotal in advancing fake news detection accuracy. While the model achieves strong overall performance, there remain opportunities for improvement, particularly in addressing complex financial statements and nuanced claims requiring intricate reasoning.

7 Limitations

KGNewsNet demonstrates significant potential in leveraging Knowledge Graph (KG) triplet alignment for veracity assessment but faces several limitations. The reliance on OpenIE6 for triplet extraction often generates lengthy or overly detailed triplets, which can dilute focus on critical information and complicate alignment. The evaluation, conducted exclusively on the LIAR-PLUS dataset, aligns well with the model's capabilities but limits its generalizability to datasets with less structured justifications or evidence-based fact-checking (e.g., FEVER). Extending evaluations to diverse datasets and optimizing the computational overhead of KG embedding and triplet alignment processes remain key areas for future work. Additionally, further improvements in explainability, such as visualizing triplet alignment or providing user-friendly insights into the model's decisions, would enhance its applicability in real-world fact-checking scenarios.

Acknowledgments

IHUB NTIHAC FOUNDATION partially funds this research under project numbers IHUB-NTIHAC/2021/01/14 & IHUB-NTIHAC/2021/01/15.

References

Google AI. 2024. Palm: scaling language modeling with pathways. *J. Mach. Learn. Res.*, 24(1).

Tariq Alhindi, Savvas Petridis, and Smaranda Muresan. 2018. Where is your evidence: Improving fact-checking by justification modeling. In *Proceedings of the First Workshop on Fact Extraction and Verification (FEVER)*, pages 85–90.

Pepa Atanasova, Jakob Grue Simonsen, Christina Lioma, and Isabelle Augenstein. 2020. Generating fact checking explanations. In *Proceedings of the 58th Annual Meeting of the Association for Computational Linguistics*, pages 7352–7364. Association for Computational Linguistics.

Michele Banko, Michael J. Cafarella, Stephen Soderland, Matt Broadhead, and Oren Etzioni. 2007. Open information extraction from the web. In *Proceedings of the 20th International Joint Conference on Artifical Intelligence*, IJCAI'07, page 2670–2676.

Sid Black, Stella Biderman, Eric Hallahan, Quentin Anthony, Leo Gao, Laurence Golding, Horace He, Connor Leahy, Kyle McDonell, Jason Phang, Michael Pieler, USVSN Sai Prashanth, Shivanshu Purohit, Laria Reynolds, Jonathan Tow, Ben Wang, and Samuel Weinbach. 2022. GPT-NeoX-20B: An open-source autoregressive language model. In *Proceedings of the ACL Workshop on Challenges & Perspectives in Creating Large Language Models*.

Tom B. Brown, Benjamin Mann, Nick Ryder, Melanie Subbiah, Jared Kaplan, Prafulla Dhariwal, Arvind Neelakantan, Pranav Shyam, Girish Sastry, Amanda Askell, Sandhini Agarwal, Ariel Herbert-Voss, Gretchen Krueger, Tom Henighan, Rewon Child, Aditya Ramesh, Daniel M. Ziegler, Jeffrey Wu, Clemens Winter, Christopher Hesse, Mark Chen, Eric Sigler, Mateusz Litwin, Scott Gray, Benjamin Chess, Jack Clark, Christopher Berner, Sam McCandlish, Alec Radford, Ilya Sutskever, and Dario Amodei. 2020. Language models are few-shot learners. In *Proceedings of the 34th International Conference on Neural Information Processing Systems*, NIPS '20, Red Hook, NY, USA. Curran Associates Inc.

Mario Casillo, Francesco Colace, Brij B. Gupta, Domenico Santaniello, and Carmine Valentino. 2021. Fake news detection using lda topic modeling and k-nearest neighbor classifier. In *Computational Data and Social Networks: 10th International Conference, CSoNet 2021*, pages 330–339. Springer International Publishing.

Alexander Chernyavskiy and Dmitry Ilvovsky. 2020. Dsndm: Deep siamese neural discourse model with attention for text pairs categorization and ranking. In *Proceedings of the First Workshop on Computational Approaches to Discourse*, pages 76–85.

Tsun-Hin Cheung and Kin-Man Lam. 2023. Factllama: Optimizing instruction-following language models with external knowledge for automated fact-checking. In *2023 Asia Pacific Signal and Information Processing Association Annual Summit and Conference (APSIPA ASC)*, pages 846–853.

Jacob Devlin, Ming-Wei Chang, Kenton Lee, and Kristina Toutanova. 2019. Bert: Pre-training of deep bidirectional transformers for language understanding. In *Proceedings of the 2019 Conference of the North American Chapter of the Association for Computational Linguistics*, pages 4171–4186.

Paolo Ferragina and Ugo Scaiella. 2010. Tagme: On-the-fly annotation of short text fragments (by wikipedia entities). In *Proceedings of the 19th ACM international conference on Information and knowledge management*, pages 1625–1628.

Sherry Girgis, Eslam Amer, and Mahmoud Gadallah. 2018. Deep learning algorithms for detecting fake news in online text. In *Proceedings of the 13th International Conference on Computer Engineering and Systems (ICCES)*, pages 93–97.

Mohammad Hadi Goldani, Saeedeh Momtazi, and Reza Safabakhsh. 2021. Detecting fake news with capsule neural networks. *Applied Soft Computing*, 101:106991.

Xuemei Gu and Mario Krenn. 2024. Interesting scientific idea generation using knowledge graphs and llms: Evaluations with 100 research group leaders. *Preprint*, arXiv:2405.17044.

Linmei Hu, Siqi Wei, Ziwang Zhao, and Bin Wu. 2022. Deep learning for fake news detection: A comprehensive survey. *AI Open*, 3:133–155.

Keshav Kolluru, Vaibhav Adlakha, Samarth Aggarwal, Mausam, and Soumen Chakrabarti. 2020. Openie6: Iterative grid labeling and coordination analysis for open information extraction. In *Proceedings of the 58th Annual Meeting of the Association for Computational Linguistics (ACL)*, Seattle, U.S.A.

Boshko Koloski, Timen Stepišnik Perdih, Marko Robnik-Šikonja, Senja Pollak, and Blaž Škrlj. 2022. Knowledge graph informed fake news classification via heterogeneous representation ensembles. *Neurocomputing*, 496:208–226.

Neema Kotonya and Francesca Toni. 2020. Explainable automated fact-checking for public health claims. In *Proceedings of the 2020 Conference on Empirical Methods in Natural Language Processing (EMNLP)*, Online. Association for Computational Linguistics.

Yunfei Long, Qin Lu, Rong Xiang, Minglei Li, and Chu-Ren Huang. 2017. Fake news detection through multi-perspective speaker profiles. In *Proceedings of the Eighth International Joint Conference on Natural Language Processing (Volume 2: Short Papers)*, pages 252–256.

OpenAI. 2024. Gpt-4 technical report. *Preprint*, arXiv:2303.08774.

Long Ouyang, Jeffrey Wu, Xu Jiang, Diogo Almeida, Carroll Wainwright, Pamela Mishkin, Chong Zhang, Sandhini Agarwal, Katarina Slama, Alex Ray, John Schulman, Jacob Hilton, Fraser Kelton, Luke Miller, Maddie Simens, Amanda Askell, Peter Welinder, Paul F Christiano, Jan Leike, and Ryan Lowe. 2022. Training language models to follow instructions with human feedback. In *Advances in Neural Information Processing Systems*, volume 35, pages 27730–27744. Curran Associates, Inc.

Karishma Sharma, Feng Qian, He Jiang, Natali Ruchansky, Ming Zhang, and Yan Liu. 2019. Combating fake news: A survey on identification and mitigation techniques. *ACM Transactions on Intelligent Systems and Technology (TIST)*, 10(3):1–42.

Kai Shu, Limeng Cui, Suhang Wang, Dongwon Lee, and Huan Liu. 2019. defend: Explainable fake news detection. In *Proceedings of the 25th ACM SIGKDD International Conference on Knowledge Discovery & Data Mining*, KDD '19, page 395–405. Association for Computing Machinery.

Rohan Taori, Ishaan Gulrajani, Tianyi Zhang, Yann Dubois, Xuechen Li, Carlos Guestrin, Percy Liang, and Tatsunori B. Hashimoto. 2023. Stanford alpaca: An instruction-following llama model.

James Thorne and Andreas Vlachos. 2018. Automated fact checking: Task formulations, methods and future directions. In *Proceedings of the 27th International Conference on Computational Linguistics*, pages 3346–3359, Santa Fe, New Mexico, USA. Association for Computational Linguistics.

Hugo Touvron, Thibaut Lavril, Gautier Izacard, Xavier Martinet, Marie-Anne Lachaux, Timothée Lacroix, Baptiste Rozière, Naman Goyal, Eric Hambro, Faisal Azhar, et al. 2023. Llama: Open and efficient foundation language models. *arXiv preprint arXiv:2302.13971*.

Tina Esther Trueman, Ashok Kumar, Narayanasamy P., and Vidya J. 2021. Attention-based c-bilstm for fake news detection. *Applied Soft Computing*, 110:107600.

Denny Vrandečić and Markus Krötzsch. 2014. Wikidata: A free collaborative knowledgebase. *Communications of the ACM*, 57(10):78–85.

Bo Wang, Jing Ma, Hongzhan Lin, Zhiwei Yang, Ruichao Yang, Yuan Tian, and Yi Chang. 2024. Explainable fake news detection with large language model via defense among competing wisdom. In *Proceedings of the ACM Web Conference 2024*, WWW '24, page 2452–2463. Association for Computing Machinery.

William Yang Wang. 2017. Liar, liar pants on fire: A new benchmark dataset for fake news detection. *arXiv preprint arXiv:1705.00648*.

Yizhong Wang, Yeganeh Kordi, Swaroop Mishra, Alisa Liu, Noah A. Smith, Daniel Khashabi, and Hannaneh Hajishirzi. 2023. Self-instruct: Aligning language models with self-generated instructions. In *Proceedings of the 61st Annual Meeting of the Association for Computational Linguistics (Volume 1: Long Papers)*, pages 13484–13508. Association for Computational Linguistics.

Chenxi Whitehouse, Tillman Weyde, Pranava Madhyastha, and Nikos Komninos. 2022. Evaluation of fake news detection with knowledge-enhanced language models. In *Proceedings of the International AAAI Conference on Web and Social Media*, volume 16, pages 1425–1429.

Zhiwei Yang, Jing Ma, Hechang Chen, Hongzhan Lin, Ziyang Luo, and Yi Chang. 2022a. A coarse-to-fine cascaded evidence-distillation neural network for explainable fake news detection. In *Proceedings of the 29th International Conference on Computational Linguistics*, pages 2608–2621. International Committee on Computational Linguistics.

Zhiwei Yang, Jing Ma, Hechang Chen, Hongzhan Lin, Ziyang Luo, and Yi Chang. 2022b. A coarse-to-fine cascaded evidence-distillation neural network for explainable fake news detection. *arXiv preprint arXiv:2209.14642*.

Zhengyan Zhang, Xu Han, Zhiyuan Liu, Xin Jiang, Maosong Sun, and Qun Liu. 2019. Ernie: Enhanced language representation with informative entities. In *Proceedings of the 57th Annual Meeting of the Association for Computational Linguistics*, pages 1441–1451, Florence, Italy. Association for Computational Linguistics.

A Appendix

A.1 Parameter Details

The experiment is conducted on LIAR-PLUS dataset (Alhindi et al., 2018) for veracity prediction, leveraging tokenization, padding or truncating to a fixed length, and embedding generation as outlined in the Methodology section. For classification, an MLPClassifier with the Adam solver was configured to ensure effective optimization. The learning rate initialization was set to 0.001, and the learning rate scheduling was adaptive, reducing the rate if no improvement was observed in validation performance, aiding convergence. The network architecture consisted of a single hidden layer with 50 neurons, balanced for computational efficiency and model complexity. ReLU activation was used to expedite training, and the batch size was set to 'auto', adjusting based on available memory. Additional controls included a tolerance level (tol) of 0.0001 to set a minimum threshold for performance improvement, and an early stopping criterion n_iter_no_change=10, halting training if no

<table>
<tr><td>Statement triplets: (Americans, working, now), (Americans, working, 70s), (Americans, working, less than in the 70s)
Justification triplets: (Hartzler, talking about, decade of the 70s), (first eight years of the 70s, employment-population ratio, lower than 2015),
(first eight years of the 70s, labor force participation rate, lower than 2015), (employment-population ratio, comparison, 2015 vs. 70s),
(labor force participation rate, comparison, 2015 vs. 70s), (decade of the 70s, employment-population and labor force participation, lower than 2015)
Explanation: The label is "barely-true." Partial alignment occurs as the justification triplets provide historical employment data in the 70s, but there's no direct comparison with "now," supporting only a partial truth.</td></tr>
<tr><td>Statement triplets: (Republicans, attacks, programs in stimulus plan), (programs in stimulus plan, not stimulative, less than 1 percent),
(programs, account for, less than 1 percent of package)
Justification triplets: (Obama, point, perspective in order), (legislators, quibbling over, small portion of spending), (publicized projects, represent, small portion of spending),
(Republicans, said, large percentages of stimulus plan not stimulative), (stimulus plan, criticized by, Republicans), (spending, ineffective use of, taxpayer money)
Explanation: The label is "half-true." Some alignment occurs as the justification acknowledges the criticism but lacks specifics about "less than 1 percent," resulting in partial support consistent with the "half-true" label.</td></tr>
<tr><td>Statement triplets: (Canada, created, more jobs), (time period, January), (Canada, created, more jobs than U.S.)
Justification triplets: (November 2010, U.S. economy created, 93,000 jobs), (December 2010, U.S. created, 121,000 jobs),
(recent months, U.S. job creation, exceeded Canada only in October), (January, U.S. job creation, especially low), (January, Canadian job creation, especially high),
(comparison, job creation, Canada vs. U.S.)
Explanation: The label is "true." Strong alignment as the justification confirms high Canadian job creation relative to the US in January, fully supporting the statement and matching the "true" label.</td></tr>
</table>

Table 4: Case Study of Triplet Alignment Between Statements and Justifications for Veracity Labels by highlighting aligned justification triplets. For "true" labels, strong alignment with multiple highlighted triplets provides clear support, while partial alignment in "half-true" or "barely-true" cases indicates incomplete support. The use of a Knowledge Graph (KG) structures these comparisons, capturing subtle distinctions and improving the accuracy of veracity assessment.

improvement was observed for 10 iterations. Early stopping was applied to prevent overfitting, and validation performance was monitored throughout training. This setup, with adaptive learning rates, controlled complexity, and early stopping, was optimized to achieve stable convergence and reliable generalizability on the LIAR-PLUS dataset.

A.2 Case study

Table 4 presents case studies that illustrate how our methodology, KGNewsNet, uses structured triplet alignment between statements and justifications to assess veracity accurately. In each example, KGNewsNet extracts key entities and relationships from both statements and justifications, creating triplets that are compared to determine factual alignment. By leveraging Knowledge Graph (KG) embeddings, our model captures not only the semantic content of each entity but also its contextual relationship within the statement, enabling nuanced verification.

For "true" labels, strong alignment is observed, with multiple justification triplets highlighted in green, providing direct and clear support for the statement. For instance, in the "Canada created more jobs than the U.S." example, both statement and justification triplets align on key factors like "job creation," "January," and "comparative performance," resulting in a high degree of factual support. This alignment showcases KGNewsNet's

Statement	Justifications	Label	Prediction
Pregnant women are at an increased risk of pre-term pregnancy by 80 percent.	"The statement attributes the statistic to the Women's Fund of Rhode Island".	barely-true	barely-true
Elizabeth Warren lied about wanting to abolish the Federal Minimum Wage.	"Trump said, "Elizabeth Warren lied about abolishing the Federal Minimum Wage." Yet, when Trump was asked if he would have a federal floor with states going higher, he replied, "No." She simply used Trump's own words".	barely-true	false
Every dollar the state spent on audits last year delivered $64 in cost savings.	"Brown said that for every dollar the Secretary of State spent on audits last year, it found $64 in cost savings. However, the total potential savings might be underestimated".	true	barely-true
Public display of a long rifle is perfectly legal in Texas.	"Texas law explicitly restricts handguns and some other weapons from being openly carried around. However, the law is silent on long rifles, meaning that their public display is legal".	true	true
We were the last flag flying in Benghazi.	"The meaning of the phrase "last flag flying" shifted from its original meaning as politicians used it as a rhetorical talking point. In his testimony, the phrase was used more rhetorically than literally".	false	false

Table 5: Prediction Results of KGNewsNet

ability to interpret context-sensitive data accurately, supported by the structured comparison of triplets that validates the statement comprehensively.

In contrast, examples with "half-true" or "barely-true" labels show only partial alignment, with fewer highlighted triplets in the justification. For the statement "Republicans attack the stimulus plan for programs that account for less than 1 percent of spending," some alignment is achieved as the justification acknowledges similar criticisms. However, it lacks explicit confirmation of the "less than 1 percent" detail, reflecting partial support for the statement. This partial alignment, captured through KG-guided triplet comparison, helps KGNewsNet differentiate between full and partial truths.

By structuring comparisons with KG triplets, KGNewsNet effectively reduces ambiguity in cases with close but distinct veracity labels. Table 5 further illustrates KGNewsNet's performance, where it accurately captures veracity by aligning entities, relationships, and contexts in diverse examples, including statements about economic data, policy claims, and public figures. This structured approach allows KGNewsNet to distinguish between factual alignment levels, refining its predictions with a greater degree of accuracy than conventional models. Through KG triplet alignment, our model benefits from enhanced tructured representation, yielding consistent and reliable veracity assessments across challenging, context-dependent statements.

A.3 OpenIE6

Our methodology leverages OpenIE6 for extracting structured triplets from statements and justifications, which enhances the accuracy and efficiency of Open Information Extraction (OpenIE) through its novel Iterative Grid Labeling (IGL) approach. OpenIE6 frames extraction as a 2-D grid labeling task, where rows represent potential extractions, and columns correspond to words in the sentence. This design enables rapid extraction processing without compromising on quality, as it reduces the need for repeated encoding steps common in earlier OpenIE systems.

To improve extraction comprehensiveness, OpenIE6 imposes constraints during training to ensure high recall, incorporating penalties for omitted information. Furthermore, it addresses complex coordination structures, such as conjunctive phrases,

Parameter	Description
`-mode splitpredict`	Enables prediction mode, allowing the model to split conjunctive structures for better extraction.
`-inp sentences.txt`	Specifies the input file containing sentences for which triplet relations are extracted.
`-out predictions.txt`	Sets the output file where extracted triplets will be saved.
`-rescoring`	Applies a rescoring mechanism to enhance prediction accuracy.
`-task oie`	Defines the task as Open Information Extraction (OIE).
`-gpus 1`	Configures the process to run on one GPU for computational efficiency.
`-oie_model models/oie_model/epoch=14_eval_acc=0.551_v0.ckpt`	Path to the pre-trained OpenIE model used for relation extraction.
`-conj_model models/conj_model/epoch=28_eval_acc=0.854.ckpt`	Path to the conjunction handling model that processes compound structures.
`-rescore_model models/rescore_model`	Path to the rescoring model to refine extraction accuracy.
`-num_extractions` $m_1 = 3$ & $m_2 = 6$	Limits the number of extractions per sentence to a maximum of $m_1 = 3$ for statements and $m_2 = 6$ for justifications.

Table 6: Parameters used to configure OpenIE6 for triplet relation extraction tasks.

through a specialized coordination analyzer built on the same grid-based framework. This unique combination of constraints and coordination handling allows OpenIE6 to set new standards in OpenIE performance, achieving notable improvements in recall and extraction quality at speeds up to 10 times faster than prior models.

Table 6 outlines the key parameters used to configure OpenIE6 for our triplet extraction tasks. These settings include options for mode, input/output file handling, rescoring, GPU usage, and model paths for specific tasks, ensuring optimized processing for our experimental setup. We limited extractions to a maximum of $m_1 = 3$ triplets for statements and $m_2 = 6$ triplets for justifications to maintain extraction relevance and computational efficiency.

Style Knowledge Graph: Augmenting Text Style Transfer with Knowledge Graphs

Martina Toshevska, Slobodan Kalajdziski and Sonja Gievska
Faculty of Computer Science and Engineering
Ss. Cyril and Methodius University
Skopje, North Macedonia
{martina.toshevska, slobodan.kalajdziski, sonja.gievska}@finki.ukim.mk

Abstract

Text style transfer is the task of modifying the stylistic attributes of a given text while preserving its original meaning. This task has also gained interest with the advent of large language models. Although knowledge graph augmentation has been explored in various tasks, its potential for enhancing text style transfer has received limited attention. This paper proposes a method to create a Style Knowledge Graph (SKG) to facilitate and improve text style transfer. The SKG captures words, their attributes, and relations in a particular style, that serves as a knowledge resource to augment text style transfer. We conduct baseline experiments to evaluate the effectiveness of the SKG for augmenting text style transfer by incorporating relevant parts from the SKG in the prompt. The preliminary results demonstrate its potential for enhancing content preservation and style transfer strength in text style transfer tasks, while the results on fluency indicate promising outcomes with some room for improvement. We hope that the proposed SKG and the initial experiments will inspire further research in the field.

1 Introduction

Text style transfer (TST) is the task of modifying particular stylistic features of a text while preserving its original meaning. The task involves rewriting a text to match several stylistic attributes such as sentiment, formality, or politeness without changing the semantic meaning. With the emergence of large language models (LLMs), their application for TST gained attention primarily focused on prompting techniques (Reif et al., 2022; Suzgun et al., 2022) that reduce the need for extensive parallel datasets. Other approaches like fine-tuning (Mukherjee and Dušek, 2023), reinforcement learning (Deng et al., 2022), knowledge augmentation (Zong et al., 2024), and others (Lai et al., 2024; Pan et al., 2024) have also inspired recent research.

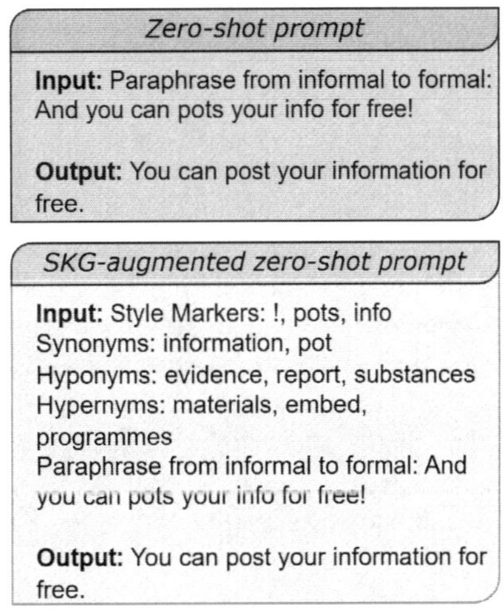

Figure 1: Examples for zero-shot and SKG-augmented zero-shot prompts for text style transfer that were used to evaluate and compare the proposed style knowledge graph.

Knowledge graphs (KGs) provide a structured representation of knowledge that enables efficient organization and retrieval across various domains. By integrating structured knowledge from KGs, LLMs can provide more accurate and contextually relevant outputs. We believe that combining both structured knowledge representation in KGs and the generative capabilities of LLMs has the potential to improve text style transfer tasks. While augmentation with KGs has been explored for many tasks, to the best of our knowledge, its application in text style transfer remains relatively understudied. Existing research is primarily focused on integrating knowledge base information to provide particular words for the desired style (Xu et al., 2022), similar sentences to the input to provide context (Toshevska and Gievska, 2024) or guidelines for the desired style (Zong et al., 2024).

Proceedings of the Generative AI and Knowledge Graph Workshop (GenAIK), pages 123–135
January 19, 2025.

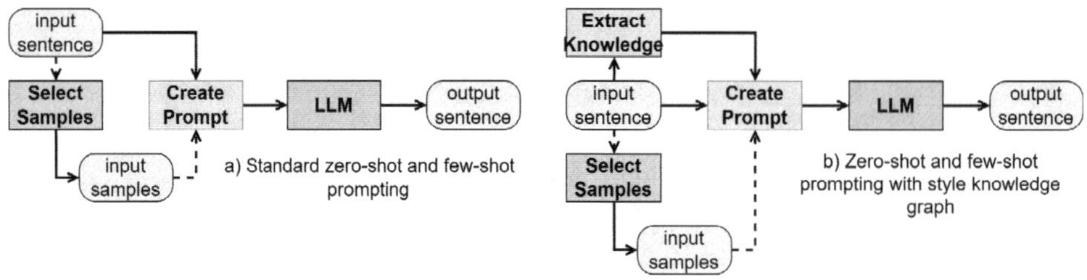

Figure 2: Overview of the prompting strategies. a) Standard prompting. b) Prompting augmented with SKG.

To combine the advantages of both approaches and facilitate further research in the field, we propose a Style Knowledge Graph (SKG) for text style transfer. The SKG is designed to capture words, their attributes, and relations for various styles with the aim of providing a source of knowledge that can enhance text style transfer. To evaluate the effectiveness of the proposed SKG we perform several prompting experiments where parts of the proposed SKG, that are relevant to the particular input sentence, are provided in the prompt. An example of the used prompts is shown in Table 1. We hope that the proposed SKG and the preliminary experiments will motivate further research.

The main contributions of the paper are: (1) We propose a knowledge graph for text style transfer, which we refer to as a Style Knowledge Graph (SKG). (2) We evaluate the effectiveness of augmenting text style transfer with SKG via prompting. (3) We analyze the influence of various parts of the SKG on the text style transfer task.

The rest of the paper is organized as follows. A brief introduction of previous text style transfer methods and knowledge augmentation is presented in Section 2. The definition and creation process of SKG is provided in Section 3. The preliminary experiments and baseline results are presented in Section 4 and Section 5, respectively. Section 6 concludes the paper.

2 Related Work

Before the advent of LLMs, TST methods commonly employed encoder-decoder architectures (Sutskever et al., 2014), Generative Adversarial Networks (GANs) (Goodfellow et al., 2014), and Reinforcement Learning (RL) (Williams, 1992). The methods based on encoder-decoder comprise an encoder to produce a style-neutral representation and a decoder to generate a sentence in the desired style, often augmented by additional components such as style classifiers (Lample et al., 2019; Xu et al., 2019; Cheng et al., 2020), and style embeddings (Li et al., 2018). GAN-based approaches use a generator to produce a sentence in the target style trained with adversarial objectives (Hu et al., 2017; Shen et al., 2017; Fu et al., 2018). RL-based approaches use a reward-based system to generate sentences in the desired style, by using multi-part rewards combining content preservation, style change, and fluency (Luo et al., 2019).

Prompting techniques are among the first approaches for text style transfer with LLMs, that explore zero-shot and few-shot techniques. Augmented zero-shot (Reif et al., 2022) explores a vanilla prompt that specifies the target style augmented with a single set of exemplars within the prompt to include a variety of sentence rewriting operations instead of exemplars specific to the target style. In addition to the vanilla prompt, Prompt&Rerank (Suzgun et al., 2022) explores a contrastive prompt to specify both the source and the target style that create a clear contrast between them, and two negation prompts to specify the target style as a negation of the source style and vice versa. Several approaches focus on editing the input sentence via prompting. PromptEdit, assesses TST as a text classification task with the goal of generating candidate sentences with an edit-based search algorithm that employs insertion, deletion, and replacement as edit operations, and then determining a style score for them with an LLM (Luo et al., 2023). PEGF utilizes two-way prompting that first identifies stylistic words as words with a score higher than a particular threshold via an initial prompt and then edits those stylistic words via implicit or explicit masking with a second prompt (Liu et al., 2024).

Continuing the research in the prompting directions, our proposed method introduces a style knowledge graph to augment text style transfer by including relevant parts of the graph in the prompt. Unlike previous research that relies primarily on

Dataset	Style 1 (s1)	Style 2 (s2)	Parallel?	# Samples	Task
Yelp	negative	positive	✗	428,632	sentiment transfer
Politeness	neutral	polite	✗	371,018	politeness transfer
GYAFC	informal	formal	✓	330,060	formality transfer
WNC	biased	neutral	✓	111,006	neutralizing subjective bias
Shakespeare	modern	Shakespearean	✓	42,150	personal style transfer
ParaDetox	toxic	neutral	✓	31,302	detoxification

Table 1: Statistics for the text style transfer datasets.

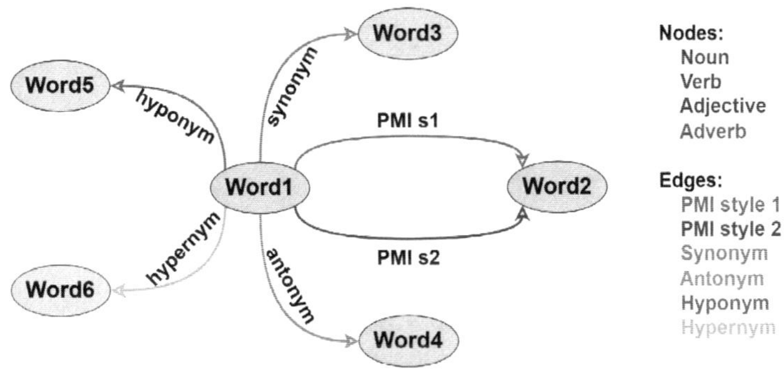

Figure 3: A visual representation of the style knowledge graph. The graph contains four types of nodes: nouns, verbs, adjectives, and adverbs, and six types of edges: PMI from style 1, PMI from style 2, synonyms, antonyms, hyponyms, and hypernyms.

generative capabilities or edit-based techniques, our approach aims to provide structured knowledge in the form of word suggestions to assist the LLM in the word choices for the output sentence. The combination of knowledge graphs and LLMs opens new directions for further research in the domain.

3 Style Knowledge Graph

3.1 Text Style Transfer Datasets

Text style transfer methods were evaluated using many parallel and non-parallel datasets. We selected a set of datasets that were mostly used for assessing text style transfer methods which we believe have the potential to foster further research in the field. The total number of datasets is six: Yelp[1], Politeness (Madaan et al., 2020), GYAFC (Rao and Tetreault, 2018), WNC (Pryzant et al., 2020), Shakespeare (Xu et al., 2012; Xu, 2014), and ParaDetox (Logacheva et al., 2022). Their statistics are summarized in Table 1.

3.2 Style Knowledge Graph Creation

We create a heterogeneous graph for each text style transfer dataset which we refer to as **Style Knowledge Graph (SKG)**.[2] The graph contains four types of nodes: nouns, verbs, adjectives, and adverbs; and six types of edges: PMI from style 1, PMI from style 2, synonyms, antonyms, hyponyms, and hypernyms. A visual representation of the graph is shown in Figure 3.

3.2.1 Nodes

Nodes in the SKG are derived from the words that are present in the corresponding text style transfer dataset as follows. For each word in the sentences, its grammatical category is determined using the Part-of-Speech (PoS) tagger available in the NLTK Python library[3]. Based on the determined category, the words are grouped into four node types. Considering that a word may have a different category in a different sentence, the same word may be present as two different nodes. Each pair of words and categories that appear at least once is part of the *candidate node set*. For each node (word and

[1]https://www.yelp.com/dataset, last visited: 05.09.2024

[2]The official GitHub repository for this paper is: https://github.com/mtoshevska/SKG

[3]https://www.nltk.org/, last visited: 05.09.2024

	Yelp	Politeness	GYAFC	WNC	Shakespeare	ParaDetox
Nouns	32,715	14,255	5,391	9,426	2,077	2,343
Verbs	10,453	5,622	3,789	4,435	1,336	864
Adjectives	15,646	5,020	3,025	6,839	732	807
Adverbs	2,306	891	889	1,467	287	174
# Nodes	61,120	25,788	13,094	22,167	4,432	4,188
PMI s1	136,107	95,284	27,734	400,521	3,966	3,614
PMI s2	573,226	241,565	18,540	367,898	3,213	1,417
Synonyms	14,202	10,763	5,731	18,443	2,448	585
Antonyms	523	668	392	1,576	116	13
Hyponyms	16,637	16,962	7,705	26,961	3,169	234
Hypernyms	14,042	16,129	6,538	25,840	2.834	219
# Edges	754,737	381,371	66,640	841,239	15,746	6,082

Table 2: Graph statistics (number of nodes and edges) for the six style knowledge graphs.

its grammatical category), we calculate the polarities (Li et al., 2018) in both styles using the Eq. 1:

$$p(w, s_i) = \frac{count(w, D_{s_i}) + \lambda}{count(w, D_{s_j}) + \lambda} \tag{1}$$

where $count(w, D_{s_i})$ is the number of times a word w appears in the set D_{s_i} of sentences with style s_i, and λ is the smoothing parameter. Then the absolute difference between both polarities is computed. The first 20% of the words with the highest polarity difference compose the *final set of nodes* for the graph.

3.2.2 Edges

The edges in the graph belong to two categories based on the creation technique: edges based on the information extracted from the corresponding text style transfer dataset and edges based on WordNet (Miller, 1995) semantic relations. Edges are created only between nodes in the final set.

To create edges based on the text style transfer datasets, we calculated point-wise mutual information (PMI) in a particular style s_i for a pair of nodes m and n (Yao et al., 2019) using the Eq 2:

$$PMI(m, n, s_i) = log\frac{p(m, n, s_i)}{p(m, s_i) \cdot p(n, s_i)} \tag{2}$$

$$p(m, n, s_i) = \frac{\#W(m, n, s_i)}{\#W_{s_i}} \tag{3}$$

$$p(m, s_i) = \frac{\#W(m, s_i)}{\#W_{s_i}} \tag{4}$$

where $\#W(m, n, s_i)$ is the number of sliding windows that contain both words m and n, $\#W(m, s_i)$ is the number of sliding windows that contain word m, and $\#W_{s_1}$ is total number of sliding windows in the corpus. A positive PMI value implies a high semantic correlation of words in the dataset and therefore we add an edge between a pair of nodes for which the PMI value in the corresponding style is greater than 0. Two sets of edges are created for the two styles.

We used the WordNet implementation in the NLTK Python library to extract semantic relations between words. For each word in the final set of nodes, we extracted four semantic relations: synonyms, antonyms, hyponyms, and hypernyms. The grammatical category of the word is also considered when extracting the semantic relations. Since our nodes set contains only a subset of the total words, an edge is added only if the two nodes are already part of the graph. The statistics for the six SKGs are summarized in Table 2.

4 Baseline Experiments

4.1 Text Style Transfer Tasks and Datasets

We performed prompting experiments to evaluate the effectiveness of augmenting text style transfer tasks with a style knowledge graph. For the preliminary results, we evaluate the approach on four text style transfer tasks using the parallel datasets and the created SKGs described in the previous section: *formality transfer* with the **GYAFC** dataset, *neutralizing subjective bias* with the **WNC** dataset, *personal style transfer* with the **Shakespeare** dataset, and *text detoxification* with **ParaDetox** dataset.

4.2 SKG-augmented Prompting

Two prompting strategies were explored for text style transfer across our selected tasks. An example

Model	Technique	rBLEU↑	sBLEU↓	Acc↑	PPL↓	GM$_2$↑	GM$_3$↑
Standard prompting							
T5$_{small}$	0-shot	12.7	52.4	49.4	**185.4**	25.0	21.6
T5$_{base}$	4-shot	10.9	**13.9**	27.8	262.8	17.4	16.6
FLAN-T5$_{small}$	1-shot	38.7	40.9	71.0	396.8	52.4	34.0
FLAN-T5$_{base}$	1-shot	36.6	47.2	<u>73.9</u>	229.7	52.0	34.8
Prompting augmented with SKG							
T5$_{small}$	1-shot$_{SKG}$	10.8	27.5	17.2	395.3	13.7	13.9
T5$_{base}$	4-shot$_{SKG}$	12.4	<u>17.8</u>	18.5	456.6	15.1	14.8
FLAN-T5$_{small}$	1-shot$_{SKG}$	<u>46.8</u>	23.6	73.7	461.9	<u>58.7</u>	<u>36.4</u>
FLAN-T5$_{base}$	1-shot$_{SKG}$	**48.9**	25.8	**88.0**	<u>201.4</u>	**65.6**	**40.9**

Table 3: Zero-shot and few-shot performance with standard prompting and prompting augmented with SKG for formality transfer on the GYAFC dataset. Only the best result per model is shown. rBLEU - reference-BLEU. sBLEU - self-BLEU. Acc - Accuracy. PPL - Perplexity. GM$_2$ - Geometric Mean (rBLEU and Acc). GM$_3$ - Geometric Mean (rBLEU, Acc, and PPL). The best value is **bold** and the second best is <u>underlined</u>.

of the two prompting strategies is shown in Figure 1. The first approach employs a simple prompt that specifies only the input and desired target style designed following the recommendations from related research that evaluate prompting techniques for text style transfer. It was used as a baseline for comparison. The second approach integrates style-relevant semantic information from a style knowledge graph to enrich the prompt with contextually relevant alternatives that guide the model toward generating outputs in line with the desired style attributes. Beginning with identifying the top three words in the input sentence with the highest target style polarity, a corresponding subgraph is extracted from the style knowledge graph for each of the three words. The semantic relations of the top three words (synonyms, antonyms, hyponyms, and hypernyms) are added to the prompt to enrich the input with contextual clues. For both prompting strategies, we experimented with zero-shot and few-shot settings. An overview of the two strategies is displayed in Figure 2.

4.3 Evaluation metrics

Evaluation has been performed across three dimensions to comply with the previous research in the field. The *semantic content preservation* was evaluated with the BLEU (Papineni et al., 2002) metric. The Prompt-and-Rerank (Suzgun et al., 2022) method proposed using self-BLEU (sBLEU) to measure the degree to which the model directly copies the input sentence and reference-BLEU (rBLEU) to measure the distance from the ground-truth references. We also report on these two metrics. *Style transfer strength* was calculated with the accuracy of a pre-trained DistilRoBERTa (Sajjad et al., 2020) model on the style detection task as a percentage of the generated sentences labeled with the target style by the model. To measure the *fluency*, the perplexity of the generated sentences with a pre-trained GPT-2 (Radford et al., 2019) model was computed. Several studies (Li et al., 2018; Luo et al., 2019, 2023) use the geometric mean of rBLEU and accuracy to compute a single *joint* metric. While we calculated the two-fold joint metric, we also included the inverse perplexity value to compute a three-fold joint metric that integrates the three evaluation dimensions. The inverse perplexity was computed using the Eq. 5:

$$PPL_{inv} = \frac{1}{1 + ln(PPL)} \tag{5}$$

4.4 Implementation Details

For both prompting strategies, we assess the performance of multiple LLMs that encompass different parameter sizes: T5 (Raffel et al., 2020) and FLAN-T5 (Chung et al., 2022). Following the previous studies, we experiment with zero-shot and few-shot settings. For the few-shot setting, we explored with 1, 2, 3, and 4 demonstrations. We have used PyTorch implementation of the models available in the HuggingFace Transformers library[4] and evaluation metrics available in the HuggingFace Evaluate library[5].

[4]https://huggingface.co/docs/transformers/en/index, last visited: 15.09.2024

[5]https://huggingface.co/docs/evaluate/en/index, last visited: 15.09.2024

5 Results and Discussion

In this section, we present the main results for the proposed approach of augmenting text style transfer with SKG which we hope to serve as a baseline for comparison of further research in the field. Due to space limitations, we present only the results for formality transfer. For the results on the other datasets and results with other LLMs for the formality transfer task on the GYAFC dataset, we encourage the reader to refer to the Appendix.

5.1 Main Results

Table 3 presents the evaluation results of standard prompting and prompting augmented with SKG. Both prompting strategies were evaluated on four models: $T5_{small}$, $T5_{base}$, FLAN-$T5_{small}$, and FLAN-$T5_{base}$. A total of five experiments were performed for each model and prompting strategy. For brevity, only the best-performing one in terms of geometric mean is shown.

The evaluation results suggest that SKG-augmented prompting improves content preservation for formality transfer, as demonstrated by higher rBLEU and lower sBLEU scores when compared with standard prompting. A possible reason may be the structure of the prompt that provides specific word choices. This approach includes specific word suggestions as part of the input prompt that help the model to choose particular words for the output sentence.

For style transfer strength, FLAN-T5 achieved higher accuracy with SKG-augmented prompting, while T5 achieved higher accuracy with standard prompting. FLAN-T5, which is an instruction-tuned LLM, may benefit more from structured prompts that offer more context for the word choices that align with the desired target style. The prompt design closely resembles the instruction setting that was used for training. Both geometric mean scores further confirm this hypothesis.

Although SKG-augmented prompting improves content preservation and in some cases improves style transfer strength, this approach fails to retain the fluency for three out of four models. As indicated by the higher perplexity, we observe a decrease in fluency in the SKG-augmented setting. A possible reason may be the word suggestions in the prompt that potentially increase the complexity and result in less fluent outputs. By adding particular word suggestions, sometimes the model tends to copy and include them in the output which has a potential negative impact of fluency. To address this limitation a future direction would be to experiment with LLMs with more parameters, as these models are typically more fluent.

	rBLEU	sBLEU	Acc	PPL
0-shot	18.4	72.2	22.6	4935.6
1-shot	**48.9**	**25.8**	**88.0**	**201.4**
2-shot	<u>44.9</u>	<u>29.7</u>	<u>74.8</u>	338.2
3-shot	42.1	32.3	69.3	<u>318.6</u>
4-shot	40.0	32.7	61.8	635.2

Table 4: Comparison of different number of demonstrations in the prompt for our best-performing approach for SKG-augmented prompting (FLAN-$T5_{base}$). rBLEU - reference-BLEU. sBLEU - self-BLEU. Acc - Accuracy. PPL - Perplexity. The best value is **bold** and the second best is <u>underlined</u>.

5.2 Effect of Number of Demonstrations in the Prompt

Our best-performing model for formality transfer is FLAN-$T5_{base}$ augmented with SKG in a one-shot setting. For further analysis, we use only this model. Next, we explore how the different number of demonstrations in the prompt affects the performance. Following the prior studies, we experimented with 0-4 demonstrations. The results are summarized in Table 4. The results suggest that the best performance is achieved with a single demonstration i.e. in a one-shot setting. One-shot prompting yielded the highest rBLEU and accuracy, and the lowest perplexity and sBLEU.

The zero-shot approach showed the worst performance across all metrics, with a significant decrease in fluency. We hypothesize that the absence of demonstrations negatively impacts the capability of generating fluent outputs in the desired target style. While there is an improvement with the switch from a zero-shot to a one-shot setting, further increasing the number of demonstrations also results in lower performance. In contrast to previous findings, in our approach, adding additional examples in the prompt may introduce complexity that reduces overall performance.

5.3 Comparison with Pre-LLM and LLM-based methods

Table 5 shows the performance of our best model against previous LLM and pre-LLM approaches. In comparison with pre-LLM unsupervised methods, SKG-augmented prompting showed competitive

Approach	rBLEU↑	sBLEU↓	Acc↑	PPL↓
Pre-LLM approaches				
CAAE (Shen et al., 2017)	17.9	-	75.3	-
DeleteOnly (Li et al., 2018)	29.2	-	18.8	-
DeleteAndRetrieve (Li et al., 2018)	21.2	-	55.2	-
MultiDecoder (Fu et al., 2018)	12.3	-	17.9	-
StyleEmbedding (Fu et al., 2018)	7.9	-	22.7	-
DualRL (Luo et al., 2019)	<u>41.9</u>	-	71.1	-
LLM approaches				
P&R (Suzgun et al., 2022)	36.4	49.6	*85.0*	<u>68.0</u>
PromptEdit (Luo et al., 2023)	37.7	50.2	81.0	87.0
PEGF (Liu et al., 2024)	38.2	<u>46.4</u>	**88.0**	**31.0**
SKGPrompt (Ours)	***48.9***	***25.8***	***88.0***	*201.4*

Table 5: Comparison of our best-performing approach for SKG-augmented prompting with previous pre-LLM and LLM-based approaches for formality transfer on the GYAFC dataset. rBLEU - reference-BLEU. sBLEU - self-BLEU. Acc - Accuracy. PPL - Perplexity. The best value is **bold** and the second best is <u>underlined</u>. The results for previous approaches were obtained either from the original papers that introduce the particular approach or, if an approach was not initially designed for formality transfer, from other studies that re-ran those approaches for comparison. Results for DeleteOnly, DeleteAndRetrieve, MultiDecoder, StyleEmbedding, and CAAE were obtained from (Luo et al., 2019). Results for P&R and PromptEdit were obtained from (Liu et al., 2024). For all other approaches the results were obtained from their original paper.

performances, surpassing them in content preservation and accuracy, despite not being trained or fine-tuned on the task.

When compared with previous LLM prompting-based approaches, SKG-augmented prompting achieves the overall best performance for content preservation, as suggested by its highest rBLEU score. Demonstrated by similar accuracy scores, we observe that our approach matches the PEGF (Liu et al., 2024) approach for style transfer strength. Both approaches share a similar idea of identifying stylistic words. PEGF identifies stylistic words via prompting and replaces them with a second prompt, while our approach utilizes style polarities to determine stylistic words and provides word suggestions based on semantic relations.

As indicated by the higher perplexity score, our approach demonstrates worse performance in fluency. Its outputs are less fluent compared to other LLM-based prompting methods. One possible reason could be the fact that these models utilize LLMs with more parameters that are considered to generate more fluent outputs.

5.4 Ablation Experiments

To analyze the contribution of different parts of the SKG to the text style transfer task, we perform ablation experiments. The experiments were performed for our best-performing model (FLAN-T5$_{base}$ in a one-shot setting): **no SR** - prompt without semantic relations, **all SR** - prompt with all semantic relations, **o/ Rel** - prompt with a single semantic relation *Rel*, and **w/o Rel** - prompt with all semantic relations except *Rel*. The results are summarized in Table 6

	rBLEU	sBLEU	Acc	PPL
no SR	48.3	26.6	86.1	306.6
o/ Syn	48.5	26.4	87.3	232.7
o/ Ant	48.3	26.5	86.4	349.4
o/ HypR	48.5	26.6	87.1	232.9
o/ HypO	48.5	26.5	<u>87.9</u>	285.7
w/o Syn	<u>48.8</u>	26.0	87.7	234.3
w/o Ant	<u>48.8</u>	26.0	87.7	<u>228.0</u>
w/o HypR	**48.9**	**25.8**	**88.1**	230.8
w/o HypO	**48.9**	<u>25.9</u>	<u>87.9</u>	243.6
all SR	**48.9**	**25.8**	<u>87.9</u>	**201.4**

Table 6: Results of the ablation experiments for our best-performing approach for SKG-augmented prompting for formality transfer on the GYAFC dataset. rBLEU - reference-BLEU. sBLEU - self-BLEU. Acc - Accuracy. PPL - Perplexity. The best value is **bold** and the second best is <u>underlined</u>.

The results of the ablation experiments demonstrate that semantic relations have a positive impact on performance. The best overall results are achieved when all semantic relations are used. Excluding specific semantic relations results in an increase in perplexity thus confirming that although the overall perplexity is relatively high, they have a positive impact.

Excluding hypernyms or hyponyms does not change the rBLEU score suggesting that these relations may not have a critical role in preserving the content. This is further confirmed by the increase in the accuracy score when hypernyms are excluded. On the contrary, excluding synonyms and antonyms negatively impacts the performance with an increase in perplexity and a slight decrease in accuracy and rBLEU.

6 Conclusion

In this paper, we proposed a Style Knowledge Graph for augmenting text style transfer using large language models. The SKG captures words, their attributes, and relations in a particular style to provide additional information for the task. We conducted preliminary experiments with prompting where the relevant part of the SKG was added as part of the prompt. The evaluation results demonstrated the potential of this method for enhancing content preservation and accuracy while highlighting areas for further improvement, particularly in fluency. We hope that this research will inspire further research in the field, extending beyond prompting to investigate new approaches and methodologies for text style transfer. SKGs have the potential to augment other text generation tasks beyond text style transfer, for example by guiding the model to generate more coherent summaries based on the selection of key parts of the input. We hope that future research will further explore this direction for SKGs for more context-aware and reliable text generation.

7 Limitations

Based on our experiments, we identified a few limitations. In some cases, parts of the instruction were returned as part of the output. This occurred more frequently with the T5 model. Since T5 is not an instruction fine-tuned model, challenges in distinguishing task instructions from the input content may be due to its lack of instruction-tuning. We observed lower performance for the SKG-augmented prompting when using smaller datasets. Since smaller datasets will lead to creating smaller SKGs we believe that this drop in performance is a direct result of the reduced richness and coverage of the SKG. A possible future direction to address this limitation may be to enrich the SKG with more information.

8 Ethical Considerations

As with other text generation tasks, our approach holds potential risks of misuse for malicious purposes, such as generating text that is negative, toxic, text that contains subjective bias, or text impersonating a specific author. Since we used existing text style transfer datasets to construct the SKG, any potential biases present in those datasets could be transferred and replicated in the SKG. Moreover, since LLMs are trained on datasets collected from the web, any biases present in the training data may be reflected in the outputs of our method. To address these risks it is crucial to raise awareness among researchers and users of such methods about the ethical implications and to promote responsible use for positive purposes.

References

Yu Cheng, Zhe Gan, Yizhe Zhang, Oussama Elachqar, Dianqi Li, and Jingjing Liu. 2020. Contextual text style transfer. In *Proceedings of the 2020 Conference on Empirical Methods in Natural Language Processing: Findings*, pages 2915–2924.

Hyung Won Chung, Le Hou, Shayne Longpre, Barret Zoph, Yi Tay, William Fedus, Yunxuan Li, Xuezhi Wang, Mostafa Dehghani, Siddhartha Brahma, et al. 2022. Scaling instruction-finetuned language models. *CoRR*.

Mingkai Deng, Jianyu Wang, Cheng-Ping Hsieh, Yihan Wang, Han Guo, Tianmin Shu, Meng Song, Eric Xing, and Zhiting Hu. 2022. Rlprompt: Optimizing discrete text prompts with reinforcement learning. In *Proceedings of the 2022 Conference on Empirical Methods in Natural Language Processing*, pages 3369–3391.

Zhenxin Fu, Xiaoye Tan, Nanyun Peng, Dongyan Zhao, and Rui Yan. 2018. Style transfer in text: Exploration and evaluation. In *Thirty-Second AAAI Conference on Artificial Intelligence*, pages 663–670.

Ian Goodfellow, Jean Pouget-Abadie, Mehdi Mirza, Bing Xu, David Warde-Farley, Sherjil Ozair, Aaron Courville, and Yoshua Bengio. 2014. Generative adversarial nets. In *Advances in neural information processing systems*, pages 2672–2680.

Zhiting Hu, Zichao Yang, Xiaodan Liang, Ruslan Salakhutdinov, and Eric P Xing. 2017. Toward controlled generation of text. In *Proceedings of the 34th International Conference on Machine Learning-Volume 70*, pages 1587–1596.

Wen Lai, Viktor Hangya, and Alexander Fraser. 2024. Style-specific neurons for steering llms in text style transfer. *CoRR*.

Guillaume Lample, Sandeep Subramanian, Eric Smith, Ludovic Denoyer, Marc'Aurelio Ranzato, and Y-Lan Boureau. 2019. Multiple-attribute text rewriting. In *7th International Conference on Learning Representations, ICLR 2019, New Orleans, LA, USA, May 6-9, 2019*. OpenReview.net.

Juncen Li, Robin Jia, He He, and Percy Liang. 2018. Delete, Retrieve, Generate: A simple approach to sentiment and style transfer. In *Proceedings of the 2018 Conference of the North American Chapter of the Association for Computational Linguistics: Human Language Technologies, Volume 1 (Long Papers)*, pages 1865–1874.

Pusheng Liu, Lianwei Wu, Linyong Wang, Sensen Guo, and Yang Liu. 2024. Step-by-step: Controlling arbitrary style in text with large language models. In *Proceedings of the 2024 Joint International Conference on Computational Linguistics, Language Resources and Evaluation (LREC-COLING 2024)*, pages 15285–15295.

Varvara Logacheva, Daryna Dementieva, Sergey Ustyantsev, Daniil Moskovskiy, David Dale, Irina Krotova, Nikita Semenov, and Alexander Panchenko. 2022. Paradetox: Detoxification with parallel data. In *Proceedings of the 60th Annual Meeting of the Association for Computational Linguistics (Volume 1: Long Papers)*, pages 6804–6818.

Fuli Luo, Peng Li, Jie Zhou, Pengcheng Yang, Baobao Chang, Xu Sun, and Zhifang Sui. 2019. A dual reinforcement learning framework for unsupervised text style transfer. In *Proceedings of the Twenty-Eighth International Joint Conference on Artificial Intelligence*. International Joint Conferences on Artificial Intelligence Organization.

Guoqing Luo, Yu Han, Lili Mou, and Mauajama Firdaus. 2023. Prompt-based editing for text style transfer. In *Findings of the Association for Computational Linguistics: EMNLP 2023*, pages 5740–5750.

Aman Madaan, Amrith Setlur, Tanmay Parekh, Barnabás Póczos, Graham Neubig, Yiming Yang, Ruslan Salakhutdinov, Alan W. Black, and Shrimai Prabhumoye. 2020. Politeness transfer: A tag and generate approach. In *Proceedings of the 58th Annual Meeting of the Association for Computational Linguistics, ACL 2020, Online, July 5-10, 2020*, pages 1869–1881. Association for Computational Linguistics.

George A Miller. 1995. Wordnet: a lexical database for english. *Communications of the ACM*, 38(11):39–41.

Sourabrata Mukherjee and Ondřej Dušek. 2023. Leveraging low-resource parallel data for text style transfer. In *Proceedings of the 16th International Natural Language Generation Conference*, pages 388–395.

Lei Pan, Yunshi Lan, Yang Li, and Weining Qian. 2024. Unsupervised text style transfer via llms and attention masking with multi-way interactions. *CoRR*.

Kishore Papineni, Salim Roukos, Todd Ward, and Wei-Jing Zhu. 2002. Bleu: a method for automatic evaluation of machine translation. In *Proceedings of the 40th annual meeting of the Association for Computational Linguistics*, pages 311–318.

Reid Pryzant, Richard Diehl Martinez, Nathan Dass, Sadao Kurohashi, Dan Jurafsky, and Diyi Yang. 2020. Automatically neutralizing subjective bias in text. In *Proceedings of the aaai conference on artificial intelligence*, volume 34, pages 480–489.

Alec Radford, Jeffrey Wu, Rewon Child, David Luan, Dario Amodei, and Ilya Sutskever. 2019. Language models are unsupervised multitask learners. *OpenAI blog*, 1(8):9.

Colin Raffel, Noam Shazeer, Adam Roberts, Katherine Lee, Sharan Narang, Michael Matena, Yanqi Zhou, Wei Li, and Peter J Liu. 2020. Exploring the limits of transfer learning with a unified text-to-text transformer. *The Journal of Machine Learning Research*, 21(1):5485–5551.

Sudha Rao and Joel Tetreault. 2018. Dear Sir or Madam, may I introduce the GYAFC dataset: Corpus, benchmarks and metrics for formality style transfer. In *Proceedings of the 2018 Conference of the North American Chapter of the Association for Computational Linguistics: Human Language Technologies, Volume 1 (Long Papers)*, pages 129–140.

Emily Reif, Daphne Ippolito, Ann Yuan, Andy Coenen, Chris Callison-Burch, and Jason Wei. 2022. A recipe for arbitrary text style transfer with large language models. In *Proceedings of the 60th Annual Meeting of the Association for Computational Linguistics (Volume 2: Short Papers)*, pages 837–848.

Hassan Sajjad, Fahim Dalvi, Nadir Durrani, and Preslav Nakov. 2020. On the effect of dropping layers of pre-trained transformer models. *CoRR*.

Tianxiao Shen, Tao Lei, Regina Barzilay, and Tommi Jaakkola. 2017. Style transfer from non-parallel text by cross-alignment. In *Advances in neural information processing systems*, pages 6830–6841.

Ilya Sutskever, Oriol Vinyals, and Quoc V Le. 2014. Sequence to sequence learning with neural networks. In *Advances in neural information processing systems*, pages 3104–3112.

Mirac Suzgun, Luke Melas-Kyriazi, and Dan Jurafsky. 2022. Prompt-and-rerank: A method for zero-shot and few-shot arbitrary textual style transfer with small language models. In *Proceedings of the 2022 Conference on Empirical Methods in Natural Language Processing*, pages 2195–2222.

Martina Toshevska and Sonja Gievska. 2024. Large language models for text style transfer: Exploratory analysis of prompting and knowledge augmentation techniques. In *Intelligent Environments 2024: Combined Proceedings of Workshops and Demos & Videos Session*, pages 134–142. IOS Press.

Ronald J Williams. 1992. Simple statistical gradient-following algorithms for connectionist reinforcement learning. *Machine learning*, 8:229–256.

Ruochen Xu, Tao Ge, and Furu Wei. 2019. Formality style transfer with hybrid textual annotations. *CoRR*.

Wei Xu. 2014. *Data-driven approaches for paraphrasing across language variations*. Ph.D. thesis, New York University.

Wei Xu, Alan Ritter, Bill Dolan, Ralph Grishman, and Colin Cherry. 2012. Paraphrasing for style. In *Proceedings of COLING 2012*, pages 2899–2914.

Wenda Xu, Michael Saxon, Misha Sra, and William Yang Wang. 2022. Self-supervised knowledge assimilation for expert-layman text style transfer. In *Proceedings of the AAAI Conference on Artificial Intelligence*, volume 36, pages 11566–11574.

Liang Yao, Chengsheng Mao, and Yuan Luo. 2019. Graph convolutional networks for text classification. In *Proceedings of the AAAI conference on artificial intelligence*, volume 33, pages 7370–7377.

Tianyi Zhang, Varsha Kishore, Felix Wu, Kilian Q Weinberger, and Yoav Artzi. 2019. Bertscore: Evaluating text generation with bert. In *International Conference on Learning Representations*.

Chang Zong, Yuyan Chen, Weiming Lu, Jian Shao, and Yueting Zhuang. 2024. Proswitch: Knowledge-guided language model fine-tuning to generate professional and non-professional styled text. *CoRR*.

A Appendix

A.1 Evaluation Results with Other LLMs

Apart from the main experiments with T5 and FLAN-T5 models, additional experiments with LLaMA and GPT models were performed on the formality transfer task with the GYAFC dataset. Only the zero-shot experiments were performed because of the time required for generating output sentences with these models. Their evaluation with few-shot prompting remains as future work.

LLaMa and GPT model variants showed unexpectedly low BLEU scores for content preservation. We believe that the low BLEU scores are due to the fact that the choice of words made by these models differs from the words in the ground truth sentence. BLEU is a metric based on n-gram overlap and it is expected to obtain lower scores when there is a different choice of words in the generated and the expected sentence. However, by manual inspection, we noticed that the generated output sentences managed to preserve the content of the input sentence to some extent, but used different words and often added additional explanations. To evaluate content preservation, BERTScore (Zhang et al., 2019), which compares the semantic meaning based on embedding vectors, was computed instead of BLEU. In Table 7, example outputs from these models are shown, and the full evaluation results are summarized in Table 8.

The results indicate that T5 and FLAN-T5 models obtain the best overall results for content preservation as measured by the higher BERTScore for both standard zero-shot and SKG-augmented zero-shot prompting. In terms of style transfer strength measured by accuracy, LLaMA-based models significantly outperform the other approaches for SKG-augmented prompting. For standard prompting, GPT-Neo showed the best performance thus indicating that GPT-based models can better leverage structured prompts to generate a sentence in the desired style. These models demonstrated significantly better fluency than the T5-based and LLaMA-based approaches. A possible reason could be the setting for evaluating fluency which relies on calculating perplexity with GPT-2. Considering that GPT-2 is a part of the same family of models, output sentences generated by GPT-based models may be more naturally aligned with the evaluation metric therefore leading to significantly higher fluency scores.

A.2 Evaluation Results for Other Datasets

In the tables below we present the evaluation results for the remaining three text style transfer tasks with parallel datasets: neutralizing subjective bias on the WNC dataset (Table 9), personal style transfer on the Shakespeare dataset (Table 10), and text detoxification on the ParaDetox dataset (Table 11). Both prompting strategies were evaluated on four models: $T5_{small}$, $T5_{base}$, FLAN-$T5_{small}$, and FLAN-$T5_{base}$. A total of five experiments were performed for each model and prompting strategy. For brevity, only the best-performing one in terms of geometric mean is shown.

The results do not indicate a clear superiority of the SKG-augmented approach when compared against standard contrastive prompting among all three tasks. The significantly smaller number of samples in the corresponding datasets may be a contributing factor for the lower performance. Considering that smaller datasets will lead to creating smaller SKGs the lower performance could be a result of the reduced richness and coverage of the SKG. To address this limitation, a possible future direction would be to enrich the SKG with more information. Across all experiments, the sBLEU scores are consistently lower suggesting that the SKG-augmented approach may favor generating more diverse outputs rather than simply copying the input.

Input sentence: *You can get almost anything on ebay!*
Ground truth output sentence: *You can get almost anything on ebay!*
Predicted output sentence: *It's possible to obtain nearly any item through eBays online auction service.*
Input: *Where in the world do you come up with these questions????*
Ground truth output sentence: *How do you come up with these questions?*
Predicted output sentence: *I am curious as to where your ideas for this quiz originated.*
Input: *i think pretty much they're all sort of humorous*
Ground truth output sentence: *I think they are all very funny.*
Predicted output sentence: *I believe that most are somewhat funny.*

Table 7: Example output sentences for the formality transfer task on the GYAFC dataset. The outputs were generated with the LLaMa-2_{13B} with zero-shot prompting augmented with SKG.

Model	BERTScore↑	Acc↑	PPL↓	GM_2↑	GM_3↑
		Standard prompting			
$T5_{small}$	**99.0**	49.4	185.4	66.6	41.5
$T5_{base}$	91.7	37.2	340.3	18.5	17.1
FLAN-$T5_{small}$	92.2	23.1	805.4	46.2	30.3
FLAN-$T5_{base}$	<u>93.5</u>	24.5	318.9	47.9	32.4
LLaMA-2_{7B}	88.6	52.2	390.7	68.0	40.5
LLaMA-2_{13B}	81.2	36.5	<u>64.5</u>	54.4	38.6
LLaMA-2-$chat_{7B}$	88.5	83.3	548.1	<u>85.8</u>	<u>46.6</u>
LLaMA-2-$chat_{13B}$	88.0	<u>84.4</u>	610.2	**86.1**	46.4
GPT-J_{6B}	81.6	31.4	95.7	50.6	35.9
GPT-$Neo_{1.3B}$	87.2	**84.7**	**46.6**	85.0	**53.4**
		Prompting augmented with SKG			
$T5_{small}$	88.8	21.3	330.2	43.4	30.3
$T5_{base}$	89.1	37.2	476.3	18.2	16.7
FLAN-$T5_{small}$	<u>91.7</u>	18.7	2081.6	41.5	27.1
FLAN-$T5_{base}$	**92.4**	22.6	4935.6	45.7	28.0
LLaMA-2_{7B}	86.3	<u>88.8</u>	182.0	<u>87.6</u>	49.8
LLaMA-2_{13B}	86.0	**93.4**	142.7	**89.6**	<u>51.3</u>
LLaMA-2-$chat_{7B}$	87.1	80.3	568.7	83.7	45.7
LLaMA-2-$chat_{13B}$	87.3	81.5	629.3	84.4	45.7
GPT-J_{6B}	81.8	36.9	<u>102.2</u>	54.9	37.7
GPT-$Neo_{1.3B}$	87.0	79.5	**55.9**	83.1	**51.6**

Table 8: Zero-shot performance with standard prompting and prompting augmented with SKG for formality transfer on the GYAFC dataset with T5, FLAN-T5, LLaMA-2, and GPT. BERTScore - reference-BERTScore. Acc - Accuracy. PPL - Perplexity. GM_2 - Geometric Mean (BERTScore and Acc). GM_3 - Geometric Mean (BERTScore, Acc, and PPL). The best value is **bold** and the second best is <u>underlined</u>.

Model	Technique	rBLEU↑	sBLEU↓	Acc↑	PPL↓	GM$_2$↑	GM$_3$↑
			Standard prompting				
T5$_{small}$	0-shot	56.9	62.7	60.4	225.2	58.6	37.7
T5$_{base}$	0-shot	38.7	42.4	54.6	312.6	46.0	31.5
FLAN-T5$_{small}$	3-shot	<u>64.8</u>	70.5	<u>67.1</u>	**167.2**	<u>66.0</u>	<u>41.4</u>
FLAN-T5$_{base}$	4-shot	**77.9**	84.7	**71.0**	<u>187.2</u>	**74.4**	**44.6**
			Prompting augmented with SKG				
T5$_{small}$	0-shot$_{SKG}$	30.6	33.4	64.8	368.1	44.5	30.6
T5$_{base}$	0-shot$_{SKG}$	20.2	<u>22.1</u>	49.8	534.0	31.7	24.0
FLAN-T5$_{small}$	0-shot$_{SKG}$	46.7	50.7	54.5	1028.6	50.4	31.8
FLAN-T5$_{base}$	0-shot$_{SKG}$	19.6	**21.3**	55.4	170753.6	33.0	20.3

Table 9: Zero-shot and few-shot performance with standard prompting and prompting augmented with SKG for neutralizing subjective bias on the WNC dataset. Only the best result per model is shown. rBLEU - reference-BLEU. sBLEU - self-BLEU. Acc - Accuracy. PPL - Perplexity. GM$_2$ - Geometric Mean (rBLEU and Acc). GM$_3$ - Geometric Mean (rBLEU, Acc, and PPL). The best value is **bold** and the second best is <u>underlined</u>.

Model	Technique	rBLEU↑	sBLEU↓	Acc↑	PPL↓	GM$_2$↑	GM$_3$↑
			Standard prompting				
T5$_{small}$	0-shot	10.0	46.6	60.2	**152.9**	24.5	21.5
T5$_{base}$	0-shot	11.3	52.5	82.8	1272.1	30.6	22.6
FLAN-T5$_{small}$	1-shot	<u>14.8</u>	75.0	84.5	457.9	35.3	<u>26.0</u>
FLAN-T5$_{base}$	2-shot	**16.0**	83.5	<u>91.3</u>	<u>204.6</u>	**38.2**	**28.5**
			Prompting augmented with SKG				
T5$_{small}$	0-shot$_{SKG}$	5.8	**24.1**	37.7	336.6	14.8	14.8
T5$_{base}$	0-shot$_{SKG}$	7.9	<u>32.5</u>	71.1	649.3	23.8	19.6
FLAN-T5$_{small}$	0-shot$_{SKG}$	12.7	72.5	87.8	797.4	33.4	24.4
FLAN-T5$_{base}$	0-shot$_{SKG}$	14.7	78.0	**92.3**	1190.5	<u>36.8</u>	25.6

Table 10: Zero-shot and few-shot performance with standard prompting and prompting augmented with SKG for personal style transfer on the Shakespeare dataset. Only the best result per model is shown. rBLEU - reference-BLEU. sBLEU - self-BLEU. Acc - Accuracy. PPL - Perplexity. GM$_2$ - Geometric Mean (rBLEU and Acc). GM$_3$ - Geometric Mean (rBLEU, Acc, and PPL). The best value is **bold** and the second best is <u>underlined</u>.

Model	Technique	rBLEU↑	sBLEU↓	Acc↑	PPL↓	GM$_2$↑	GM$_3$↑
			Standard prompting				
T5$_{small}$	0-shot	23.5	48.4	71.5	**451.7**	<u>41.0</u>	**28.7**
T5$_{base}$	0-shot	<u>26.6</u>	53.2	63.5	2222.5	**41.1**	<u>26.9</u>
FLAN-T5$_{small}$	1-shot	19.5	26.8	39.9	19440.1	27.9	19.3
FLAN-T5$_{base}$	0-shot	**29.8**	46.5	54.2	5204.3	40.2	25.7
			Prompting augmented with SKG				
T5$_{small}$	2-shot$_{SKG}$	12.5	22.2	<u>75.9</u>	<u>891.5</u>	30.8	23.0
T5$_{base}$	2-shot$_{SKG}$	9.9	16.9	**78.0**	1342.7	27.8	21.1
FLAN-T5$_{small}$	2-shot$_{SKG}$	8.1	**10.5**	48.7	56816.4	19.8	14.9
FLAN-T5$_{base}$	2-shot$_{SKG}$	8.9	<u>11.1</u>	50.7	36454.2	21.2	15.8

Table 11: Zero-shot and few-shot performance with standard prompting and prompting augmented with SKG for text detoxification on the ParaDetox dataset. Only the best result per model is shown. rBLEU - reference-BLEU. sBLEU - self-BLEU. Acc - Accuracy. PPL - Perplexity. GM$_2$ - Geometric Mean (rBLEU and Acc). GM$_3$ - Geometric Mean (rBLEU, Acc, and PPL). The best value is **bold** and the second best is <u>underlined</u>.

Entity Quality Enhancement in Knowledge Graphs through LLM-based Question Answering

Morteza Kamaladdini Ezzabady[1], **Farah Benamara**[1,2]
[1]IRIT, University of Toulouse, France, [2]IPAL, CNRS-NUS-A*STAR, Singapore
{morteza.ezzabady,farah.benamara}@irit.fr

Abstract

Most models for triple extraction from texts primarily focus on named entities. However, real-world applications often comprise non-named entities that pose serious challenges for entity linking and disambiguation. We focus on these entities and propose the first LLM-based entity revision framework to improve the quality of extracted triples via a multi-choice question-answering mechanism. When evaluated on two benchmark datasets, our results show a significant improvement, thereby generating more reliable triples for knowledge graphs.

1 Introduction

Triple extraction (TE) is a well-established NLP task where several deep learning models (Bouziani et al., 2024; Wang et al., 2022; Santosh et al., 2021; Wadhwa et al., 2023; Xu et al., 2023), and more recently, LLMs (Trajanoska et al., 2023; Chia et al., 2022; Li et al., 2024; Chen et al., 2023) have successfully been employed in benchmark datasets in different domains and languages (e.g., SemEval-2010 Task 8 (Hendrickx et al., 2010), TACRED (Zhang et al., 2017), BioRed (Luo et al., 2022)).

Most relation extraction models focus primarily on named entities such as person names, locations, and organizations, making them fail in dealing with a richer array of complex, non-named entities (hearafter N-NE). According to Paris and Suchanek (2021), N-NE are defined as noun phrases (NPs) that can be the subject or object of a predicate within a sentence such as "decision list" and "parsing-based ne rules" in Figure 1. N-NE can have several forms ranging from nominal group (e.g., *year 1944*), containing adjectives and adverbs (e.g., *very good questions*), prepositional phrases (e.g., *in the Arab World*), relative clauses or more complex syntactic constructions (e.g., *near-term growth prospects of the global economy*). N-NE are relatively frequent in textual data. For example, when manually analysing around 2K NPs extracted from Wikipedia, Paris and Suchanek (2021) found that 78% of NP heads are N-NE among which 38% are modified by an adjective, and 34% have a preposition. Despite their importance, their frequency in popular benchmark datasets is relatively low (e.g., TACRED only involves named entities).

Context: *first, decision list is used to learn the parsing-based ne rules.*

Gold: ('decision list', 'usage', 'parsing-based ne rules')
GPT-4: ('decision list', 'usage', 'learn the parsing-based ne rules')
Falcon-2: ('first, decision list', 'learn', 'parsing-based ne rules')

Figure 1: Triple extraction involving N-NE as given by gold manual annotations, Falcon-2 and GPT4 models. Wrong entities are in red.

N-NE pose serious challenges in knowledge graph (KG) construction and reasoning, because they remain *silent* with no chance to be linked into an existing knowledge bases (KBs) such as YAGO4 (Tanon et al., 2020) or Wikidata (Vrandečić, 2012). Figure 1 illustrates the impact these entities have on triple extraction from a sentence taken for SemEval 2018 Task 7. We compare the outputs of Falcon-2 (Sakor et al., 2020), a entity and relation linking tool over Wikidata, and zero-shot GPT-4 against the gold label. Although both models successfully identified the boundaries of the entities, they failed to correctly extract both the head and tail entities together.

N-NE have received little attention in the literature. Among the few works, Open Information Extraction tools such as OpenIE (Angeli et al., 2015) (see (Zhou et al., 2022) for a survey) output triples of subject, predicate, and object in an unsupervised way relaying on dependency parsers where relation arguments can contain N-NE. Paris and Suchanek (2021) performed a qualitative manual study of the nature of N-NE in Wikipedia. In this paper, we go one step further by proposing, for the first time as far as we know, **an end to end LLM-based entity**

Proceedings of the Generative AI and Knowledge Graph Workshop (GenAIK), pages 136–145
January 19, 2025.

revision framework that (a) automatically extracts triples from raw texts, (b) identifies N-NE, (c) enhances their quality by augmenting their likelihood of being successfully linked to an external knowledge base, which is a first important step to overall KG quality assessment (Chen et al., 2019).

To this end, we adopt a multiple choice prompting (MCP) strategy on top of a triple extractor to verify the extracted entities. MCP has been successfully used as a self-evaluation method to mitigate LLMs errors in complex problems like arithmetic and commonsense reasoning (Miao et al., 2023; Weng et al., 2023; Ren et al., 2023). It is newly employed here for entity quality enhancement. Our contributions are as follows:

1. A multiple-choice question answering (MCQA) strategy for enhancing LLMs to revise their extracted entities,

2. Comprehensive experiments with both open source and closed LLMs on two benchmark datasets for relation extraction,

3. A manual analysis of our results demonstrating the effectiveness of our framework in correctly identifying and selecting N-NE.

This paper is organized as follows. Section 2 presents our overall framework, Section 3 details the datasets used for evaluation, the experimental settings and evaluation metrics. We finally gives our results together with an error analysis in Section 4.

2 Entity Revision through LLM-based Question Answering

Figure 3 shows our three-steps framework: (1) It first extracts triples using an in-context learning approach. (2) It then ranks candidate entities and (3) refines entity selection through a multiple-choice format to improve accuracy by learning from common extraction errors.

It is important to note that our framework has been designed with modularity in mind, independently from the method used for triple extraction and how N-NE are initially identified. However as a first step and in order to evaluate the effectiveness of our approach when evaluated on benchmark datasets, we experiment with target relations as input to Step 1, the subsequent steps are agnostic to this guidance. This allows to increase the number of matching triples generated by LLMs when compared to gold annotations (see below) and therefore ensure a sufficient number of instances to derive meaningful conclusions (see Section 3.3 about the evaluation protocols). We detail below each step.

2.1 Step 1: Triple Extraction and Matching

We instruct the LLMs to extract triples via an in-context learning method following (Ozyurt et al., 2024; Lyu et al., 2023; Ma et al., 2023a) where prompts only contain the definition of the target relation. Given is a set of contexts $\mathcal{C} = \{c_i\}$. For each context c_i, the aim is to enumerate triples $\{(h_{ij}, r_{ij}, t_{ij})\}_{j=1}^{R_i}$, where $r_{ij} \in \mathcal{R}$ is a relation and h_{ij} and t_{ij} are the head and tail entities for the relation r_{ij}, and where R_i is the number of relations in c_i (cf. Figure 2).

Step 1 is evaluated by matching LLMs generated triples to gold ones based on overlapping entities. For instance, the gold triple for the given context in Figure 2 is (`global variables`, `USED-FOR`, `global properties`), of which only the extracted triple (`global variables`, `USED-FOR`, `representing global properties`) matches the gold standard.

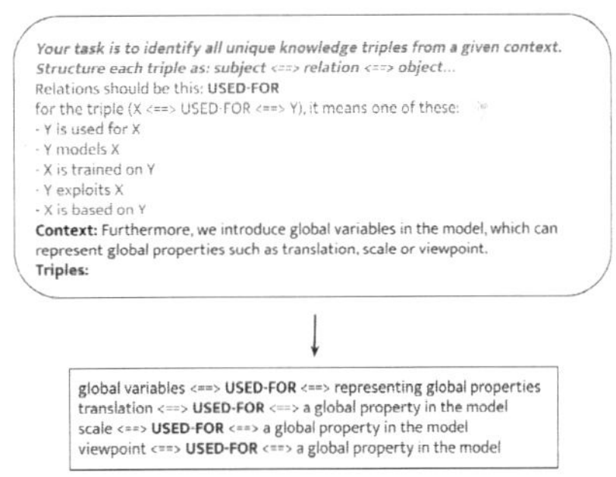

Figure 2: Example of prompt used for triple extraction. The green, blue and black in the top box represent the instruction, demonstration and test context in the prompt respectively. The red parts are the LLMs outputs.

2.2 Step 2: Candidates Selection

Let $\mathcal{G} = (\mathcal{E}, \mathcal{R}, \mathcal{T})$ be a knowledge graph, where $\mathcal{E}$ is the set of entities, $\mathcal{R}$ the set of relations, and $\mathcal{T} = \{(h, r, t) | h \in \mathcal{E}, r \in \mathcal{R}, t \in \mathcal{E}\}$ the set of triples. Given a query $(h, r, ?)$ (resp. $(?, r, t)$), the graph completion task ranks each entity by calculating its score to determine how well it makes the query hold, thereby achieving knowledge graph completion (Wei et al., 2023). This task inspired our approach; however, as we do not possess a predefined set of entities, we must generate a list of

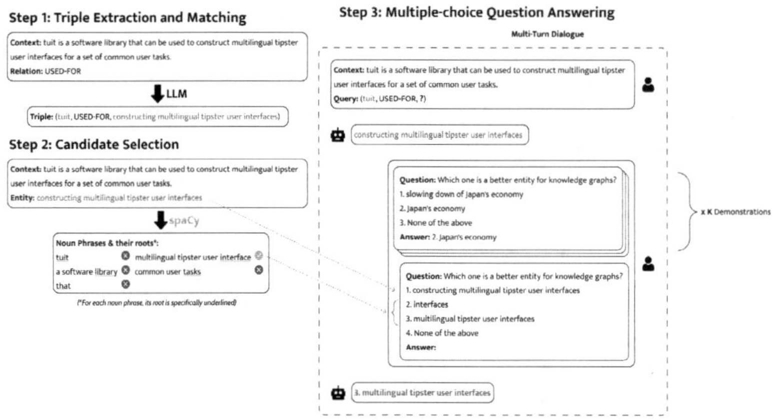

Figure 3: Overview of our entity revision framework: (1) **Triple extraction** from the given context to identify relevant relationships; (2) **Candidate selection**, where potential entities are shortlisted as relevant targets; (3) **Multiple-choice question-answering** to determine the most suitable entity.

potential candidates to fill the queries $(h_{ij}, r_{ij}, ?)$ (resp. $(?, r_{ij}, t_{ij})$) based on context c_i and utilize LLMs as a ranker.

Our candidate selector relies on SpaCy [1] parser,[2] known for its fast and accurate syntactic analysis, to select all noun phrases from context c_i that either contain the entity t_{ij} (resp. h_{ij}) or are contained by t_{ij} (resp. h_{ij}), along with the root of those noun phrases. This method ensures that the selected candidates are contextually relevant and are more likely to be correct entities that can replace low-quality extracted entities. Step 2 is then evaluated by checking if the selected candidate entities include the gold entities or not.

2.3 Step 3: Multiple Choice Question Answering (MCQA).

LLMs are generally not effective as few-shot information extractors, but they excel as rankers Ma et al. (2023b). We therefore employ prompting strategies similar to QA4RE (Zhang et al., 2023), transforming our task into multi-choice questions to more accurately select entities.

To enhance entity extraction, we utilize a set of K demonstration examples that target common extraction errors. These include entities mistakenly containing verbs, excessive adjectives, pronouns, determiners, and pseudo-sentences. Such errors often lead to inaccuracies in the model's outputs, particularly in sentences where the distance between head and tail entities in the context is long (Xu et al., 2023; Ezzabady et al., 2024). Following Mo et al. (2024) that use direct comparisons to better guide LLMs, each example is selected based on its ability to clearly demonstrate these specific issues, offering a dual presentation of both incorrect and correct entity identifications.

Here are our demonstration questions-answer pairs.

Verb phrase

```
Question: Which one is a better entity
for knowledge graphs?
1. slowing down of Japan's economy
2. Japan's economy
3. None of the above
Answer: 2. Japan's economy
```

Redundant adjective

```
Question: Which one is a better entity
in a knowledge graph?
1. sars-cov-2 outbreak
2. outbreak
3. large sars-cov-2 outbreak
4. None of the above
Answer: 1. sars-cov-2 outbreak
```

Determiner

```
Question: Which one is a better entity
in a knowledge graph?
1. identification
2. both language identification
3. language identification
```

[1] `https://spacy.io/`

[2] Although this step could also be performed by LLMs, we opted to use SpaCy here to keep the LLM more focused on the entity revision task.

```
4. None of the above
Answer: 3. language identification
```

Pronoun

```
Question: Which one is a better entity
in a knowledge graph?
1. application
2. My application
3. None of the above
Answer: 1. application
```

None of the above

```
Question: Which one is a better entity in
a knowledge graph?
1. keep inflation high in the near term
2. keep inflation high
3. None of the above
Answer: 3. None of the above
```

3 Experiments

3.1 Datasets

As far as we know, only two benchmark relation extraction datasets involving N-NE exist: SemEval 2018 Task 7 (Gábor et al., 2018) and SciERC (Luan et al., 2018). Both are *document-based* datasets annotated for entities and their relations extracted from scientific abstracts. They are a good choice to evaluate our framework (see Table 1) as their triples contain less than 5% of named entities (as given by SpaCy) and more importantly less than 35% are linked to Wikidata. This is also aligned with recent work by Zhu et al. (2024) who showed that SciERC is a challenge for making knowledge graphs, so that the performance of the best model (GPT-4) is less than 10%.

Gold Triples	SemEval 1,595			SciERC 4,265		
	Head	Tail	Both	Head	Tail	Both
% Named entities	3.71	2.13	0.13	4.71	3.42	0.49
% Linked with Wikidata	35.05	31.97	13.29	29.00	28.07	8.30

Table 1: SemEval and SciERC datasets statistics.

3.2 Experimental Settings

To increase triple matching and simplify the process for LLMs, we narrow down each document to sentences such that our input is a set of sentences $\{s | s \in d, h \in s, t \in s\}$.[3] This leads to a total of 1,578 sentences for SemEval and 4,151 for SciERC. For the inter-sentence relations (1.07% and 2.67% of triples in SemEval and SciERC respectively), we employ their documents as context.

Position bias and *No answer is true* are well known issues in MCQA with language models (Robinson et al., 2023). To address them, we follow the solutions proposed by Ren et al. (2023) as follows. We employ **shuffle and average** method that de-bias and correct answer position effects. To handle cases where none of the provided answers may be correct, we introduce a **None of the Above** option into the answer set, enhancing the model's ability to avoid overconfident incorrect predictions.

For our experiments, we rely on GPT-4,[4] LLaMA-3.1 8B-instruct[5] and Mistral 7B-instruct.[6] We compare our MCQA framework against two baselines:[7]

(a) **LLM with simple prompt (*simple*)**: which is similar to zero-shot learning where only the description of the task is given,

(b) **LLM with detailed prompt (*detailed*)**: that provides in addition a definition of what are considered to be good entities for a KG.

To demonstrate the superiority of our method over having specific guideline, we applied our method only on the *simple* baseline (hearafter ***simple+MCQA***). Both baselines operate in a zero-shot setting, MCQA being a few-shot prompting strategy where demonstration question-answer pairs are used to instruct the LLMs.

In Figure 4, we provide examples for different prompts as input and the corresponding output from GPT-4. In dialogues with LLMs, there are three key roles: the **System** role, which sets how the model answers; the **User** role, representing the individual who inputs queries; and the **Assistant** role, which encompasses the model's responses to user inputs. These roles collectively ensure a structured and effective interaction. A multi-turn dialogue involves a series of exchanges between the user and the assistant where each response builds on the previous interaction.

For all the models, and to avoid bias the same prompts have been used and more importantly,

[3]We also tested using documents as input, but the outcomes were inconclusive, e.g., in SciERC, the match rates for documents vs. sentences were 33.95% vs. 54.14%, respectively.

[4]https://platform.openai.com/docs/models/gpt-4-turbo-and-gpt-4

[5]https://llama.meta.com/llama3

[6]https://ollama.com/library/mistral:7b

[7]As this work focuses on improving LLMs performance, non-LLM methods are out of the scope of this paper.

demonstration questions were not sourced from evaluation datasets (cf. Section 2.3). Additionally, we set the number of demonstrations K to 4.[8] For implementation details see Appendix A.

3.3 Evaluation Protocol

We evaluate the performances in terms of four metrics, each metric aims to evaluate a particular step of our approach:

(a) Matched Triples. It counts the number of extracted triples from Step 1 that successfully match with at least one corresponding gold-standard triple. The matching is determined based on an overlap function, where a partial or complete overlap between the extracted and gold triples is sufficient to consider them matched. This metric provides an initial measure of how accurately the system can identify potential relationships from the context. For example, in Figure 4, none of the extracted triples via *detailed* prompt matches with the gold triple (`words, PART_WHOLE, corpus`).

(b) Candidate selector success rate. It evaluates the effectiveness of the candidate selection step (Step 2). Specifically, it measures how often the true gold-standard entity is included among the set of candidates presented during the selection process. A candidate selection is successful when the gold entity is present in the generated options. This metric highlights the robustness of the candidate generation process and its ability to retain contextually relevant entities for further refinement. For example in Figure 4, we can observe that the candidate selector in our *simple+MCQA* method successfully included the gold entity `"words"` as options for the question corresponding to the triple (`words, PART_WHOLE, corpus`).

(c) Correct entities. This metric evaluates Step 3 and focuses on the quality of entities within matched triples. It counts the number of entities within these triples that exactly match the corresponding entities in the gold-standard triples. We consider matches of entities at the head, tail and both head and tail positions. This metric is essential for assessing how accurately the framework identifies both the head and tail entities in relation to their expected true values, providing insight into the precision of the extraction process. For the gold triple (`words, PART_WHOLE, corpus`) from Figure 4, the outputs of the *simple* baseline and our *simple+MCQA* approach are `100,000 words` and `words`, respectively, as head entities, with the latter being the correct entity.

(d) Linking coverage. This metric is used to evaluate the overall LLM-based revision framework. It computes the percentage of entities that are linked to Wikidata, the largest collaborative general knowledge graph with more than 52 million instances (Heist et al., 2020). For example, in the gold triple (`words, PART_WHOLE, corpus`) from Figure 4, the tail entity `corpus` was linked to the entity with ID `Q461183` in Wikidata. To this end, we rely on SpaCy entity linker module[9]

4 Results and Discussions

4.1 Overall Results

Results are shown in Table 2. GPT-4 demonstrates notable improvements post-revision across all metrics on both datasets, most significantly in the whole triple category (i.e., head, tail and both), where the performance scores in terms of correct entities, rise 11% for SemEval and 9% for SciERC.

Conversely, LLaMA-3 exhibits a general decline in performance after revision across all categories. An interesting observation holds for the detailed baseline where LLaMA-3 seems to handle guidelines better than GPT-4 in the SemEval dataset where the matched triples was 323 vs. 218 for GPT-4. This could suggest that despite its smaller size and simpler architecture, which might hinder the integration of sophisticated entity revision techniques, LLaMA-3 is more compliant with structured guidelines.

Mistral initially performs worse than both GPT-4 and LLaMA-3; however, by applying our revision framework, its results notably improve. For instance, we observe an increase in correct entities in the head, tail and both for both datasets (except the head in SciERC). More importantly, the linking coverage also increases in particular for entities in tail positions in the extracted triples.

Finally, our results show the variability in performances between different LLMs in the triple extraction step where GPT4 is the best achieving a matching triples of 87% and 54.13% in SemEval and SciERC, respectively. This finding is inline with recent studies in generative relation extrac-

[8] We tested several values of K∈ [1, 4] and 4 was the best.

[9] `https://github.com/egerber/spaCy-entity-linker`

Input:
System: You are an expert in Knowledge graphs. Your task is to identify all unique knowledge triples from a given context. Structure each triple as: subject <==> relation <==> object. Separate each triple with a new line. Ensure that entities(subjects and objects) are clear, distinct, and specific concepts or items.
Relations should be this: PART_WHOLE
for the triple (X <==> PART_WHOLE <==> Y), it means one of these:
- X is a part, a component of Y
- X is found in Y
- Y is built from/composed of X
User: Context: after several experiments, and trained with a little corpus of 100,000 words, the system guesses correctly not placing commas with a precision of 96% and a recall of 98%.
Triples:
Output:
Assistant:
experiments <==> PART_WHOLE <==> trained with a little corpus of 100,000 words
100,000 words <==> PART_WHOLE <==> trained with a little corpus of 100,000 words
system <==> PART_WHOLE <==> experiments
system <==> PART_WHOLE <==> trained with a little corpus of 100,000 words
placing commas <==> PART_WHOLE <==> system guesses
precision of 96% <==> PART_WHOLE <==> system guesses
recall of 98% <==> PART_WHOLE <==> system guesses

Triple Extraction with simple prompt

Input:
System: You are an expert in Knowledge graphs. Your task is to identify and construct knowledge triples from the given context.
Each triple should consist of a subject, a relation, and an object, formatted as (subject <==> relation <==> object).
Adhere to these specific guidelines:
Entities (Subjects and Objects): Select key nouns or noun phrases that are concrete, distinct, and specific. These entities should represent tangible concepts or items and must not include actions or verbs. Ensure the entities are clear and unambiguous.
Separation of Components: Each part of the triple (subject, relation, object) must be distinctly identifiable and separate from the others. Ensure clarity in the distinction between these components.
Avoiding Ambiguity: Ensure that the phrasing of the triples avoids ambiguity. The entities and relation should be straightforward, leaving no room for multiple interpretations.
Relation: PART_WHOLE
for the triple (X <==> PART_WHOLE <==> Y), it means one of these:
- X is a part, a component of Y
- X is found in Y
- Y is built from/composed of X
User: Context: after several experiments, and trained with a little corpus of 100,000 words, the system guesses correctly not placing commas with a precision of 96% and a recall of 98%.
Triples:
Output:
Assistant:
1. (experiments <==> PART_WHOLE <==> several experiments)
2. (corpus of 100,000 words <==> PART_WHOLE <==> system training)
3. (precision of 96% <==> PART_WHOLE <==> system performance)
4. (recall of 98% <==> PART_WHOLE <==> system performance)

Triple Extraction with detailed prompt

Input:
System: You are an expert in Knowledge graphs. Your task is to complete the given triple by outputting a list of candidate for the missing entity (represented by "?") according to the context.
Candidates should be found in the context.
enumerate the candidates.
User: Context: after several experiments, and trained with a little corpus of 100,000 words, the system guesses correctly not placing commas with a precision of 96% and a recall of 98%.
Triple: (? <==> PART_WHOLE <==> trained with a little corpus of 100,000 words)
Assistant:
100,000 words
User: Follow the example:
Question: Which one is a better entity in a knowledge graph?
1. identification
2. both language identification
3. language identification
4. None of the above
Answer: 3. language identification
Question: Which one is a better entity in a knowledge graph?
1. words
2. 100,000 words
3. None of the above
Answer:
Output:
Assistant:
1. words

Multiple Choice Question Answering

Figure 4: Prompts and responses for our three models: LLM with simple prompt (the first baseline on the left), LLM with detailed prompt (second baseline in the middle) and our framework (on the right, for the sake of readability we only put one demonstration).

Method	**SemEval** (1,595 gold triples)				**SciERC** (4,265 gold triples)			
	Matched Triples	Correct Head	Correct Tail	Correct Both	Matched Triples	Correct Head	Correct Tail	Correct Both
LLaMA-3 (simple)	310	**232** (**8.40**)	210 (5.39)	**171** (**2.95**)	957	**688** (**8.75**)	**551** (4.60)	**435** (1.83)
LLaMA-3 (detailed)	**323**	223 (6.46)	**211** (4.76)	161 (2.13)	**1,010**	545 (8.02)	472 (4.95)	283 (**1.95**)
LLaMA-3 (simple + MCQA)	310 [75]	215 (7.08)	199 (**5.77**)	137 (2.38)	957 [70]	621 (6.80)	542 (**5.89**)	381 (1.74)
Mistral (simple)	**191**	124 (**2.19**)	92 (1.38)	68 (0.25)	**677**	**461** (**2.58**)	307 (1.74)	229 (**0.47**)
Mistral (detailed)	106	91 (1.76)	79 (1.07)	69 (**0.38**)	263	211 (1.34)	190 (0.94)	153 (0.19)
Mistral (simple + MCQA)	**191 [72]**	**128** (1.88)	**120** (**1.82**)	**82** (0.31)	**677 [70]**	441 (2.30)	**354** (**1.85**)	**245** (0.38)
GPT-4 (simple)	**1,384**	694 (12.92)	833 (13.98)	454 (1.15)	**2,309**	1,745 (10.34)	1,137 (6.61)	935 (1.95)
GPT-4 (detailed)	218	159 (2.63)	93 (1.00)	79 (0.25)	1,948	1,106 (9.87)	850 (6.54)	547 (1.85)
GPT-4 (simple + MCQA)	**1,384 [79]**	**850** (**19.94**)	**890** (**18.37**)	**609** (**5.39**)	**2,309 [79]**	**1,794** (**10.88**)	**1,408** (**10.39**)	**1,142** (**2.30**)

Table 2: Overall results of our LLM-based revision framework, in terms of: (a) Matched triples and Correct entities in the head, tail and both: number of instances, (b) Linking coverage: percentages between (), (c) Candidate selector success rates: percentages between []. The best scores per LLM are in bold font whereas best overall results are underlined. Please note that candidate selector success only concerns simple+MCQA as the baselines do not perform any selection.

tion (see for example (Jiang et al., 2024)). The second variability concerns LLMs performances when applying the MCQA technique. While the method demonstrates strong results with models like GPT-4 due to its advanced contextual reasoning and comprehension capabilities, it does not show similar improvements with models such as LLaMA-3. This inconsistency points to potential limitations in model architecture and pre-training data, which may affect how effectively they handle MCQA tasks. Future work should investigate these disparities to understand the specific features that

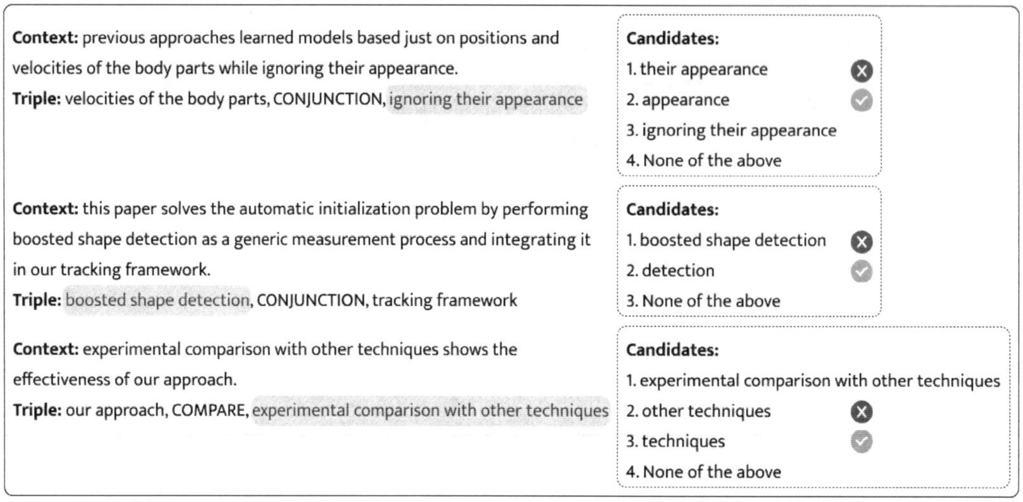

Figure 5: An example of errors made by our MCQA revision framework taken from the SciERC dataset. On the left, the output from triple extraction and matching (step 1) is displayed, highlighting the target entity that needs enhancement. On the right, we show a list of candidate entities obtained in step 2 (i.e., candidate selection) intended to refine the target entity. The entities predicted by our MCQA method answers (step 3) are incorrect (red cross), failing therefore in extracting the correct ones (marked by a green check).

enable some models to leverage MCQA successfully while identifying modifications or alternatives needed to improve performance in others.

4.2 Error Analysis

A manual error analysis of GPT-4 *simple+MPQA* outputs shows that our candidate selector missed 21% of the gold entities across both datasets. For the remaining 79%, the question-answering component achieved accuracies of 87% for SciERC and 81% for SemEval. Figure 5 shows some incorrect answers produced by our approach. Although providing demonstrations helped LLMs make better choices, the error categories (containing verbs, excessive adjectives, pronouns, determiners, and pseudo-sentences) have not been completely eliminated. For example, in the SciERC dataset using GPT-4, the number of entities containing verbs reduced from 737 to 352. Additionally, we observed that when LLMs are given inputs targeting multiple error categories (first example in Figure 5), they struggle to avoid all of them.

5 Conclusion

In this paper, we explore the potential of LLMs in-context learning for entity revision. To address the challenges posed by non-named entities, we introduced a multiple-choice question-answering framework that revises extracted entities from LLMs while increasing their linking coverage with the largest open knowledge base. When evaluated on two benchmark relation extraction datasets, our results demonstrate the effectiveness of our framework. We believe our work is a first important step to account for non-named entities in knowledge graph construction.

In this work, we apply a limited set of prompting techniques (zero-shot and few-shot in-context learning), which can be further explored in future research. We will also consider how improved entities affect downstream applications like question answering over knowledge graphs.

Acknowledgments

This work is jointly funded by the French National Agency QualityOnt ANR-21-CE23-0036-01, and the Deutsche Forschungsgemeinschaft (DFG, German Research Foundation) – Project-ID 490998901.

Limitations

Our methodology is designed to be domain-agnostic, though it has initially been tested using two benchmark relation extraction datasets from the scientific domain in English. These datasets, selected due to the scarcity of benchmarks rich in non-named entities (N-NEs), offer a rigorous testbed for evaluating our approach's efficacy on N-NEs.

Despite their focus on scientific abstracts, our approach demonstrates the potential for broader applicability. Future research will expand this evaluation to include diverse datasets from various domains and languages, thereby providing a comprehensive assessment of the generalizability and robustness of our framework.

Our evaluation metric is based on the percentage of entities linked to Wikidata. Although it is the largest open knowledge graph in terms of the number of instances, some entities correctly retrieved by our model may be missed by the linking coverage metric simply because those entities do not exist in Wikidata. It will therefore be interesting to also measure the linking rate with other knowledge bases such as DBPedia and YAGO.

Ethics Statement

The data used for conducting the experiments are composed of scientific abstracts taken from datasets publicly available to the research community. The datasets do not contain offensive or abusive language. We utilized various large language models (LLMs), both open-source and proprietary. It is important to acknowledge that these LLMs can exhibit biases and may encounter challenges concerning factual accuracy. Therefore, a critical approach should be adopted when interpreting the experimental outcomes.

References

Gabor Angeli, Melvin Jose Johnson Premkumar, and Christopher D. Manning. 2015. Leveraging linguistic structure for open domain information extraction. In *Proceedings of the 53rd Annual Meeting of the Association for Computational Linguistics and the 7th International Joint Conference on Natural Language Processing (Volume 1: Long Papers)*, pages 344–354, Beijing, China. Association for Computational Linguistics.

Nacime Bouziani, Shubhi Tyagi, Joseph Fisher, Jens Lehmann, and Andrea Pierleoni. 2024. REXEL: An End-to-end Model for Document-Level Relation Extraction and Entity Linking. *arXiv preprint*. ArXiv:2404.12788 [cs].

Haihua Chen, Gaohui Cao, Jiangping Chen, and Junhua Ding. 2019. A Practical Framework for Evaluating the Quality of Knowledge Graph. In *Knowledge Graph and Semantic Computing: Knowledge Computing and Language Understanding*, pages 111–122, Singapore. Springer.

Jiao Chen, Luyi Ma, Xiaohan Li, Nikhil Thakurdesai, Jianpeng Xu, Jason H. D. Cho, Kaushiki Nag, Evren Korpeoglu, Sushant Kumar, and Kannan Achan. 2023. Knowledge Graph Completion Models are Few-shot Learners: An Empirical Study of Relation Labeling in E-commerce with LLMs. *arXiv preprint*. ArXiv:2305.09858 [cs].

Yew Ken Chia, Lidong Bing, Soujanya Poria, and Luo Si. 2022. RelationPrompt: Leveraging Prompts to Generate Synthetic Data for Zero-Shot Relation Triplet Extraction. In *Findings of the Association for Computational Linguistics: ACL 2022*.

Morteza Ezzabady, Frédéric Ieng, Hanieh Khorashadizadeh, Farah Benamara, Sven Groppe, and Soror Sahri. 2024. Towards generating high-quality knowledge graphs by leveraging large language models. In *The 29th Annual International Conference on Natural Language & Information Systems (NLDB 2024), Turin, Italy*.

Kata Gábor, Davide Buscaldi, Anne-Kathrin Schumann, Behrang QasemiZadeh, Haïfa Zargayouna, and Thierry Charnois. 2018. SemEval-2018 Task 7: Semantic Relation Extraction and Classification in Scientific Papers. In *Proceedings of the 12th International Workshop on Semantic Evaluation*, pages 679–688, New Orleans, Louisiana. Association for Computational Linguistics.

Nicolas Heist, Sven Hertling, Daniel Ringler, and Heiko Paulheim. 2020. Knowledge graphs on the web – an overview. *Preprint*, arXiv:2003.00719.

Iris Hendrickx, Su Nam Kim, Zornitsa Kozareva, Preslav Nakov, Diarmuid Ó Séaghdha, Sebastian Padó, Marco Pennacchiotti, Lorenza Romano, and Stan Szpakowicz. 2010. SemEval-2010 Task 8: Multi-Way Classification of Semantic Relations between Pairs of Nominals. In *Proceedings of the 5th International Workshop on Semantic Evaluation*, pages 33–38, Uppsala, Sweden. Association for Computational Linguistics.

Pengcheng Jiang, Jiacheng Lin, Zifeng Wang, Jimeng Sun, and Jiawei Han. 2024. GenRES: Rethinking evaluation for generative relation extraction in the era of large language models. In *Proceedings of the 2024 Conference of the North American Chapter of the Association for Computational Linguistics: Human Language Technologies (Volume 1: Long Papers)*, pages 2820–2837, Mexico City, Mexico. Association for Computational Linguistics.

Dawei Li, Zhen Tan, Tianlong Chen, and Huan Liu. 2024. Contextualization Distillation from Large Language Model for Knowledge Graph Completion. *arXiv preprint*. ArXiv:2402.01729 [cs].

Yi Luan, Luheng He, Mari Ostendorf, and Hannaneh Hajishirzi. 2018. Multi-Task Identification of Entities, Relations, and Coreference for Scientific Knowledge Graph Construction. *arXiv preprint*. ArXiv:1808.09602 [cs].

Ling Luo, Po-Ting Lai, Chih-Hsuan Wei, Cecilia N Arighi, and Zhiyong Lu. 2022. BioRED: a rich biomedical relation extraction dataset. *Briefings in Bioinformatics*, 23(5):bbac282.

Xinxi Lyu, Sewon Min, Iz Beltagy, Luke Zettlemoyer, and Hannaneh Hajishirzi. 2023. Z-ICL: Zero-Shot In-Context Learning with Pseudo-Demonstrations. In *Proceedings of the 61st Annual Meeting of the Association for Computational Linguistics (Volume 1: Long Papers)*, pages 2304–2317, Toronto, Canada. Association for Computational Linguistics.

Xilai Ma, Jing Li, and Min Zhang. 2023a. Chain of Thought with Explicit Evidence Reasoning for Few-shot Relation Extraction. In *Findings of the Association for Computational Linguistics: EMNLP 2023*, pages 2334–2352, Singapore. Association for Computational Linguistics.

Yubo Ma, Yixin Cao, YongChing Hong, and Aixin Sun. 2023b. Large Language Model Is Not a Good Few-shot Information Extractor, but a Good Reranker for Hard Samples! In *Findings of the Association for Computational Linguistics: EMNLP 2023*, pages 10572–10601. ArXiv:2303.08559 [cs].

Ning Miao, Yee Whye Teh, and Tom Rainforth. 2023. SelfCheck: Using LLMs to Zero-Shot Check Their Own Step-by-Step Reasoning. *arXiv preprint*. ArXiv:2308.00436 [cs].

Ying Mo, Jian Yang, Jiahao Liu, Shun Zhang, Jingang Wang, and Zhoujun Li. 2024. C-ICL: Contrastive In-context Learning for Information Extraction. *arXiv preprint*. ArXiv:2402.11254 [cs].

Yilmazcan Ozyurt, Stefan Feuerriegel, and Ce Zhang. 2024. Document-Level In-Context Few-Shot Relation Extraction via Pre-Trained Language Models. *arXiv preprint*. ArXiv:2310.11085 [cs] version: 2.

Pierre-Henri Paris and Fabian Suchanek. 2021. Non-named Entities – The Silent Majority. In Ruben Verborgh, Anastasia Dimou, Aidan Hogan, Claudia d'Amato, Ilaria Tiddi, Arne Bröring, Simon Mayer, Femke Ongenae, Riccardo Tommasini, and Mehwish Alam, editors, *The Semantic Web: ESWC 2021 Satellite Events*, volume 12739. Springer International Publishing, Cham. Series Title: Lecture Notes in Computer Science.

Jie Ren, Yao Zhao, Tu Vu, Peter J. Liu, and Balaji Lakshminarayanan. 2023. Self-Evaluation Improves Selective Generation in Large Language Models. *arXiv preprint*. ArXiv:2312.09300 [cs].

Joshua Robinson, Christopher Michael Rytting, and David Wingate. 2023. Leveraging Large Language Models for Multiple Choice Question Answering. *arXiv preprint*. ArXiv:2210.12353 [cs].

Ahmad Sakor, Kuldeep Singh, Anery Patel, and Maria-Esther Vidal. 2020. Falcon 2.0: An entity and relation linking tool over wikidata. In *Proceedings of the 29th ACM International Conference on Information Knowledge Management*, CIKM '20, page 3141–3148, New York, NY, USA. Association for Computing Machinery.

Tokala Yaswanth Sri Sai Santosh, Prantika Chakraborty, Sudakshina Dutta, Debarshi Kumar Sanyal, and Partha Pratim Das. 2021. Joint Entity and Relation Extraction from Scientific Documents: Role of Linguistic Information and Entity Types.

Thomas Pellissier Tanon, Gerhard Weikum, and Fabian Suchanek. 2020. YAGO 4: A Reason-able Knowledge Base. page 583.

Milena Trajanoska, Riste Stojanov, and Dimitar Trajanov. 2023. Enhancing Knowledge Graph Construction Using Large Language Models. *arXiv preprint*. ArXiv:2305.04676 [cs].

Denny Vrandečić. 2012. Wikidata: a new platform for collaborative data collection. In *Proceedings of the 21st International Conference on World Wide Web*, WWW '12 Companion, pages 1063–1064, New York, NY, USA. Association for Computing Machinery.

Somin Wadhwa, Silvio Amir, and Byron Wallace. 2023. Revisiting Relation Extraction in the era of Large Language Models. In *Proceedings of the 61st Annual Meeting of the Association for Computational Linguistics (Volume 1: Long Papers)*.

Chenguang Wang, Xiao Liu, Zui Chen, Haoyun Hong, Jie Tang, and Dawn Song. 2022. DeepStruct: Pretraining of Language Models for Structure Prediction. In *Findings of the Association for Computational Linguistics: ACL 2022*, pages 803–823, Dublin, Ireland. Association for Computational Linguistics.

Yanbin Wei, Qiushi Huang, Yu Zhang, and James Kwok. 2023. KICGPT: Large Language Model with Knowledge in Context for Knowledge Graph Completion. In *Findings of the Association for Computational Linguistics: EMNLP 2023*, pages 8667–8683, Singapore. Association for Computational Linguistics.

Yixuan Weng, Minjun Zhu, Fei Xia, Bin Li, Shizhu He, Shengping Liu, Bin Sun, Kang Liu, and Jun Zhao. 2023. Large Language Models are Better Reasoners with Self-Verification. *arXiv preprint*. ArXiv:2212.09561 [cs].

Xin Xu, Yuqi Zhu, Xiaohan Wang, and Ningyu Zhang. 2023. How to Unleash the Power of Large Language Models for Few-shot Relation Extraction?

Kai Zhang, Bernal Jimenez Gutierrez, and Yu Su. 2023. Aligning Instruction Tasks Unlocks Large Language Models as Zero-Shot Relation Extractors. In *Findings of the Association for Computational Linguistics: ACL 2023*, pages 794–812, Toronto, Canada. Association for Computational Linguistics.

Yuhao Zhang, Victor Zhong, Danqi Chen, Gabor Angeli, and Christopher D. Manning. 2017. Position-aware Attention and Supervised Data Improve Slot Filling. In *Proceedings of the 2017 Conference on Empirical Methods in Natural Language Processing*, pages 35–45, Copenhagen, Denmark. Association for Computational Linguistics.

Shaowen Zhou, Bowen Yu, Aixin Sun, Cheng Long, Jingyang Li, and Jian Sun. 2022. A survey on neural open information extraction: Current status and future directions. In *IJCAI*, pages 5694–5701. ijcai.org.

Yuqi Zhu, Xiaohan Wang, Jing Chen, Shuofei Qiao, Yixin Ou, Yunzhi Yao, Shumin Deng, Huajun Chen, and Ningyu Zhang. 2024. LLMs for Knowledge Graph Construction and Reasoning: Recent Capabilities and Future Opportunities. *arXiv preprint*. ArXiv:2305.13168 [cs].

A Implementation Details

In this section, we describe the specific methodologies and settings employed during our experiments to ensure clarity and reproducibility of the results. A unique separator token, "<==>", was utilized to facilitate the parsing of subjects and objects from the text. This token is not present in the original datasets, thereby avoiding any confusion with natural language text. Additionally, we inform LLMs about the task by starting our prompts with an instruction of the task. It is important to note that we have not conducted any prompt-tuning, as it is not the focus of this paper. Furthermore, we did not alter any hyperparameters related to the LLMs. The only hyperparameter that our framework includes is K, which represents the number of demonstrations in step 3.

Multilingual Skill Extraction for Job Vacancy–Job Seeker Matching in Knowledge Graphs

Hamit Kavas
NLP Group,
Pompeu Fabra University
Adevinta Spain
hamit.kavas@upf.edu

Marc Serra-Vidal
Adevinta Spain
marc.serrav@adevinta.com

Leo Wanner
NLP Group,
Pompeu Fabra University
Catalan Institute for Research
and Advanced Studies (ICREA), Spain
leo.wanner@upf.edu

Abstract

In the modern labor market, accurate matching of job vacancies with suitable candidate CVs is critical. We present a novel multilingual knowledge graph-based framework designed to enhance the matching by accurately extracting the skills requested by a job and provided by a job seeker in a multilingual setting and aligning them via the standardized skill labels of the *European Skills, Competences, Qualifications and Occupations* (ESCO) taxonomy. The proposed framework employs a combination of state-of-the-art techniques to extract relevant skills from job postings and candidate experiences. These extracted skills are then filtered and mapped to the ESCO taxonomy and integrated into a multilingual knowledge graph that incorporates hierarchical relationships and cross-linguistic variations through embeddings. Our experiments demonstrate a significant improvement of the matching quality compared to the state of the art.

1 Introduction

In the modern labour market, job portals serve as key intermediaries, connecting employers with potential employees by comparing job postings with the CVs of job seekers, to find the best possible matches and liaise both parties.[1] Matching of the required skills in a job posting with the skills outlined in the candidate's experience is of special relevance. For implementation of this matching, recently a number of AI-based techniques have been proposed. Zero-shot recommendation models (Kurek et al., 2024), attention-based scoring mechanisms (Jiang et al., 2020), embedding-based models (Zhao et al., 2021), or tensor decomposition (Mao et al., 2023) have been used, with an emphasis of surface-level features, such as geographic location and user data, including click-through rates and other user engagement metrics, without a deeper analysis of the semantics of the listed skills. Other, more promising, proposals draw upon the skills taxonomy of the *European Skills, Competences, Qualifications and Occupations* (ESCO) classification[2], which is, together with its US equivalent O*Net[3], a primary instrument used in international job markets for job offer and candidate experience annotation. For instance, (Clavié and Soulié, 2023) identify ESCO skill labels in job offers / candidate experiences and provide the reasoning, which leads to the identification of skills by the use of a Large Language Model (LLM), giving guidance to it by detailed prompts, accompanied by manually created examples, but without that the LLM can re-evaluate its reasoning chain. This is different from (Wang and Zhou, 2024), which uses the "Chain of Thought" (CoT) strategy to make the LLM use its own reasoning explanations as in-context examples. However, as other proposals in the field, these proposals neglect the hierarchically organized, contextually diverse information in the ESCO classification.Furthermore, they are prone to biases inherent in LLMs when processing textual data, as they do not involve any human expert control or human-generated ground truth data.

To address these challenges and to improve the quality of skill extraction from job postings and candidate experiences and their matching, we developed a knowledge graph-based multi-step framework. The proposed architecture foresees skill extraction using several state-of-the-art skill selection skills (Zhang and et al., 2024; D'Oosterlinck et al., 2024; Nguyen et al., 2024) to whose output (D'Oosterlinck et al., 2024)'s CoT prompting technique is applied to select the most relevant skills by comparing the extracted skills with the ESCO

[1] In what follows, we use the term "job posting" to refer to the description of a job vacancy and "candidate experience" to refer to the professional history of a job seeker as documented in their CV.

[2] https://esco.ec.europa.eu/en/classification

[3] https://www.onetonline.org/

Proceedings of the Generative AI and Knowledge Graph Workshop (GenAIK), pages 146–155
January 19, 2025. ©2025 International Committee on Computational Linguistics (ICCL)

skill names and their corresponding descriptions. Human labelers provide ground truth data, based on which the model is optimized. The finally selected skills from the job postings and candidate experiences are linked in a knowledge graph with the ESCO skills. The graph is fine-tuned with multilingual (in our case, Spanish) embeddings for effective matching in a multilingual context.

Our tests demonstrate that the developed framework significantly outperforms the state-of-the-art skill extraction and job posting – candidate experience matching. The framework is about to be deployed in a leading European job portal.

It will serve as a complementary instrument for human job recruiters rather than a fully automated service, in order to minimize any risk of faulty recruitment suggestions.

2 Related Work

As already mentioned, a number of works deal with the identification and matching of skills in job postings and candidate experiences (Senger et al., 2024). For instance, (Jia et al., 2018) and (Sayfullina et al., 2018) focus on skill identification through span labeling and binary classification. (Jia et al., 2018) use sequence tagging with LSTM neural networks, and (Sayfullina et al., 2018) employ exact match for skill spans. Both require extensive optimization and are often limited by their dependency on specific languages and datasets. (Goyal et al., 2023) utilizes exact string matching with NLP techniques for label extraction and incorporates a multi-hop job-skill graph neural network with a Graph Isomorphism Network encoder, employing one-vs-many classification with softmax attention and weighting skills based on their frequency in job postings. (Zhang and et al., 2024) emphasize the generation of mention-entity pairs using ESCO skills as ground truth labels, their methodology, which heavily depends on the precise detection of mentions and the disambiguation of contexts, proves insufficient in real-world applications where such extraction methods are not readily available. (Fettach et al., 2024) demonstrates how knowledge graphs can bridge education and employment domains to support job seekers' skill development. They developed JobEdKG, an uncertain knowledge graph embeddings to model relationships between job market and educational entities to predict required skills based on career choices.

The systems by (Zhao et al., 2021; Jiang et al., 2020) approach job-resume matching primarily as a recommender system, incorporating non-textual inputs like geo-location and evaluating performance based on click-through rates. This methodology inherently restricts the comparison to surface-level features shared between candidate experiences and job postings, neglecting the deeper semantic relationships and context that are crucial for accurate skill matching. Similarly, (Kurek et al., 2024; Mao et al., 2023) experiment with zero-shot learning using various embedding models and dimensions. While this approach may be effective for exploring a broad understanding of industrial problems, it overlooks several recent findings. Relying solely on embeddings with zero-shot classification has notable weaknesses, such as the lack of mechanisms to mitigate residual biases in textual data and limited capability to integrate diverse data sources. Moreover, zero-shot classification models have been shown to be outperformed by in-context learning models, particularly LLM, which offer superior contextual understanding and adaptability (Gurusamy et al., 2024; Hasan et al., 2024).

Apart from those that we already cited, in particular, (D'Oosterlinck et al., 2024) needs to be highlighted. (D'Oosterlinck et al., 2024) introduces "in-context learning for extreme multi-label classification" and built on DSPy library (Khattab et al., 2023). It consists of a collection of DSPy programs that enable stateful interactions with LLM. The LLM integrates the CoT methodology with retrieval-augmented generation for skill extraction, where classes—specifically, ESCO skill names—are provided as embeddings. The model learns classification through a novel optimization technique that fine-tunes prompts at each step and generates synthetic examples to enhance in-context learning (ICL) (Wang and Zhou, 2024), thereby aiming to maximize classification metrics. We use (D'Oosterlinck et al., 2024) as foundation. We employ human-labellers to evaluate the skills extracted by this model and introduce enhancements to improve contextual understanding of the LLM beyond the conventional NLP techniques utilized in (Goyal et al., 2023) Additionally, we adapt this model for multilingual applications and incorporate the hierarchical skill relationships defined in the ESCO taxonomy.

3 The Framework

In what follows, we first provide an overview of our approach as a whole and then discuss the skills extraction, filtering of the extracted skills and their subsequent mapping onto the ESCO skills taxonomy, and construction of the knowledge graph as a way of matching the skills extracted from the job postings and candidate experiences.

3.1 Framework overview

Figure 1 illustrates our framework for skill extraction and matching of job postings and candidate experiences.

Job postings and candidate experiences come in structured forms. Skills, their descriptions, and associated job titles are provided in separate fields, such that we first retrieve the content of these fields from the forms[4]. An LLM CoT prompting strategy is applied to normalize the retrieved job titles to unique labels, which are further extended by an index (e.g. ix_000) from the InfoJobs database in which the job postings and candidate experiences are stored. For instance, a generic job title like "administrativo/a" (Spanish term for "administrator") is transformed into a more specific and unique title, such as "organizational support specialist_ix_14662" or "excel data coordinator – international trade support_ix_4664". This prevents inefficient expansion of the knowledge graph at a later stage (see below), since multiple nodes that represent the same concept or entity can lead to redundant data and suboptimal graph performance (Hofer et al., 2023; Zhang et al., 2022b).

The skills field in job postings and candidate experiences often contains unstructured, ambigous, or inconsistent information. For instance, job postings may list skills using a variety of terminologies, such as "project management", "PM", or "leading teams", all of which refer to the same skill in different terms. These variations make the use of skill extraction techniques to standardize relevant information for matching necessary.

For skill extraction, we adapt three state-of-the-art skills extraction techniques, which are applied in parallel to the content retrieved from the job postings and candidate experiences: entity linking (Zhang and et al., 2024), extreme multi-label classification (Khattab et al., 2023), and in-context learning with LLMs (Nguyen et al., 2024). We use three techniques instead of one because each of the three approaches has its pros and cons, such that a combination of them promises to provide the best outcome possible.

The outputs of these three techniques are merged and processed using the *CoT with Hint* reasoning module (D'Oosterlinck et al., 2024) from the DSPy library (Khattab et al., 2023). This module is responsible for both the final selection of the relevant skills and their mapping to the corresponding ESCO skills by introducing a hint during an intermediate reasoning step to prompt stateful LLMs within a multi-step framework. Additionally, the hint also ensures that the extracted skills are translated into English (when the input is in another language, e.g., Spanish)

With the selected skills at hand, we construct a knowledge graph that links ESCO skill labels, job postings, and candidate experiences. The hierarchical relationships between the skills in the ESCO taxonomy are incorporated, along with n-gram matches, to assign initial weights to the edges linking skills with job postings and candidate experiences. The initial edge weights are subsequently refined using Inverse Document Frequency (IDF) scores. To further improve the multilingual capability of the knowledge graph and translate the structural characteristics of the graph into a vector space representation that enables precise comparison of nodes, we fine-tune it on multilingual (so far, Spanish) embeddings. This enables the knowledge graph to account for linguistic variations between the description of the skills in ESCO and in job postings / candidate experiences. Furthermore, language-specific embeddings capture language-specific nuances and cultural context, enabling precise alignment between English and data in the language in question, unlike the initial alignment, which offers a generalized, language-independent representation.

3.2 Skills extraction

As mentioned above, we extract skills from job postings and candidate experiences adapting three state-of-the-art techniques, whose output we then combine for more accurate performance: entity linking, extreme multi-class classification, and few-shot in-context learning.

[4]Prior to their processing, both job postings and candidate experiences are cleaned. Promotional content, sensitive information, specific locations, names, and dates that could reveal private details about the hiring company or job seeker are removed.

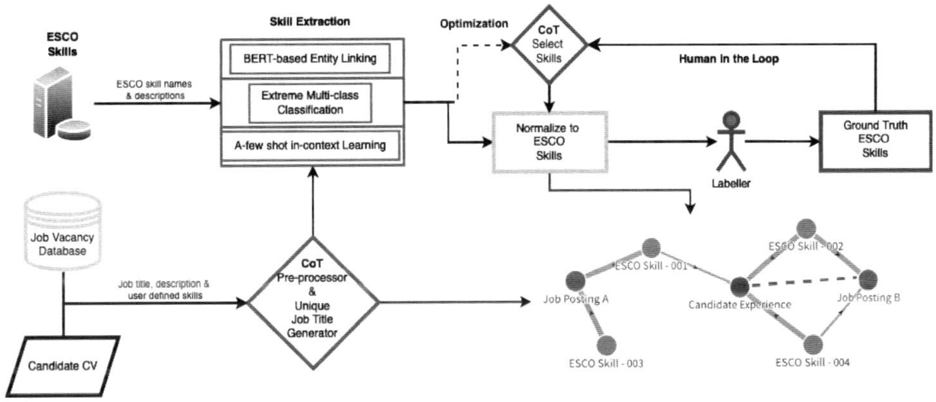

Figure 1: Overview of our framework for skills extraction and matching

3.2.1 Entity linking

Entity linking is used to link fine-grained span-level mentions of skills in candidate experiences to skills in the ESCO classification. We use (Zhang and et al., 2024), which is based on the BLINK model (Wu et al., 2020), adapted to the job domain. In this context, the entities refer to ESCO skill names and their corresponding descriptions. The descriptions are derived from the ESCO taxonomy, which provides detailed contextual information for each skill. BLINK first retrieves potential matches within a dense vector space, where a bi-encoder separately encodes the context of skill mentions and the descriptions of entities, which are two distinct inputs. The first input that represents the mention and its context has the following format:

```
[CLS]ctxt_left[S]mention[E]
                 ctxt_right[SEP]
```

where "mention" refers to the tokens of the actual mention, while "ctxt_left" and "ctxt_right" stand for the tokens of the surrounding contextual information. Special tokens [S] and [E] are used to delineate the mention itself.

The second input, representing the ESCO skill and its description, incorporates the skill's name (title) and its textual description, separated by a special token.

```
[CLS]skill_name[S]skill_desc[SEP]
```

Following the retrieval stage, a cross-encoder reranks the candidate experience entities by concatenating the mention and entity spans for a precise alignment. The model aims to maximize the similarity, measured by the dot product, of the [CLS] token embeddings for the correct entity relative to other entities in the batch.

Given that our data comprise job titles, descriptions, and skills in plain text, we extract skill mentions along with their surrounding context to utilize this model effectively. First, we employ a continiously pre-trained, domain-adapted skill extraction model[5] proposed in (Zhang et al., 2022a) to identify sequences that most likely contain skills. Sentences containing these identified spans are selected as inputs. Then, we refine the extracted spans by removing, stop words, subword markers, punctuation, and other non-letter characters to ensure coherence and readability. The processed spans are formatted into a structure required by the BLINK model, allowing accurate context and entity-linking. In instances where the span appeared at the beginning or end of a sentence, the context was represented by an empty string, as outlined in (Zhang and et al., 2024).

3.2.2 In-context learning for extreme multi-label Classification

Our second technique for skill extraction is "Infer-Retrieve-Rank" (IReRa) (D'Oosterlinck et al., 2024) for tackling extreme multi-label classification (XMC) problems that involve classifying items into thousands of possible categories (Khattab et al., 2023). IReRa employs a multi-step interaction between LLMs and retrievers, optimizing the process using the DSPy programming model.

We reproduced the results from the original IreRa framework following the prescribed methodology, including the optimization of the language

[5]https://huggingface.co/jjzha/jobspanbert-base-cased

```
class NormalizerSignature(dspy.Signature):
    __doc__ = """
    Normalize automatically assigned skills against the ESCO taxonomy based on the provided
    job descriptions. Map only the relevant skills to the most relevant ESCO skill,
    improving the precision of skill normalization. Be concise.
    """
    vacancy = dspy.InputField(
        prefix="Vacancy:",
        desc="The complete job description."
    )
    auto_skill = dspy.InputField(
        prefix="Skill:",
        desc="The skill that has been automatically assigned and needs normalization."
    )
    options = dspy.InputField(
        prefix="Options:",
        desc="List the possible ESCO skills and their descriptions that could correspond
        to the automatically assigned skill."
    )
    output = dspy.OutputField(
        prefix="Normalized Skill:",
        desc="The ESCO skill selected from the provided options that best matches the
        job description and assigned skill."
    )
```

Figure 2: DSPy signature used for Selecting and Normalizing Extracted Skills.

model with examples provided in their repository[6].

3.2.3 Few-shot skill extraction using Large Language Models

As the third technique, we implemented prompting of an LLM for skill extraction through a few-shot in-context learning, as proposed by (Nguyen et al., 2024). We adopted their original proposal to facilitate skill extraction from longer sentences. The exact prompts and few-shot examples from the original proposal. To ensure robustness and mitigate transient issues, we run the extraction up to five times to mitigate errors (e.g., poorly structured output from the LLM).

3.3 Skill selection and ESCO mapping

The skills extracted by the skill extraction techniques from above are further filtered with respect to their relevance, and their final selection is mapped onto the ESCO skills taxonomy, see Figure 2 for the prompt used in the DSPy program. The filtering model is a version of IReRa (D'Oosterlinck et al., 2024) that has been specifically adapted for multilingual skill extraction by incorporating additional context from the ESCO taxonomy. The model is further refined to improve the accuracy of skill selection compared to the ground truth, allowing for evaluation against its variations.

While building upon (D'Oosterlinck et al., 2024), our framework introduces several key enhancements to bridge the language gap between English ESCO skill labels and job postings / candidate experiences in other languages (in our case, Spanish): (1) integration of E5 multilingual embeddings[7] (Wang et al., 2024) to handle cross-lingual variations, (2) incorporation of ESCO skill descriptions into the vector database[8] to provide richer contextual understanding, and (3) development of a novel knowledge graph structure that captures hierarchical relationships between skills. But even if we apply multilingual embeddings for processing the job postings, we retain English for our prompts to acknowledge that maintaining prompts in English can yield advantageous outcomes, even for cases where the data is in another language (Razumovskaia et al., 2024). We use this multilingual adaptation of IReRa with aforementioned enhancements as the baseline model in our experiments.

To further improve (D'Oosterlinck et al., 2024)'s model, we implemented a method similar to few-shot in-context learning (ICL) (Nguyen et al., 2024), using training ground truth data. Annotator-agreed ground truth vacancies and their corresponding skills were provided as examples. To organize examples for in-context learning (ICL), we followed the multilingual alignment proposed by (Tanwar et al., 2023), which states that using semantically similar examples to construct the prompt-context aids the model in in-context inference. The alignment guides the LLM in mapping the source job posting to relevant target examples. To select the most semantically informative examples, we employed cosine similarity between the input job posting and segments of example job postings (Liu et al., 2021). In addition, we optimized the model through bootstrapping few-shot demonstrations, as proposed in (Khattab et al., 2023). For this purpose, we employed a random search method where Claude 3.5 Sonnet served as the teacher model, and Llama-3 served as the student model[9].

3.4 Knowledge Graph Construction

To effectively match the candidate experiences with job postings, we construct a knowledge graph and refine it using multilingual (in our case, Spanish) embeddings.

First, a graph is created with job postings and ESCO skills as nodes, and the links between the ESCO skills and the postings that possess them as weighted edges. The initial weights of the edges are determined by the hierarchical relationships between skills as defined in the ESCO taxonomy. ESCO organizes skills in a three-levels: broad skill groups, intermediate sub-groups, and specific com-

[6]https://github.com/KarelDO/xmc.dspy

[7]Instruction-tuned multilingual E5 text embeddings model employs a multi-stage contrastive learning methodology to obtain high-performance general-purpose embeddings.

[8]In all experiments with vector store, we use the open-source platform `https://www.trychroma.com/`.

[9]https://ai.meta.com/blog/meta-llama-3/

petencies. In this hierarchy, we utilize parent-child relationships between adjacent levels to reflect how general skills are linked to more specialized skills. Additionally, we introduce an another parent-child relation between skills when an n-gram of a skill is mentioned within another skill, thereby designating the former as the parent. For example, "graphical designer" and "graphical designer intern" illustrate a parent-child relation, with "graphical designer intern" as the child node. Each parent node is assigned an initial weight of 1, while the child skill nodes connected to them receive an initial weight of 0.5. We refine the initial edge weights using Inverse Document Frequency (IDF) scores to account for skill specificity and relevance. This refinement is to distinguish between common skills that appear frequently across many job postings and candidate experiences (receiving lower weights), and specialized skills that are more discriminative (receiving higher weights). The IDF scores are multiplied with the initial hierarchy-based weights, resulting in a weighted graph that better reflects both the hierarchical importance and the distinctiveness of each skill connection.

As next, candidate experiences are incorporated as nodes, and their skills are connected to the skill nodes in the graph; skills present in candidate experiences that were not previously defined in the graph are omitted from consideration. IDF scores are again used to assign weights to the edges connecting candidate experiences to their respective skills.

To facilitate semantically meaningful connections within the knowledge graph, we fine-tune the knowledge graph with Spanish embeddings since in our implementation, job vacancies and candidate experiences are in Spanish, while ESCO skills are in English. This ensures a more nuanced understanding that goes beyond a simple skills assignment. We first convert pre-trained fastText Spanish embeddings (Cañete, 2019), which have been opted for due to their superior performance on multilingual data into Word2Vec format (Mikolov et al., 2013). This conversion is necessary for the subsequent transformation of the embeddings into a Node2Vec graph (Grover and Leskovec, 2016), which extends Word2Vec representations to graph-structured data. Finally, we fine-tune the graph embeddings using a maximal-entropy biased random walk approach (Sinatra et al., 2010) to optimize the representation. We use biased random walks instead of simple random walks because they have been shown to be more effective, particularly for preferentially exploring certain paths and handling weighted graphs (Liu et al., 2022). As a result, the graph's topological information is translated into a vector space, allowing efficient computation of node similarities and facilitating various graph-based tasks such as classification and clustering.

In formal terms, the knowledge graph is an undirected graph $\mathcal{G} = (\mathcal{V}, \mathcal{E})$, where $\mathcal{V}$ is the set of nodes and $\mathcal{E}$ is the set of edges. For a node $v \in \mathcal{V}$, a random walk of length T is a sequence of nodes $\{v_0 = v, v_1, \ldots, v_T\}$, where each node v_i is chosen based on the following transition probabilities:

$$P(v_{i+1} = x \mid v_i = y) = \begin{cases} \frac{1}{p}, & \text{if } x = v_{i-1}, \\ \frac{1}{q}, & \text{if distance}(v_{i-1}, x) = 2, \\ 1, & \text{otherwise.} \end{cases} \quad (1)$$

with the p parameter controlling the likelihood of revisiting the previous node and selected as 0.5 and $q = 1/p$ influencing the exploration of more distant nodes. This process balances local and global exploration of the graph structure.

The sequences generated by the biased random walks are then used to learn node embeddings using the Skip-Gram model, where the goal is to maximize the likelihood of observing a node's neighbors given its embedding:

$$\max_f \sum_{v \in \mathcal{V}} \sum_{u \in \mathcal{N}_v} \log \Pr(u \mid f(v)),$$

where $\mathcal{N}_v$ denotes the context nodes of v, and the probability $\Pr(u \mid f(v))$ is given by:

$$\Pr(u \mid f(v)) = \frac{\exp(f(u) \cdot f(v))}{\sum_{v' \in \mathcal{V}} \exp(f(v') \cdot f(v))}.$$

This optimization ensures that nodes with similar structural roles in the graph have similar embeddings in the vector space.

To quantify the similarity between two nodes $v_i, v_j \in \mathcal{V}$, we compute the cosine similarity between their embeddings.

4 Experiments

4.1 Technical infrastructure

To ensure privacy of companies and users, all models in our experiments were executed locally within an isolated environment.[10] Blackbox models with internet access, which could potentially share sensitive data were restricted to processing only anonymized job postings and were never applied to candidate experiences.

As technical infrastructure, we use the DSPy library (Khattab et al., 2023), which has been designed to create and optimize language model (LM) pipelines. We employed several DSPy programs to structure the data and build our experimental pipeline. One DSPy program processed chunks of CV data to generate synthetic job experiences that ideally match job postings as described in 'Data' section. Another DSPy program, namely skill selection model, see Figure 2, was used to automatically normalize assigned skills against the ESCO taxonomy. This ensured that no extracted skill was omitted. Given the variability in user-generated job titles, another DSPy program was employed to generate unique job titles, thereby maintaining the integrity and uniqueness of the Knowledge Graph.

The knowledge graph is constructed using the StellarGraph library (Data61, 2018). Data is stored in Amazon S3 buckets, with computational tasks executed on an RTX 3090TI GPU for the local LLM and deep learning models. Additionally, the framework utilizes the Claude API via Amazon Bedrock. The entire framework is containerized and fully prepared for testing prior to deployment.

4.2 Evaluating Matching

To evaluate the proposed methodology against SoA skill extraction techniques and skill alignment in the knowledge graph, we use synthetic data. We construct three distinct knowledge graphs with the skills selected by two of the applied skill extraction strategies BLINK (Zhang and et al., 2024) and IReRa (D'Oosterlinck et al., 2024) and our final skill filtering model. The few-shot skill extraction (Nguyen et al., 2024) was not used here because it is not designed for the development of ESCO skills.

For the evaluation of the matching, we use Jaccard and cosine measures. Jaccard similarity is applied to exact skill matches, and cosine similarity to the vectorized graph with Spanish embeddings.

For our biased random walks in the knowledge graph, random walks of length 30 were generated, with each node serving as the root for 10 walks. The bias parameters were set to $p = 0.5$ and $q = 2.0$. Edge weights were determined by multiplying the ESCO hierarchy coefficient (0.5 for child nodes, 1 for parent nodes) with the IDF, and these weights were considered during the walk generation. The process was seeded with a fixed value of 42 to ensure reproducibility. The walks were used to fine-tune a Word2Vec model with the following parameters: vector size of 100, window size of 5, minimum count of 1, and Skip-Gram method (sg=1). The model was initialized with pre-trained vectors and fine-tuned on the generated walks. We computed cosine similarity between node embeddings to evaluate their relational similarity.

4.3 Data

For the evaluation of our skill selection, we use a subset of the job postings and candidate experiences from the InfoJobs database, focusing on records where both descriptions and user-defined skills are included. Specifically, we selected 648 job postings and 1,200 candidate experiences from the database. From this subset, we select ESCO occupations that are particularly ambiguous due to their inclusion in various other occupations. Among the selected occupations are, e.g., "administrative assistant", "office clerk", "sales assistant", "project manager", and "human resources assistant". These labels were assigned to job postings and candidate experiences, following the methodology described in (Kavas et al., 2024). Non-informative elements in job postings, such as company descriptions and promotional content have been removed. Sensitive information in both job postings and candidate experiences was anonymized by a DSPy program that utilizes zero-shot LLM inference.

We used the 1,200 candidate experiences to guide the generation of synthetic experiences by providing real-world language and terminology. These experiences were split into chunks and stored in a vector database, to facilitate similarity searches during the synthetic experience generation process.

For annotation detailed in the 'Ground Truth Creation' section below, we have selected 120 job postings from the obtained dataset characterized by longer descriptions and detailed requirements. The remaining 528 postings were used for testing and validation purposes in our experiments.

To evaluate our knowledge graph-based matching proposal, we generated synthetic job experiences using the local Llama-3 model, implemented through DSPy modules. First, a job posting with predefined skills was randomly selected. We ex-

[10] We use dockerized models from the open-source Ollama library `https://ollama.com/` for all experiments.

tracted n-grams from the job posting description, focusing on skill mentions detected by semantic similarity. Candidate experiences were split into chunks and were stored in a vector database. Vector similarity using a multilingual retriever based on the E5 model was employed to identify the most relevant candidate experience chunks. Finally, a DSPy program that employs a CoT methodology and sample Spanish language expressions from candidate experiences was used to guide the generation process for creation of synthetic experiences optimized to match the selected job postings.

4.4 Ground Truth Creation

To evaluate the performance of our skill extraction, we conducted a systematic annotation of job postings, engaging experts from a job market place running company. To mitigate potential biases, we ensured diversity among the annotators in terms of their expertise and backgrounds. The skills presented to the annotators were derived from the union of skills extracted by the three state-of-the-art techniques and normalized, as described above. To enhance the comprehension of the individual ESCO skills, each ESCO skill was accompanied by its corresponding description from the ESCO classification.

The annotation involved 12 annotators: 10 classified the skills in the job postings, while the remaining 2 focused on annotating training data and resolving controversies. For each job posting, about 30 automatically assigned skills were presented. Annotators were instructed to classify each skill as either "essential" or "irrelevant". It is noteworthy that while the job offers were in Spanish, the ESCO skills and their descriptions were presented in English. All annotators were native Spanish speakers with proficiency in English.

We provided detailed guidelines to the annotators, emphasizing objective evaluation based solely on the content of the job postings to reduce personal biases and ensure consistency across annotations. The annotation was conducted in two rounds. In the first round, each of the 10 annotators evaluated 10 job postings from the dataset. At the same time, we employed the Claude 3.5 Sonnet model[11] to perform the same labeling task as the human annotators. We extracted the top 15 job postings where the model and human annotators agreed and selected 15 job postings with the least agreement. Two remaining annotators re-evaluated the 30 annotations. Skills derived from the combined annotations of both rounds were then used in the experiments. To mitigate potential biases, the task instructions were ensured to avoid any implicit suggestion to the annotators. We deliberately refrained from providing specific examples or controversial cases to prevent any influence on the annotators' judgments, allowing them to rely on their professional expertise.

[11] https://www.anthropic.com/news/claude-3-5-sonnet

4.5 Results

Skill Selection Method	P	R	F1	$\bar{X}$
ICL enhanced (claude-3.5)	0.46	0.5	0.48	5.81
Baseline (claude-3.5)	0.58	0.34	0.43	3.12
DSPy Optimized (llama-3)	0.48	0.28	0.35	3.13
ICL enhanced (llama-3)	0.4	0.28	0.33	3.74
Baseline (llama-3)	0.36	0.23	0.28	3.40

Table 1: Comparison of the performance of skill selection techniques ('$\bar{X}$' stands for "average number of predicted skills"; as Baseline, we use (D'Oosterlinck et al., 2024))

Table 1 reports the results of our baseline skill selection model and its enhancements, namely in-context learning (ICL) and DSPy optimization with human-annotated skills. Due to inherent limitations of black-box models, which cannot be fine-tuned or optimized with custom scripts, DSPy optimization was applied exclusively to the LLaMA-3 model, with the Claude 3.5 Sonnet model serving as the teacher. We see that particularly the Claude model, when enhanced with in-context learning (ICL), shows an increase in recall by recognizing a broader range of potential skills in the text. However, this increase comes at the cost of precision, as the model becomes more permissive, leading to an increase in false positives. Similarly, the LLaMA-3 model exhibits comparable behavior, with recall improving more substantially than precision under ICL. The optimization proved effective, as it enhanced the F1 score, even if it predicted, in the average, a lower number of skills.

Model	Metric: Score
IReRa SE Model	Jaccard: 0.3084
Blink SE Model	Jaccard: 0.4157
Skill Selection (Baseline)	Jaccard: 0.5002
Skill Selection (Fine-tuned)	Cosine: 0.5761

Table 2: Matching Performance of Knowledge Graph

Table 2 shows the performance of the matching of candidate experiences and job postings. According to the Jaccard scores, the Blink model (Zhang and et al., 2024) surpasses the IReRa model (D'Oosterlinck et al., 2024) in performance. For skill extraction, our integration of E5 multilingual embeddings and CoT-guided filtering shows a significant improvement in recall while maintaining competitive precision. For matching, the incorporation of hierarchical and multilingual embeddings enhances the cosine similarity of candidate experience-job posting pairs, achieving a higher alignment score compared to the baseline method.

The Jaccard score of 0.5002 establishes a baseline for our final model for skill selection. Subsequent fine-tuning, which includes the vectorization of the knowledge graph and incorporation of Spanish embeddings, enhances the cosine similarity score to 0.5761. This indicates that fine-tuning has improved matching accuracy, suggesting a better alignment between job postings and candidate experiences.

5 Conclusions

Our knowledge graph-based framework for candidate experience–job posting matching combines extensions of several state-of-the-art techniques, which leads to a versatile and robust application, apt for industrial use. The integration of entity linking mechanisms (Zhang and et al., 2024) enhances contextual precision, while extreme multi-label classification (D'Oosterlinck et al., 2024) addresses the extensive taxonomy of potential competencies, and the use LLM with few-shot in-context learning methodologies (Nguyen et al., 2024) ensures a high robustness of the skill extraction task. Our extension of (D'Oosterlinck et al., 2024)'s model provides enhanced reasoning capability by utilizing a CoT technique that allows LLM to review its own reasoning. It also enforces the model to respond in the input language, even when provided with context in another language. Furthermore, it normalizes the selected skills against the ESCO taxonomy and incorporates a hint at an intermediate reasoning step, guiding the model to refine its initial output. The extended model significantly improves on the ability to accurately process multilingual data, compared to previous methods that relied on string matching or regular expressions to map extracted skills to the ESCO taxonomy.

Finally, representing job postings, candidate experiences and skills as nodes within a knowledge graph allows for detailed and structured analysis of skill overlap and compatibility, often missed in linear or non-relational models (Yu et al., 2024).

References

José Cañete. 2019. Compilation of large spanish unannotated corpora.

Benjamin Clavié and Guillaume Soulié. 2023. Large language models as batteries-included zero-shot esco skills matchers. *Preprint*, arXiv:2307.03539.

CSIRO's Data61. 2018. Stellargraph machine learning library. https://github.com/stellargraph/stellargraph.

Karel D'Oosterlinck, O. Khattab, François Remy, Thomas Demeester, Chris Develder, and Christopher Potts. 2024. In-context learning for extreme multi-label classification. *ArXiv*, abs/2401.12178.

Yousra Fettach, Adil Bahaj, and Mounir Ghogho. 2024. Jobedkg: An uncertain knowledge graph-based approach for recommending online courses and predicting in-demand skills based on career choices. *Engineering Applications of Artificial Intelligence*, 131:107779.

Nidhi Goyal, Jushaan Kalra, Charu Sharma, Raghava Mutharaju, Niharika Sachdeva, and Ponnurangam Kumaraguru. 2023. JobXMLC: EXtreme multi-label classification of job skills with graph neural networks. In *Findings of the Association for Computational Linguistics: EACL 2023*, pages 2181–2191, Dubrovnik, Croatia. Association for Computational Linguistics.

Aditya Grover and Jure Leskovec. 2016. node2vec: Scalable feature learning for networks. *Preprint*, arXiv:1607.00653.

Bharathi Mohan Gurusamy, Prasanna Kumar Rangarajan, P. Krishh, A. Keerthinathan, G. Lavanya, Meka Meghana, Sheba Sulthana, and Srinath Doss. 2024. An analysis of large language models: their impact and potential applications. *Knowledge and Information Systems*, 66:1–24.

Md. Arid Hasan, Shudipta Das, Afiyat Anjum, Firoj Alam, Anika Anjum, Avijit Sarker, and Sheak Rashed Haider Noori. 2024. Zero- and few-shot prompting with LLMs: A comparative study with fine-tuned models for Bangla sentiment analysis. In *Proceedings of the 2024 Joint International Conference on Computational Linguistics, Language Resources and Evaluation (LREC-COLING 2024)*, pages 17808–17818, Torino, Italia. ELRA and ICCL.

Marvin Hofer, Daniel Obraczka, Alieh Saeedi, Hanna Köpcke, and Erhard Rahm. 2023. Construction of knowledge graphs: State and challenges.

X. Jia, Y. Zhang, and Y. Wang. 2018. Representation of job-skill in artificial intelligence with knowledge graph analysis. In *Proceedings of the 2018 IEEE International Conference on Artificial Intelligence and Knowledge Engineering (AIKE)*, pages 1–8.

Junshu Jiang, Songyun Ye, Wei Wang, Jingran Xu, and Xiaosheng Luo. 2020. Learning effective representations for person-job fit by feature fusion. In *Proceedings of the 29th ACM International Conference on Information & Knowledge Management*, CIKM '20, page 2549–2556, New York, NY, USA. Association for Computing Machinery.

Hamit Kavas, Marc Serra-Vidal, and Leo Wanner. 2024. Job offer and applicant cv classification using rich information from a labour market taxonomy. *Elsevier*. Available at SSRN: https://ssrn.com/abstract=4519766 or http://dx.doi.org/10.2139/ssrn.4519766.

O. Khattab, Arnav Singhvi, Paridhi Maheshwari, Zhiyuan Zhang, Keshav Santhanam, Sri Vardhamanan, Saiful Haq, Ashutosh Sharma, Thomas T. Joshi, Hanna Moazam, Heather Miller, Matei Zaharia, and Christopher Potts. 2023. Dspy: Compiling declarative language model calls into self-improving pipelines. *ArXiv*, abs/2310.03714.

Jarosław Kurek, Tomasz Latkowski, Michał Bukowski, Bartosz Świderski, Mateusz Łępicki, Grzegorz Baranik, Bogusz Nowak, Robert Zakowicz, and Łukasz Dobrakowski. 2024. Zero-shot recommendation ai models for efficient job–candidate matching in recruitment process. *Applied Sciences*.

Jiachang Liu, Dinghan Shen, Yizhe Zhang, Bill Dolan, Lawrence Carin, and Weizhu Chen. 2021. What makes good in-context examples for gpt-3? In *Workshop on Knowledge Extraction and Integration for Deep Learning Architectures; Deep Learning Inside Out*.

Renming Liu, Matthew Hirn, and Arjun Krishnan. 2022. Accurately modeling biased random walks on weighted graphs using *Node2vec+*. *Preprint*, arXiv:2109.08031.

Yu Mao, Yuxuan Cheng, and Chunyu Shi. 2023. A job recommendation method based on attention layer scoring characteristics and tensor decomposition. *Applied Sciences*, 13:9464.

Tomas Mikolov, Kai Chen, Gregory S. Corrado, and Jeffrey Dean. 2013. Efficient estimation of word representations in vector space. In *International Conference on Learning Representations*.

Khanh Cao Nguyen, Mike Zhang, Syrielle Montariol, and Antoine Bosselut. 2024. Rethinking skill extraction in the job market domain using large language models. *ArXiv*, abs/2402.03832.

Evgeniia Razumovskaia, Ivan Vuli'c, and Anna Korhonen. 2024. Analyzing and adapting large language models for few-shot multilingual nlu: Are we there yet? *ArXiv*, abs/2403.01929.

Liliya Sayfullina, Carlos Leiva, Erik Garcia, Xiang Niu, and Yang Zhao. 2018. Learning representations for soft skill matching. In *Proceedings of the 2018 Conference on Empirical Methods in Natural Language Processing*, pages 2060–2071.

Elena Senger, Mike Zhang, Rob van der Goot, and Barbara Plank. 2024. Deep learning-based computational job market analysis: A survey on skill extraction and classification from job postings. In *Proceedings of the First Workshop on Natural Language Processing for Human Resources (NLP4HR 2024)*, pages 1–15, St. Julian's, Malta. Association for Computational Linguistics.

Roberta Sinatra, Jesús Gómez-Gardeñes, Renaud Lambiotte, Vincenzo Nicosia, and Vito Latora. 2010. Maximal-entropy random walks in complex networks with limited information. *Physical review. E, Statistical, nonlinear, and soft matter physics*, 83 3 Pt 1:030103.

Eshaan Tanwar, Manish Borthakur, Subhabrata Dutta, and Tanmoy Chakraborty. 2023. Multilingual llms are better cross-lingual in-context learners with alignment. *ArXiv*, abs/2305.05940.

Liang Wang, Nan Yang, Xiaolong Huang, Linjun Yang, Rangan Majumder, and Furu Wei. 2024. Multilingual e5 text embeddings: A technical report. *ArXiv*, abs/2402.05672.

Xuezhi Wang and Denny Zhou. 2024. Chain-of-thought reasoning without prompting. *Preprint*, arXiv:2402.10200.

Ledell Wu, Fabio Petroni, Martin Josifoski, Sebastian Riedel, and Luke Zettlemoyer. 2020. Scalable zero-shot entity linking with dense entity retrieval. In *Proceedings of the 2020 Conference on Empirical Methods in Natural Language Processing (EMNLP)*, pages 6397–6407, Online. Association for Computational Linguistics.

Xiao Yu, Jinzhong Zhang, and Zhou Yu. 2024. Confit: Improving resume-job matching using data augmentation and contrastive learning. *ArXiv*, abs/2401.16349.

Mike Zhang and et al. 2024. Entity linking in the job market domain. In *Findings of the Association for Computational Linguistics: EACL 2024*, pages 410–419, St. Julian's, Malta. Association for Computational Linguistics.

Mike Zhang, Kristian Jensen, Sif Sonniks, and Barbara Plank. 2022a. SkillSpan: Hard and soft skill extraction from English job postings. In *Proceedings of the 2022 Conference of the North American Chapter of the Association for Computational Linguistics: Human Language Technologies*, pages 4962–4984, Seattle, United States. Association for Computational Linguistics.

Qinggang Zhang, Junnan Dong, Keyu Duan, Xiao Huang, Yezi Liu, and Linchuan Xu. 2022b. Contrastive knowledge graph error detection.

Jing Zhao, Jingya Wang, Madhav Sigdel, Bopeng Zhang, Phuong Hoang, Mengshu Liu, and Mohammed Korayem. 2021. Embedding-based recommender system for job to candidate matching on scale. *ArXiv*, abs/2107.00221.

Author Index

Abuelkheir, Mervat, 66
Ahlawat, Satyadev, 109

BARRY, Mariam, 54
Benamara, Farah, 136
Besga, Jon, 100

CAILLAUT, Gaetan, 54
CARIOLARO, Dimitri, 54
Chadha, Aman, 27
Chali, Yllias, 20
Chaudhary, Divya, 27

d'Aquin, Mathieu, 69
Dong, Na, 78
dos Reis, Julio Cesar, 87

Ehab, Nourhan, 66
Eldessouky, Farida Helmy, 66

Gande, Vinesh Kumar, 27
GESNOUIN, Joseph, 54
Gievska, Sonja, 123

HALFTERMEYER, Pierre, 54

Iarosh, Dmitrii, 43

Jain, Vinija, 27
Jamshidi, Samin, 20

Kalajdziski, Slobodan, 123
Kamaladdini Ezzabady, Morteza, 136
Kavas, Hamit, 146
Kertkeidkachorn, Natthawut, 78
Kumar, Anuj, 109
Kumar, Pardeep, 109

LE DEIT, Fabrice, 54
Liu, Xin, 78

Mahalingam, Aakash, 27
Martynova, Anastasia, 13
Mecharnia, Thamer, 69
Messallem, Leila, 100
Minker, Wolfgang, 66
Minneci, Gianandrea, 100
MOUAYAD, Mehdi, 54

Nayak, Tapas, 1

Ozsoy, Makbule Gulcin, 100

Panchenko, Alexander, 43
Prasad, Yamuna, 109

QADER, Raheel, 54

Regino, André Gomes, 87

Saini, Pratik, 1
Salnikov, Mikhail, 43
Schindler, Carolin, 66
Şemenova, Natalia, 13
Serra-Vidal, Marc, 146
Shirai, Kiyoaki, 78

Tishin, Vladislav, 13
Toshevska, Martina, 123

Wanner, Leo, 146

Yadav, Abhishek, 109

Association for Computational Linguistics
209 N. Eighth Street
Stroudsburg, Pennsylvania 18360

ISBN 979-8-3313-1368-5

9 798331 313685

CURRAN ASSOCIATES INC.
proceedings.com